American
24-Karat Gold

24 Classic American Short Stories

Yvonne Collioud Sisko

Middlesex County College

Illustrations by
John Seymour and Ted Sisko

Longman

New York • San Francisco • Boston
London • Toronto • Sydney • Tokyo • Singapore • Madrid
Mexico City • Munich • Paris • Cape Town • Hong Kong • Montreal

To George and Teddy and Laura,
who give me joy every day of my life.

Vice President/Editor-in-Chief: Joseph Opiela
Senior Acquisitions Editor: Steven Rigolosi
Marketing Manager: Melanie Craig
Supplements Editor: Donna Campion
Production Manager: Denise Phillip
Project Coordination, Text Design, and
    Electronic Page Makeup: Thompson Steele, Inc.
Cover Design Manager: John Callahan
Cover Designer: Laura Shaw
Cover Photo: © Steve Hathaway/Workbook
Manufacturing Buyer: Al Dorsey
Printer and Binder: Courier—Stoughton
Cover Printer: John P. Pow

For permission to use copyrighted material, grateful acknowledgment is made to
the copyright holders on p. 456, which are hereby made part of this copyright page.

Library of Congress Cataloging-in-Publication Data
Sisko, Yvonne Collioud.
    American 25-karat gold : 24 classic American short stories / Yvonne Collioud
Sisko ; illustrations by John Seymour and Ted Sisko.
        p. cm
    Includes bibliographical references and index.
    ISBN 0-321-8330-X (alk. paper)
        1. College readers. 2. English language--Rhetoric--Problems, exercises, etc.
3. Report writing--Problems, exercises, etc. 4. Short stories, American. I. Title:
American twenty-four-karat gold. II. Title.

PE1417 .S454 2001
808'.0427--dc21   2001029337

Please visit our website at http://www.ablongman.com

ISBN 0-321-08330-X

1 2 3 4 5 6 7 8 9 10—CRS—04 03 02 01

Contents

Old Phoenix overcomes challenge after challenge as she takes the reader on a journey to town.

In this wonderful weaving of female personalities, family triumphs even over death.

Mark Twain *Strong Temptations—Strategic Movements—The Innocents Beguiled*   **120**

Told with humor and irony, this is the classic tale of Tom Sawyer painting the fence.

Edgar Allan Poe *The Cask of Amontillado*   **134**

Poe again walks the reader through the homicidal mind in this classic story of family revenge where darkness increases with the subterranean descent.

Jack London *To Build a Fire*   **149**

Arctic conditions test the knowledge of man and dog.

Shirley Jackson *The Lottery*   240

Jackson questions the very construct of cultural tradition as the reader walks through the characters' plight.

Flannery O'Connor *Good Country People*   256

This macabre tale plays on human frailties and questions assumptions about relationships.

CHAPTER 4 Irony   283

Kate Chopin *The Story of an Hour*   284

Chopin turns marital assumptions upside down with her ironic twist.

CHAPTER 5   Extended Short Story Study   365

Nathaniel Hawthorne   *Dr. Heidegger's Experiment*   366

In this tale set amid dark and ominous surroundings, Hawthorne questions change with light humor, irony, and even a touch of sarcasm.

William Faulkner   *A Rose for Emily*   386

The reader experiences the very wretchedness of Faulkner's decaying South through Emily and her relationships.

Edgar Allan Poe   *The Masque of the Red Death*   404

Writing over one hundred years ago, Poe uses the supernatural with a vengeance ominous of today's plight with AIDS.

Herman Melville   *The Bell-Tower*   420

In this powerful tale written long before modern machinery, Melville exposes a man's self-glorifying pride in his own resourcefulness.

Intent and/or Tone
Contents

Here is a general listing of stories by theme, although most of these stories do not easily fit one category or another. For instance, Twain's story of Tom Sawyer painting the fence can as easily be placed in *Irony, Triumph of the Spirit, Social Commentary,* or *Humor.*

TRIUMPH OF THE SPIRIT

These stories inspire and offer insight into the human condition.

HUMOR

These stories tickle the reader's funny bone.

IRONY

These stories come with unexpected twists.

SOCIAL COMMENTARY

These stories examine social and/or cultural issues.

EERIE

These stories visit the worlds of the macabre and the supernatural.

BY ITSELF

This is a story in a class by itself.

Chronological
Contents

Foreword

S tarting with an idea, this book became a dynamic process. The original idea for this collection came out of necessity. While teaching courses on world literature, freshman composition, and developmental studies simultaneously, I searched far and wide for a concise collection of affordable American short stories that would be a logical culmination in New World Study for World Literature, provide rich prompts for composition, and supply a literary answer to the question, "But what do they *read?*" for developmental studies. I found none. Instead, I found comprehensive monographs (all O. Henry, and so forth), ponderous tomes for short story courses per se, or weighty collections of esoteric writings by obscure writers. Nowhere was there a concise and diverse collection of America's best. *American 24-Karat Gold* proposes to fill this void.

After selecting the literature, I decided to focus on the developmental student, and the process of creating effective pedagogical materials began. During this process, so many have been helpful, understanding, and supportive. First, I deeply thank Lucille Alfieri, Betty Altruda, John Bakum, Jim Bernarducci, Debbie Brady, Santi Buscemi, Wilson Class, Gert Coleman, Jamie Daley, Sallie DelVecchio, Evelyn and Kristin Honey, Vernie Jarocki, Jane Lasky, Albert Nicolai, Renee Price, Rich Strugala, Helena Swanicke, Shirley Wachtel, and Nancy Zavoluk—friends and colleagues at Middlesex—for their ever-ready interest, guidance, and patience. Next, I deeply thank Bernie Weinstein, Dan O'Day, Eileen Kennedy, Bill Evans, and Howard Didsbury—my mentors—who continually push me further and further. Very special thanks go to the many students who have field-tested these materials and who have taught and continue to teach me what works and what does not work. And, extraordinarily special thanks go to my editor, Steven Rigolosi, whose vision truly shaped this book.

Special thanks also go to my sisters, Michelle, Dodee, and Alice; to my parents, Ted and Margaret, for understanding my committed time; and to my brother-in-law, John, whose illustrations light this book. And, of course, very special thanks go to my husband, George, and to my children, Teddy and Laura, who have often lost a mother and have heard, "Not now! I just lost a file," oh so many times during this process. I would also like to thank the many reviewers who provided extended commentary on every phase of the book, from proposal through final draft:

Kim Ballard, Ivy Technical State College
Susan Bernstein, Shippensburg University of Pennsylvania
Shirley Berry, Cape Fear Community College
Caroline Birden, Community College of Philadelphia

Rick Branscomb, Salem State College
Julie Hanks, Cabrillo College
Kevin Hayes, Essex County College
Christine Heilman, Cincinnati State Technical
    and Community College
Charles Hood, Antelope Valley College
Daniel O'Day Jr., Kean University
Barbara Powers, Al Collins Graphic Design School
Dee Pruitt, Florence Darlington Technical College
Kim Stringer-Zernechel, Minneapolis Community
    and Technical college
Shirley Wachtel, Middlesex County College
John Zuern, University of Hawaii

This book has been a wonderful journey. I honestly hope you enjoy using this book as much as I have enjoyed developing it.

—Yvonne Collioud Sisko
Matawan, New Jersey

Preface

To the Student

It seems that human beings have always loved a good story. In fact, anthropologists tell us that story telling has been used to teach rules and ideas for centuries.

This book is filled with good stories, or narratives or narrations, from some of post–Columbian America's greatest story tellers. Read these stories to gain knowledge about past and present American attitudes. Read them to gain knowledge about yourself, for a good story always offers us some information about ourselves. But most of all, read these stories to enjoy them. Stories have a way of taking us into new worlds, offering universals (feelings we all can understand).

However, the stories in this book are designed to do more than just expose you to each story itself. Each story in *American 24-Karat Gold* is surrounded with exercises that will help you better understand each story. Each story includes:

- **Vocabulary Exercises**—Vocabulary exercises help you define the words you need to know for the story, before you even read it.
- **Questions**—Questions help guide you through the story.
- **Biography**—A biography of the story's author provides you information about the author's style and other works.
- **Journal**—After reading, you can record and organize your thoughts about the story in a journal.
- **Follow-up Questions**—You can demonstrate what you've learned about the story in follow-up questions.
- **Writing Ideas**—Writing ideas help guide your own writing.

To better understand how this book works, turn to the Sample Lesson on page 1, and work your way through it. You'll find that you will be actively participating in this book, which will make understanding and appreciating the stories easier and more rewarding for you.

Welcome to *American 24-Karat Gold!* Read this book, study it, and—most of all—enjoy it.

To the Teacher

The greatest assets of *American 24-Karat Gold* are its participatory lessons and the many options these lessons offer you. Certainly, the literature is the core of this book, but the pedagogical materials that surround every story require students to actively participate in every story. Simultaneously, these materials offer a choice of multiple, administratively efficient diagnostic and assessment tools. Each story is a self-contained lesson, and all the stories are consistently formatted, thereby offering students clear expectations and offering you multiple options.

Sample Lesson

American 24-Karat Gold starts out with an applied **Sample Lesson.** The Sample Lesson can be used in class, *or* it can be assigned as homework. Written in simple and accessible language, this introductory lesson walks students through the basic story format, using Kate Chopin's "Ripe Figs." This lesson, as all lessons, opens with Pre-Reading Vocabulary—Context and Pre-Reading Vocabulary—Word Attack to help students define important words used in the story. Pre-Reading Questions set purpose, and an author biography supplies relevant background information.

After reading "Ripe Figs," students learn notation strategies that they can then apply to the subsequent readings. With the story completed, students move on to the Journal exercises, which are comprehensive and participatory studies of the story. The Sample Lesson explains the tasks in each Journal section, offers sample answers to get students started, and introduces relevant literary terminology.

With the Journal completed, students now have an active, working understanding of "Ripe Figs." They can then move on to three sets of Follow-up Questions. These questions consistently use multiple assessment formats: (1) ten multiple-choice questions objectively assessing comprehension, (2) five significant quotations subjectively assessing comprehension; and (3) two essay questions subjectively assessing comprehension. Each story ends with Writing suggestions. In the Sample Lesson, students are introduced to pre-writing and outlining strategies. In subsequent stories, students will find multiple writing prompts.

I suggest that you work through the Sample Lesson in class for it is here that you will find the dynamics and possibilities of this book encapsulated.

Chapter Structure

The stories in *American 24-Karat Gold* are arranged into five topical chapters, based on and reinforcing the literary terminology the student has already encountered in the Sample Lesson. While all stories contain combinations of these terms and/or elements, each of the chapters focuses on a specific term(s) and/or element(s) by beginning with a restatement of the term(s) and then by presenting the stories that have been specifically chosen to demonstrate the term(s) and/or element(s). Chapter 1 focuses on characters and conflicts, Chapter 2 focuses on setting and props, Chapter 3 focuses on plot and foreshadowing, and Chapter 4 focuses on irony. Chapter 5 focuses on symbolism, but Chapter 5 is different from the other chapters. The more complex stories in Chapter 5 bring together all that students have learned in earlier chapters and are intended to challenge advanced students.

Within each chapter, you have many options:

1. You can assign these chapters in any order.
2. You can also assign the stories within each chapter in any order. Generally, the stories within each chapter progress from more accessible to more difficult; but the strengths of each class vary, and what may seem more accessible to one group may be more difficult for another.
3. You can assign all the stories in a chapter or any number you prefer.
4. You can ignore all these suggestions and assign any story at your discretion.
5. You can use one of the alternative tables of contents. Selecting from the *Intent and/or Tone Contents* can make for interesting study. The *Chronological Contents* offers an historical perspective for more thematic or sophisticated study, wherein the stories move, generally, from Puritan moral and supernatural concerns to laic human affairs and, with Jackson and O'Connor, back to moral concerns. In this context, students visit the Mississippi with Twain, the Civil War with Bierce, the suburban movement with Thurber, the disillusionment after World War I with the modernists, and discrimination and/or cultural concerns with contemporary writers.

Story Structure

Each story in *American 24-Karat Gold* is set amid carefully designed teaching materials, and because the format is consistent, you will be able to find material easily. These materials were discussed generally in the overview of the Sample Lesson above, but here we look at the materials more closely.

Pre-Reading Materials

Each story selection begins with pre-reading materials. The pre-reading materials prepare students for reading stories while offering you insights into their vocabulary mastery and study habits.

Pre-Reading Vocabulary—Context presents words that are crucial to understanding the story. These words have been chosen to make the story accessible to students and may or may not be the most sophisticated words in the story. For more sophisticated study, all potentially trouble-some words in any given story are presented in the Instructor's Manual, where you will find words listed in the order in which they appear in the story so that you can easily locate them and identify them for students in the story's text.

Pre-Reading Vocabulary—Word Attack offers structural analysis exercises. These words were chosen not for their sophistication, but because they help students apply structural analysis skills. Thus, before students start the story, they have defined at least 20 words in context and 10 to 30 words by structural analysis. The need for distracting glossed words and marginal definitions is thereby eliminated, because students are well pre-pared by the pre-reading vocabulary to attack the story.

Third, Pre-Reading Questions offer food for thought as students enter the story. The author's Biography offers not only biographical background, but also additional information about the author's other works.

Journal

After students have read and annotated the story, the Journal then draws them into active reflection and participation.

- *MLA Works Cited*—Students record the story in MLA Works Cited entry format, using the generic model provided.
- *Main Characters(s)*—Students separate, describe, and defend the char-acter(s) they have selected as main character(s) (applying and reinforc-ing the separation of main ideas from supporting details).
- *Supporting Characters*—Students separate, describe, and defend the characters they have selected as supporting characters (applying and reinforcing the separation of main ideas from supporting details).
- *Setting*—Students describe and decide if they can change the setting (applying and reinforcing inference skills).
- *Sequence*—Students outline the story's events in order (applying and reinforcing sequencing and outlining skills).
- *Plot*—Students summarize the story's events in no more than three sentences (applying and reinforcing the separation of main ideas from supporting details, as well as summary skills).
- *Conflicts*—Students identify and explain the relevant conflicts (apply-ing and reinforcing inference and judgment skills).
- *Significant Quotations*—Students explain the importance of quota-tions that are central to the story (applying and reinforcing inference skills).
- *Foreshadowing, irony, or symbolism*—There may be a section to dis-cuss foreshadowing, irony, or symbolism. Students explain foreshad-owing, irony, or symbolism (applying and reinforcing inference and judgment skills).

The Journal is a comprehensive cognitive workout for students. In the Journal, students reflect on the story, sort out the details, and organize the story's components while applying and/or reinforcing the comprehension skills noted above. You can collect any part or all of the Journal to check on student progress. The wealth of diagnostic information in the Journal will enable you to spot misunderstandings, illogical thinking, and so forth, that may compromise comprehension. Requiring a completed Journal for classroom participation also assures you of students prepared to discuss the story.

Follow-up Questions

The Journal is followed by three follow-up question formats. The Follow-up Questions are designed for assessment, but can also be used for small-group or class discussion. All of these questions are intended to measure comprehension; they purposely avoid literary controversy.

- **10 Short Questions** offers ten multiple-choice questions.
- **5 Significant Quotations** asks students to explain the importance of five quotations that are always central to the story and usually different from the five quotations in the Journal.
- **2 Comprehensive Essay Questions** provides two essay prompts.

The Follow-up Questions offer you multiple, efficient assessment options. You may decide to use some questions for discussion or some for testing. If you are trying to establish standardization, the section of 10 Short Questions is applicable for standardization, measuring comprehension efficiently by psychometrically employing 10 questions with 3 choices each (only 6 are needed for accurate measurement).

Writing Prompts

Each story concludes with options for **Writing.** Here, two prompts for personal writing are included. Then, under **Further Writing,** you will find prompts for more advanced, research-oriented writing. These prompts may be literary (compare and contrast this story with another in this book, with another by this author, with one by another author, and so forth) or topical research suggestions.

Instructor's Manual

The **Instructor's Manual (IM)** offers valuable resources for teachers. In addition to an overview of the book's pedagogy, the IM offers additional information on each story.

1. The entry for each story starts with a brief overview and suggestions for appropriate readers.

2. Next, each entry offers an extensive list of all potentially troublesome words in the story, assembled with both the native speaker and the ESL student in mind. Words are listed in the order they appear in the story for easy location.

3. Under plot, each story is condensed to one sentence; you may find these summaries useful in selecting stories for assignment.

4. Suggested answers to the Journal and Follow-up Questions are provided. The suggested answers—suggested because these are, after all, literary pursuits and students answers will vary—set parameters for correctness. The only areas that have clearly right and/or wrong answers are the MLA Works Cited entry and 10 Short Questions.

To order a copy of the Instructor's Manual, contact your Longman sales representative and request ISBN 0-321-08331-8.

Some Final Notes

The materials in *American 24-Karat Gold*—the context and structural vocabulary exercises, the journal format, the three assessment options, as well as many of the writing prompts—have been extensively field-tested by 2,000 students. These field tests have taken place in one of the most culturally diverse counties in the nation—Middlesex County, New Jersey. Two results have occurred. First, the story lessons have not only increased all students' competencies but have also come to serve as a basis for acculturation discussions with ESL and/or international students. Second, the pedagogical materials have been streamlined to maximize learning efficacy and to minimize administrative inefficiency.

It should also be noted that, although copyright restrictions apply, we have elided offensive words wherever feasible.

Last, but certainly not least, we must address the stories themselves. The richness of the literature speaks for itself, and the stories have been carefully chosen to present the best of American short stories by some of America's foremost writers. Increasingly, we are seeing students who have never heard of O. Henry or Mark Twain, let along Faulkner, Hurston, or Hughes. This collection sets out to expand the basic literary lexicon of today's entering student.

Two criteria were used to select the stories in this anthology: first, that the author is a recognized American writer and, second, that the story is important, accessible, or interesting. Tom Sawyer painting the fence? It's in here. The irony of O. Henry and the macabre aura of Poe. They're in here. This is America and America's best.

I sincerely hope you and your students enjoy reading these stories as much as I have enjoyed discovering them, rediscovering them, and working with them.

—Yvonne Collioud Sisko
Matawan, New Jersey

Sample Lesson

Ripe Figs

by

Kate Chopin

The best way to learn how to use something is to do just that—to use it. This sample lesson presents a very short work, "Ripe Figs" by Kate Chopin, to demonstrate how this book works. This sample lesson presents all the materials that surround each story. Generally, each story starts with pre-reading activities, which are designed to make your reading easier, and ends with a journal, follow-up questions, and writing assignments that are designed to improve your understanding. This sample lesson also introduces the elements of a short story—elements that you will be using throughout this book.

Let's begin.

Ripe Figs

KATE CHOPIN

PRE-READING VOCABULARY
CONTEXT

Use context clues to define these words before reading. Use a dictionary as needed.

The words that are critical for your understanding of the story are presented at the beginning of each story. These are not necessarily the most difficult words. Rather, they are words that you will need to know to read the story more easily.

The **Pre-reading Vocabulary—Context** exercises present words in sentences. You should try to define each word by using the **context clues** in the sentence. Note that the first eight words have been defined as examples for you. Look at question 1. The word here is "fig," and the clues let you know that this is something "small" and "purple" that grows "on a tree" and is "delicious." Since "delicious" implies it is something to eat and since fruit grows on a tree, we can define a "fig" as "a small, purple fruit that grows on a tree." Using this same strategy, check the meanings of the next seven words. Then use the clues and define the remaining words.

1. The small, purple *figs* grow on a tree and are delicious. *Fig* means

   a small, purple fruit that grows on a tree .

2. Some may say "mom" or "mama" for "mother," while the French may say *"mère"* or *"maman"*. *Maman* means _a name for "mother"_ .

3. The campers rowed their boat slowly through the reeds along the side of the *bayou. Bayou* means _a slow-moving body of water_ .

4. The children licked the long *sugar cane* they found in the field. *Sugar cane* means _a stick-like food_ .

5. The elderly person's fingers seemed to cross each other in *gnarled* knots from old age and arthritis. *Gnarled* means

   knotted and crisscrossed .

6. Ted is so *patient*; he doesn't mind if Laura takes two hours to do her hair. *Patient* means <u>willing to wait</u>.

7. There is a stone *statue* of a little boy in the middle of the garden. *Statue* means <u>a carved or sculpted figure</u>.

8. The tiny *hummingbird's* wings moved so quickly that you could not see them. *Hummingbird* means <u>a small bird with rapidly moving wings</u>.

9. José was *disconsolate* after he lost the championship game. *Disconsolate* means _____.

10. Kings and queens usually walk in a very upright and *stately* manner. *Stately* means _____.

11. Furniture is often first covered in a simple *muslin* under the fine fabric to protect the fabric. *Muslin* means _____.

12. The haze of color often drawn around a saint's head is called a halo or *aureole*. *Aureole* means _____.

13. In spite of all the upset and confusion, Luis stayed cool and *placid*. *Placid* means _____.

14. The bride's dishes are fine *porcelain* decorated with tiny flowers and trimmed in gold. *Porcelain* means _____.

15. I will go to see my aunt, *Tante* Lena, to celebrate her birthday. *Tante* means _____.

16. I love the large yellow *chrysanthemums* that bloom in a fall garden. *Chrysanthemum* means _____.

PRE-READING VOCABULARY
WORD ATTACK

Define these words by solving the parts. Use a dictionary as needed.

The **Pre-reading Vocabulary—Word Attack** exercises present words that you know but that may look strange or have altered meanings because of added parts. Here you will want to look for and define the **root,** or core, word. Then look for and define the **prefix,** or part added to the front of the word. Finally, look for and define the **suffix,** or part added to the end of the word.

Prefixes (added to the front) and suffixes (added to the end) are called **affixes.** By defining the root and the affixes, you should be able to define each of these words with little trouble. For instance, look at question 1. The very simple word "ripe" has two suffixes (–en, –ing) that can be added to it, which change the word's meaning from "ready" or "mature" to "getting ready" or "maturing." Using this same strategy, take each word apart, and define it by using the roots and affixes. The next three words are defined for you also. Try the last three on your own. See Glossary (page 449) for affix definitions.

1. ripening   *becoming ripe or mature*
2. la Madone   *mother or Holy Mother*
3. restless   *active; cannot rest*
4. summertime
5. godmother
6. plumpest

PRE-READING QUESTIONS

Try answering these questions as you read.

Now that you have defined words that might prevent you from understanding the story, you are ready to turn to the story. Before reading, it is always helpful to start with a purpose. Use the story's title and any other relevant information to set up questions to answer while you are reading. Answering these questions will make your reading easier and more efficient, so that you do not have to reread and reread to understand the story.

Each story starts with **Pre-Reading Questions** to set your purpose. Keep these questions in mind as you read.

Who are the main characters? Supporting characters?

What does Babette want?

What does Maman want?

What does the title mean?

Ripe Figs

KATE CHOPIN

Before each story, a brief biography provides some information about the author. In addition to learning about the author's life, you may also pick up information that will help you in reading the story. The biography may also list other works by the author, in case you would like to read more by the author.

Read Kate Chopin's biography. It tells you, among other things, that she writes about the people she met in Louisiana and that she likes to use "symbols and images from nature." Both of these pieces of information will come in handy as you read "Ripe Figs."

Kate O'Flaherty Chopin was born in St. Louis in 1851 to an affluent family. Although her father died when she was young, her widowed mother gave young Kate a taste of independence. In 1870 Chopin married Oscar Chopin and moved to New Orleans and then Natchitoches Parish. Here she met the Creoles, Arcadians, and southern African Americans she would later write about. However, Oscar died in 1882, and by 1884 she sold the plantation, gathered her five children, and returned home to St. Louis, where she began to write for popular women's magazines. Influenced noticeably by de Maupassant's sense of irony and Ibsen's social comment, Chopin wrote stories, often touched with rich symbols and images from nature, that question societal assumptions and dictates. Her brief novel *The Awakening* remains her master work, although stories such as "Desiree's Baby" and "The Kiss" offer Chopin at her most terse. Chopin died in 1904.

Now it is time to turn to the story. As you read, keep the following suggestions in mind. Don't just let your eyes go over words. Instead, *get involved—get out a pen or pencil and highlighters, and use them!*

1. First, circle the name of each character, or highlight each in a different color. The first step in understanding a story is knowing *whom* it is about.
2. Second, underline or highlight in yet another color all the hints that let you know where and when the story takes place. The second step in understanding a story is knowing *where* and *when* it takes place.
3. Third, number each event in the story as it occurs. Number these events in the margin or right in the text. The third step in understanding a story is knowing *what* is happening.
4. Fourth, make notes—ideas, questions to be answered later, and so on—in the margin. These are ideas you can return to later, and they may help you understand the *how* and/or *why* of the story.
5. Fifth, but certainly not least, always reread the title. The title often gives you information that is helpful in understanding the story.

Maman-Nainaine said that when the figs were ripe Babette might go to visit her cousins down on the Bayou-Lafourche where the sugar cane grows. Not that the ripening of figs had the least thing to do with it, but that is the way Maman-Nainaine was.

2   It seemed to Babette a very long time to wait; for the leaves upon the trees were tender yet, and the figs were like little hard, green marbles.

3   But warm rains came along and plenty of strong sunshine, and though Maman-Nainaine was as patient as the statue of la Madone, and Babette as restless as a humming-bird, the first thing they both knew it was hot summertime. Every day Babette danced out to where the fig-trees were in a long line against the fence. She walked slowly beneath them, carefully peering between the gnarled, spreading branches. But each time she came disconsolate away again. What she saw there finally was something that made her sing and dance the whole long day.

4   When Maman-Nainaine sat down in her stately way to breakfast, the following morning, her muslin cap standing like an aureole around her white, placid face, Babette approached. She bore a dainty porcelain platter, which she set down before her godmother. It contained a dozen purple figs, fringed around with their rich, green leaves.

5   "Ah," said Maman-Nainaine arching her eyebrows, "how early the figs have ripened this year!"

6   "Oh," said Babette. "I think they have ripened very late."

7   "Babette," continued Maman-Nainaine, as she peeled the very plumpest figs with her pointed silver fruit-knife, "you will carry my love to them all down on Bayou-Lafourche. And tell your Tante Frosine I shall look for her at Toussaint—when the chrysanthemums are in bloom."

Now turn to the marked copy of "Ripe Figs" in Figure 1. The first half has already been noted for you. Take out your pen, pencil, and/or highlighters, and using the strategies listed above, complete the notes on "Ripe Figs." Note how effective the notations in Figure 1 are. It's important to know that Chopin uses nature to reflect life, so this is underlined in the biography. The title is "Ripe Figs," so figs (which are a delicate fruit) must somehow relate to the story. Babette and Maman-Nainaine are in the center of the story, and the cousins and Tante Toussaint are also involved. Hints like "figs" and "Bayou," as well as information in the biography, all indicate that this story is probably taking place in the South, in Louisiana. The events are numbered in sequence: (1) Babette wants to go visiting, but Maman says not yet; (2) Babette must wait for the figs to ripen; (3) the figs ripen, and Babette now can go; and (4) Maman will go in the fall. Now it is easier to see that two things are ripening or maturing here: Babette and the figs. Thus, the ripening figs reflect Babette's maturing. When the figs are ripe, she is also ripe, or mature enough to go visiting. By using the information from the biography and title and combining this information with the story's characters, setting, and events, you can see that as the figs ripen, Babette grows older and becomes ready to travel. Add your own notes in paragraphs 4 through 7.

FIGURE 1
Marked Copy of "Ripe Figs"

Ripe Figs

KATE CHOPIN

Kate O'Flaherty Chopin was born in St. Louis in 1851 to an affluent family. Although her father died when she was young, her widowed mother gave young Kate a taste of independence. In 1870 Chopin married Oscar Chopin and moved to New Orleans and then Natchitoches Parish. Here she met the Creoles, Arcadians, and southern African-Americans she would later write about. However, Oscar died in 1882, and by 1884 she sold the plantation, gathered her five children, and returned home to St. Louis, where she began to write for popular women's magazines. Influenced noticeably by de Maupassant's sense of irony and Ibsen's social comment, Chopin wrote stories, often touched with rich symbols and images from nature, that question societal assumptions and dictates. Her brief novel *The Awakening* remains her master work, although stories such as "Desiree's Baby" and "The Kiss" offer Chopin at her most terse. Chopin died in 1904.

1. Maman-Nainaine said that when the figs were ripe Babette
might go to visit her cousins down on the Bayou-Lafourche
where the sugar cane grows. Not that the ripening of figs had the
least thing to do with it, but that is the way Maman-Nainaine was.

— 1. CAN VISIT WHEN FIGS RIPEN

2.   It seemed to Babette a very long time to wait; for the leaves upon the trees were tender yet, and the figs were like little hard, green marbles.

3.   But warm rains came along and plenty of strong sunshine, and though Maman-Nainaine was as patient as the statue of la Madone, and Babette as restless as a humming-bird, the first thing they both knew it was hot summertime. Every day Babette danced out to where the fig-trees were in a long line against the fence. She walked slowly beneath them, carefully peering between the gnarled, spreading branches. But each time she came disconsolate away again. What she saw there finally was something that made her sing and dance the whole long day.

— 2. WAIT FOR FIGS TO GROW

4.   When Maman-Nainaine sat down in her stately way to breakfast, the following morning, her muslin cap standing like an aureole around her white, placid face, Babette approached. She bore a dainty porcelain platter, which she set down before her godmother. It contained a dozen purple figs, fringed around with their rich, green leaves.

5.   "Ah," said Maman-Nainaine arching her eyebrows, "how early the figs have ripened this year!"

6.   "Oh," said Babette. "I think they have ripened very late."

7.   "Babette," continued Maman-Nainaine, as she peeled the very plumpest figs with her pointed silver fruit-knife, "you will carry my love to them all down on Bayou-Lafourche. And tell your Tante Frosine I shall look for her at Toussaint—when the chrysanthemums are in bloom."

Ripe Figs

JOURNAL

Once you have finished reading and making your notes on the story, the **Journal** allows you to record and organize all the relevant information. Here you will be able to record, to organize, to reflect upon, and to make sense of all the details that can make a story challenging.

1. MLA Works Cited

Using this model, record your reading here.

Author's Last Name, First Name. "Title of the Story." <u>Title of the Book</u>. *Ed. First Last Name. City: Publisher, year. Pages of the story.*

Whenever you refer to or use anyone else's words or ideas, you must give that person credit. Failing to give credit is called **plagiarism.** Plagiarism can result in failing an assignment, failing a course, and even being removed from school.

To give credit appropriately, it is helpful to learn the format used to credit works of literature, and short stories are literature. This format was created by the MLA, which is short for Modern Language Association. The **MLA Works Cited entry** you use here is the same form you will be using in your other English classes.

The MLA entry is really a very simple form. All you have to do is follow the model given. Note that, unlike paragraphs, the first line starts at the left margin and each line *after* that is indented. Try doing this on your own. When you finish, your MLA Works Cited entry should look like the following.

Chopin, Kate. "Ripe Figs." <u>American 24 Karat Gold</u>. Ed. Yvonne C. Sisko. New York: Longman, 2002. 6.

2. Main Character(s)

Characters are the creatures that create, move, or experience the actions of a story. We normally thinks of characters as alive, animated beings, such as humans or animals, who can participate in the action, although some characters in this book will surprise you. A character may also be called an **actor, player, person, personage,** or **persona.**

Characters fall into two categories: main characters and supporting characters. Generally, a **main character** is central to the action. A **supporting character** may encourage the action and is usually not present as much, or as central to the action, as the main character. Sometimes it is difficult to decide if a character is main or supporting. For instance, in a murder mystery, the victim may appear at the beginning or not at all, but the entire story is about solving his or her murder. Is the victim a main character because the entire story is all about her or him, or is s/he a supporting character because s/he is simply not around much? Both answers may be correct. In literature there are not always so much right or wrong answers as there are explanations, analyses, and debates. The correctness of your answers depends on how well you explain your choices.

Characters may also be considered protagonists or antagonists. "Pro" means "for," and the **protagonist** is the hero or heroine, the character we **empathize** with or share feelings with, the character we root for. "Anti" means "against," and the **antagonist** is the villain, the enemy of the protagonist, the character we do not like, the character we root against. In "Ripe Figs" our sympathies are with Babette and her longing for adventure; she is the protagonist. Maman, who sets limits on Babette, is the antagonist. Here, these two characters are members of a seemingly close family and love each other, but in other stories the protagonist and antagonist will not be such close friends.

The author speaks to us through her or his characters. When an author writes using "I" or "we," this is called a **first-person narration**. The first person makes a story very immediate. The character who tells the story is called the **narrator.** If the author addresses the reader directly using "you," this narrative technique is called the **second-person narration.** Second person is not used often in American literature. Finally, if the author uses "he," "she," "it," or "they" to tell the story, this narrative technique is called the **third-person narration.** This is the most common narrative form, with the author seeming to be more of an observer and less of a participant in the story. In "Ripe Figs" both Babette and Maman are observed as "she." The story is thus told in the third person; the author is the narrator who observes but does not enter the story.

With these understandings, turn to the *Main* and *Supporting Character(s)* entries in the Journal. Note that we have already filled in Babette, briefly describing her and noting her important place in the story. Who else should be here? Add an entry in which you describe and defend Maman as a main character.

Note: When discussing literature, always use the present tense. Although a story may have been written a thousand years ago, each time a story is read the characters and actions come to life and are alive right now, so keep your discussion of the characters and events in the present tense.

Describe each main character, and explain why you think each is a main character.

Babette is a young girl who lives with her godmother and wants to go visit her cousins. She is a main character because the story is about her wants and her godmother's rules.

3. Supporting Characters

> Now fill in the *Supporting Characters* entry. This has been started for you. Certainly, the cousins support the action because they are the reason Babette wants to travel. Who else should be here? Add an entry in which you describe and defend Tante Frosine as a supporting character. Remember from your context studies that "tante" means "aunt," so Tante Frosine is probably the cousins' mother.

Describe each supporting character, and explain why you think each is a supporting character.

Babette's cousins are supporting characters. Although we never see them, they are the reason for the story's conflict.

4. Setting

> **Setting** is a catch-all term that describes the time, place, and surroundings of a story. In a short story, the setting is usually, although not always, limited. The story usually takes place in a shorter amount of time than in a longer work, and fewer places are involved.
>
> **Props** go along with the setting. Props (short for "properties") are the inanimate objects in a story. Props sometimes take on the qualities of characters.
>
> Now turn to the *Setting* entry. You already have a head start because the place, Louisiana, is described. But you still have several things to do. First, you need to add when the story takes place. Check the biography for when Chopin lived, and remember that traveling seems to be a very big accomplishment in this story, unlike it is in today's world of easy car transportation. Second, think about props and mention the figs, which are certainly part of this story. Third, decide if you can change this setting and, if so, to where or when. Think of some other place and/or time in which the story could be set, and explain your thinking. You will need, for instance, a place where delicate fruit can grow during a warm season.

Describe the setting. Decide if this setting could be changed and, if so, to where and when.

This must be set in the South because figs are a delicate fruit, because the French words sound like words spoken in Louisiana, and because the biography says that Chopin wrote about the South.

5. Sequence

A story is based around a simple skeleton of events called a **plot.** Around this basic plot, a logical order of events or **sequence** occurs that builds tension or, in mysteries, suspense. In stories we call all the events in the sequence a **story line.** The plot is the bare framework, while the sequence supplies the details that make each story unique.

Have you ever gone to the movies and watched the end credits roll while you were still waiting for the movie to get going? You looked at the person sitting next to you, felt cheated, and asked, "What happened?" What happened is that somewhere along the line, the storyteller failed.

In a well-written story, one event logically leads to another, and then to another, and so on, so that each word and action counts and builds tension that carries your interest. The tension peaks at the **climax** and then resolves in the **dénouement.** When any of these pieces is missing, poorly developed, or unbelievable, we are disappointed. (Movie sequels, in fact, purposely stop at the climax and before the dénouement so that we will return for the next episode.) A very simple story line appears in Figure 2.

FIGURE 2
Simple Story Line

Use information about sequence and plot in the Journal. In the *Sequence* entry, you are asked to relate all the events in order. The outline is started for you, with Babette's desire to go visiting and Maman's restriction. Now look at your numbered notes on the story, and complete the outline. Add as many events as you feel are necessary.

Relate the events of the story in order.

     I. Babette wants to go visiting, but Maman-Nainaine says she must wait for the ripe figs.

    II.

    III.

    IV.

6. Plot

> Next, in the *Plot* entry, summarize all these events into one sentence. Summarizing makes you look back over the story and reflect on what you have read. Remember this is the bare framework of the story, so keep it short.

Tell the story in no more than one sentence.

7. Conflicts

> **Conflicts** are the disagreements between the characters. Conflicts build the tension in a story. Many types of conflict are possible. The conflict may be **human versus human,** as when a character(s) is pitted against another character(s). The conflict may be **human versus society,** as when a character(s) struggles against a group, community, or social structure. The conflict may be **human versus technology,** as when a character(s) vies with the tools of science or machines of his society. The conflict may be **human versus nature,** as when a character(s) battles with the forces of nature. The conflict may be **human versus the supernatural,** as when a character(s) vies with God or gods or demons. Finally, the conflict may be **human versus her/himself,** as when a character wrestles with his or her own internal and self-defeating **flaw.** More often than not, a story will contain a combination of these conflicts.
>
> Let's now turn to the *Conflicts* entry. Human versus human, in Babette's struggle with Maman's restriction, is already noted. What other types of conflicts are present in the story? How about human versus nature in Babette's wanting to mature rapidly, and human versus herself in Babette's impatience? Add these to and explain them in your Journal entry.

Identify and explain the conflicts involved here.

Human versus human applies to Babette wanting to go and Maman-Nainaine stopping her.

8. Significant Quotations

By now, you already understand the story well. You have identified the pieces and pulled them together. Now you need to reflect on the story. In this section, you will find quotations from key parts of the story. By explaining why each quotation is important to the story, you can deepen your understanding.

First, look up the quotation in the story text. Underline and note what is important about this moment in the story. Then, record the importance of this moment. Tell who is speaking and why this quotation is important to the action in the story. The first one has been done for you. Now, complete the rest. Record the page number for practice with MLA parenthetical notation.

Explain the importance of each of these quotations. Record the page number in the parentheses.

a. "Maman-Nainaine said that when the figs were ripe Babette might go to visit her cousins down on the Bayou-Lafourche where the sugar cane grows" (7).

This quotation sets the tension in the story between Babette and Maman-Nainaine and between Babette and nature. Babette wants to visit her cousins, but she must wait until the figs—and she—are ripe or mature enough to go.

b. "Every day Babette danced out to where the fig-trees were in a long line against the fence" (   ).

c. "What she saw there finally was something that made her sing and dance the whole long day" (   ).

d. "'Ah,' said Maman-Nainaine arching her eyebrows, 'how early the figs have ripened this year!'" (   ).

e. "'And tell your Tante Frosine I shall look for her at Toussaint—when the chrysanthemums are in bloom'" (   ).

9. Foreshadowing, Irony, or Symbolism

Other elements that may enhance a story are foreshadowing, irony, and symbolism.

Foreshadowing is a technique some authors use to help explain or predict events to come. The author may sprinkle information or hints throughout the story to help predict actions that are yet to happen.

Irony is found in the difference between what *is* and what *should be*. Irony may be bitter—you work and work and work, and someone new, who has done nothing, arrives at your job and gets the promotion you deserve. Irony may be humorous—you wake up late and race around knowing you will be late for class, only to get to school and find out that your class has been canceled. Irony may even be providential—you sleep in and miss your bus only to find out that the bus was in an accident and you are still safe at home. Think of ironies as unexpected twists in time, places, or events.

Symbols are objects or characters that represent something beyond their face value. For instance, an American flag is really nothing more than pieces of cloth sewn together, but the American flag represents the pride and glory and industry of America. By looking beyond the surface, you will find many symbols in literature.

In the *Foreshadowing, Irony,* or *Symbolism* entry, you will often be asked to discuss one of these elements. Here, you are asked to discuss the symbols in this story, and there are several. First and foremost, the figs represent maturity and reflect Babette's growth. Second, the seasons are relevant here. Summer is youthful Babette's time, while fall is the older Maman's and Tante Frosine's time. In literature, spring may represent birth or rebirth or youth; summer may represent youth or the full blossom of life; fall may represent middle age; and winter may represent the later years. Here Chopin gives us clues to the ages by using the seasons. The chrysanthemums (flowers that bloom in the fall) represent the time for Babette's elders.

Although foreshadowing and irony are not particularly relevant to this story, be aware that Kate Chopin is known for her ironic twists. "The Story of an Hour" (page 287) takes a wonderfully unexpected turn. And, of course, here the ripening figs foreshadow Babette's growth.

Identify and explain the symbols Chopin uses.

FOLLOW-UP QUESTIONS

10 SHORT QUESTIONS

Follow-up questions are designed to measure your comprehension of each story. In the first set of questions, **10 Short Questions,** you will see ten multiple-choice questions aimed at measuring your comprehension.

Notice that you are instructed to "select the <u>best</u> answer." In some stories, more than one answer will be correct; it is your job to choose the *best* answer. The first five have been done for you here.

The answer to question 1 is "a" because Babette is the younger of the two. We know this because Babette's actions and the information from the story—Maman means "mother" and Maman is Babette's godmother—imply that Babette is younger and Maman is older. The answer to question 2 is "b" for the same reasons listed in the answer to question 1. The answer to question 3 is "c" because we are clearly told that Maman is the godmother. The cousins are in Babette's age group and are whom she wants to visit; there is no mention of a sister in the story. The answer to question 4 is "a" because, as the story implies, figs need a warm summer and rain to grow; neither "cold" nor "desert" fit the story's setting. The answer to question 5 is "c," because we are clearly told about Babette's "restlessness" as opposed to Maman's "patience."

Now complete questions 6 through 10 on your own. The correct answers appear on page 20.

Select the <u>best</u> answer for each.

<u>a</u> 1. Babette is
    a. younger than Maman.
    b. older than Maman.
    c. the same age as Maman.

<u>b</u> 2. Maman-Nainaine is
    a. younger than Babette.
    b. older than Babette.
    c. the same age as Babette.

<u>c</u> 3. Maman-Nainaine is Babette's
    a. sister.
    b. cousin.
    c. godmother.

<u>a</u> 4. "Ripe Figs" is probably set in
    a. a warm climate.
    b. a cold climate.
    c. a desert climate.

<u>c</u> 5. Babette
    a. does not wait for the figs.
    b. waits calmly for the figs.
    c. waits impatiently for the figs.

____ 6. Maman
    a. does not wait for the figs.
    b. waits calmly for the figs.
    c. waits impatiently for the figs.

____ 7. The figs symbolize
    a. Maman's maturing.
    b. Babette's maturing.
    c. Babette's cousins' maturing.

_____ 8. We can infer that Maman is
relatively
a. poor.
b. middle class.
c. well off.

_____ 9. We can infer that the cousins
live
a. nearby.
b. a distance away.
c. very, very far away.

_____ 10. The chrysanthemums tell us
that Maman is
a. very young.
b. very old.
c. in her middle years.

5 SIGNIFICANT QUOTATIONS

Approach these **5 Significant Quotations** the same way you approached the
significant quotations in the Journal. Usually, the quotations in the Journal and
the quotations here are different, but all are important and central to the story.
Remember you are demonstrating how well you have understood the story, so
explain why each quotation is important as completely as you can.

The first quotation here has already been done for you. Now, explain the
significance of the remaining four. (The answers are on page 20.)

Explain the importance of each of these quotations.

1. "Maman-Nainaine said that when the figs were ripe Babette might go
   to visit her cousins down on the Bayou-Lafourche where the sugar
   cane grows."

   This sentence sets the tension in the story between Babette and
   Maman-Nainaine and between Babette and nature. Babette wants to
   visit her cousins, but she must wait until the figs—and she—are ripe
   or mature enough.

2. "It seemed to Babette a very long time to wait [. . .]."

3. "But warm rains came along and plenty of strong sunshine, and
   though Maman-Nainaine was as patient as the statue of la Madone,
   and Babette as restless as a humming-bird, the first thing they knew it
   was hot summertime."

4. "It [the platter] contained a dozen purple figs, fringed around with
   their rich, green leaves."

5. " 'Babette,' continued Maman-Nainaine, as she peeled the very
   plumpest figs with her pointed silver fruit-knife, 'you will carry my
   love to them all down on Bayou-LaFourche.' "

2 COMPREHENSION ESSAY QUESTIONS

The *2 Comprehension Essay Questions* offer opportunities for extended essays. Your teacher may assign one or both for individual assignment or for group discussion. Gather your thoughts and respond, demonstrating what you have learned from the story. Note that none of these questions asks how well you liked the story or even if you liked it at all. The intention here is very simply to find out what you have understood in the story.

Note that the directions ask you to "use specific details and information from the story." This does not mean that you have to memorize the story, but it does mean that you should know the characters and events in the story. Look at question 1. It asks you to explain the title, so for this essay question, you will want to review the story's events and the relevance of the figs. Now look at question 2. It asks you to focus on the ages involved in the story, and for this you will want to discuss the ages of Babette and her cousins as opposed to those of Maman and Tante Frosine, remembering the references to summer and fall in the story.

Use specific details and information from the story to answer these as completely as possible.

1. How does the title relate to the story? Explain the significance of the title using specific details and information from the story.

2. Explain the relevance of age in this story. Use specific details and information from the story to support your explanation.

WRITING

Each story ends with a final section of **Writing** prompts. The first two prompts offer suggestions for personal writing. The prompts under Further Writing are designed with research in mind. These may suggest comparing and contrasting the story with other stories in this book or with other stories the author or another author has written, or they may suggest other research topics. Your teacher will guide you through the writing process.

At this point, a few words about the writing process are in order. Writing does not start with a pen or pencil; it starts with ideas. Before you start writing, jot down ideas, and then organize them. Here are two **pre-writing strategies** to get the ideas flowing:

1. On a clean sheet of paper, write one key word from the topic you plan to write about. Now look at the key word, and start listing every word that this key word brings to mind. Avoid sentences or even phrases, as they take longer to write and can break your train of thought. Just write words—lots of words, the more the merrier. When you run out of words, look back at the key word, and write more words. When you finish, you will have a whole list of ideas to start thinking about for your essay. This process is called **free associating** or **brainstorming**.

2. On a clean sheet of paper, draw a circle. Inside that circle, write one key word from the topic you plan to write about. Now look at the key word, and start tagging other, related words onto the circle. Then tag words onto the tag words, and so on. When you get stuck, look back at the key word, and add more words. When you finish, you will have groups of words—ideas—to start thinking about for your essay. This process is called **grouping, networking,** or **clustering.**

Once you have the ideas—and you should have plenty from either of these pre-writing strategies—the next step is to organize them into an **outline.** Do not worry about Roman numerals at this stage. Rather, develop logical groupings of these ideas into a working outline. You may find that there are words/ideas in your pre-write that you do not want to use. Cross these out. You may also find ideas in your outline that are out of place. Number and renumber the groups to make them work for you. (Your instructor may want you to formalize your outline later, but at this point the important thing is to find an organization that works for you.)

Look at the first writing prompt on page 20. It asks you, first, to discuss one specific maturing process you have experienced and, second, to relate this process to a reflective image, much like the figs in our story. In Figure 3 both a cluster and an outline on the topic, "Getting a License," is demonstrated, but you may want to try "Learning to Ride a Bike" or "Graduating High School" or any other maturing process you prefer.

FIGURE 3
Sample Cluster and Outline

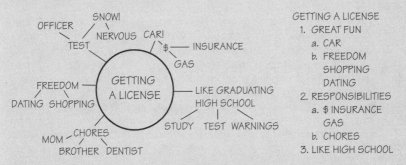

To prepare the pre-writing cluster and outline shown in Figure 3, we first tagged ideas onto "License" and then tagged ideas onto ideas. Second, we looked for a logical order and numbered and renumbered the cluster. Third, we transferred these numbers into the informal, working outline. Finally, we looked back over what we had and decided that getting a license was like attending high school, because of all the preparation and responsibility involved in getting a license. With these ideas initiated and organized, we are now ready to write an intelligent and orderly essay.

Now try your hand at the other writing prompts.

Use these ideas for writing an essay.

1. We all go through maturing processes. Think of a specific process you have experienced. Then think of something that reflects your process, much like the figs reflect Babette's growth. Write an essay on your growing up process, relating it to a continuing symbol.

2. Age has an effect on all of us. Write about a specific incident when age affected you or someone you know.

Further Writing

1. Read Kate Chopin's "The Storm" (which can be found in a library), and compare and contrast the images of nature in "The Storm" with those in "Ripe Figs."

2. Read Kate Chopin's "The Kiss" (which can be found in a library), and compare the women in "The Kiss" and those in "The Storm."

Answers to
10 Short Questions

6. b. We are clearly told Maman is "patient" and not "impatient."
7. b. We know Babette is the one growing and "maturing."
8. c. Their genteel life, her leisurely breakfast, and the "silver fruit-knife" all imply wealth.
9. b. Bayou-Lafourche, in Louisiana, and Maman's reluctance to let Babette go at all both imply that this is, on the one hand, not "near by" and, on the other hand, not "very, very far away." The middle choice is the best choice here.
10. c. Again, we have discussed literary seasons and the middle choice is the best choice here. Spring or summer would refer to youth, and winter would refer to old age. Chrysanthemums are fall, and fall is middle age.

Answers to
5 Significant Quotations

2. You should note that this sets up the central tension of Babette having to wait for the figs to ripen so that she can go visiting.
3. You should comment on Babette's "restlessness" and Maman's patience. This is not an easy wait for Babette.
4. You should explain that this is the moment of climax. The figs are ripe. You should explain that the ripe figs represent Babette's maturing and she now is old enough/mature enough/ripe enough to travel to her cousins'.
5. You should note that this is the story's resolution, the dénouement. Babette may now travel.

1

Characters
and Conflicts

Characters are the creatures that create, move, or experience the actions of a story. We normally think of characters as alive, animated beings, such as humans or animals, who can participate in the action. A character may also be called an **actor, player, person, persona,** or **personage.**

Characters fall into two categories: main characters and supporting characters. Generally, a **main character** is central to the action. A **supporting character** may encourage the action and is usually not present as much, or as central to the action, as the main character. Sometimes, it is difficult to decide if a character is main or supporting. For instance, in a murder mystery the victim may only appear at the beginning of the story or not at all, but the entire story is about solving his or her murder. Is the victim a main character because the entire story is about her or him, or is s/he a supporting character because s/he simply is not present? Both answers may be correct. In literature there are not always so much right or wrong answers as there are explanations, analyses, and debates. The correctness of your answers depends on how well you explain your choices.

The author speaks to us through his or her characters. When an author writes using "I" or "we," this is called a **first-person narration.** The first person makes a story very immediate. The character who tells the story is called the **narrator.** If the author addresses the reader directly using "you," this narrative technique is called the **second-person narration.** The second person is not used often in American literature. Finally, if the author uses "he," "she," "it," or "they" to tell the story, this narrative technique is called the **third-person narration.** This is the most common narrative form, with the author seeming to be more of an observer and less of a participant in the story. In this chapter, all of the stories, except Edgar Allan Poe's "The Tell-Tale Heart," are told in the third person. Notice how immediate and how different Poe's story is.

Characters may also be considered protagonists or antagonists. "Pro" means "for," and the **protagonist** is the hero or heroine, the character we empathize with, or share feelings with, the character we root for. "Anti" means "against," and the antagonist is the villain, the enemy of the protagonist, the character we do not like, the character we root against. Be aware that authors like to play with these roles. You may be sympathetic to one character and then find that the author turns things upside down and you no longer like the character.

When we talk about protagonists and antagonists, we need to talk about conflicts. Conflicts are the disagreements between characters. Conflicts build the tension in a story. Many types of conflicts are possible. The conflict may be human versus human, as when a character(s) is pitted against another character(s). Notice the conflict between the old man and the narrator in "The Tell-Tale Heart." The conflict may be human versus society, as when a character(s) struggles against a group, community, or social structure. Notice how Walter Mitty solves his conflict with his suburban world. The conflict may be human versus herself/himself, as when a character wrestles with her or his own internal and self-defeating flaw. Notice the flaw in the narrator of "The Tell-Tale Heart." The conflict may be human versus technology, as when a character(s) vies with the tools of science or machines of her or his society. This conflict is at the very core of "There Will Come Soft Rains." The conflict may be human versus nature, as when a character(s) battles with the forces of nature. Notice Old Phoenix's struggle in "A Worn Path." Finally, the conflict may be human versus the supernatural, as when a character(s) vies with God or gods or demons. You will discover this conflict when you read the stories of Poe and Melville in Chapter 5. More often than not, a story will contain a combination of these conflicts.

Stories in this chapter focus on characters and are called character studies. In a character study, the emphasis is on getting to know each character, and the action of the story is used to help you understand each character better. Eudora Welty takes you through Old Phoenix's persistence, Roberta Fernandez through Zulema's cares, and James Thurber through Walter Mitty's fantasies. Then Edgar Allan Poe, whose stories are invariably character studies, works his sinister magic as he walks you through insanity. In reading Poe, keep asking yourself which character is the protagonist and which is the antagonist. And finally, Ray Bradbury turns all our assumptions about characters upside down as inanimate things and machines take on the qualities of characters. The living, breathing family and even the dog become mere support or properties in this story centered on things.

Now it is time to turn to the stories. Enjoy the characters you meet.

A Worn Path

EUDORA WELTY

PRE-READING VOCABULARY
CONTEXT

Use context clues to define these words before reading. Use a dictionary as needed.

1. The cook wore a full *apron* to cover the front of his clothes. *Apron* means _____.

2. The *thicket* of bushes was so dense that only the little rabbits could live under it. *Thicket* means _____.

3. When he walked, the elderly man used a slender *cane* made of oak to steady himself. *Cane* means _____.

4. The land was quite even until it dipped into a *hollow* near the stream. *Hollow* means _____.

5. The *thorn* on the rose stem stuck Gert in the finger. *Thorn* means

   _____.

6. When Laura performed in front of hundreds of people, she was so nervous that her hands were *trembling. Trembling* means

   _____.

7. Whether Teddy could pass chemistry or not became a personal *trial* for him. *Trial* means _____.

8. As the lions finished their meal, the *buzzards* flew overhead and then waited to finish the rest. *Buzzard* means _____.

9. A figure made of straw stuffed into clothes so that it will look like a person and keep birds out of a field is called a *scarecrow. Scarecrow* means _____.

10. The cool water bubbled up from below, making a *spring* at the top.
    Spring means _____.

11. Tashika was lost in thought as she *meditated* on her new job.
    Meditate means _____.

12. The tall building looked like a tower as it stood so straight and *erect*.
    Erect means _____.

13. George knew he was close to home when he saw the tall, cone-shaped
    steeple on top of the church. *Steeple* means _____.

14. Workers worked for three years to build the tall *tower* with the clock
    at the top. *Tower* means _____.

15. Whenever she can, Sallie donates *charity*, in time and money, to the
    poor. *Charity* means _____.

16. When Lucille felt ill, she went to the drugstore and bought
    medicine she could take to feel better. *Medicine* means

    _____.

17. Graduation ceremonies, with their formal speeches and many well-
    dressed people, are very *dignified* events. *Dignified* means

    _____.

18. The *lye* Tim was mixing to make soap got on his skin and ate the skin
    away. *Lye* means _____.

19. He is so *obstinate* and never wants to do anything anyone else wants
    to do. *Obstinate* means _____.

20. Jamie decided to buy a *windmill*, a hand-held toy with paddles that
    turn in the wind, for Megan. *Windmill* means _____.

Pre-reading Vocabulary
Word Attack

Define these words by solving the parts. Use a dictionary as needed.

1. pinewoods
2. shoe-laces
3. numberless
4. pearly
5. acceptable
6. barbed-wire

7. overhead
8. gunshot
9. crisscrossed
10. clockwork
11. forgiveness

Pre-reading Questions

Try answering these questions as you read.

Who is Old Phoenix?

What does she do?

What do her actions tell you about her?

A Worn Path

Eudora Welty

Eudora Welty was born in Jackson, Mississippi, in 1909. After studying at Mississippi State College for Women, the University of Wisconsin, and the Columbia University Graduate School of Business, she returned to the South and eventually turned to writing. Her writing presents a much more pleasant view of the South than Faulkner's, and the triumphs of her always-interesting characters inspire us all. Her other works include *The Collected Stories of Eudora Welty* and *The Optimist's Daughter*, which won the Pulitzer Prize in 1972.

It was December—a bright frozen day in the early morning. Far out in the country there was an old Negro woman with her head tied in a red rag, coming along a path through the pinewoods. Her name was Phoenix Jackson. She was very old and small and she walked slowly in the dark pine shadows, moving a little from side to side in her steps, with the balanced heaviness and lightness of a pendulum in a grandfather clock. She carried a thin, small cane made from an umbrella, and with this she kept tapping the frozen earth in front of her. This made a grave and persistent noise in the still air, that seemed meditative like the chirping of a solitary little bird.

2   She wore a dark striped dress reaching down to her shoe tops, and an equally long apron of bleached sugar sacks, with a full pocket: all neat and tidy, but every time she took a step she might have fallen over her shoe-laces, which dragged from her unlaced shoes. She looked straight ahead. Her eyes were blue with age. Her skin had a pattern all its own of numberless branching wrinkles and as though a whole little tree stood in the middle of her forehead, but a golden color ran underneath, and the two knobs of her cheeks were illuminated by a yellow burning under the dark. Under the red rag her hair came down on her neck in the frailest of ringlets, still black, and with an odor like copper.

3   Now and then there was a quivering in the thicket. Old Phoenix said, "Out of my way, all you foxes, owls, beetles, jack rabbits, coons, and wild animals! . . . Keep out from under these feet, little bobwhites. . . . Keep the big wild hogs out of my path. Don't let none of those come running my direction. I got a long way." Under her small black-freckled hand her cane, limber as a buggy whip, would switch at the brush as if to rouse up any hiding things.

4   On she went. The woods were deep and stiff. The sun made the pine needles almost too bright to look at, up where the wind rocked. The cones dropped as light as feathers. Down in the hollow was the mourning dove—it was not too late for him.

5   The path ran up a hill. "Seem like there is chains about my feet, time I get this far," she said, in the voice of argument old people keep to use with themselves. "Something always take a hold of me on this hill—pleads I should stay."

6   After she got to the top she turned and gave a full, severe look behind her where she had come. "Up through pines," she said at length. "Now down through oaks."

7   Her eyes opened their widest, and she started down gently. But before she got to the bottom of the hill a bush caught her dress.

8   Her fingers were busy and intent, but her skirts were full and long, so that before she could pull them free in one place they were caught in another. It was not possible to allow the dress to tear. "I in the thorny bush," she said. "Thorns, you doing your appointed work. Never want to let folks pass—no sir. Old eyes thought you was a pretty little *green* bush."

9   Finally, trembling all over, she stood free, and after a moment dared to stoop for her cane.

10   "Sun so high!" she cried, leaning back and looking, while the thick tears went over her eyes. "The time getting all gone here."

11   At the foot of this hill was a place where a log was laid across the creek.

12   "Now comes the trial," said Phoenix.

13   Putting her right foot out, she mounted the log and shut her eyes. Lifting her skirt, levelling her cane fiercely before her, like a festival figure in some parade, she began to march across. Then she opened her eyes and she was safe on the other side.

14   "I wasn't as old as I thought," she said.

15   But she sat down to rest. She spread her skirts on the bank around her and folded her hands over her knees. Up above her was a tree in a pearly cloud of mistletoe. She did not dare to close her eyes, and when a little boy brought her a little plate with a slice of marble-cake on it she spoke to him. "That would be acceptable," she said. But when she went to take it there was just her own hand in the air.

16   So she left that tree, and had to go through a barbed-wire fence. There she had to creep and crawl, spreading her knees and stretching her fingers like a baby tying to climb the steps. But she talked loudly to herself: she could not let her dress be torn now, so late in the day, and

she could not pay for having her arm or leg sawed off if she got caught fast where she was.

17   At last she was safe through the fence and risen up out in the clearing. Big dead trees, like black men with one arm, were standing in the purple stalks of the withered cotton field. There sat a buzzard.

18   "Who you watching?"

19   In the furrow she made her way along.

20   "Glad this not the season for bulls," she said, looking sideways, "and the good Lord made his snakes to curl up and sleep in the winter. A pleasure I don't see no two-headed snake coming around that tree, where it come once. It took a while to get by him, back in the summer."

21   She passed through the old cotton and went into a field of dead corn. It whispered and shook and was taller than her head. "Through the maze now," she said, for there was no path.

22   Then there was something tall, black, and skinny there, moving before her.

23   At first she took it for a man. It could have been a man dancing in the field. But she stood still and listened, and it did not make a sound. It was as silent as a ghost.

24   "Ghost," she said sharply, "who be you the ghost of? For I have heard of nary death close by."

25   But there was no answer—only the ragged dancing in the wind.

26   She shut her eyes, reached out her hand, and touched a sleeve. She found a coat and inside that an emptiness, cold as ice.

27   "You scarecrow," she said. Her face lighted. "I ought to be shut up for good," she said with laughter. "My senses is gone, I too old. I the oldest people I ever know. Dance, old scarecrow," she said, "while I dancing with you."

28   She kicked her foot over the furrow, and with mouth drawn down, shook her head once or twice in a little strutting way. Some husks blew down and whirled in streamers about her skirts.

29   Then she went on, parting her way from side to side with the cane, through the whispering field. At last she came to the end, to a wagon track where the silver grass blew between the red ruts. The quail were walking around like pullets, seeming all dainty and unseen.

30   "Walk pretty," she said. "This the easy place. This the easy going."

31   She followed the track, swaying through the quiet bare fields, through the little strings of trees silver in their dead leaves, past cabins silver from weather, with the doors and windows boarded shut, all like old women under a spell sitting there. "I walking in their sleep," she said, nodding her head vigorously.

32   In a ravine she went where a spring was silently flowing through a hollow log. Old Phoenix bent and drank. "Sweet-gum makes the water sweet," she said, and drank more. "Nobody know who made this well, for it was here when I was born."

33   The track crossed a swampy part where the moss hung as white as lace from every limb. "Sleep on, alligators, and blow your bubbles." Then the track went into the road.

34   Deep, deep the road went down between the high green-colored banks. Overhead the live oaks met, and it was as dark as a cave.

35   A black dog with a lolling tongue came up out of the weeds by the ditch. She was meditating, and not ready, and when he came at her she only hit him a little with her cane. Over she went in the ditch, like a little puff of milk-weed.

36   Down there, her senses drifted away. A dream visited her, and she reached her hand up, but nothing reached down and gave her a pull. So she lay there and presently went to talking. "Old woman," she said to herself, "that black dog come up out of the weeds to stall you off, and now there he sitting on his fine tail, smiling at you."

37   A white man finally came along and found her—a hunter, a young man, with his dog on a chain.

38   "Well, Granny!" he laughed. "what are you doing there?"

39   "Lying on my back like a June-bug waiting to be turned over, mister," she said, reaching up her hand.

40   He lifted her up, gave her a swing in the air, and set her down. "Anything broken, Granny?"

41   "No sir, them old dead weeds is springy enough," said Phoenix, when she had got her breath. "I thank you for your trouble."

42   "Where do you live, Granny?" he asked, while the two dogs were growling at each other.

43   "Away back yonder, sir, behind the ridge. You can't even see it from here."

44   "On your way home?"

45   "No, sir, I going to town."

46   "Why, that's too far! That's as far as I walk when I come out myself, and I get something for my trouble." He patted the stuffed bag he carried, and there hung down a little closed claw. It was one of the bob-whites, with its beak hooked bitterly to show it was dead. "Now you go on home, Granny!"

47   "I bound to go to town, mister," said Phoenix. "The time come around."

48   He gave another laugh, filling the whole landscape. "I know you old colored people! Wouldn't miss going to town to see Santa Claus!"

49   But something held Old Phoenix very still. The deep lines in her face went into a fierce and different radiation. Without warning, she had seen with her own eyes a flashing nickel fall out of the man's pocket onto the ground.

50   "How old are you, Granny?" he was saying.

51   "There is no telling, mister," she said, "no telling."

52   Then she gave a little cry and clapped her hands and said, "Git on away from here, dog! Look! Look at that dog!" She laughed as if in admiration. "He ain't scared of nobody. He a big black dog." She whispered, "Sic him!"

53   "Watch me get rid of that cur," said the man. "Sic him, Pete! Sic him!"

54   Phoenix heard the dogs fighting, and heard the man running and throwing sticks. She even heard a gunshot. But she was slowly bending forward by that time, further and further forward, the lids stretched down over her eyes, as if she were doing this in her sleep. Her chin was lowered almost to her knees. The yellow palm of her hand came out from the fold of her apron. Her fingers slid down and along the ground under the piece of money with the grace and care they would have in lifting an egg from under a sitting hen. Then she slowly straightened up, she stood erect, and the nickel was in her apron pocket. A bird flew by. Her lips moved. "God watching me the whole time. I come to stealing."

55   The man came back, and his own dog panted about them. "Well, I scared him off that time," he said, and then he laughed and lifted his gun and pointed it at Phoenix.

56   She stood straight and faced him.

57   "Doesn't the gun scare you?" he said, still pointing it.

58   "No, sir, I seen plenty go off closer by, in my day, and for less than what I done," she said, holding utterly still.

59   He smiled, and shouldered the gun. "Well, Granny," he said, "You must be a hundred years old, and scared of nothing. I'd give you a dime if I had any money with me. But you take my advice and stay home, and nothing will happen to you."

60   "I bound to go on my way, mister," said Phoenix. She inclined her head in the red rag. Then they went in different directions, but she could hear the gun shooting again and again over the hill.

61   She walked on. The shadows hung from the oak trees to the road like curtains. Then she smelled wood-smoke, and smelled the river, and she saw a steeple and the cabins on their steep steps. Dozens of little black children whirled around her. There ahead was Natchez shining. Bells were ringing. She walked on.

62   In the paved city it was Christmas time. There were red and green electric lights strung and crisscrossed everywhere, and all turned on in the daytime. Old Phoenix would have been lost if she had not distrusted her eyesight and depended on her feet to know where to take her.

63   She paused quietly on the sidewalk where people were passing by. A lady came along in the crowd, carrying an armful of red-, green-, and silver-wrapped presents; she gave off perfume like the red roses in hot summer, and Phoenix stopped her.

64   "Please, missy, will you lace up my shoe?" She held up her foot.

65   "What do you want, Grandma?"

66   "See my shoe," said Phoenix. "Do all right for out in the country, but wouldn't look right to go in a big building."

67   "Stand still then, Grandma," said the lady. She put her packages down on the sidewalk beside her and laced and tied both shoes tightly.

68   "Can't lace 'em with a cane," said Phoenix. "Thank you, missy. I doesn't mind asking a nice lady to tie up my shoe, when I gets out on the street."

69   Moving slowly and from side to side, she went into the big building and into a tower of steps, where she walked up and around and around until her feet knew to stop.

70   She entered a door, and there she saw nailed up on the wall the document that had been stamped with the gold seal and framed in the gold frame, which matched the dream that was hung up in her head.

71   "Here I be," she said. There was a fixed and ceremonial stiffness over her body.

72   "A charity case, I suppose," said an attendant who sat at the desk before her.

73   But Phoenix only looked above her head. There was sweat on her face, the wrinkles in her skin shone like a bright net.

74   "Speak up, Grandma," the woman said. "What's your name? We must have your history, you know. Have you been here before? What seems to be the trouble with you?"

75   Old Phoenix only gave a twitch to her face as if a fly were bothering her.

76   "Are you deaf?" cried the attendant.

77   But then the nurse came in.

78   "Oh, that's just old Aunt Phoenix," she said. "She doesn't come for herself—she has a little grandson. She makes these trips just as regular as clockwork. She lives away back off the old Natchez Trace." She bent down. "Well, Aunt Phoenix, why don't you just take a seat? We won't keep you standing after your long trip." She pointed.

79   The old woman sat down, bolt upright in the chair.

80   "Now, how is the boy?" asked the nurse.

81   Old Phoenix did not speak.

82   "I said, how is the boy?"

83   But Phoenix only waited and stared straight ahead, her face very solemn and withdrawn into rigidity.

84   "Is his throat any better?" asked the nurse. "Aunt Phoenix, don't you hear me? Is your grandson's throat any better since the last time you came for the medicine?"

85   With her hands on her knees, the old woman waited, silent, erect and motionless, just as if she were in armor.

86   "You mustn't take up our time this way, Aunt Phoenix," the nurse said. "Tell us quickly about your grandson, and get it over. He isn't dead, is he?"

87   At last there came a flicker and then a flame of comprehension across her face, and she spoke.

88   "My grandson. It was my memory had left me. There I sat and forgot why I made my long trip."

89   "Forgot?" The nurse frowned. "After you came so far?"

90   Then Phoenix was like an old woman begging a dignified forgiveness for waking up frightened in the night. "I never did go to school, I was too old at the Surrender," she said in a soft voice. "I'm an old woman without an education. It was my memory fail me. My little grandson, he is just the same, and I forgot it in the coming."

91   "Throat never heals, does it?" said the nurse, speaking in a loud, sure voice to Old Phoenix. By now she had a card with something written on it, a little list. "Yes. Swallowed lye. When was it—January—two-three years ago—"

92   Phoenix spoke unasked now. "No, missy, he not dead, he just the same. Every little while his throat begin to close up again, and he not able to swallow. He not get his breath. He not able to help himself. So the time come around, and I go on another trip for the soothing medicine."

93   "All right. The doctor said as long as you came to get it, you could have it," said the nurse. "But it's an obstinate case."

94   "My little grandson, he sit up there in the house all wrapped up, waiting by himself," Phoenix went on. "We is the only two left in the world. He suffer and it don't seem to put him back at all. He got a sweet look. He going to last. He wear a little patch quilt and peep out holding his mouth open like a little bird. I remembers so plain now. I

not going to forget him again, no, the whole enduring time. I could tell him from all the others in creation."

95   "All right." The nurse was trying to hush her now. She brought her a bottle of medicine. "Charity," she said, making a check mark in a book.

96   Old Phoenix held the bottle close to her eyes and then carefully put it into her pocket.

97   "I thank you," she said.

98   "It's Christmas time, Grandma," said the attendant. "Could I give you a few pennies out of my purse?"

99   "Five pennies is a nickel," said Phoenix stiffly.

100   "Here's a nickel," said the attendant.

101   Phoenix rose carefully and held out her hand. She received the nickel and then fished the other nickel out of her pocket and laid it beside the new one. She stared at her palm closely, with her head on one side.

102   Then she gave a tap with her cane on the floor.

103   "This is what come to me to do," she said. "I going to the store and buy my child a little windmill they sells, made out of paper. He going to find it hard to believe there such a thing in the world. I'll march myself back where he waiting, holding it straight up in his hand."

104   She lifted her free hand, gave a little nod, turned round, and walked out of the doctor's office. Then her slow step began on the stairs, going down.

A Worn Path

JOURNAL

1. MLA Works Cited

Using this model, record this story here.

Author's Last Name, First Name. "Title of the Story." <u>Title of the Book</u>. Ed. First Last Name. City: Publisher, year. Pages of the story.

2. Main Character(s)

Describe each main character, and explain why you think each is a main character.

3. Supporting Characters

Describe each supporting character, and explain why you think each is a supporting character.

4. Setting

Describe the setting. Decide if this setting can be changed and, if so, to where and when.

5. **Sequence**

   Relate the events of the story in order.

6. **Plot**

   Tell the story in no more than two sentences.

7. **Conflicts**

   Identify and explain the conflicts involved here.

8. **Significant Quotations**

   Explain the importance of each of these quotations. Record the page number in the parentheses.

   a. "She wore a dark striped dress reaching down to her shoe tops, and an equally long apron of bleached sugar sacks [. . .]" (   ).

b. "Without warning, she had seen with her own eyes a flashing nickel fall out of the man's pocket onto the ground" (   ).

c. "Old Phoenix would have been lost if she had not distrusted her eyesight and depended on her feet to know where to take her" (   ).

d. "'Oh, that's just old Aunt Phoenix,' she said. [. . .] 'She makes these trips just as regular as clockwork'" (   ).

e. "'I going to the store and buy my child a little windmill they sells, made out of paper'" (   ).

FOLLOW-UP QUESTIONS

10 SHORT QUESTIONS

Select the best answer for each.

B 1. Old Phoenix probably is wearing
   a. fine clothing.
   b. old clothing.
   c. formal clothing.

C 2. Old Phoenix probably
   a. does not care about her clothing.
   b. wants to buy new clothing.
   c. is concerned about her clothing.

C 3. The hunter
   a. hands a nickel to Old Phoenix.
   b. drops the nickel on purpose.
   c. does not hand the coin to Old Phoenix.

a 4. When Old Phoenix sees the coin, she
   a. quietly takes the coin.
   b. does not see the coin.
   c. returns the coin to the hunter.

a 5. Old Phoenix's journey to town is
   a. a difficult trip for her.
   b. an easy trip for her.
   c. an uneventful trip for her.

B 6. Old Phoenix's trip to town is
   a. a short trip.
   b. a long trip.
   c. a weekly trip.

a 7. Old Phoenix
   a. has been to the doctor's office before.
   b. has never been to the doctor's office before.
   c. does not get into the doctor's office.

C 8. Old Phoenix
   a. offers the nickel for the medicine.
   b. does not get the medicine.
   c. gets the medicine for free.

a 9. Old Phoenix
   a. is willing to accept charity.
   b. insists on paying for all she receives.
   c. accepts only what she finds.

B 10. Old Phoenix is probably
   a. rich.
   b. poor.
   c. middle class.

5 SIGNIFICANT QUOTATIONS

Explain the importance of each of these quotations.

Line

3 1. "Old Phoenix said, 'Out of my way, all you foxes, owls, beetles, jack rabbits, coons, and wild animals! [. . .] I got a long way.'"

37 2. "A white man finally came along and found her—a hunter, a young man, with his dog on a chain."

61   3.   "Then she smelled wood-smoke, and smelled the river, and she saw a steeple and the cabins on their steep steps."

70   4.   "She entered the door, and there she saw nailed up on the wall the document that had been stamped with the gold seal and framed in the gold frame [. . .]."

103 5.   " 'I going to the store and buy my child a little windmill they sells, made out of paper.' "

2 Comprehension Essay Questions

Use specific details and information from the story to answer these as completely as possible.

1.   The Phoenix is a mythical bird that could not die. After it flew into fire, it would come alive again with new life. Explain why Welty named her character "Old Phoenix" using specific details and information from the story.

2.   How does the title relate to the story? Explain the significance of the title using specific details and information from the story.

Writing

Use each of these ideas for writing an essay.

1.   Often students want to describe a person by looks, but here we learn about Old Phoenix through her actions. Write an essay describing someone you know, using mainly conversation with or the words of that person.

2.   No matter what, Old Phoenix persists. Write an essay describing a time when you or someone you know persisted in achieving something.

Further Writing

1.   Compare and contrast this story with William Faulkner's "A Rose for Emily" (page 390).

2.   Compare and contrast Old Phoenix with Tom Sawyer in the story by Mark Twain (page 123).

Zulema

ROBERTA FERNANDEZ

PRE-READING VOCABULARY
CONTEXT

Use context clues to define these words before reading. Use a dictionary as needed.

1. Howard spent all his paycheck as soon as he got it; as a *consequence* he was broke. *Consequence* means _____.

2. When America fought Great Britain to get our independence, we conducted a *revolution*. *Revolution* means _____.

3. When Carol was waiting for the important phone call, she kept *vigil* by the phone all night. *Vigil* means _____.

4. Michelle's flowing hot pink scarf and bright gold shoes were *flamboyant* compared to the quiet colors she usually wears. *Flamboyant* means _____.

5. Mike was *apprehensive* about what would happen to his delivery job if he were to lose his license. *Apprehensive* means

_____.

6. Sean felt *abandoned* when all his friends went to the movies and left him home alone. *Abandoned* means

_____.

7. Whenever Suraj is on stage, he overacts and is very *melodramatic*. *Melodramatic* means _____.

8. To think about death all the time is *morbid*. *Morbid* means

_____.

9. Akim was trying to get to work on time when he *inadvertently* missed the bus. *Inadvertently* means _____.

10. Santi went *rummaging* through the attic trying to find his old yearbook. *Rummaging* means _____.

11. When the new puppy came home, Dodee placed many *restrictions* on where he could go until he was trained. *Restrictions* means

_____.

12. It was *essential* that Evelyn find her car keys so that she could drive to school. *Essential* means _____.

13. The bride's gown, trimmed in tiny crystals and pearls, was *exquisite*. *Exquisite* means _____.

14. Alice gave *extravagant* gifts and then had no money left for herself. *Extravagant* means _____.

15. Using bright yellows and reds, Wilson produced a *vivid* picture. *Vivid* means _____.

16. Much to José's *astonishment*, everyone liked the meal he threw together in ten minutes. *Astonishment* means _____.

17. After the funeral, Barb followed the cars to watch the burial at the *cemetery*. *Cemetery* means _____.

18. Anthony is attending medical school because his *aspiration* is to become a doctor. *Aspiration* means _____.

19. War is an upsetting and *tumultuous* affair. *Tumultuous* means

_____.

20. Watching rhythmic waves on the ocean may put you in a trance and *mesmerize* you. *Mesmerize* means _____.

Pre-reading Vocabulary
Word Attack

Define these words by solving the parts. Use a dictionary as needed.

1. unfamiliar
2. recall
3. departed
4. unexpected
5. entangled
6. unfinished
7. uncontrollably
8. war-weary
9. outstretched
10. finality
11. ensnared
12. unknowingly
13. semi-darkness
14. cinnamoned
15. encrusted
16. sizeable
17. enclosed
18. tombstone
19. leatherbound
20. envision

Try solving the Spanish words in this story by going to the library and using an English/Spanish dictionary or by working with a Spanish-speaking classmate.

Pre-reading Questions

Try answering these questions as you read.

What are the characters like?

What do they talk about?

What stories do they tell?

What do the stories tell you about them?

Zulema

ROBERTA FERNANDEZ

> **Roberta Fernandez** was born in Laredo, Texas, in 1940. Educated in
> Texas, she went on to receive her doctorate in romance languages and
> literatures from the University of California at Berkeley. Since then,
> she has taught and/or conducted research at Howard University,
> Carleton College, the University of California at Santa Barbara, the
> University of Houston, the University of Massachusetts, and Mills
> College. Deeply sympathetic to the arts of women, she interweaves
> the stories in "Zulema" as intricately as Nenita weaves the red ribbons
> in Zulema's hair. "Zulema" is taken from Fernandez's *Itaglio: A Novel
> in Six Stories.*

I

The story Zulema heard that November morning in 1914 changed her forever, and for the rest of her life she had to deal with the consequences of what she was told on that long-ago Tuesday morning. All during the previous night she listened to sporadic gunshots across the river where the *Federales* were shooting at the *Villistas*. The noise and the unfamiliar bed had made her wake up long before the bells of San Augustine Church pealed their daily calling to the faithful, and at six o'clock when the first sounds from the belfry echoed in the distance, Zulema got up, blessed herself, then knelt down to say her morning prayers. She heard her aunt Mariana moving around in the next room and wondered if the disturbances in the night had also made her get up earlier than usual.

2   Mariana looked different that morning, puffy around the eyes and rather tense as she prepared the coffee and tortillas. Zulema sensed she had interrupted her aunt as she came into the kitchen but Mariana instinctively left her *comal* to kiss the child. "I have a lot to tell you," Mariana whispered as she put her arms around Zulema's slender body. Then, as she moved back to the stove and stirred the chocolate she was preparing for the child, Mariana told her the story.

3   Her voice sounded a little forced and her face looked weary. Zulema would later try to recall the scene but all she could remember was Mariana's palor and the voice that had been pitched higher than normal. In this tone Mariana had told her that her new brother had arrived during the night, tired from his journey but happy and fat and kicking with gusto.

4   The night had been full of activity, she continued, for not only had the new baby arrived and the shooting continued on the other side but a messenger had also come from San Antonio. He had informed Zulema's mother that her other sister, Carmen, had come down with a serious case of pneumonia. Isabel had left right away with the messenger, leaving her new-born baby behind with the rest of the family. "Give my Zulemita and Miguelito a kiss and tell them I'll be home soon." Those had been her last words as she departed, Mariana said.

5   "You will stay with me for a while," she continued. Miguel would stay with his father and his grandmother, and the baby would remain with Doña Julia who lived across the street and also had a small infant she was nursing. It had all been arranged.

II

6   Thirty-five years later, sitting on some thick pillows Zulema had spe-
cial-made for me, I heard many different versions of what I later realized
was the same story. During my afternoon visits I listened to Zulema's
calm, deep voice as she invented one tale after another with superbly
eccentric characters who continued to dance and whirl about in my own
accelerated imagination. Some of the stories were simple duplications
of tales Mariana had told her but most of the narratives were Zulema's
own inventions. Often Mariana would join us, sitting on the rocking
chair with her eyes closed as though she were reliving the episodes
which Zulema was describing.

7   Now and then Mariana would open her eyes, then lean forward to
listen more closely. Then she would shake her head and correct
Zulema. *"No, no fue así,"* and she would turn to me with her own version of the story I had just heard. It was difficult for me to decide whose
narrative I liked the most, for they each had their way with description
and knew just when to pause for the maximum of effect but I suppose
at that time I tended to think that Mariana's *"bola de años,"* as she
referred to her advancing age, gave her an edge over Zulema's rendition.

8   I soon learned that Zulema had a favorite story. It was the one
about the camp follower Victoriana, who, at the height of the revolution, had crossed to this side to wait for her lover Joaquín. For a while
people coming from her pueblo in Zacatecas confirmed her belief that
Joaquín was still alive but as the years passed, everyone simply forgot
about Victoriana. She continued her vigil until that unexpected afternoon when the people had found her thirty years later, sitting in the
same chair where she had first sat down to wait, covered with cobwebs
and red dust but with a glowing expression on her face and her rusted
rifle at her feet.

9   I never got tired of Zulema's *cuento,* for each time she'd recite it,
she would pretend it was the first time she had confided to me about
Victoriana and she would embellish the story with a few more details.
The climax was always the same, though, as she'd describe how Victoriana was unable to recognize the man whose memory she had loved
all those years, for when the newspapers had printed the story about
her long wait, out of curiosity, Joaquín had come to see Victoriana and
she had not singled him out from all the other visitors she had greeted
that afternoon. No longer the *campesino* she had fallen in love with
but a very important businessman, Joaquín was alternately amused
and mortified by all of the moths and butterflies entangled among the
cobwebs in her silvered hair.

10   Zulema would conclude the story with Victoriana boarding the Ferrocarriles Nacionales Mexicaños, while the townspeople waved a sad farewell to the splendid and flamboyant figure who had enlivened their routine lives for a brief while. She, too, waved to the people as the train pulled away, taking her back to her *pueblo* where she hoped to locate some of the relatives she had last seen in Bachimba claiming their rifles and riding off into the distance to be swept into the force of the revolution.

11   Unknown endings, unfinished lives. That was the subject of most of Zulema's narratives but I cannot remember when I first began to notice this. On the day after my sixth birthday I sensed something different, for Zulema changed the story from fantasy to biography and for the first time mentioned Isabel to me. She took a photograph from her missal and passed the edge-worn picture to me. "Do you know who she is?"

12   Immediately I recognized the photo as a copy of one my mother had. "*Es tu mamá,*" I responded right away. "*Mí abuelita Isabel.*"

13   I often opened the top drawer of my mother's dresser just to steal a peep at the young woman in the tucked lace blouse who looked back at me with soft, gentle eyes. No one had ever told me much about her except that she was my father's mother who had died when my uncle Luis was born. Each of the boys had been reared by different relatives who did not find it appropriate to talk to them about Isabel, possibly to spare the children from the memories the adults did not want them to have. Up to then I knew very little about her.

14   "She died when she was only twenty-four. I was six then," Zulema spoke very deliberately. "Mariana really pulled the wool over my eyes, telling me Mamá had gone away with Tía Carmen."

15   Zulema's shoulders began to rise up and down. Suddenly she started to sob uncontrollably, holding the photo to her breast. Through my own tears I heard her describe how she had waited for days on end for her mother's return during that first winter when Isabel had gone away without a word to her. The minute she'd hear people pass by on the street she'd run to the door on the chance her mother would be with them. The streetcar that clanged in front of the house seemed to sound especially for her and every time she'd see Julia nursing the baby she'd wonder if Luisito was hungry for his own mother. Feeling abandoned she began to talk about her feelings; yet, everyone maintained the story which Mariana had uttered. When, when, when she had asked her aunt, and Mariana had finally said, "When the war is over, she'll be back."

16   And so the eight-year old Zulema had become interested in the war. At night whenever she heard gunshots or sirens she'd cry herself

to sleep. The bugles of the infantry across the river woke her up every morning and in the afternoons after class she'd go down to the river to look across its banks at the war-weary nation on the other side. Then she would wish the war away, praying with her eyes closed while she imagined her mother running towards her with outstretched arms. But Zulema could sense that Isabel would not be back for a long time, for every day she was aware of the dozens of people who crossed the bridge with their belongings in wheelbarrows or in suitcases of every sort. Some even had knapsacks slung across their back, looking tired and worn from the personal anxieties they too were experiencing. Sometimes her father would give work around the store or at the ranch to some of the people who had just arrived, and before they moved on farther north, Zulema would take advantage of their personal accounts to ask them questions about the war. No one had any idea when the fighting would end and many of them no longer cared about the revolution except for the manner in which it had altered the course of their lives. They were mostly preoccupied with the death and destruction over which they had absolutely no control.

17   With all the talk of death, Zulema soon became apprehensive. When the newly-arrived talked about the death of their loved ones, she began to associate their experiences with her own loss and slowly began to doubt the story about her mother's return. On her ninth birthday, in 1917, she had let everyone know she realized the war was supposed to be over and still her mother had not come back. "I know she is lost," she concluded. Then she looked directly at Mariana and stated in a tone of finality. "I no longer have a mother."

18   And that same day she had started to tell her own stories. She took Miguelito and Luisito, to her room and sat them down on the floor, while she lay on her bed looking up at the ceiling. "*Les voy a contar un cuento de nunca acabar,*" she began, then started to narrate her own version of the Sleeping Beauty, who had been put under a spell by her wicked stepmother. Sleeping Beauty was supposed to be awakened by the kiss of a gorgeous prince but that never really happened. She turned to her brothers and asked them if they knew why the prince had not found Sleeping Beauty. Then, without giving them a chance to answer, for this was supposed to be her very own story, she continued with melodramatic gestures.

19   The prince could not find Sleeping Beauty, she whispered, because a revolution broke out just as he was setting out on his journey. Word soon arrived that his white horse had been confiscated by Emiliano Zapata. So now the prince had to find his way around on foot, and not being accustomed to looking out for himself, he had no idea what

direction he should take. Finally, he headed towards his castle but when he got there he found that it had been blown to pieces, and the revolutionaries had proclaimed that he could no longer be a prince. And so he was unable to complete his mission. Poor Sleeping Beauty was left forgotten in the woods but since she could not live without the prince, for they needed each other to exist, she simply had no future and remained out there in the dark woods forever and ever. Pretty soon no one could remember, much less care, about the troubles of that poor little Sleeping Beauty, foolish enough to think she needed to live with a prince in a castle. So, without realizing what they had done, the revolutionaries got rid of all those charming princes and the silly, pampered Sleeping Beauties as well.

20   That afternoon I listened for a long time as Zulema recited one such story after another. From the beginning, she said, her brothers did not like her plots because they considered her endings to be strange, even morbid at times. Once in a while she had tried to tell her stories to her father but he did not seem the least bit interested in them. Mariana, who perhaps best understood what she was really trying to say, assumed she could change her endings. So, for lack of an audience Zulema felt she had been fated to keep them to herself all those years. I was the only one who had let her tell the stories the way she wanted.

21   "Zulema, I like your stories," I reassured her as I undid her braids, then ran my small fingers through her hair.

22   I then looked at her in a whole new way. Unlike Mariana and the picture we had of Isabel, Zulema seemed quite ordinary, with her long hair parted in the middle and plaited into thick braids which she wore criss-crossed on top of her head. She did not look like my mother either, whose hair was swept up, away from her face and wrapped around a hair piece that was pinned around her head in keeping with the fashion of the day. I much preferred Zulema's hair, which I loved to unbraid, then brush out in waves which reached down to her waist.

23   That afternoon I gave her particular attention weaving a red satin ribbon into her braids which made her look prettier than usual. Finally animated, she continued with the narrative that had gone unshared all those years. She skipped the elaboration she gave to her other tales and was direct and terse as she described the main event that had shaped her life. She really could not blame Mariana or her father, she said, for they had simply been trying to save her from the very pain they had inadvertently caused. By the time she was twelve she had given up altogether on her mother's return although occasionally when she opened a door in her father's house, for an instant she felt she had caught a glimpse of her mother sitting there in her rocking

chair. That was about the time she took to leaving all the doors in the house ajar. Gradually she became fascinated with opening trunks and boxes as well.

24   One day while she was visiting her father and Amanda she found herself alone in the room where he kept his papers. Slowly, she began to poke into his desk and in a drawer, underneath some photos, she uncovered the announcement which she unknowingly had been searching for all those months. She picked up the card, looked at its black borders, then read: *ISABEL MENDOZA-DEL VALLE, esposa de José Maria Cárdenas*—1890–1914. The rest of the announcement stated that Isabel was survived by three children—Zulema, Miguel, and Luis.

25   Zulema put the card back where she had found it. After that she lost her interest in rummaging through boxes and drawers. She began to rise at six o'clock in order to attend daily mass where she remained until it was time for school. Gradually she began to lose interest in her classes, and one day she decided to stay in church all day. For several weeks she sat in the immense church where the incense soothed her memories and the candles she lit brightened the semi-darkness. Soon el Padre Salinas began to notice the disappearance of the candles. Concerned that almost no money was being left in the offering box to cover their cost, he staked out the various altars and, shortly thereafter, caught her sitting in the front pew facing the virgin and child. He watched as she lighted two or three candles at once, then when those burned down, he saw her light new ones.

26   Just about the time el Padre Salinas approached Mariana about the expense, the teacher paid José María a visit. José María did not take the trouble to discuss the matter with his daughter; instead, he talked to Mariana who related to Zulema that her father now wished to keep her at home, for she could no longer be trusted to go out on her own. From then on she would not be allowed to go anywhere without being accompanied either by one of the cousins or the aunts.

27   Zulema had not minded the restrictions at all. In fact, for the first time she felt she was the object of everyone's attention. Mariana taught her the secrets that went into cooking traditional dishes. For their *mole de gallina* they would spend a good part of a day grinding sesame seeds, peanuts and *pastillas de chocolate* on the *metate* and once the ingredients for the sauce were ready, they would simmer it for hours. It was then that they would go to the chicken coop to pick out two or three chickens. At first Zulema was squeamish but she learned to wring a chicken by the neck before chopping off its head with a *machete*. For dessert she loved to make *capirotada* and *leche quemada*

and the first time she prepared the entire meal for a table of twelve, she relished all the compliments she got for her *calabaza con puerco.*

28   Doña Julia taught her to crochet, little squares at first, then larger items like tablecloths and bedspreads which she made as gifts for *fiestas de quinceañeras,* engagement showers and weddings. When she turned fifteen she too was honored with a dance attended by all the relatives, their friends and friends of her father. Everyone danced to the music of a local band until the early hours of the morning and between dances they kept going back for more *tamales* and steaming cups of cinnamoned coffee. Before the night was over, all the spread on the table—*barbacoa, guacamole, arroz, frijoles borracbos* and freshly grilled *gorditas*—had been eaten up.

29   That was the first time she had met Carlos who danced all evening with her. A few days later, he had called on her father requesting permission to visit with her at home. Soon she began to be kidded about having a sweetheart and when the *comadres* in Mariana's quilt-making group asked her about Carlos, Zulema smiled and pretended to be concentrating on her stitches. After a while, she filled her trunk with the essentials for her future life and when she married Carlos, she brought to her new home all the exquisite handmade items that a seventeen-year-old bride needed. A few weeks after Zulema's and Carlos's first child was born, Mariana came to live with them, and for more than twenty years the three of them saw the family expand, then contract again, as the older sons went off to study at the university and the youngest daughter married, at seventeen, like her mother.

30   Zulema had tried to get each one of her children interested in listening to her stories but all four thought the stories were silly and repetitive. So, it wasn't until I started making requests for recitations about her extravagant characters that she began to ponder about this particular vacuum in her life.

31   Now, as the afternoon light softly faded, Zulema paused to reflect on everything she had told me. Finally, she sighed, "Telling stories. That's what I've enjoyed the most."

32   "Me too," I smiled, tucking at her red ribbons.

33   Just then the door opened and my cousin Maruca turned on the light. Surprised, she asked "How come you're sitting in the dark?"

34   Neither of us answered her. Then, she burst out, "Ay, *Mamá,* why are you wearing those silly ribbons? You look as if you were about to dance *el jarabe tapatío.*

35   "She looks great with her hair like this," I responded.

36   Maruca waved her hands as if to brush my comment aside. "You two live in your special little world, with all your *cuentos.* Come

join us now. I've brought a big trayful of fried chicken and potato salad."

37   "We'll come in a minute," Zulema answered. "Just let us finish here."

38   As soon as we were alone again, Zulema looked at me very intently, tapping her index finger against her mouth. "Nenita, let's keep this to ourselves. Poor Mariana. It's been such a long time since mother died. There's no point in creating problems now. All this was just between you and me, okay?"

III

39 Earlier that day, my sister Patricia had called to inform me about the heart attack. In my rush to the bus station I had forgotten my sunglasses and the bright light of the afternoon was now blinding me. Closing my eyes, I tried to sort out my feelings but I couldn't focus on anything. Instead, I tried leafing through the magazine I had picked up at the Greyhound shop. News of Czechoslovakia, Viet Nam and Cambodia flashed by me. A picture of Joan Baez. Many anti-war demonstrators. Unable to concentrate, I set the magazine aside.

40   Leaning against the bus window I stretched out my legs across the two seats and studied the passengers closest to me. Two rows up on my left was a woman with very teased hair. She reminded me of Florinda's Cuban mother whom I knew only through my sister's vivid description. I looked around at the other people, then fidgeted with the journal I had on my lap. Feeling its smooth leather cover, I remembered how pleased I had been the previous Christmas when Mariana and Zulema had given it to me. On its first page, they had inscribed: "Make this a memory book of your very own dreams and aspirations." It was the first thing I grabbed when I started to pack for this journey home but at the moment I did not feel like looking at it.

41   I concentrated instead on the woman with the teased hair. Florinda's mother must have looked like that when she left Cuba ten years ago. In anticipation of the day when the family would leave the island, she let her hair grow for more than a year. Then when the moment for their departure arrived, she had carefully teased her hair, then divided it into three layers. The first section had been twisted into a tight French roll fastened with pins encrusted with precious gems. A small fortune, I was told. The tiny twist had been covered with a larger one held up by more jeweled hairpins. Finally, the top outer layer neatly covering the cache had been sprayed several times with a heavy lacquer. As if to mock fate, she had attached thin wires with pink and

white gauze butterflies all over her hair. According to my sister, Florinda had said that her mother looked so outrageous no one bothered much with her and she had smuggled a sizeable sum which the family had used to set up a fabric store. Several years later, it was a thriving business.

42   For reasons I didn't quite understand, Florinda's mother's story always made me anxious. So, I lit a cigarette and watched the smoke whirl upwards. From the angle the sun was hitting me, the smoke resembled the tumultuous vapors in the film version of "Pedro Páramo." In that film, as Juan Preciado searched for his father, the vapors kept getting thicker and thicker the more he travelled inside the land of the dead.

43   "This is my favorite novel," I had pointed out to Zulema and Mariana on the previous Thanksgiving holiday. "But I'm sure there's a lot in this novel I don't understand," I had warned as I introduced them to the spirits, the *espíritus*, of Comala.

44   We had been reading from the paperback copies of *Pedro Páramo* that I had given to each of them. Mariana and I did most of the reading, although Zulema sometimes took her turn. Sipping Cuervo *añejo*, we had commented on the novel, pointing out the scenes we had particularly enjoyed. Mariana, especially, was enthralled with the characters at the Rancho Media Luna, for they were part of a period she still remembered well. And Zulema, as I had expected, identified with Susana, the character whose fate had also been shaped by the early death of her mother.

45   "The spirits always continue to influence those who live after them," Mariana had sighed. "Just right here, we have the example of Zulema, who suffered so much after the death of Isabel."

46   Zulema and I had glanced at one another. Fifty-five years after the death of her sister, Mariana was finally commenting on it.

47   "Why do you say that?" I had softly questioned.

48   "It's just that the murmurs get stronger by the day," she had answered, extending her hands on the armrest. She had closed her eyes rocking herself back and forth letting us know the conversation had ended for the moment. Finally, she had murmured, "It is time now" and to our astonishment she said she would take us to Isabel's burial place.

49   As I drove to the cemetery in silence, my mind was full of questions. Like the rest of the family, I had succumbed to the story of Isabel's departure and had not even asked where she had been buried. For twenty years, since Zulema had told me her version of her mother's death, I had learned to think of Isabel as a spirit living the

special life of the dead. I wondered if Zulema was as shocked as I was since she too had not uttered a word.

50   *"Vamos por este camino."* Mariana led us through the old part of the cemetery to an enclosed plot. There, a red tin can with a cluster of marigolds lay half-buried in front of a tombstone marked with the same inscription as on the death announcement which Zulema had read so long ago: ISABEL MENDOZA-DEL VALLE, 1890–1914.

51   I was stunned, realizing that for all these years, Isabel had been within reach. Zulema's lower lip started to tremble and little whimpering sounds began to come out of her mouth. Mariana put her arm around Zulema's shoulder, then rested her head on it.

52   "I never knew how to remedy what had happened," Mariana said simply. It was obvious she finally wanted to break the silence surrounding Isabel and in order to get her off her feet, we moved to a nearby bench.

53   For awhile we sat quietly. Then Mariana began to tell us about the difficulty she had experienced in repeating the story the family had chosen for the children on the night Isabel had died. From the very beginning she had made adjustments in her life, for she had stayed home with Zulema while the rest of the family attended the novena for her sister. Later, when the child's suspicions were aroused, she had started to doubt the decision to protect Zulema from the truth.

54   Yet, after a few years they themselves had almost accepted the story as fact and tacitly believed it would be much more difficult to adjust to a new reality than to live with the pattern that had been set. "I don't know what to do," Mariana repeated over and over.

55   Then she told us about her weekly visits to the cemetery and how she considered those visits her personal ritual in keeping the memory of Isabel alive. For years she had snuck away on the bus with her little bouquet of marigolds. But, as she got older, her visits became more and more sporadic. Still, only a few days before, she had brought the flowers we had just seen.

56   I looked at Mariana's rheumatic limbs and wondered how she had managed to honor her sister for so long.

57   *"Uno hace lo que tiene que hacer,"* she affirmed as they headed back to the car. I repeated those words to myself, "One simply does what one has to do."

58   For the rest of the day I tried to fit together all the pieces of the story and started to write long entries about Mariana, Isabel and Zulema in a loose-leaf journal. When I got back to my apartment I continued writing and one day in early December, I stuffed my notes into an envelope and mailed it off to them, with instructions to save the

pages for me. A few weeks after that, they gave me my blue leather-bound book as a present.

59   I reached over to feel it, then opened my eyes. We had arrived. As soon as we pulled into the terminal I saw my sister Patricia waiting for me.

60   "How is she doing?" I asked.

61   "She's been hanging on but she won't last much longer. Late this morning she had another heart attack and the doctor does not think she'll pull through this time."

IV

62   As I opened the door I heard Father Murphy reciting the prayers of Extreme Unction and saw him blessing the small body on the hospital bed. My mother leaned towards me and whispered as she put her arm around me, "I'm so sorry. She died about fifteen minutes ago."

63   I felt everyone's eyes on me as I walked up to the bed. As tears streamed down my face I kissed the smooth sallow cheeks, then looked at the body for a long time without saying anything. It was useless for me to remain there, I thought, and slowly I began to envision what it was I had to do.

64   In my sister's car I drove across the border to the church by the first plaza, then walked towards the adjacent small shop which sold religious articles. As I had hoped, its window display was full of saints with tin *milagros* pinned to their clothing. Inside I found hundreds of *milagros* for sale in many different shapes, sizes and materials. Immediately I by-passed the larger ones and the gold ones which I could not afford. Looking at the half-inch tin offerings, I carefully selected from those in the shape of human profiles, hearts and tongues of fire. The volunteer at the shop seemed surprised when I said I wanted five dozen of each, then waited patiently while I made my selection. Eventually, she divided the offerings into small plastic bags.

65   With the *milagros* on my lap I drove a few blocks to the flower market. There I purchased bunches of marigolds and asked the vendor to divide them up into small bouquets which he tied together with white ribbons. They took up most of the back seat, making the custom inspector remark on my collection of *flores para los muertos.* My next stop was the stationery shop where I bought a small box of red cinnamonscented candles. Then, on my way to the funeral parlor I passed by a record shop. Slamming on the brakes, I double-parked and ran in to inquire if they sold small 45s that were blank. The clerk thought they had three such records left over from an old special order. As soon as he

found them I rushed back to the car and made my way to the funeral parlor. The administrator listened rather dubiously to my plans, then reluctantly gave me permission to do as I wished.

66   I went home to rest for a while, then at the agreed-upon hour I returned to the funeral parlor and for the next three hours I carried out my task. My back hurt from being bent for so long as, between tears, I carefully sewed the milagros on the white satin which lined the inside cover of the casket. Applying three stitches through the tiny hole on each tin sculpture I made a design of three arcs—the faces were on the outer row, the tongues in the middle and the hearts on the inner row. Once I finished with the *milagros* I stepped back to get a better view. Seeing how pretty they looked, each with its accompanying tiny red ribbon, I cried once more, yet felt a little relief from my sorrow knowing that when the lid was closed the *milagros* would be a lovely sight to behold from inside. Then, with the marigolds, I created a halo effect on the space above the corpse, hoping its spirit could savor the smell of the flowers. I arranged the candles in a row in front of the casket and felt myself tremble as I placed the three records on the left side of the body. *"Llénalos con tus cuentos favoritos,"* I whispered. "Fill them with your favorite stories."

67   For a long time I sat in the semi-darkness, mesmerized by the smell of the flowers and perfumed glow of the candles. Recalling the many *cuentos* which had inspired my youthful imagination, I felt I could stay there forever. But I knew I did not want to see anyone tonight, and soon someone would be coming to sit out the early morning vigil.

68   Slowly, I got up and walked to the coffin once again. The *milagros* and the flowers looked splendid but I wondered what the rest of the family would say when they saw them. I touched the dear figure for the last time, then walked out into the night knowing I would not be going to the burial ceremony the next afternoon.

69   Instead I went home and immediately began to write in my journal. For two days I wrote, filling all its pages. Then I gave my thick blue book to Patricia so she could read what I had just finished.

70   She started reading right away and did not move from her chair for hours. At times I would see her shake her head and make almost audible sounds. Finally, when she finished, she closed the book but kept her hand on its cover.

71   "No," she said. "No *fue así.*" A stern expression crossed her face. "It's not been at all the way you've presented it. You've mixed up some

of the stories Mariana and Zulema have told you, which might not even be true in the first place. I've. heard other versions from Tía Carmen and, in fact, from Zulema herself. Mariana would never even recognize herself if you ever show this to her."

72   "I'm not sure what you are trying to do," Patricia continued, "but what you have here is not at all what really happened."

73   *"Lo que tienes aquí no es lo que pasó."*

74   I smiled at Patricia, then took my journal back. As I did so, I remembered that my mother always said that her own memory book had been a collection of images of our family's past both as it was and as we all would have liked that past to have been.

75   "You know I responded. *"Uno cuenta de la feria según lo que ve en ella.* Each of us tell it as we see it."

Zulema

JOURNAL

1. MLA Works Cited

Using this model, record this reading.

Author's Last Name, First Name. "Title of the Story." <u>Title of the Book</u>. Ed. First Last Name. City: Publisher, year. Pages of the story.

2. Main Character(s)

Describe each main character, and explain why you think each is a main character.

3. Supporting Characters

Describe each supporting character, and explain why you think each is a supporting character.

4. Setting

Describe the setting. Decide if this setting can be changed and, if so, to where and when.

5. Sequence

Relate the events of the story in order.

6. Plot

Tell the story in no more than three sentences.

7. Conflicts

Identify and explain the conflicts involved here.

8. Significant Quotations

Explain the importance of each of these quotations. Record the page number in the parentheses.

a. "The night had been full of activity, she continued, for not only had the new baby arrived and the shooting continued on the other side but a messenger had also come from San Antonio. [. . .] Isabel left right away with the messenger, leaving her new-born baby behind with the rest of the family" (   ).

b. "And so the eight-year old Zulema had become interested in the war" (   ).

c. "Then she looked directly at Mariana and stated in a tone of finality, 'I no longer have a mother' " (   ).

d. " 'I never knew how to remedy what had happened,' Mariana said simply" (   ).

e. "Seeing how pretty they looked, each with its accompanying tiny red ribbon [. . .].
    "For a long time I sat in the semi-darkness, mesmerized by the smell of the flowers and perfumed glow of the candles" (   ).

FOLLOW-UP QUESTIONS

10 SHORT QUESTIONS

Select the <u>best</u> answer for each.

1. Mariana is Zulema's
   a. mother.
   b. aunt.
   c. sister.

2. Isabel is Zulema's
   a. mother.
   b. aunt.
   c. sister.

3. Zulema is Nenita's
   a. mother.
   b. aunt.
   c. sister.

4. Isabel probably died
   a. in the war.
   b. in childbirth.
   c. at home.

5. Zulema
   a. is told right away that her mother has died.
   b. learns later that her mother has died.
   c. is happy that her mother is still alive.

6. Zulema's brothers
   a. wait for her stories.
   b. enjoy her stories.
   c. dislike her stories.

7. The narrator probably
   a. does not enjoy Zulema's stories.
   b. is one of many who enjoy Zulema's stories.
   c. is one of few who enjoy Zulema's stories.

8. Mariana
   a. likes to talk about Isabel.
   b. refuses to talk about Isabel.
   c. rarely talks about Isabel.

9. Patricia probably
   a. is as sad as her sister.
   b. is not as sad as her sister.
   c. is unsympathetic to her sister.

10. In the end, the person who dies is probably
    a. Zulema.
    b. Nenita.
    c. Patricia.

5 SIGNIFICANT QUOTATIONS

Explain the importance of each of these quotations.

1. " 'Give my Zulemita and Miguelito a kiss and tell them I'll be home soon.' Those had been her [Isabel's] last words as she departed, Mariana said."

2. "That afternoon I gave her particular attention weaving a red satin ribbon into her braids [. . .]."

3. "A few weeks after that, they gave me my blue leatherbound book as a present."

4. " 'She's been hanging on but she won't last much longer. Late this morning she had another heart attack and the doctor does not think she'll pull through this time.' "

5. "Seeing how pretty they looked, each with its accompanying red ribbons [. . .].
   "For a long time I sat in the semi-darkness, mesmerized by the smell of the flowers and perfumed glow of the candles."

2 COMPREHENSION ESSAY QUESTIONS

Use specific details and information from the story to answer these as completely as possible.

1. Choose another title for this story, and explain your choice using specific details and information from the story.

2. Describe each of the characters in this story. Tell what you think they look like, how old they are, how you think they act, and so forth. Use specific details and information from the story to support your descriptions.

WRITING

Use each of these ideas for writing an essay.

1. Fernandez portrays passing family lore on through stories as women's art. Tell a story from your family to teach a family value or memory to a younger member of your family.

2. Focus on a memorable time with a parent, aunt, uncle, or grandparent. Tell the story of this memorable time, remembering that the audience knows nothing about your family.

Further Writing

1. Read Zore Neale Hurston's "Sweat" (page 348), and compare the storytelling in "Sweat" with that in "Zulema."

2. Anthropological research into cultural transmission, or how children are taught about their society, reveals many interesting similarities to as well as differences from that in "Zulema." Discuss the similarities and differences.

The Secret Life of Walter Mitty

JAMES THURBER

PRE-READING VOCABULARY
CONTEXT

Use context clues to define these words before reading. Use a dictionary as needed.

1. The leader of a group is often called the *commander,* the one in command. *Commander* means _____.

2. The photographer took a picture of the movie star with the star's coat flowing *rakishly* behind him. *Rakishly* means _____.

3. The angry boy was *spoiling* for a fight. *Spoiling* means

   _____.

4. The *pilot* landed the plane smoothly. *Pilot* means _____.

5. Georgiana was *astonished* at her surprise party. *Astonished* means _____.

6. After awhile, the bright colors of flowers *fade. Fade* means

   _____.

7. Because Ajay was not sure how to use the standard shift, the car suddenly *lurched* ahead. *Lurch* means _____.

8. One is often *intimate* with one's best friends. *Intimate* means

   _____.

9. The boy was *distraught* over his poor grade and lost his appetite for days. *Distraught* means _____.

10. The child genius was so *brilliant* that he passed high school courses with all A's. *Brilliant* means _____.

11. When Susan had to have dental surgery, the dentist made her unconscious with an *anaesthetizer*. *Anaesthetizer* means

_____.

12. As a new doctor, Jason had to serve as an *intern* in the emergency room. *Intern* means _____.

13. Debbie *muttered* so quietly that I could not hear or understand her. *Mutter* means _____.

14. The deer *vaulted* over the fence with ease. *Vault* means

_____.

15. In severe snow conditions, one puts linked *chains* around tires to get better contact with the road. *Chains* means _____.

16. To get the law they wanted, the people used their rights of *initiative and referendum* to initiate the law. *Initiative and referendum* means

_____.

17. Because of her sister's new car, Aruna *insinuated* that her sister is more favored than she is. *Insinuate* means _____.

18. *Pandemonium* and *bedlam* broke out when someone yelled, "Fire!" *Pandemonium* and/or *bedlam* mean _____.

19. The winning players *cannonaded* their coaches with an endless supply of sparkling water. *Cannonade* means _____.

20. The *inscrutable* note was so poorly written that it was impossible to understand. *Inscrutable* means _____.

Pre-reading Vocabulary
Word Attack

Define these words by solving the parts. Use a dictionary as needed.

1. full-dress
2. unfamiliar
3. overshoes
4. millionaire
5. nervously

6. parking-lot
7. garageman
8. firearms
9. firing squad
10. undefeated

Pre-reading Questions

Try answering these questions as you read.

Who is the main character in the story?

Why is this called his "secret life"?

What is real and unreal?

What does Mitty's behavior tell you about him?

The Secret Life of Walter Mitty

JAMES THURBER

> James Thurber was born in Columbus, Ohio, in 1894 and attended college at Ohio State University. He was briefly in Paris with the U.S. State Department and then turned to journalism as a reporter for the Columbus *Dispatch*, then the Paris desk of the Chicago *Tribune*, and then the New York *Evening Post*. In 1927, he joined the *New Yorker* magazine, where most of his writing and short stories were published. Urbane, vigorous, and eventually blind—but writing until the end—Thurber left an array of books, stories, and single-line sketches that celebrate optimistic survival through courageous humor and include *Fables of Our Time* and *Thurber Country*. He died in New York in 1961.

We're going through!" The Commander's voice was like thin ice breaking. He wore his full-dress uniform, with the heavily braided white cap pulled down rakishly over one cold gray eye. "We can't make it, sir. It's spoiling for a hurricane, if you ask me." "I'm not asking you, Lieutenant Berg," said the Commander. "Throw on the power lights! Rev her up to 8,500! We're going through!" The pounding of the cylinders increased: ta-pocketa-pocketa-pocketa-*pocketa-pocketa*. The Commander stared at the ice forming on the pilot window. He walked over and twisted a row of complicated dials. "Switch on No. 8 auxiliary!" he shouted. "Switch on No. 8 auxiliary!" repeated Lieutenant Berg. "Full strength in No. 3 turret!" shouted the Commander. "Full strength in No. 3 turret!" The crew, bending to their various tasks in the huge, hurtling eight-engined Navy hydroplane, looked at each other and grinned. "The Old Man'll get us through," they said to one another. "The Old Man ain't afraid of Hell!" . . .

2   "Not so fast! You're driving too fast!" said Mrs. Mitty. "What are you driving so fast for?"

3   "Hmm?" said Walter Mitty. He looked at his wife, in the seat beside him, with shocked astonishment. She seemed grossly unfamiliar, like a strange woman who had yelled at him in a crowd. "You were up to fifty-five," she said. "You know I don't like to go more than forty. You were up to fifty-five." Walter Mitty drove on toward Waterbury in silence, the roaring of the SN202 through the worst storm in twenty years of Navy flying fading in the remote, intimate airways of his mind. "You're tensed up again," said Mrs. Mitty. "It's one of your days. I wish you'd let Dr. Renshaw look you over."

4   Walter Mitty stopped the car in front of the building where his wife went to have her hair done. "Remember to get those overshoes while I'm having my hair done," she said. "I don't need overshoes," said Mitty. She put her mirror back into her bag. "We've been through that," she said, getting out of the car. "You're not a young man any longer." He raced the engine a little. "Why don't you wear your gloves? Have you lost your gloves?" Walter Mitty reached in a pocket and brought out the gloves. He put them on, but after she had turned and gone into the building and he had driven on to a red light, he took them off again. "Pick it up, brother!" snapped a cop as the light changed, and Mitty hastily pulled on his gloves and lurched ahead. He drove around the streets aimlessly for a time, and then he drove past the hospital on his way to the parking lot.

5   . . . "It's the millionaire banker, Wellington McMillan," said the pretty nurse. "Yes?" said Walter Mitty, removing his gloves slowly. "Who has the case?" "Dr. Renshaw and Dr. Benbow, but there are two specialists here, Dr. Remington from New York and Dr. Pritchard-Mitford from London. He flew over." A door opened down a long, cool corridor and Dr. Renshaw came out. He looked distraught and haggard. "Hello, Mitty," he said. "We're having the devil's own time with McMillan, the millionaire banker and close personal friend of Roosevelt. Obstreosis of the ductal tract. Tertiary. Wish you'd take a look at him." "Glad to," said Mitty.

6   In the operating room there were whispered introductions: "Dr. Remington, Dr. Mitty. Dr. Pritchard-Mitford, Dr. Mitty." "I've read your book on streptothricosis," said Pritchard-Mitford, shaking hands. "A brilliant performance, sir." "Thank you," said Walter Mitty. "Didn't know you were in the states, Mitty," grumbled Remington. "Coals to Newcastle, bringing Mitford and me up here for a tertiary." "You are very kind," said Mitty. A huge, complicated machine, connected to the operating table, with many tubes and wires, began at this moment to go pocketa-pocketa-pocketa. "The new anaesthetizer is giving away!" shouted an intern. "There is no one in the East who knows how to fix it!" "Quiet, man!" said Mitty, in a low, cool voice. He sprang to the machine, which was now going pocketa-pocketa-queep-pocketa-queep. He began fingering delicately a row of glistening dials. "Give me a fountain pen!" he snapped. Someone handed him a fountain pen. He pulled a faulty piston out of the machine and inserted the pen in its place. "That will hold for ten minutes," he said. "Get on with the operation." A nurse hurried over and whispered to Renshaw, and Mitty saw the man turn pale. "Coreopsis has set in," said Renshaw nervously. "If you would take over, Mitty?" Mitty looked at him and at

the craven figure of Benbow, who drank, and at the grave, uncertain faces of the two great specialists. "If you wish," he said. They slipped a white gown on him; he adjusted a mask and drew on thin gloves; nurses handed him shining . . .

7   "Back it up, Mac! Look out for that Buick!" Walter Mitty jammed on the brakes. "Wrong lane, Mac," said the parking-lot attendant, looking at Mitty closely. "Gee. Yeh," muttered Mitty. He began cautiously to back out of the lane marked "Exit Only." "Leave her sit there," said the attendant. "I'll put her away." Mitty got out of the car. "Hey, better leave the key." "Oh," said Mitty, handing the man the ignition key. The attendant vaulted into the car, backed it up with insolent skill, and put it where it belonged.

8   They're so darn cocky, thought Walter Mitty, walking along Main Street; they think they know everything. Once he had tried to take his chains off, outside New Milford, and he had got them wound around the axles. A man had had to come out in a wrecking car and unwind them, a young, grinning garageman. Since then Mrs. Mitty always made him drive to a garage to have the chains taken off. The next time, he thought, I'll wear my right arm in a sling; they won't grin at me then. I'll have my right arm in a sling and they'll see I couldn't possibly take the chains off myself. He kicked at the slush on the sidewalk. "Overshoes," he said to himself and he began looking for a shoe store.

9   When he came out into the street again, with the overshoes in a box under his arm, Walter Mitty began to wonder what the other thing was his wife had told him to get. She had told him twice before they set out from their house for Waterbury. In a way he hated these weekly trips to town—he was always getting something wrong. Kleenex, he thought. Squibb's, razor blades? No. Toothpaste, toothbrush, bicarbonate, carborundum, initiative and referendum? He gave it up. But she would remember it. "Where's the what's-its-name?" she would ask. "Don't tell me you forgot the what's-its-name." A newsboy went by shouting something about the Waterbury trial.

10   . . . "Perhaps this will refresh your memory." The District Attorney suddenly thrust a heavy automatic at the quiet figure on the witness stand, "Have you ever seen this before?" Walter Mitty took the gun and examined it expertly. "This is my Webley-Vickers 50.80," he said calmly. An excited buzz ran around the courtroom. The Judge rapped for order. "You are a crack shot with any sort of firearms, I believe?" said the District Attorney, insinuatingly. "Objection!" shouted Mitty's attorney. "We have shown that he wore his right arm in a sling on the night of the fourteenth of July." Walter Mitty raised his hand briefly and the bickering attorneys were stilled. "With any

known make of gun," he said evenly, "I could have killed Gregory Fitzhurst at three hundred feet *with my left hand.*" Pandemonium broke loose in the courtroom. A woman's scream rose above the bed-lam and suddenly a lovely, dark-haired girl was in Walter Mitty's arms. The District Attorney struck at her savagely. Without rising from his chair, Mitty let the man have it on the point of the chin. "You miser-able cur!"

11   "Puppy biscuit," said Walter Mitty. He stopped walking and the buildings of Waterbury rose up out of the misty courtroom and sur-rounded him again. A woman who was passing laughed. "He said 'Puppy biscuit,'" she said to her companion. "That man said 'Puppy biscuit' to himself." Walter Mitty hurried on. He went into an A. & P., not the first one he came to but a smaller one farther up the street. "I want some biscuit for small, young dogs," he said to the clerk. "Any special brand, sir?" The greatest pistol shot in the world thought a moment. "It says 'Puppies Bark for It!' on the box," said Walter Mitty.

12   His wife would be through at the hairdresser's in fifteen minutes, Mitty saw in looking at his watch, unless they had trouble drying it; sometimes they had trouble drying it. She didn't like to get to the hotel first; she would want him to be there waiting for her as usual. He found a big leather chair in the lobby, facing a window, and he put the over-shoes and the puppy biscuit on the floor beside it. He picked up an old copy of *Liberty* and sank down into the chair. "Can Germany Conquer the World Through the Air?" Walter Mitty looked at the pictures of bombing planes and of ruined streets.

13   . . . "The cannonading has got the wind up in young Raleigh, sir," said the sergeant. Captain Mitty looked up at him through tousled hair. "Get him to bed," he said wearily, "with the others. I'll fly alone." "But you can't, sir," said the sergeant anxiously. "It takes two men to handle that bomber and the Archies are pounding hell out of the air. Von Richtman's circus is between here and Saulier." "Some-body's got to get that ammunition dump," said Mitty. "I'm going over. Spot of brandy?" He poured a drink for the sergeant and one for him-self. War thundered and whined around the dugout and battered at the door. There was a rending of wood, and splinters flew through the room. "A bit of a near thing," said Captain Mitty carelessly. "The box barrage is closing in," said the sergeant. "We only live once, Sergeant," said Mitty, with his faint, fleeting smile. "Or do we?" He poured another brandy and tossed it off. "I never see a man could hold his brandy like you, sir," said the sergeant. "Begging your pardon, sir." Captain Mitty stood up and strapped on his huge Webley-Vickers auto-matic. "It's forty kilometres through hell, sir," said the sergeant, Mitty

finished one last brandy. "After all," he said softly, "what isn't?" The pounding of the cannon increased; there was the rat-tat tatting of machine guns, and from somewhere came the menacing pocketa-pocketa-pocketa of the new flame throwers. Walter Mitty walked to the door of the dugout humming "Auprès de Ma Blonde." He turned and waved to the sergeant. "Cheerio!" he said. . . .

14   Something struck his shoulder. "I've been looking all over this hotel for you," said Mrs. Mitty. "Why do you have to hide in this old chair? How did you expect me to find you?" "Things close in," said Walter Mitty vaguely. "What?" Mrs. Mitty said. "Did you get the what's-its-name? The puppy biscuit? What's in that box?" "Overshoes," said Mitty. "Couldn't you have put them on in the store?" "I was thinking," said Walter Mitty. "Does it ever occur to you that I am sometimes thinking?" She looked at him. "I'm going to take your temperature when I get you home," she said.

15   They went out through the revolving doors that made a faintly derisive whistling sound when you pushed them. It was two blocks to the parking lot. At the drugstore on the corner she said, "Wait here for me. I forgot something. I won't be a minute." She was more than a minute. Walter Mitty lighted a cigarette. It began to rain, rain with sleet in it. He stood up against the wall of the drugstore smoking. . . . He put his shoulders back and his heels together. "To hell with the handkerchief," said Walter Mitty scornfully. He took one last drag on his cigarette and snapped it away. Then, with that faint, fleeting smile playing about his lips, he faced the firing squad; erect and motionless, proud and disdainful, Walter Mitty, the Undefeated, inscrutable to the last.

The Secret Life of Walter Mitty

JOURNAL

1. MLA Works Cited

Using this model, record this story here.

Author's Last Name, First Name. "Title of the Story." <u>Title of the Book</u>. Ed. First Last Name. City: Publisher, year. Pages of the story.

2. Main Character(s)

Describe each main character, and explain why you think each is a main character.

3. Supporting Characters

Describe each supporting character, and explain why you think each is a supporting character.

4. **Setting**

   Describe the setting. Decide if the setting can be changed and, if so, to where and when.

5. **Sequence**

   Relate the events of the story in order.

6. **Plot**

   Tell the story in no more than three sentences.

7. **Conflicts**

   Identify and explain the conflicts involved here.

8. **Significant Quotations**

   Explain the importance of each of these quotations. Record the page number in the parentheses.

a. " 'Not so fast! You're driving too fast!' said Mrs. Mitty" (   ).

b. "[. . .] he drove past the hospital on his way to the parking lot" (   ).

c. "A newsboy went by shouting something about the Waterbury trial" (   ).

d. "He picked up an old copy of *Liberty* and sank down into the chair" (   ).

e. "Then, with a faint, fleeting smile playing about his lips, he faced the firing squad; erect and motionless, proud and disdainful, Walter Mitty, the Undefeated, inscrutable to the last" (   ).

FOLLOW-UP QUESTIONS

10 SHORT QUESTIONS

Select the <u>best</u> answer for each.

____ 1. Mitty
   a. is in the Navy.
   b. thinks he is in the Navy.
   c. daydreams he is in the Navy.

____ 2. The boss in the family seems to be
   a. Mitty.
   b. his wife.
   c. the Captain.

____ 3. Gloves signal
   a. a hospital.
   b. a courtroom.
   c. a bomber station.

____ 4. Mitty
   a. is a renown surgeon.
   b. thinks he is a renown surgeon.
   c. daydreams he is a renown surgeon.

____ 5. Mitty
   a. wants to wear the gloves.
   b. does not want to wear the gloves.
   c. wants to buy the gloves.

____ 6. A newsboy signals
   a. a courtroom.
   b. a hospital.
   c. a bomber station.

____ 7. Mitty really
   a. is on trial.
   b. is not on trial.
   c. is a lawyer.

____ 8. Mitty
   a. is a "crack shot."
   b. knows he is a "crack shot."
   c. daydreams he is "crack shot."

____ 9. A magazine article signals
   a. a hospital.
   b. a courtroom.
   c. a bomber station.

____ 10. Mitty
   a. is a fighter pilot.
   b. thinks he is a fighter pilot.
   c. daydreams he is a fighter pilot.

5 SIGNIFICANT QUOTATIONS

Explain the importance of each of these quotations.

1. "Walter Mitty drove on toward Waterbury in silence, the roaring of the SN202 through the worst storm in twenty years of Navy flying fading in the remote, intimate airways of his mind."

2. "A door opened down a long, cool corridor and Dr. Renshaw came out. He looked distraught and haggard. 'Hello, Mitty,' he said."

3. "Walter Mitty took the gun and examined it expertly."

4. " 'Can Germany Conquer the World Through the Air?' Walter Mitty looked at the pictures of bombing planes and of ruined streets."

5. " 'I was thinking,' said Walter Mitty. 'Does it ever occur to you that I am sometimes thinking?' "

2 COMPREHENSION ESSAY QUESTIONS

Use specific details and information from the story to answer these as completely as possible.

1. How does the title relate to the story? Explain the significance of the title using specific details and information from the story.

2. Describe Walter Mitty in terms of looks, personality, and general manner. Describe his wife in terms of looks, personality, and general manner. Use specific details and information from the story in your descriptions.

WRITING

Use each of these ideas for writing an essay.

1. Write a narrative essay about a time you have been caught off guard in a daydream and about the consequences.

2. We all use safe escapes. Write an essay illustrating one of your safe escapes.

Further Writing

1. Compare and contrast Ambrose Bierce's "An Occurrence at Owl Creek Bridge" (page 106) with "The Secret Life of Walter Mitty."

2. Read and compare Margot in Ernest Hemingway's "The Short Happy Life of Francis Macomber" (which can be found in a library) with Mrs. Mitty.

The Tell-Tale Heart

EDGAR ALLAN POE

PRE-READING VOCABULARY
CONTEXT

Use context clues to define these words before reading. Use a dictionary as needed.

1. The movie was so terrible that it was *dreadful. Dreadful* means

   __aufull__.

2. The smell of dinner may *sharpen* one's appetite. *Sharpen* means

   __highten__.

3. After too much use, the knife became *dull. Dull* means

   __not sharp__.

4. A *vulture* circled overhead, waiting to eat the dead animal. *Vulture*

   means __Scavenger bird__.

5. Trying to catch a bus and a train and a plane all at the same time is

   just plain *mad. Mad* means __Crazy__.

6. To see down the dark hallway, Betty used a *lantern. Lantern* means

   __lamp; a light__.

7. The cat *cunningly* hid in the closet so that she could jump out and

   scare us. *Cunningly* means __Sneaky__.

8. The sudden, loud noise *startled* Juan. *Startle* means

   __frighten__.

9. Albert bought new wooden *shutters* to filter the light in each window.

   Shutters means __wooden covers for window__.

10. Renee was in *awe* when she actually met the rock superstar. *Awe* means _Surprise_.

11. Shirley was *furious* when her dog tore up her favorite, brand new shoes. *Furious* means _angry_.

12. The smog *enveloped* the city making it very hard to see. *Envelop* means _Coverd_.

13. As he got tired of waiting, Jim's tapping fingers beat a continual *tattoo* on the countertop. *Tattoo* means _pattern_.

14. When Kathy saw the mouse run across her foot, she let out a loud *shriek*. *Shriek* means _Scream_.

15. John *muffled* the loud noise with earplugs. *Muffle* means _Covered over_.

16. After the funeral, the *corpse* was buried in the old cemetery. *Corpse* means _body_.

17. After running the mile, Aimee could feel her heart beat and sensed its every *pulsation*. *Pulsation* means _beat_.

18. The mechanic had to *dismember* the car to get to the fan belt. *Dismember* means _take apart_.

19. After money suddenly was found to be continuously missing, we developed a *suspicion* that the new employee was stealing. *Suspicion* means _idea_.

20. Although Bruce was very upset after his accident, he *dissembled* well and had us all believing that he was not upset at all. *Dissemble* means _take apart kept cool_.

Pre-reading Vocabulary
Word Attack

Define these words by solving the parts. Use a dictionary as needed.

1. causeless
2. unperceived
3. stealthily
4. distinctness
5. motionless

6. uncontrollable
7. precaution
8. concealment
9. hastily

Pre-reading Questions

Try answering these questions as you read.

Who are the characters in the story?

How does the narrator want you to feel about him?

Sanity is defined as being able to recognize reality, while insanity is defined as not being able to recognize reality. What does this tell you about the narrator?

What hints does Poe give you for the startling ending?

The Tell-Tale Heart

EDGAR ALLAN POE

Edgar Allan Poe was born in 1809 and orphaned at a young age. He was adopted by John Allan, a rather militaristic businessman from Richmond, Virginia. Adoption by a person of means was not uncommon and would have been fortunate for the young Poe, except that his free spirit and his father's precision clashed. John Allan provided Poe with study at the University of Virginia—but Poe withdrew, due to drinking problems—and then at West Point—but Poe was dismissed, due to a disciplinary problem. Poe later married his very young cousin, Virginia Clemm, but the probable nonconsummation of this marriage and the early death of young Virginia contributed to Poe's idealization of both real and imagined women. His life, in fact, was one of continual disappointments. After Virginia's death, Poe sank into intermittent depressions, suffered bouts of insanity, and experienced hallucinations. Writing for many others, he wanted to publish his own magazine, but this dissolved in financial failure. He eventually died in Baltimore in 1849.

However, it is from these very problems that Poe's genius soars. He envelops the reader with his perceived worlds of the sane and insane, the rational and macabre, with equal ease. Credited with developing the modern mystery form, Poe's every word and every action draw the reader in, mixing reality with irreality, sane with insane. His other works include "The Pit and the Pendulum" and "The Fall of the House of Usher."

True! nervous—very, very dreadfully nervous I had been and am; but why *will* you say that I am mad? The disease had sharpened my senses—not destroyed—not dulled them. Above all was the sense of hearing acute. I heard all things in the heaven and in the earth. I heard many things in hell. How, then, am I mad? Hearken! and observe how healthily—how calmly I can tell you the whole story.

2   It is impossible to say how first the idea entered my brain; but once conceived, it haunted me day and night. Object there was none. Passion there was none. I loved the old man. He had never wronged me. He had never given me insult. For his gold I had no desire. I think it was his eye! yes, it was this! He had the eye of a vulture—a pale blue eye, with a film over it. Whenever it fell upon me, my blood ran cold; and so by degrees—very gradually—I made up my mind to take the life of the old man, and thus rid myself of the eye forever.

3   Now this is the point. You fancy me mad. Madmen know nothing. But you should have seen *me.* You should have seen how wisely I proceeded—with what caution—with what foresight—with what dissimulation I went to work! I was never kinder to the old man than during the whole week before I killed him. And every night, about midnight, I turned the latch of his door and opened it—ah, so gently! And then, when I had made an opening sufficient for my head, I put in a dark lantern, all closed, closed, so that no light shone out, and then I thrust in my head. Oh, you would have laughed to see how cunningly I thrust it in! I moved it slowly—very, very slowly, so that I might not disturb the old man's sleep. It took me an hour to place my whole head within the opening so far that I could see him as he lay upon his bed. Ha!—would a madman have been so wise as this? And then, when my head was well in the room, I undid the lantern cautiously—oh, so cautiously—cautiously (for the hinges creaked)—I undid it just so much that a single thin ray fell upon the vulture eye. And this I did for seven long nights—every night just at midnight—but I found the eye always closed; and so it was impossible to do the work; for it was not the old man who vexed me, but his Evil Eye. And every morning, when the day broke, I went boldly into the chamber, and spoke courageously to him, calling him by name in a hearty tone, and inquiring how he had passed the night. So you see he would have been a very profound old man, indeed, to suspect that every night, just at twelve, I looked in upon him while he slept.

4   Upon the eighth night I was more than usually cautious in opening the door. A watch's minute hand moves more quickly than did mine. Never, before that night, had I *felt* the extent of my own powers—of my sagacity. I could scarcely contain my feelings of triumph. To think

that there I was, opening the door, little by little, and he not even to dream of my secret deeds or thoughts. I fairly chuckled at the idea; and perhaps he heard me; for he moved on the bed suddenly, as if startled. Now you may think that I drew back—but no. His room was as black as pitch with the thick darkness (for the shutters were close fastened, through fear of robbers), and so I knew that he could not see the opening of the door, and I kept pushing it on steadily, steadily.

5   I had my head in, and was about to open the lantern, when my thumb slipped upon the tin fastening, and the old man sprang up in bed, crying out, "Who's there?" I kept quite still and said nothing. For a whole hour I did not move a muscle, and in the meantime I did not hear him lie down. He was still sitting up in the bed listening—just as I have done, night after night, hearkening to the death watches in the wall.

6   Presently I heard a slight groan, and I knew it was the groan of mortal terror. It was not a groan of pain or of grief—oh, no!—it was the low stifled sound that rises from the bottom of the soul when overcharged with awe. I knew the sound well. Many a night, just at midnight, when all the world slept, it has welled up from my own bosom, deepening, with its dreadful echo, the terrors that distracted me. I say I knew it well. I knew what the old man felt, and pitied him, although I chuckled at heart. I knew that he had been lying awake ever since the first slight noise, when he had turned in his bed. His fears had been ever since growing upon him. He had been trying to fancy them causeless, but could not. He had been saying to himself—"It is nothing but the wind in the chimney—it is, only a mouse crossing the floor," or "It is merely a cricket which has made a single chirp." Yes, he had been trying to comfort himself with these suppositions: but he had found all in vain. *All in vain;* because Death, in approaching him, had stalked with his black shadow before him, and enveloped the victim. And it was the mournful influence of the unperceived shadow that caused him to feel—although he neither saw nor heard—to *feel* the presence of my head within the room.

7   When I had waited a long time, very patiently, without hearing him lie down, I resolved to open a little—a very, very little crevice in the lantern. So I opened it—you cannot imagine how stealthily, stealthily—until at length a single dim ray, like the thread of the spider, shot from out the crevice and fell upon the vulture eye.

8   It was open—wide, wide open—and I grew furious as I gazed upon it. I saw it with perfect distinctiveness—all a dull blue, with a hideous veil over it that chilled the very marrow in my bones; but I could see nothing else of the old man's face or person; for I had directed the ray as if by instinct, precisely upon the damned spot.

9   And have I not told you that what you mistake for madness is but overacuteness of the senses?—Now, I say, there came to my ears a low, dull, quick sound, such as a watch makes when enveloped in cotton. I knew *that* sound well, too. It was the beating of the old man's heart. It increased my fury, as the beating of a drum stimulates the soldier into courage.

10   But even yet I refrained and kept still. I scarcely breathed. I held the lantern motionless. I tried how steadily I could maintain the ray upon the eye. Meantime the hellish tattoo of the heart increased. It grew quicker and quicker, and louder and louder every instant. The old man's terror *must* have been extreme! It grew louder, I say louder every moment!—do you mark me well? I have told you that I am nervous: so I am. And now at the dead hour of the night, amid the dreadful silence of that old house, so strange a noise as this excited me to uncontrollable terror. Yet, for some minutes longer I refrained and stood still. But the beating grew louder, louder. I thought the heart must burst. And now a new anxiety seized me—the sound would be heard by a neighbor! The old man's hour had come! With, a loud yell, I threw open the lantern and leaped into the room. He shrieked once—once only. In an instant I dragged him to the floor, and pulled the heavy bed over him. I then smiled gaily, to find the deed so far done. But, for many minutes, the heart beat on with a muffled sound. This, however, did not vex me; it would not be heard through the wall. At length it ceased. The old man was dead. I removed the bed and examined the corpse. Yes, he was stone, stone dead. I placed my hand upon the heart and held it there many minutes. There was no pulsation. He was stone dead. His eye would trouble me no more.

11   If still you think me mad, you will think so no longer when I describe the wise precautions I took for the concealment of the body. The night waned, and I worked hastily, but in silence. First of all I dismembered the corpse. I cut off the head and the arms and the legs.

12   I then took up three planks from the flooring of the chamber, and deposited all between the scantlings. I then replaced the boards so cleverly, so cunningly, that no human eye—not even his—could have detected anything wrong. There was nothing to wash out—no stain of any kind—no blood spot whatever. I had been too wary for that. A tub had caught all—ha! ha!

13   When I had made an end of these labors, it was four o'clock—still dark as midnight. As the bell sounded the hour, there came a knocking at the street door. I went down to open it with a light heart—for what had I *now* to fear? There entered three men, who introduced themselves, with perfect suavity, as officers of the police. A shriek had been

heard by a neighbor during the night; suspicion of foul play had been aroused; information had been lodged at the police office, and they (the officers) had been deputed to search the premises.

14   I smiled—for *what* had I to fear? I bade the gentlemen welcome. The shriek, I said, was my own in a dream. The old man, I mentioned, was absent in the country. I took my visitors all over the house. I bade them search—search *well*. I led them, at length, to *his* chamber. I showed them his treasures, secure, undisturbed. In the enthusiasm of my confidence, I brought chairs into the room, and desired them *here* to rest from their fatigues, while I myself, in the wild audacity of my perfect triumph, placed my own seat upon the very spot beneath which reposed the corpse of the victim.

15   The officers were satisfied. My *manner* had convinced them. I was singularly at ease. They sat, and while I answered cheerily, they chatted of familiar things. But, erelong, I felt myself getting pale and wished them gone. My head ached, and I fancied a ringing in my ears: but still they sat and still chatted. The ringing became more distinct— it continued and became more distinct; I talked more freely to get rid of the feeling; but it continued and gained definiteness—until, at length, I found that the noise was *not* within my ears.

16   No doubt I now grew *very* pale—but I talked more fluently, and with a heightened voice. Yet the sound increased—and what could I do? It was *a low, dull, quick sound—much such a sound as a watch makes when enveloped in cotton.* I gasped for breath—and yet the officers heard it not. I talked more quickly—more vehemently; but the noise steadily increased. I arose and argued about rifles, in a high key and with violent gesticulations; but the noise steadily increased. Why *would* they not be gone? I paced the floor to and fro with heavy strides, as if excited to fury by the observations of the men—but the noise steadily increased. Oh, God! what *could* I do? I foamed—I raved—I swore! I swung the chair upon which I had been sitting, and grated it upon the boards, but the noise arose over all and continually increased. It grew louder—louder—*louder!* And still the men chatted pleasantly, and smiled. Was it possible they heard not? Almighty God!—no, no! They heard!—they suspected!—they *knew!*—they were making a mockery of my horror!—this I thought, and this I think. But anything was better than this agony! Anything was more tolerable than derision! I could bear those hypocritical smiles no longer! I felt that I must scream or die! and now—again!—hark! louder! louder! louder! *louder!*

17   "Villains!" I shrieked, "dissemble no more! I admit the deed!—tear up the planks! here, here!—it is the beating of his hideous heart!"

The Tell-Tale Heart

JOURNAL

1. MLA Works Cited

Using this model, record this reading here.

Author's Last Name, First Name. "Title of the Story." <u>Title of the Book</u>. *Ed. First Last Name. City: Publisher, year. Pages of the story.*

2. Main Character(s)

Describe each main character, and explain why you think each is a main character.

3. Supporting Characters

Describe each supporting character, and explain why you think each is a supporting character.

4. Setting

Describe the setting. Decide if this setting can be changed and, if so, to where and when.

5. Sequence

Relate the events of the story in order.

6. Plot

Tell the story in no more than two sentences.

7. Conflicts

Identify and explain the conflicts involved here.

8. Significant Quotations

Explain the importance of each of these quotations. Record the page number in the parentheses.

a. "The disease had sharpened my senses—not destroyed—not dulled them" (   ).

b. "He had the eye of a vulture—a pale blue eye, with a film over it"(   ).

c. "Upon the eighth night I was more than usually cautious in opening the door" (   ).

d. "And have I not told you that what you mistake for madness is but overa-cuteness of the senses?—Now, I say, there came to my ears a low, dull, quick sound, such as a watch makes when enveloped in cotton" (   ).

e. "I gasped for breath—and yet the officers heard it not" (   ).

9. Foreshadowing
   Identify and explain the hints Poe gives to predict the action.

FOLLOW-UP QUESTIONS

10 SHORT QUESTIONS

Select the <u>best</u> answer for each.

___ 1. The narrator thinks
a. he is sane.
b. he is insane.
c. he is normal.

C 2. The narrator wants you to think
a. he is sane.
b. he is insane.
c. he is sane and more clever than most.

C 3. At first, the narrator is
a. kind to the old man.
b. unkind to the old man.
c. unfeeling toward the old man.

B 4. The old man is.
a. unkind to the narrator.
b. like a father figure to the narrator.
c. the narrator's brother.

A 5. The narrator probably shares
a. no relationship with the old man.
b. a formal working relationship with the old man.
c. a family-like relationship with the old man.

C 6. The narrator
a. hates the old man.
b. loves the old man.
c. does not care about the old man.

A 7. The narrator
a. hates the old man's eye.
b. loves the old man's eye.
c. does not care about the old man's eye.

A 8. The narrator
a. has planned well.
b. has not planned well.
c. does not tell the reader about his plans.

C 9. The only person(s) who can hear the heartbeat is (are)
a. the police.
b. the old man.
c. the narrator.

B 10. At first, the police
a. do not suspect the narrator.
b. do suspect the narrator.
c. know the old man is dead

5 SIGNIFICANT QUOTATIONS

Explain the importance of each of these quotations.

1. "True! nervous—very, very dreadfully nervous I had been and am; but why *will* you say that I am mad?"

2. "I think it was his eye! yes, it was this!"

3. "You fancy me mad. Madmen know nothing. But you should have seen *me*."

4. "And this I did for seven long nights—every night just at midnight—but I found the eye always closed; and so it was important to do the work [. . .]."

5. " 'Villains!' I shrieked, 'dissemble no more! I admit the deed!—tear up the planks! here, here!—it is the beating of his hideous heart!' "

2 COMPREHENSION ESSAY QUESTIONS

Use specific details and information from the story to answer these as completely as possible.

1. How does the title relate to the story? Explain the significance of the title using specific details and information from the story.

2. Explain all the events that happen during the narrator's confession. Use specific details and information from the story for your explanation.

WRITING

Use each of these ideas for writing an essay.

1. At one time or another, we have all been so scared that we could hear our own heartbeat. Tell the story of a time when you were so scared that you could hear your heartbeat.

2. The narrator is very sure that what he is doing very clever. Describe a time when you or someone you know was sure of being right when, in fact, what he or she was doing was wrong.

Further Writing

1. Compare and contrast the narrator in this story with Montresor in Edgar Allan Poe's "The Cask of Amontillado" (page 137).

2. Research today's use of the insanity plea in criminal actions. Poe's story offers an insightful anecdote for this study.

There Will Come Soft Rains

RAY BRADBURY

PRE-READING VOCABULARY
CONTEXT

Use context clues to define these words before reading. Use a dictionary as needed.

1. The principal *ejected* the student who was always in trouble from school. *Eject* means _____.

2. The *relay* runners passed the torch from one runner to the next. *Relay* means _____.

3. When rabbits live underground, they live in what is called a *warren*. *Warren* means _____.

4. The scientist created a *robot* with arms like a man to put the dishes in the dishwasher. *Robot* means _____.

5. The atomic bomb gave off deadly *radioactive* particles. *Radioactive* means _____.

6. The chef baked the rolls too long and *charred* all the bottoms of the rolls. *Char* means _____.

7. A *silhouette* is usually a picture of a black profile set on a white background. *Silhouette* means _____.

8. The extremely large wave was of *titanic* size. *Titanic* means

    _____.

9. When Ted studied *mechanical* engineering, he learned how machines work and how to invent machines. *Mechanical* means

    _____.

10. Saying a prayer before dinner is our family *ritual. Ritual* means

    _____.

11. The air flowed through the open *vent. Vent* means

    _____.

12. To get rid of excess trash, the township burned the trash in an
    incinerator. Incinerator means _____.

13. Sonia sunbathed on the lovely concrete *patio* in back of her house.
    Patio means _____.

14. Cinderella's busy mice rapidly *scurried* past the sleeping cat. *Scurry*
    means _____.

15. The glass shattered into a million dangerous and flying pieces like
    shrapnel when it broke. *Shrapnel* means _____.

16. The hot water *scalded* the young plants. *Scald* means

    _____.

17. When Kristin called for silence, all the talking *ceased. Cease* means

    _____.

18. Hundreds of rocks fell down the mountainside in a roaring *avalanche.*
    Avalanche means _____.

19. The *frantic* mother searched everywhere for her lost child until she
    found him. *Frantic* means _____.

20. After the building burned to the ground, the workers returned
    to search through the *rubble* for valuables. *Rubble* means

    _____.

Pre-reading Vocabulary
Word Attack

Define these words by solving the parts. Use a dictionary as needed.

1. emptiness
2. payable
3. acrawl
4. windowpane
5. self-protection

6. senselessly
7. uselessly
8. summer-starched
9. trapdoor
10. remote-control

Pre-reading Questions

Try answering these questions as you read.

Who or what are the characters in the story?

What has happened?

What is happening now?

What is the scene Bradbury is painting?

There Will Come Soft Rains

Ray Bradbury

Ray Bradbury was born in 1920 in Waukegan, Illinois, but was raised in Los Angeles. Already writing science fiction in high school, he published his first story in 1941. With a continuing dialectic dynamic, his writings discuss the relationship between humans and the machines and/or destruction we create. Taken from *The Martian Chronicles*, this story remains one of his more noted short stories.

The house was a good house and had been planned and built by the people who were to live in it, in the year 1980. The house was like many another house in that year; it fed and slept and entertained its habitants, and made a good life for them. The man and wife and their two children lived at ease there, and lived happily, even while the world trembled. All of the fine things of living, the warm things, music and poetry, books that talked, beds that warmed and made themselves, fires that built themselves in the fireplaces of evenings, were in this house, and living there was a contentment.

2   And then one day the world shook and there was an explosion followed by ten thousand explosions and red fire in the sky and a rain of ashes and radioactivity, and the happy time was over.

3   In the living room the voice clock sang, *tick-tock, seven A.M. o'clock, time to get up!* as if it were afraid nobody would. The house lay empty. The clock talked on into the empty morning.

4   The kitchen stove sighed and ejected from its warm interior eight eggs, sunny side up, twelve bacon slices, two coffees, and two cups of hot cocoa. *Seven nine, breakfast time, seven nine.*

5   "Today is April 28th, 1985," said a phonograph voice in the kitchen ceiling. "Today, remember, is Mr. Featherstone's birthday. Insurance, gas, light, and water bills are due."

6   Somewhere in the walls, relays clicked, memory tapes glided under electric eyes. Recorded voices moved beneath steel needles:

7   *Eight one, run, run, off to school, off to work, run, run, tick-tock, eight one o'clock!*

8   But no doors slammed, no carpets took the quick tread of rubber heels. Outside, it was raining. The voice of the weather box on the front door sang quietly: "Rain, rain, go away, rubbers, raincoats for today." And the rain tapped on the roof.

9   At eight thirty the eggs were shriveled. An aluminum wedge scraped them into the sink, where hot water whirled them down a metal throat which digested and flushed them away to the distant sea.

10   *Nine fifteen,* sang the clock, *time to clean.*

11   Out of warrens in the wall, tiny mechanical mice darted. The rooms were acrawl with the small cleaning animals, all rubber and metal. They sucked up the hidden dust, and popped back in their burrows.

12   *Ten o'clock.* The sun came out from behind the rain. The house stood alone on a street where all the other houses were rubble and ashes. At night, the ruined town gave off a radioactive glow which could be seen for miles.

13   *Ten fifteen.* The garden sprinkler filled the soft morning air with golden fountains. The water tinkled over the charred west side of the house where it had been scorched evenly free of its white paint. The entire face of the house was black, save for five places. Here, the silhouette, in paint, of a man mowing a lawn. Here, a woman bent to pick flowers. Still farther over, their images burned on wood in one titanic instant, a small boy, hands flung in the air—higher up, the image of a thrown ball—and opposite him a girl, her hands raised to catch a ball which never came down.

14   The five spots of paint—the man, the woman, the boy, the girl, the ball—remained. The rest was a layer of charcoal.

15   The gentle rain of the sprinkler filled the garden with falling light.

16   Until this day, how well the house had kept its peace. How carefully it had asked, "Who goes there?" and getting no reply from rains and lonely foxes and whining cats, it had shut up its windows and drawn the shades. If a sparrow brushed a window, the shade snapped up. The bird, startled, flew off! No, not even an evil bird must touch the house.

17   And inside, the house was like an altar with nine thousand robot attendants, big and small, servicing, attending, singing in choirs, even though the gods had gone away and the ritual was meaningless.

18   A dog whined, shivering, on the front porch.

19   The front door recognized the dog's voice and opened. The dog padded in wearily, thinned to the bone, covered with sores. It tracked mud on the carpet. Behind it whirred the angry robot mice, angry at having to pick up mud and maple leaves, which, carried to the burrows, were dropped down cellar tubes into an incinerator which sat like an evil Baal in a dark corner.

20   The dog ran upstairs, hysterically yelping at each door. It pawed the kitchen door wildly.

21   Behind the door, the stove was making pancakes which filled the whole house with their odor.

22   The dog frothed, ran insanely, spun in a circle, biting its tail, and died.

23   It lay in the living room for an hour.

24   *One o' clock.*

25   Delicately sensing decay, the regiments of mice hummed out of the walls, soft as blown leaves, their electric eyes glowing.

26   *One fifteen.*

27   The dog was gone.

28   The cellar incinerator glowed suddenly and a whirl of sparks leaped up the flue.

29   *Two thirty-five.*

30   Bridge tables sprouted from the patio walls. Playing cards fluttered onto pads in a shower of pips. Martinis appeared on an oaken bench.

31   But the tables were silent, the cards untouched.

32   At four thirty the tables folded back into the walls.

33   *Five o'clock.* The bathtubs filled with clear hot water. A safety razor dropped into a wall mold, ready.

34   *Six, seven, eight, nine o'clock.*

35   Dinner made, ignored, and flushed away; dishes washed; and in the study, the tobacco stand produced a cigar, half an inch of gray ash on it, smoking, waiting. The hearth fire bloomed up all by itself, out of nothing.

36   *Nine o'clock.* The beds began to warm their hidden circuits, for the night was cool.

37   A gentle click in the study wall. A voice spoke from above the crackling fireplace:

38   "Mrs. McClellan, what poem would you like to hear this evening?"

39   The house was silent.

40   The voice said, "Since you express no preference, I'll pick a poem at random." Quiet music rose behind the voice. "Sara Teasdale. A favorite of yours, as I recall."

41   *There will come soft rains and the smell of*
42   *the ground,*
43   *And swallows circling with their shimmering*
44   *sound;*

45   *And frogs in the pools singing at night,*
46   *And wild plum-trees in tremulous white.*

47   *Robins will wear their feathery fire*
48   *Whistling their whims on a low fence-wire;*

49   *And not one will know of the war, not one*
50   *Will care at last when it is done.*

51   *Not one would mind, neither bird nor tree,*
52   *If mankind perished utterly.*

53   *And Spring herself, when she woke at dawn,*
54   *Would scarcely know that we were gone.*

55   The voice finished the poem. The empty chairs faced each other between the silent walls, and the music played.
56   At ten o'clock, the house began to die.
57   The wind blew. The bough of a falling tree smashed the kitchen window. Cleaning solvent, bottled, crashed on the stove.
58   "Fire!" screamed voices. "Fire!" Water pumps shot down water from the ceilings. But the solvent spread under the doors, making fire as it went, while other voices took up the alarm in chorus.
59   The windows broke with heat and the wind blew in to help the fire. Scurrying water rats, their copper wheels spinning, squeaked from the walls, squirted their water, ran for more.
60   Too late! Somewhere, a pump stopped. The ceiling sprays stopped raining. The reserve water supply, which had filled baths and washed dishes for many silent days, was gone.
61   The fire crackled upstairs, ate paintings, lay hungrily in the beds! It devoured every room.
62   The house was shuddering, oak bone on bone, the bared skeleton cringing from the heat, all the wires revealed as if a surgeon had torn the skin off to let the red veins quiver in scalded air. Voices screamed, *"Help, help, fire, run!"* Windows snapped open and shut, like mouths, undecided. *Fire, run!* the voices wailed a tragic nursery rhyme, and the silly Greek chorus faded as the sound-wires popped their sheathings. Ten dozen high, shrieking voices died, as emergency batteries melted.
63   In the other parts of the house, in the last instant under the fire avalanche, other choruses could be heard announcing the time, the weather, appointments, diets; playing music, reading poetry in the fiery study, while doors opened and slammed and umbrellas appeared

at the doors and put themselves away—a thousand things happening like the interior of a clockshop at midnight, all clocks striking, a merry go-round of squeaking, whispering, rushing, until all the film spools were burned and fell, and all the wires withered and the circuits cracked.

61   In the kitchen, an instant before the final collapse, the stove, hysterically hissing, could be seen making breakfasts at a psychopathic rate, ten dozen pancakes, six dozen loaves of toast.

62   The crash! The attic smashing kitchen down into cellar and subcellar. Deep freeze, armchairs, film tapes, beds, were thrown in a cluttered mound deep under.

63   Smoke and silence.

64   Dawn shone faintly in the east. In the ruins, one wall stood alone. Within the wall, a voice said, over and over again and again, even as the sun rose to shine upon the heaped rubble and steam:

65   "Today is April 29th, 1985. Today is April 29th, 1985. Today is . . ."

There Will Come Soft Rains
JOURNAL

1. MLA Works Cited

Using this model, record this story.

Author's Last Name, First Name. "Title of the Story." <u>Title of the Book</u>. Ed. First Last Name. City: Publisher, year. Pages of the story.

2. Main Character(s)

Describe each main character, and explain why you think each is a main character.

3. Supporting Characters

Describe each supporting character, and explain why you think each is a supporting character.

4. Setting

Describe the setting. Decide if this setting can be changed and, if so, to where and when.

5. Sequence

Relate the events of the story in order.

6. Plot

Tell the story in no more than three sentences.

7. Conflicts

Identify and explain the conflicts involved here.

8. Significant Quotations

Explain the importance of each of these quotations. Record the page number in the parentheses.

a. "The house stood alone on a street where all the other houses were rubble and ashes" (   ).

b. "Here the silhouette, in paint, of a man mowing a lawn. Here, a woman bent to pick flowers" (   ).

c. "Delicately sensing decay, the regiments of mice hummed out of the walls, soft as blown leaves, their electric eyes glowing" (   ).

d. " 'There will come soft rains and the smell of
    the ground, [. . .]
And Spring herself, when she woke at dawn,
Would scarcely know that we were gone' " (   ).

e. "Somewhere, a pump stopped" (   ).

FOLLOW-UP QUESTIONS

10 SHORT QUESTIONS

Select the <u>best</u> answer for each.

____ 1. The mice are
   a. animals.
   b. robots.
   c. rodents.

____ 2. The house works
   a. by human command.
   b. by human touch.
   c. automatically.

____ 3. Breakfast is made by
   a. humans.
   b. machines.
   c. animals.

____ 4. The house is cleaned by
   a. humans.
   b. machines.
   c. animals.

____ 5. The family is
   a. dying.
   b. alive.
   c. vaporized.

____ 6. The massive destruction is
   caused by
   a. a fire.
   b. a thunderstorm.
   c. a nuclear explosion.

____ 7. The dog is
   a. ill and dies.
   b. healthy and lives.
   c. unaffected.

____ 8. The dog is
   a. incinerated.
   b. buried.
   c. fed.

____ 9. The house
   a. continues to stand.
   b. burns to the ground.
   c. explodes.

____ 10. The poem predicts that
   a. nature will go on.
   b. the world is destroyed.
   c. the house will be rebuilt.

5 SIGNIFICANT QUOTATIONS

Explain the importance of each of these quotations.

1. "And then one day the world shook and there was [. . .] a rain of ashes and radioactivity, and the happy time was over."

2. "Out of the warrens in the wall, tiny mechanical mice darted."

3. "The entire face of the house was black, save for five places."

4. " 'There will come soft rains and the smell of
        the ground, [. . .]

    And Spring herself, when she woke at dawn,
    Would scarcely know that we were gone.' "

5. "The bough of a falling tree smashed the kitchen window. Cleaning
    solvent, bottled, crashed on the stove."

2 COMPREHENSION ESSAY QUESTIONS

*Use specific details and information from the story to answer these as completely
as possible.*

1. One of Bradbury's themes is the destruction of war. Explain how he
    demonstrates this using specific details and information from the
    story.

2. Another of Bradbury's themes is that the machines we create will
    destroy us. Explain how he demonstrates this using specific details
    and information from the story.

WRITING

Use each of these ideas for writing an essay.

1. Select one or two machines, and tell how they help you. Explain your
    dependence on these machines.

2. Select one or two machines, and tell how they hinder you. Explain
    your dependence on these machines.

Further Writing

1. This story portrays the effects of war. Compare and contrast this
    story with Ambrose Bierce's "An Occurrence at Owl Creek Bridge"
    (page 106).

2. We do not need Bradbury's calamity to ruin our world. Research ozone
    depletion, the greenhouse effect, or an endangered major animal, all of
    which are man-made problems.

2

Setting and Props

Setting is the catch-all term that describes the time, place, and surroundings of a story. The surroundings include the mood or the tone of the story and even the inanimate objects that support the action of the story. In a short story, the setting is usually, although not always, limited. The story usually takes place in a shorter amount of time than in a longer work, and fewer places are involved.

The **time** during which a story takes place may be an historical period, such as the ancient, medieval, or modern period, or it may be an era, such as the Roaring Twenties, the Depression, the Civil War, or a world war. The time period may be a season—spring, summer, winter, or fall—or it may be a rainy, sunny, planting, or harvesting period or part of a day, such as daytime or nighttime. "An Occurrence at Owl Creek Bridge," for instance, will make more sense to you if you know that it is set during the Civil War.

Place is the location where a story is set. That "An Occurrence at Owl Creek Bridge" is set by a military installation in the South, that "Strong Temptations—Strategic Movements—The Innocents Beguiled" is set on a fenced property in the South, that "The Cask of Amontillado" is set in a large home in Italy, that "To Build a Fire" is set to the far north, and that "Everyday Use" is set in a welcoming home are important to the events of each story.

Mood or **tone** sets the general feeling of the story. A bright setting that is filled with sunlight and light breezes sets a much different mood or tone than a decaying, haunted house. Think of setting *Pet Cemetery* on a bright, sun-filled beach; it would not work. Notice in "An Occurrence at Owl Creek Bridge" that the mood of military formality and threat gives way to that of a welcoming homecoming—a mood that tricks the reader. In "Strong Temptations—Strategic Movements—The Innocents Beguiled," the outdoor setting is bright and airy and sets a lighthearted feeling. Edgar Allan Poe, a master of overwhelming atmospheres, draws the reader deeper and deeper into dampness and gloom; in "To Build a Fire" the pristine beauty of the outdoors creates the very threat of the story; and the comfortable home in which "Everyday Use" is set makes Dee's actions all the more outrageous.

Props (short for "properties") are the inanimate objects in a story. Props sometimes take on the qualities of characters. In a story of renown by the French master, Guy de Maupassant, a woman loses a diamond necklace and then devotes ten years of her life to paying for the replacement necklace, only to find that the original necklace was a fake and she has wasted ten years of her life for nothing. The prop, the necklace, is the very core of the story. In the stories in this chapter, the bridge is necessary in "An Occurrence at Owl Creek Bridge," the fence is crucial in "Strong Temptations—Strategic Movements—The Innocents Beguiled," the wine is essential to "The Cask of Amontillado," the energy of fire is central in "To Build a Fire," and the quilts are the core of "Everyday Use."

Enjoy the times and places to which these stories take you.

An Occurrence at Owl Creek Bridge

AMBROSE BIERCE

PRE-READING VOCABULARY
CONTEXT

Use context clues to define these words before reading. Use a dictionary as needed.

1. The serial murderer faced death by injection for his *execution.*

   Execution means _____.

2. The guard stood as *sentinel* at the closed gate. *Sentinel* means

   _____.

3. Rich asked the carpenter to put new *planking* on his deck. *Planking*

   means _____.

4. The fort was far from the city as an *outpost* to protect travelers.

   Outpost means _____.

5. Shannon slipped while climbing the muddy *bank* of the river. *Bank*

   means _____.

6. When Keith considered joining the *military,* he called the Army,

   Navy, Air Force, and Marines. *Military* means _____.

7. Jerry decided not to join the military and to remain a *civilian. Civilian*

   means _____.

8. Years ago, a murderer was executed by putting a rope around his neck

   and *hanging* him to death. *Hang* means _____.

9. The judge *condemned* the robber to ten years in prison. *Condemn*

   means _____.

10. When someone dies and the church bells ring, this is called that person's *death knell. Death knell* means _____.

11. A rope tied with a loop at the end is called a *noose. Noose* means

    _____.

12. *Secessionists* wanted the southern United States to be a country separate from the northern United States. *Secessionist* means

    _____.

13. Dan silently nodded his head to agree in thoughtful *assent. Assent* means _____.

14. The Germans shot from one side of the *front* and the French from the other side of the *front. Front* means _____.

15. The fishermen paid a local man to be their *scout* so that he would help them find the best fishing areas. *Scout* means _____.

16. The broken bone jutted out through the skin and caused severe *agony. Agony* means _____.

17. The fortune teller *presaged* Ellen's wedding, telling her she would marry in a year. *Presage* means _____.

18. The quietness and peacefulness of the sun softly setting on the calm lake gave a feeling of *tranquillity. Tranquillity* means

    _____.

19. Angela sipped coffee under the stars on the stone *veranda* overlooking the golf course. *Veranda* means _____.

20. As Licia fell forward in the car accident, she suffered a severe *blow* to her head. *Blow* means _____.

PRE-READING VOCABULARY
WORD ATTACK

Define these words by solving the parts. Use a dictionary as needed.

1. railroad
2. encircled
3. cross-timber
4. unnatural
5. inclining
6. stonily
7. motionless
8. fixity
9. cross-ties
10. bandaged
11. driftwood
12. metallic
13. immeasurably
14. progressively
15. unclosed
16. unnecessary
17. inglorious
18. gray-clad
19. horseman
20. commandant
21. unaccompanied

22. encompassed
23. suddenness
24. frightful
25. restored
26. superhuman
27. insupportable
28. veining
29. dewdrop
30. dragon-fly
31. unarmed
32. counter-swirl
33. pitilessly
34. singularly
35. rapidity
36. woodman
37. untraveled
38. unfamiliar
39. unknown
40. doubtless
41. recover

PRE-READING QUESTIONS

Try answering these questions as you read.

What is happening to the main character in the story?

What role does the scout serve?

Where is the man at first? Later? Still later?

An Occurrence at Owl Creek Bridge

AMBROSE BIERCE

Ambrose Bierce was born in Ohio in 1842. He served as an officer in the Union Army during the Civil War and then moved to San Francisco where he became a journalist. After traveling to England, he returned to San Francisco and progressed from a journalist to a columnist for Hearst publishing. After retiring in 1913, he followed Pancho Villa, a Mexican revolutionary, as an observer and was no longer heard from after 1913. His Civil War experiences often had an impact on his work, including "One of the Missing," and he is often compared to Poe because of his fascination with horror, death, and life after death.

A man stood upon a railroad bridge in northern Alabama, looking down into the swift water twenty feet below. The man's hands were behind his back, the wrists bound with a cord. A rope closely encircled his neck. It was attached to a stout cross-timber above his head and the slack fell to the level of his knees. Some loose boards laid upon the sleepers supporting the metals of the railway supplied a footing for him and his executioners—two private soldiers of the Federal army, directed by a sergeant who in civil life may have been a deputy sheriff. At a short remove upon the same temporary platform was an officer in the uniform of his rank, armed. He was a captain. A sentinel at each end of the bridge stood with his rifle in the position known as "support," that is to say, vertical in front of the left shoulder, the hammer resting on the forearm thrown straight across the chest—a formal and unnatural position, enforcing an erect carriage of the body. It did not appear to be the duty of these two men to know what was occurring at the centre of the bridge; they merely blockaded the two ends of the foot planking that traversed it.

2   Beyond one of the sentinels nobody was in sight; the railroad ran straight away into a forest for a hundred yards, then, curving, was lost to view. Doubtless there was an outpost farther along. The other bank of the stream was open ground—a gentle acclivity topped with a stockade of vertical tree trunks, loop-holed for rifles, with a single embrasure through which protruded the muzzle of a brass cannon commanding the bridge. Midway of the slope between bridge and fort were the spectators—a single company of infantry in line, at "parade rest," the butts of the rifles on the ground, the barrels inclining slightly

backward against the right shoulder, the hands crossed upon the stock. A lieutenant stood at the right of the line, the point of his sword upon the ground, his left hand resting upon his right. Excepting the group of four at the centre of the bridge, not a man moved. The company faced the bridge, staring stonily, motionless. The sentinels, facing the banks of the stream, might have been statues to adorn the bridge. The captain stood with folded arms, silent, observing the work of his subordinates, but making no sign. Death is a dignitary who when he comes announced is to be received with formal manifestations of respect, even by those most familiar with him. In the code of military etiquette silence and fixity are forms of deference.

3   The man who was engaged in being hanged was apparently about thirty-five years of age. He was a civilian, if one might judge from his habit, which was that of a planter. His features were good—a straight nose, firm mouth, broad forehead, from which his long, dark hair was combed straight back, falling behind his ears to the collar of his well-fitting frock-coat. He wore a mustache and pointed beard, but no whiskers; his eyes were large and dark gray, and had a kindly expression which one would hardly have expected in one whose neck was in the hemp. Evidently this was no vulgar assassin. The liberal military code makes provision for hanging many kinds of persons, and gentlemen are not excluded.

4   The preparations being complete, the two private soldiers stepped aside and each drew away the plank upon which he had been standing. The sergeant turned to the captain, saluted and placed himself immediately behind that officer, who in turn moved apart one pace. These movements left the condemned man and the sergeant standing on the two ends of the same plank, which spanned three of the cross-ties of the bridge. The end upon which the civilian stood almost, but not quite, reached a fourth. This plank had been held in place by the weight of the captain; it was now held by that of the sergeant. At a signal from the former the latter would step aside, the plank would tilt and the condemned man go down between two ties. The arrangement commended itself to his judgment as simple and effective. His face had not been covered nor his eyes bandaged. He looked a moment at his "unsteadfast footing," then let his gaze wander to the swirling water of the stream racing madly beneath his feet. A piece of dancing driftwood caught his attention and his eyes followed it down the current. How slowly it appeared to move! What a sluggish stream!

5   He closed his eyes in order to fix his last thoughts upon his wife and children. The water, touched to gold by the early sun, the brooding mists under the banks at some distance down the stream, the fort, the

soldiers, the piece of drift—all had distracted him. And now he became conscious of a new disturbance. Striking through the thought of his dear ones was a sound which he could neither ignore nor understand, a sharp, distinct, metallic percussion like the stroke of a blacksmith's hammer upon the anvil; it had the same ringing quality. He wondered what it was, and whether immeasurably distant or near by—it seemed both. Its recurrence was regular, but as slow as the tolling of a death knell. He awaited each stroke with impatience and—he knew not why—apprehension. The intervals of silence grew progressively longer; the delays became maddening. With their greater infrequency the sounds increased in strength and sharpness. They hurt his ear like the thrust of a knife; he feared he would shriek. What he heard was the ticking of his watch.

6   He unclosed his eyes and saw again the water below him. "If I could free my hands," he thought, "I might throw off the noose and spring into the stream. By diving I could evade the bullets and, swimming vigorously, reach the bank, take to the woods and get away home. My home, thank God, is as yet outside their lines; my wife and little ones are still beyond the invader's farthest advance."

7   As these thoughts, which have here to be set down in words, were flashed into the doomed man's brain rather than evolved from it, the captain nodded to the sergeant. The sergeant stepped aside.

8   Peyton Farquhar was a well-to-do planter, of an old and highly respected Alabama family. Being a slave owner and, like other slave owners, a politician, he was naturally an original secessionist and ardently devoted to the Southern cause. Circumstances of an imperious nature, which it is unnecessary to relate here, had prevented him from taking service with the gallant army that had fought the disastrous campaigns ending with the fall of Corinth, and he chafed under the inglorious restraint, longing for the release of his energies, the larger life of the soldier, the opportunity for distinction. That opportunity, he felt, would come, as it comes to all in war time. Meanwhile he did what he could. No service was too humble for him to perform in aid of the South, no adventure too perilous for him to undertake if consistent with the character of a civilian who was at heart a soldier, and who in good faith and without too much qualification assented to at least a part of the frankly villainous dictum that all is fair in love and war.

9   One evening while Farquhar and his wife were sitting on a rustic bench near the entrance to his grounds, a gray-clad soldier rode up to the gate and asked for a drink of water. Mrs. Farquhar was only too happy to serve him with her own white hands. While she was fetching

the water her husband approached the dusty horseman and inquired eagerly for news from the front.

10   "The Yanks are repairing the railroads," said the man, "and are getting ready for another advance. They have reached the Owl Creek bridge, put it in order and built a stockade on the north bank. The commandant has issued an order, which is posted everywhere, declaring that any civilian caught interfering with the railroad, its bridges, tunnels or trains will be summarily hanged. I saw the order

11   "How far is it to the Owl Creek bridge?" Farquhar asked.

12   "About thirty miles."

13   "Is there no force on this side the creek?"

14   "Only a picket post half a mile out, on the railroad, and a single sentinel at this end of the bridge."

15   "Suppose a man—a civilian and student of hanging—should elude the picket post and perhaps get the better of the sentinel," said Farquhar, smiling, "what could he accomplish?"

16   The soldier reflected. "I was there a month ago," he replied. "I observed that the flood of last winter had lodged a great quantity of driftwood against the wooden pier at this end of the bridge. It is now dry and would burn like tow."

17   The lady had now brought the water, which the soldier drank. He thanked her ceremoniously, bowed to her husband and rode away. An hour later, after nightfall, he repassed the plantation, going northward in the direction from which he had come. He was a Federal scout.

18   As Peyton Farquhar fell straight downward through the bridge he lost consciousness and was as one already dead. From this state he was awakened—ages later, it seemed to him—by the pain of a sharp pressure upon his throat, followed by a sense of suffocation. Keen, poignant agonies seemed to shoot from his neck downward through every fibre of his body and limbs. These pains appeared to flash along well-defined lines of ramification and to beat with an inconceivably rapid periodicity. They seemed like streams of pulsating fire heating him to an intolerable temperature. As to his head, he was conscious of nothing but a feeling of fullness—of congestion. These sensations were unaccompanied by thought. The intellectual part of his nature was already effaced; he had power only to feel, and feeling was torment. He was conscious of motion. Encompassed in a luminous cloud, of which he was now merely the fiery heart, without material substance, he swung through unthinkable arcs of oscillation, like a vast pendulum.

19   Then all at once, with terrible suddenness, the light about him shot upward with the noise of a loud plash; a frightful roaring was in

his ears, and all was cold and dark. The power of thought was restored; he knew that the rope had broken and he had fallen into the stream. There was no additional strangulation; the noose about his neck was already suffocating and kept the water from his lungs. To die of hanging at the bottom of a river!—the idea seemed to him ludicrous. He opened his eyes in the darkness and saw above him a gleam of light, but how distant, how inaccessible! He was still sinking, for the light became fainter and fainter until it was a mere glimmer. Then it began to grow and brighten, and he knew that he was rising toward the surface—knew it with reluctance, for he was now very comfortable. "To be hanged and drowned," he thought, "that is not so bad; but I do not wish to be shot. No; I will not be shot; that is not fair."

20   He was not conscious of an effort, but a sharp pain in his wrist apprised him that he was trying to free his hands. He gave the struggle his attention, as an idler might observe the feat of a juggler, without interest in the outcome. What splendid effort! What magnificent, what superhuman strength! Ah, that was a fine endeavor! Bravo! The cord fell away; his arms parted and floated upward, the hands dimly seen on each side in the growing light. He watched them with a new interest as first one and then the other pounced upon the noose at his neck. They tore it away and thrust it fiercely aside, its undulations resembling those of a watersnake. "Put it back, put it back!" He thought he shouted these words to his hands, for the undoing of the noose had been succeeded by the direst pang that he had yet experienced. His neck ached horribly; his brain was on fire; his heart, which had been fluttering faintly, gave a great leap, trying to force itself out at his mouth. His whole body was racked and wrenched with an insupportable anguish! But his disobedient hands gave no heed to the command. They beat the water vigorously with quick, downward strokes, forcing him to the surface. He felt his head emerge; his eyes were blinded by the sunlight; his chest expanded convulsively, and with a supreme and crowning agony his lungs engulfed a great draught of air, which instantly he expelled in a shriek!

21   He was now in full possession of his physical senses. They were, indeed, preternaturally keen and alert. Something in the awful disturbance of his organic system had so exalted and refined them that they made record of things never before perceived. He felt the ripples upon his face and heard their separate sounds as they struck. He looked at the forest on the bank of the stream, saw the individual trees, the leaves and the veining of each leaf—saw the very insects upon them: the locusts, the brilliant-bodied flies, the gray spiders stretching their webs from twig to twig. He noted the prismatic colors in all the dew-

drops upon a million blades of grass. The humming of the gnats that danced above the eddies of the stream, the beating of the dragon-flies' wings, the strokes of the waterspiders' legs, like oars which had lifted their boat—all these made audible music. A fish slid along beneath his eyes and he heard the rush of its body parting the water.

22   He had come to the surface facing down the stream; in a moment the visible world seemed to wheel slowly round, himself the pivotal point, and he saw the bridge, the fort, the soldiers upon the bridge, the captain, the sergeant, the two privates, his executioners. They were in silhouette against the blue sky. They shouted and gesticulated, pointing at him. The captain had drawn his pistol, but did not fire; the others were unarmed. Their movements were grotesque and horrible, their forms gigantic.

23   Suddenly he heard a sharp report and something struck the water smartly within a few inches of his head, spattering his face with spray. He heard a second report, and saw one of the sentinels with his rifle at his shoulder, a light cloud of blue smoke rising from the muzzle. The man in the water saw the eye of the man on the bridge gazing into his own through the sights of the rifle. He observed that it was a gray eye and remembered having read that gray eyes were keenest, and that all famous marksmen had them. Nevertheless, this one had missed.

24   A counter-swirl had caught Farquhar and turned him half round; he was again looking into the forest on the bank opposite the fort. The sound of a clear, high voice in a monotonous singsong now rang out behind him and came across the water with a distinctness that pierced and subdued all other sounds, even the beating of the ripples in his ears. Although no soldier, he had frequented camps enough to know the dread significance of that deliberate, drawing, aspirated chant; the lieutenant on shore was taking a part in the morning's work. How coldly and pitilessly—with what an even, calm intonation, presaging and enforcing tranquillity in the men—with what accurately measured intervals fell those cruel words:

25   "Attention, company! . . . Shoulder arms! . . . Ready! . . . Aim! . . . Fire!"

26   Farquhar dived—dived as deeply as he could. The water roared in his ears like the voice of Niagara, yet he heard the dulled thunder of the volley and, rising again toward the surface, met shining bits of metal, singularly flattened, oscillating slowly downward. Some of them touched him on the face and hands, then fell away, continuing their descent. One lodged between his collar and neck; it was uncomfortably warm and he snatched it out.

27   As he rose to the surface, gasping for breath, he saw that he had been a long time under water; he was perceptibly farther down stream—nearer to safety. The soldiers had almost finished reloading; the metal ramrods flashed all at once in the sunshine as they were drawn from the barrels, turned in the air, and thrust into their sockets. The two sentinels fired again, independently and ineffectually.

28   The hunted man saw all this over his shoulder; he was now swimming vigorously with the current. His brain was as energetic as his arms and legs; he thought with the rapidity of lightning.

29   "The officer," he reasoned, "will not make that martinet's error a second time. It is as easy to dodge a volley as a single shot. He has probably already given the command to fire at will. God help me, I cannot dodge them all!"

30   An appalling plash within two yards of him was followed by a loud, rushing sound, *diminuendo,* which seemed to travel back through the air to the fort and died in an explosion which stirred the very river to its deeps! A rising sheet of water curved over him, fell down upon him, blinded him, strangled him! The cannon had taken a hand in the game. As he shook his head free from the commotion of the smitten water he heard the deflected shot humming through the air ahead, and in an instant it was cracking and smashing the branches in the forest beyond.

31   "They will not do that again," he thought, "The next time they will use a charge of grape. I must keep my eye upon the gun; the smoke will apprise me—the report arrives too late; it lags behind the missile. That is a good gun."

32   Suddenly he felt himself whirled round and round—spinning like a top. The water, the banks, the forests, the now distant bridge, fort and men—all were commingled and blurred. Objects were represented by their colors only; circular horizontal streaks of color—that was all he saw. He had been caught in a vortex and was being whirled on with a velocity of advance and gyration that made him giddy and sick. In a few moments he was flung upon the gravel at the foot of the left bank of the stream—the southern bank—and behind a projecting point which concealed him from his enemies. The sudden arrest of his motion, the abrasion of one of his hands on the gravel, restored him, and he wept with delight. He dug his fingers into the sand, threw it over himself in handfuls and audibly blessed it. It looked like diamonds, rubies, emeralds; he could think of nothing beautiful which it did not resemble. The trees upon the bank were giant garden plants; he

noted a definite order in their arrangement, inhaled the fragrance of their blooms. A strange, roseate light shone through the spaces among their trunks and the wind made in their branches the music of aeolian harps. He had no wish to perfect his escape—was content to remain in that enchanting spot until retaken.

33   A whiz and rattle of grapeshot among the branches high above his head roused him from his dream. The baffled cannoneer had fired him a random farewell. He sprang to his feet, rushed up the sloping bank, and plunged into the forest.

34   All that day he traveled, laying his course by the rounding sun. The forest seemed interminable; nowhere did he discover a break in it, not even a woodman's road. He had not known that he lived in so wild a region. There was something uncanny in the revelation.

35   By nightfall he was fatigued, footsore, famishing. The thought of his wife and children urged him on. At last he found a road which led him in what he knew to be the right direction. It was as wide and straight as a city street, yet it seemed untraveled. No fields bordered it, no dwelling anywhere. Not so much as the barking of a dog suggested a human habitation. The black bodies of the trees formed a straight wall on both sides, terminating on the horizon in a point, like a diagram in a lesson in perspective. Overhead, as he looked up through this rift in the wood, shone great golden stars looking unfamiliar and grouped in strange constellations. He was sure they were arranged in some order which had a secret and malign significance. The wood on either side was full of singular noises, among which—once, twice, and again—he distinctly heard whispers in an unknown tongue.

36   His neck was in pain and lifting his hand to it he found it horribly swollen. He knew that it had a circle of black where the rope had bruised it. His eyes felt congested; he could no longer close them. His tongue was swollen with thirst; he relieved its fever by thrusting it forward from between his teeth into the cold air. How softly the turf had carpeted the untraveled avenue—he could no longer feel the roadway beneath his feet!

37   Doubtless, despite his suffering, he had fallen asleep while walking, for now he sees another scene—perhaps he has merely recovered from a delirium. He stands at the gate of his own home. All is as he left it, and all bright and beautiful in the morning sunshine. He must have traveled the entire night. As he pushes open the gate and passes up the wide white walk, he sees a flutter of female garments; his wife, looking fresh and cool and sweet, steps down from the veranda to meet him. At

the bottom of the steps she stands waiting, with a smile of ineffable joy, an attitude of matchless grace and dignity. Ah, how beautiful she is! He springs forward with extended arms. As he is about to clasp her he feels a stunning blow upon the back of the neck; a blinding white light blazes all about him with a sound like the shock of a cannon— then all is darkness and silence!

38   Peyton Farquhar was dead; his body, with a broken neck, swung gently from side to side beneath the timbers of the Owl Creek bridge.

An Occurrence at Owl Creek Bridge

JOURNAL

1. MLA Works Cited

Using this model, record this reading.

Author's Last Name, First Name. "Title of the Story." Title of the Book. Ed. First Last Name. City: Publisher, year. Pages of the story.

2. Main Character(s)

Describe each main character, and explain why you think each is a main character.

3. Supporting Character

Describe each supporting character, and explain why you think each is a supporting character.

4. Setting

Describe the setting. Decide if this setting can be changed and, if so, to where and when.

5. Sequence

Relate the events of the story in order.

6. Plot

Tell the story in no more than three sentences.

7. Conflicts

Identify and explain the conflicts involved here.

8. Significant Quotations

Explain the importance of each of these quotations. Record the page number in the parentheses.

a. "Death is a dignitary who when he comes announced is to be received with formal manifestations of respect, even by those most familiar with him" (   ).

b. "He was a civilian, if one might judge from his habit, which was that of a planter" (   ).

c. " 'By diving I could evade the bullets and, swimming vigorously, reach the bank, take to the woods and get away home' " (   ).

d. " 'The commandant has issued an order, which is posted everywhere, declaring that any civilian caught interfering with the railroad, its bridges, tunnels or trains will be summarily hanged' " (   ).

e. "He stands at the gate of his own home" (   ).

Follow-up Questions

10 Short Questions

Select the <u>best</u> answer for each.

____ 1. The soldiers at Owl Creek
Bridge are
a. Federal (northern).
b. Confederate
(southern).
c. of unclear loyalty.

____ 2. The man is being
prepared
a. to be shot.
b. to be drowned.
c. to be hanged.

____ 3. The bridge is
a. a railroad bridge.
b. a roadway bridge.
c. a military bridge.

____ 4. Peyton Farquhar is
a. a southerner.
b. a northerner.
c. of unclear
residence.

____ 5. Peyton Farquhar is
a. a civilian.
b. a lieutenant.
c. a captain.

____ 6. The visiting soldier is
a. a southerner.
b. a northerner.
c. of unclear loyalty.

____ 7. Farquhar probably tried to
a. burn the house.
b. shoot at the soldiers.
c. burn the bridge.

____ 8. Farquhar's visit to his home is
a. real.
b. imagined.
c. unwelcomed.

____ 9. Farquhar
a. escapes into the woods.
b. escapes under the bridge.
c. does not escape.

____ 10. Farquhar dies
a. in the woods.
b. at home.
c. on the bridge.

5 Significant Quotations

Explain the importance of each of these quotations.

1. "Excepting the group of four at the centre of the bridge, not a man moved."

2. "The liberal military code makes provision for hanging many kinds of persons, and gentlemen are not excluded."

3. " 'By diving I could evade the bullets and, swimming vigorously, reach the bank, take to the woods and get away home.' "

4. " 'I observed that the flood of last winter had lodged a great quantity of

driftwood against the wooden pier at this end of the bridge. It is now dry and would burn like tow.' "

5. "As he pushes open the gate and passes up the wide white walk, he sees a flutter of female garments; his wife, looking fresh and cool and sweet, steps down from the veranda to meet him."

2 COMPREHENSION ESSAY QUESTIONS

Use specific details and information from the story to answer these as completely as possible.

1. Describe what occurs at Owl Creek Bridge. Use specific details and information from the story to support your description.

2. Separate fantasy from reality in this story. Use specific details and information from the story to support your points.

WRITING

Use each of these ideas for writing an essay.

1. Tell the story of a dream you have had that has affected your life.

2. Take the place of a friend or sibling you argue with, and tell the story of an argument from his or her standpoint.

Further Writing

1. Compare and contrast this story with Ray Bradbury's "There Will Come Soft Rains" (page 90).

2. Research the Civil War, and use this story by Ambrose Bierce and one by Bruce Catton (which can be found in a library) to offer literary insight.

Strong Temptations—
Strategic Movements—
The Innocents Beguiled

MARK TWAIN

PRE-READING VOCABULARY
CONTEXT

Use context clues to define these words before reading. Use a dictionary as needed.

1. The children poured the water in a *bucket* in order to carry the water to the pool. *Bucket* means _____.

2. Ken painted the house using a watery paint called *whitewash*. *Whitewash* means _____.

3. The *continents* of Asia, North America, and South America are all tremendous land masses. *Continent* means _____.

4. Little Missy and Carrie had a wonderful time playing on the beach and just generally *skylarking* together. *Skylarking* means

   _____.

5. Emanuel was not sure which suit to buy and *wavered* when he was at the counter, still unsure about which to buy. *Waver* means

   _____.

6. The sad woman looked so *melancholy* after she lost her dog. *Melancholy* means _____.

7. Robert went to *fetch* his mother at the train station. *Fetch* means

   _____.

8. During the cruise, Jane got off the ship to take many exciting *expeditions* ashore. *Expedition* means _____.

9. In an even trade, the boys *exchanged* one baseball glove for another. *Exchange* means _____.

10. Corey improved his *straightened means* when he took a job and finally had money to spend. *Straightened means* means

_____.

11. The idea of painting the lawn green came as a great *inspiration* to Joe. *Inspiration* means _____.

12. During a lazy afternoon of floating around the pool, RoseAnn *tranquilly* ran her fingers slowly through the water. *Tranquilly* means _____.

13. Helena is a good friend and never *ridicules* or makes fun of any of her friends. *Ridicule* means _____.

14. Pilar was so interested in the book that she became completely *absorbed* and did not notice anything around her. *Absorbed* means

_____.

15. You could see the lazy boy's *reluctance* to help with all the work. *Reluctance* means _____.

16. Ali responded to the wonderful invitation to see Springsteen for free with *alacrity. Alacrity* means _____.

17. Little children, who are true *innocents,* are so pure and trusting; they believe everyone. *Innocents* means _____.

18. Don has always been able to earn a lot of money; he has never been *poverty-stricken. Poverty-stricken* means _____.

19. When Harold won all the money at the poker game, he *bankrupted* the other players. *Bankrupt* means _____.

20. After he took the job, Mohammed was *obliged* to show up on time. *Obliged* means _____.

Pre-reading Vocabulary Word Attack

Define these words by solving the parts. Use a dictionary as needed.

1. long-handled
2. topmost
3. steamboat
4. carelessly
5. poverty-stricken
6. passenger-coach

Pre-reading Questions

Try answering these questions as you read.

What are the "temptations?"

What are the "strategic movements?"

Who are "the innocents?"

What does Tom do?

What does Tom get everyone else to do?

Strong Temptations— Strategic Movements— The Innocents Beguiled

MARK TWAIN

Mark Twain was born Samuel Langhorne Clemens in 1835. Growing up in Hannibal, Missouri, he enjoyed a childhood filled with the glamour of riverboats and the mysteries of the Mississippi. His father died when he was twelve, and he became a printer's apprentice. For ten years he set type for newspapers from Iowa to New York. In 1857 he returned to the Mississippi and became a riverboat pilot. With the coming of the Civil War and decreased river traffic, he headed west and became a journalist. While working for a Nevada newspaper, he adopted the name "Mark Twain," a term riverboat crews used in recording depth measures. In 1869 he journeyed to Europe. In 1890 he married Olivia Langdon and moved to her hometown of Elmira, New York, where they built a sizable estate that, arguably, contributed to his later financial problems. During the 1890s he suffered the loss of his wife and a daughter as well as financial problems. He died in 1910.

Twain developed a uniquely American style, unstifled by European dictates, that reflected the frontier he explored. His happiest works are set in his fictional St. Petersburg, Missouri, and include *Tom Sawyer* and *The Adventures of Huckleberry Finn*. The death of his wife and daughter led to what is generally agreed as darker and more obscure writing, but this story from *Tom Sawyer* is a classic tale recognized as part of American lore, a story of American ingenuity at its best.

Saturday morning was come, and all the summer world was bright and fresh, and brimming with life. There was a song in every heart; and if the heart was young the music issued at the lips. There was cheer in every face and a spring in every step. The locust trees were in bloom and the fragrance of the blossoms filled the air. Cardiff Hill, beyond the village and above it, was green with vegetation, and it lay just far enough away to seem a Delectable Land, dreamy, reposeful, and inviting.

2   Tom appeared on the sidewalk with a bucket of whitewash and a long-handled brush. He surveyed the fence, and all gladness left him and a deep melancholy settled down upon his spirit. Thirty yards of board fence nine feet high. Life to him seemed hollow, and existence but a burden. Sighing he dipped his brush and passed it along the top-most plank; repeated the operation; did it again; compared the insignificant whitewashed streak with the far-reaching continent of unwhitewashed fence, and sat down on a tree-box discouraged. Jim came skipping out at the gate with a tin pail, and singing "Buffalo Gals." Bringing water from the town pump had always been hateful work in Tom's eyes, before, but now it did not strike him so. He remembered that there was company at the pump. White, mulatto, and negro boys and girls were always there waiting their turns, resting, trading playthings, quarreling, fighting, skylarking. And he remembered that although the pump was only a hundred and fifty yards off, Jim never got back with a bucket of water under an hour—and even then somebody generally had to go after him. Tom said:

3   "Say, Jim, I'll fetch the water if you'll whitewash some."

4   Jim shook his head and said:

5   "Can't, Mars Tom. Ole missis, she tole me I got to go an' git dis water an' not stop foolin' roun' wid anybody. She say she spec' Mars Tom gwine to ax me to whitewash, an' so she tole me go 'long an' 'tend to my own business—she 'lowed *she'd* 'tend to de whitewashin'."

6   "Oh, never you mind what she said, Jim. That's the way she always talks. Gimme the bucket—I won't be gone only a minute. *She* won't ever know."

7   "Oh, I dasn't Mars Tom. Ole missis she'd take an' tar de head off'n me. 'Deed she would."

8   "*She!* She never licks anybody—whacks 'em over the head with her thimble—and who cares for that, I'd like to know. She talks awful, but talk don't hurt—anyways it don't if she don't cry. Jim, I'll give you a marvel. I'll give you a white alley!"

9   Jim began to waver.

10   "White alley, Jim! And it's a bully taw."

11   "My! Dat's a mighty gay marvel, *I* tell you! But Mars Tom I's powerful 'fraid ole missis—"

12   "And besides, if you will I'll show you my sore toe."

13   Jim was only human—this attraction was too much for him. He put down his pail, took the white alley, and bent over the toe with absorbing interest while the bandage was being unwound. In another moment he was flying down the street with his pail and a tingling rear, Tom was whitewashing with vigor, and Aunt Polly was retiring from the field with a slipper in her hand and triumph in her eye.

14   But Tom's energy did not last. He began to think of the fun he had planned for this day, and his sorrows multiplied. Soon the free boys would come tripping along on all sorts of delicious expeditions, and they would make a world of fun of him for having to work—the very thought of it burnt him like fire. He got out his worldly wealth and examined it—bits of toys, marbles, and trash; enough to buy an exchange of *work* maybe, but not half enough to buy so much as half an hour of pure freedom. So he returned his straightened means to his pocket, and gave up the idea of trying to buy the boys. At this dark and hopeless moment an inspiration burst upon him! Nothing less than a great, magnificent inspiration.

15   He took up his brush and went tranquilly to work. Ben Rogers hove in sight presently—the very boy, of all boys, whose ridicule he had been dreading. Ben's gait was the hop-skip-and-jump—proof enough that his heart was light and his anticipations high. He was eating an apple, and giving a long, melodious whoop, at intervals, followed by a deep-toned ding-dong-dong, ding-dong-dong, for he was personating a steamboat. As he drew near, he slackened speed, took the middle of the street, leaned far over to starboard and rounded to ponderously and with laborious pomp and circumstance—for he was personating the "Big Missouri," and considered himself to be drawing nine feet of water. He was boat, and captain, and engine-bells combined, so he had to imagine himself standing on his own hurricane-deck giving the orders and executing them:

16   "Stop her, sir! Ting-a-ling-ling!" The headway ran almost out and he drew up slowly toward the side-walk.

17   "Ship up to back! Ting-a-ling-ling!" His arms straightened and stiffened down his sides.

18   "Set her back on the stabboard! Ting-a-ling-ling! Chow! ch-chow-wow! Chow!" His right hand, meantime, describing stately circles—for it was representing a forty-foot wheel.

19   "Let her go back on the labboard! Ting-a-ling-ling! Chow-ch-chow-chow!" The left hand began to describe circles.

20   "Stop the stabboard! Ting-a-ling-ling! Stop the labboard! Come ahead on the stabboard! Stop her! Let your outside turn over slow! Ting-a-ling-ling! Chow-ow-ow! Get out that head-line! *Lively* now! Come—out with your spring-line—what're you about there! Take a turn round that stump with the bight of it! Stand by that stage, now—let her go! Done with the engines, sir! Ting-a-ling-ling! *Sh't! sh't! sh't!*" (trying the gauge-cocks.)

21   Tom went on whitewashing—paid no attention to the steamboat. Ben stared a moment and then said:

22   "Hi-*yi! You're* up a stump, ain't you!

23   No answer. Tom surveyed his last touch with the eye of an artist; then he gave his brush another gentle sweep and surveyed the result, as before. Ben ranged up alongside of him. Tom's mouth watered for the apple, but he stuck to his work. Ben said:

24   "Hello, old chap, you got to work, hey?"

25   Tom wheeled suddenly and said:

26   "Why it's you Ben! I warn't noticing."

27   "Say—*I*'m going in a swimming, *I* am. Don't you wish you could? But of course you'd druther *work*—wouldn't you? Course you would!"

28   Tom contemplated the boy a bit, and said:

29   "What do you call work?"

30   "Why ain't *that* work?"

31   Tom resumed his whitewashing, and answered carelessly:

32   "Well, maybe it is, and maybe it ain't. All I know, is, it suits Tom Sawyer."

33   "Oh come, now, you don't mean to let on that you *like* it?"

34   The brush continued to move.

35   "Like it? Well I don't see why I oughtn't to like it. Does a boy get a chance to whitewash a fence every day?"

36   That put the thing in a new light. Ben stopped nibbling his apple. Tom swept his brush daintily back and forth—stepped back to note the effect—added a touch here and there—criticised the effect again—Ben watching every move and getting more and more interested, more and more absorbed. Presently he said:

37   "Say, Tom, let *me* whitewash a little."

38   Tom considered, was about to consent; but he altered his mind:

39   "No—no—I reckon it wouldn't hardly do, Ben. You see, Aunt Polly's awful particular about this fence—right here on the street, you know—but if it was the back fence I wouldn't mind and *she* wouldn't. Yes, she's awful particular about this fence; it's got to be done very

careful; I reckon there ain't one boy in a thousand, maybe two thousand, that can do it the way it's got to be done."

40   "No—is that so? Oh come, now—lemme just try. Only just a little—I'd let *you*, if you was me, Tom."

41   "Ben, I'd like to, honest injun; but Aunt Polly—well Jim wanted to do it, but she wouldn't let him; Sid wanted to do it, and she wouldn't let Sid. Now don't you see how I'm fixed? If you was to tackle this fence and anything was to happen to it—"

42   "Oh, shucks, I'll be just as careful. Now lemme try. Say—I'll, give you the core of my apple."

43   "Well, here—. No Ben, now don't. I'm afeard—"

44   "I'll give you *all* of it!"

45   Tom gave up the brush with reluctance in his face but alacrity in his heart. And while the late steamer "Big Missouri" worked and sweated in the sun, the retired artist sat on a barrel in the shade close by, dangled his legs, munched his apple, and planned the slaughter of more innocents. There was no lack of material; boys happened along every little while; they came to jeer, but remained to whitewash. By the time Ben was fagged out, Tom had traded the next chance to Billy Fisher for a kite, in good repair; and when *he* played out, Johnny Miller bought in for a dead rat and a string to swing it with—and so on, and so on, hour after hour. And when the middle of the afternoon came, from being a poor poverty-stricken boy in the morning, Tom was literally rolling in wealth. He had beside the things before mentioned, twelve marbles, part of a jews-harp, a piece of blue bottle-glass to look through, a spool cannon, a key that wouldn't unlock anything, a fragment of chalk, a stopper of a decanter, a tin soldier, a couple of tadpoles, six firecrackers, a kitten with only one eye, a brass door-knob, a dogcollar—but no dog—the handle of a knife, four pieces of orange peel, and a dilapidated old window-sash.

46   He had had a nice, good, idle time all the while—plenty of company—and the fence had three coats of whitewash on it! If he hadn't run out of whitewash, he would have bankrupted every boy in the village.

47   Tom said to himself that it was not such a hollow world, after all. He had discovered a great law of human action, without knowing it—namely, that in order to make a man or a boy covet a thing, it is only necessary to make the thing difficult to attain. If he had been a great and wise philosopher, like the writer of this book, he would now have comprehended that Work consists of whatever a body is *obliged* to do,

and that Play consists of whatever a body is not obliged to do. And this would help him to understand why constructing artificial flowers or performing on a treadmill is work, while rolling ten-pins or climbing Mont Blanc is only amusement. There are wealthy gentlemen in England who drive four-horse passenger-coaches twenty or thirty miles on a daily line, in the summer, because the privilege costs them considerable money; but if they were offered wages for the service, that would turn it into work and then they would resign.

48   The boy mused a while over the substantial change which had taken place in his worldly circumstances, and then wended toward headquarters to report.

Strong Temptations—
Strategic Movements—
The Innocents Beguiled

JOURNAL

1. MLA Works Cited

Using this model, record this reading here.

*Author's Last Name, First Name. "Title of the Story." <u>Title of the Book</u>. Ed.
First Last Name. City: Publisher, year. Pages of the story.*

2. Main Character(s)

*Describe each main character, and explain why you think each is a main
character.*

3. Supporting Characters

*Describe each supporting character, and explain why you think each is a
supporting character.*

4. Setting

Describe the setting. Decide if this setting can be changed and, if so, to where and when.

5. Sequence

Relate the events of the story in order.

6. Plot

Tell the story in no more than two sentences.

7. Conflicts

Identify and explain the conflicts involved here.

8. Significant Quotations

Explain the importance of each of these quotations. Record the page number in the parentheses.

a. "He surveyed the fence, and all gladness left him [. . .]" (   ).

b. "At this dark and hopeless moment an inspiration burst upon him! Nothing less than a great, magnificent inspiration" (   ).

c. " 'Like it? Well I don't see why I oughtn't to like it. Does a boy get a chance to whitewash a fence every day?' " (   ).

d. " 'Now don't you see how I'm fixed? If you was to tackle this fence and any-thing was to happen to it—'
   " 'Oh, shucks, I'll be just as careful. Now lemme try. Say—I'll give you the core of my apple. [. . .]'
   " 'I'll give you *all* of it!' " (   ).

e. "And when the middle of the afternoon came, from being a poor poverty-stricken boy in the morning, Tom was literally rolling in wealth" (   ).

Follow-up Questions

10 Short Questions

Select the best answer for each.

____ 1. It is a
   a. sunny day.
   b. rainy day.
   c. cold day.

____ 2. Tom
   a. does not paint the fence at all.
   b. wants to paint the fence.
   c. does not want to paint the fence.

____ 3. Before, Tom had thought going to pump water was
   a. a chore.
   b. fun.
   c. a good escape.

____ 4. Now, Tom would rather
   a. do chores.
   b. paint the fence.
   c. go to get water.

____ 5. Ben seems to be
   a. a stranger to Tom.
   b. Tom's good friend.
   c. Tom's rival.

____ 6. Ben is
   a. piloting a riverboat.
   b. pretending to pilot a riverboat.
   c. on a riverboat.

____ 7. The boys consider riverboats to be
   a. fun and adventuresome.
   b. hard work.
   c. boring and dull.

____ 8. Tom tells Ben Aunt Polly is "particular"
   a. to scare him away.
   b. to insult him.
   c. to lure him in.

____ 9. Ben is
   a. the only painter.
   b. not the only painter.
   c. the only other boy.

____ 10. Tom
   a. does trick the other boys into painting the fence.
   b. does not trick the other boys into painting the fence.
   c. cannot trick the other boys into painting the fence.

5 Significant Quotations

Explain the importance of each of these quotations.

1. "Sighing he dipped his brush and passed it along the topmost plank; repeated the operation; did it again; compared the insignificant whitewashed streak with the far-reaching continent of unwhitewashed fence, and sat down on a tree-box discouraged."

2. "Bringing water from the town had always been hateful work in Tom's eyes, before, but now it did not strike him so."

3. "That put the thing in a new light. [. . .]
     " 'Say, Tom, let *me* whitewash a little.' "

4. "Tom gave up the brush with reluctance in his face but alacrity in his heart."

5. "There are wealthy gentlemen in England who drive four-horse passenger-coaches twenty and thirty miles on a daily line, in the summer, because the privilege costs them considerable money; but if they were offered wages for the service, that would turn it into work and then they would resign."

2 Comprehension Essay Questions

Use specific details and information from the story to answer these as completely as possible.

1. The fence is central to this story. Explain the significance of the fence using specific details and information from the story.

2. Explain how Tom tricks the boys. Use specific details and information from the story to support your explanation.

Writing

Use each of these ideas for writing an essay.

1. "Whitewashing" means to paint a surface with thin, white paint. "Whitewashing" has also come to mean getting someone to do your undesirable work. Compare a time you used someone to do your undesirable work or a time someone used you to do his or her dirty work to Tom's trickery.

2. "Whitewashing" also means to cover unpleasant facts with white lies or half-truths. Tell the story of a time you or someone you know whitewashed facts.

Further Writing

1. Tom Sawyer in this story and Dee in "Everyday Use" by Alice Walker (page 175) use ruses or pretenses to try to get what they want. Compare and contrast their manipulations and their goals.

2. Research the animal rights movement, and include a discussion of Twain's "A Dog's Tale" (which can be found in a library), one of the most poignant and compelling pieces written germane to animal treatment.

The Cask of Amontillado

Edgar Allan Poe

PRE-READING VOCABULARY
CONTEXT

Use context clues to define these words before reading. Use a dictionary as needed.

1. Treating Jacky, who is very smart, as if she has no brains is an *insult* to her intelligence. *Insult* means _____.

2. Because they lost the World Series, the Yankees will seek *revenge* against the Tigers. *Revenge* means _____.

3. After defeating the Tigers 21–0, the Yankees felt *avenged*. *Avenged* means _____.

4. The ability to identify fine things, such as art or wine, shows Matt's *connoisseurship*. *Connoisseurship* means _____.

5. Loretta went on the rides and ate lots of cotton candy at the *carnival*. *Carnival* means _____.

6. The queen stored her jewels in a secure *vault* in the palace. *Vault* means _____.

7. Either potassium or sodium combined with nitrate make a nasty smelling substance called *nitre*. *Nitre* means _____.

8. Giorgio lives in a magnificent *palazzo* with forty rooms surrounded by colorful gardens. *Palazzo* means _____.

9. Edith lighted the citronella *flambeaux* that were set on stands around the pool. *Flambeaux* mean _____.

10. Ancient Christians buried their dead in the *catacombs'* cave-like tunnels under Rome. *Catacomb* means _____.

11. Ricki stopped at the wine store to buy a fine bottle of *Medoc* for dinner. *Medoc* means _____.

12. The *masons* built the wall, brick by brick. *Mason* means

_____.

13. To build the brick wall, the masons spread the cement between the bricks with a *trowel. Trowel* means _____.

14. Brendan wore a large velvet *cloak* over his tuxedo for the opening night. *Cloak* means _____.

15. The prince was buried in a *crypt* under the rose garden behind the castle. *Crypt* means _____.

16. The masons working on the brick wall used *mortar* to seal the bricks together. *Mortar* means _____.

17. Lisa hid her secret diary in a little *niche* under the window seat in her room. *Niche* means _____.

18. The masons placed the bricks one layer after another, *tier* by *tier. Tier* means _____.

19. Roberta was able to put the thread through the small *aperture* in the needle. *Aperture* means _____.

20. Because we will die one day, we are called *mortals. Mortal* means

_____.

Pre-reading Vocabulary
Word Attack

Define these words by solving the parts. Use a dictionary as needed.

1. definitiveness
2. unredressed
3. conical

4. intermingling
5. foulness
6. unsheathing

Use context clues Poe gives you to define this word.

" 'It is this,' I answered, producing a trowel from beneath the folds of my *roquelaire.*"

Roquelaire means _____.

Pre-reading Questions

Try answering these questions as you read.

Who are the main characters in the story?

What role does Luchesi play?

Where does the story take place?

What is happening in the story?

The Cask of Amontillado

EDGAR ALLAN POE

Edgar Allan Poe was born in 1809 and orphaned at a young age. He was adopted by John Allan, a rather militaristic businessman from Richmond, Virginia. Adoption by a person of means was not uncommon and would have been fortunate for the young Poe, except that Poe's free spirit and his father's precision clashed. John Allan provided Poe with study at the University of Virginia—but Poe withdrew due to drinking problems—and then at West Point—but Poe was dismissed due to a disciplinary problem. Poe later married his very young cousin, Virginia Clemm, but the probable nonconsummation of this marriage and the early death of young Virginia contributed to Poe's idealization of both real and imagined women. His life, in fact, was one of continual disappointments. After Virginia's death, Poe sank into intermittent depressions, suffered bouts of insanity, and experienced hallucinations. Writing for many others, he wanted to publish his own magazine, but this dissolved in financial failure. He eventually died in Baltimore in 1849.

However, it is from these very problems that Poe's genius soars. He envelops the reader with his perceived worlds of the sane and the insane, the rational and macabre, with equal ease. Credited with developing the modern mystery form, Poe's every word and every action draws the reader in, mixing reality with irreality, sane with insane. His other works include "The Pit and the Pendulum" and "The Fall of the House of Usher."

T he thousand injuries of Fortunato I had borne as I best could; but when he ventured upon insult, I vowed revenge. You, who so well know the nature of my soul, will not suppose, however, that I gave utterance to a threat. *At length* I would be avenged; this was a point definitely settled—but the very definitiveness with which it was resolved, precluded the idea of risk. I must not only punish, but punish with impunity. A wrong is unredressed when retribution overtakes its redresser. It is equally unredressed when the avenger fails to make himself felt as such to him who has done the wrong.

2   It must be understood, that neither by word nor deed had I given Fortunato cause to doubt my good-will. I continued, as was my wont, to smile in his face, and he did not perceive that my smile *now* was at the thought of his immolation.

3   He had a weak point—this Fortunato—although in other regards he was a man to be respected and even feared. He prided himself on his connoisseurship in wine. Few Italians have the true virtuoso spirit. For the most part their enthusiasm is adopted to suit the time and opportunity—to practise imposture, upon the British and Austrian millionaires. In painting and gemmary Fortunato, like his countrymen, was a quack—but in the matter of old wines he was sincere. In this respect I did not differ from him materially: I was skilful in the Italian vintages myself, and bought largely whenever I could.

4   It was about dusk, one evening during the supreme madness of the carnival season, that I encountered my friend. He accosted me with excessive warmth, for he had been drinking much. The man wore motley. He had on a tight-fitting parti-striped dress, and his head was surmounted by the conical cap and bells. I was so pleased to see him, that I thought I should never have done wringing his hand.

5   I said to him: "My dear Fortunato, you are luckily met. How remarkably well you are looking to-day! But I have received a pipe of what passes for Amontillado, and I have my doubts."

6   "How?" said he. "Amontillado? A pipe? Impossible! And in the middle of the carnival!"

7   "I have my doubts," I replied; "and I was silly enough to pay the full Amontillado price without consulting you in the matter. You were not to be found, and I was fearful of losing a bargain."

8   "Amontillado!"

9   "I have my doubts."

10   "Amontillado!"

11   "And I must satisfy them."

12   "Amontillado!"

13   "As you are engaged, I am on my way to Luchesi. If any one has a critical turn, it is he. He will tell me—"

14   "Luchesi cannot tell Amontillado from Sherry."

15   "And yet some fools will have it that his taste is a match for your own."

16   "Come, let us go."

17   "Whither?"

18   "To your vaults."

19   "My friend, no; I will not impose upon your good nature. I perceive you have an engagement. Luchesi—"

20   "I have no engagement;—come."

21   "My friend, no. It is not the engagement, but the severe cold with which I perceive you are afflicted. The vaults are insufferably damp. They are encrusted with nitre."

22   "Let us go, nevertheless. The cold is merely nothing. Amontillado! You have been imposed upon. And as for Luchesi, he cannot distinguish Sherry from Amontillado."

23   Thus speaking, Fortunato possessed himself of my arm. Putting on a mask of black silk, and drawing a *roquelaire* closely about my person, I suffered him to hurry me to my palazzo.

24   There were no attendants at home; they had absconded to make merry in honor of the time. I had told them that I should not return until the morning, and had given them explicit orders not to stir from the house. These orders were sufficient, I well knew, to insure their immediate disappearance, one and all, as soon as my back was turned.

25   I took from their sconces two flambeaux, and giving one to Fortunato, bowed him through several suites of rooms to the archway that led into the vaults. I passed down a long and winding staircase, requesting him to be cautious as he followed. We came at length to the foot of the descent, and stood together on the damp ground of the catacombs of the Montresors.

26   The gait of my friend was unsteady, and the bells upon his cap jingled as he strode.

27   "The pipe?" said he.

28   "It is farther on," said I; "but observe the white webwork which gleams from these cavern walls."

29   He turned toward me, and looked into my eyes with two filmy orbs that distilled the rheum of intoxication.

30   "Nitre?" he asked, at length.

31   "Nitre," I replied. "How long have you had that cough?"

32   "Ugh! ugh! ugh!—ugh! ugh! ugh!—ugh! ugh! ugh!—ugh! ugh! ugh!—ugh! ugh! ugh!"

33   My poor friend found it impossible to reply for many minutes.

34   "It is nothing," he said, at last.

35   "Come," I said with decision, "we will go back; your health is precious. You are rich, respected, admired, beloved; you are happy, as once I was. You are a man to be missed. For me it is no matter. We will go back; you will be ill, and I cannot be responsible. Besides, there is Luchesi—"

36   "Enough," he said; "the cough is a mere nothing; it will not kill me. I shall not die of a cough."

37   "True—true," I replied; "and, indeed, I had no intention of alarming you unnecessarily; but you should use all proper caution. A draught of this Medoc will defend us from the damps."

38   Here I knocked off the neck of a bottle which I drew from a long row of its fellows that lay upon the mould.

39   "Drink," I said, presenting him the wine.

40   He raised it to his lips with a leer. He paused and nodded to me familiarly, while his bells jingled.

41   "I drink," he said, "to the buried that repose around us."

42   "And I to your long life."

43   He again took my arm, and we proceeded.

44   "These vaults," he said, "are extensive."

45   "The Montresors," I replied, "were a great and numerous family."

46   "I forget your arms."

47   "A huge human foot d'or, in a field azure; the foot crushes a serpent rampant whose fangs are imbedded in the heel."

48   "And the motto?"

49   *"Nemo me impune lacessit."*

50   "Good!" he said.

51   The wine sparkled in his eyes and the bells jingled. My own fancy grew warm with the Medoc. We had passed through walls of piled bones, with casks and puncheons intermingling, into the inmost recesses of the catacombs. I paused again, and this time I made bold to seize Fortunato by an arm above the elbow.

52   "The nitre!" I said; "see, it increases. It hangs like moss upon the vaults. We are below the river's bed. The drops of moisture trickle among the bones. Come, we will go back ere it is too late. Your cough—"

53   "It is nothing," he said; "let us go on. But first, another draught of the Medoc."

54   I broke and reached him a flagon of De Grâve. He emptied it at a breath. His eyes flashed with a fierce light. He laughed and threw the bottle upward with a gesticulation I did not understand.

55   I looked at him in surprise. He repeated the movement—a grotesque one.

56   "You do not comprehend?" he said.

57   "Not I," I replied.

58   "Then you are not of the brotherhood."

59   "How?"

60   "You are not of the masons."

61   "Yes, yes," I said; "yes, yes."

62   "You? Impossible! A mason?"

63   "A mason," I replied.

64   "A sign," he said.

65   "It is this," I answered, producing a trowel from beneath the folds of my *roquelaire.*

66   "You jest," he exclaimed, recoiling a few paces. "But let us proceed to the Amontillado."

67   "Be it so," I said, replacing the tool beneath the cloak, and again offering him my arm. He leaned upon it heavily. We continued our route in search of the Amontillado. We passed through a range of low arches, descended, passed on, and descending again, arrived at a deep crypt, in which the foulness of the air caused our flambeaux rather to glow than flame.

68   At the most remote end of the crypt there appeared another less spacious. Its walls had been lined with human remains, piled to the vault overhead, in the fashion of the great catacombs of Paris. Three sides of this interior crypt were still ornamented in this manner. From the fourth the bones had been thrown down, and lay promiscuously upon the earth, forming at one point a mound of some size. Within the wall thus exposed by the displacing of the bones, we perceived a stiff interior recess, in depth about four feet, in width three, in height six or seven. It seemed to have been constructed for no especial use within itself, but formed merely the interval between two of the colossal supports of the roof of the catacombs, and was backed by one of their circumscribing walls of solid granite.

69   It was in vain that Fortunato, uplifting his dull torch, endeavored to pry into the depth of the recess. Its termination the feeble light did not enable us to see.

70   "Proceed," I said; "herein is the Amontillado. As for Luchesi—"

71   "He is an ignoramus," interrupted my friend, as he stepped unsteadily forward, while I followed immediately at his heels. In an instant he had reached the extremity of the niche, and finding his progress arrested by the rock, stood stupidly bewildered. A moment more and I had fettered him to the granite. In its surface were two iron

staples, distant from each other about two feet, horizontally. From one of these depended a short chain, from the other a padlock. Throwing the links about his waist, it was but the work of a few seconds to secure it. He was too much astounded to resist. Withdrawing the key I stepped back from the recess.

72   "Pass your hand," I said, "over the wall; you cannot help feeling the nitre. Indeed it is *very* damp. Once more let me *implore* you to return. No? Then I must positively leave you. But I must first render you all the little attentions in my power."

73   "The Amontillado!" ejaculated my friend, not yet recovered from his astonishment.

74   "True," I replied; "the Amontillado."

75   As I said these words I busied myself among the pile of bones of which I have before spoken. Throwing them aside, I soon uncovered a quantity of building stone and mortar. With these materials and with the aid of my trowel, I began vigorously to wall up the entrance of the niche.

76   I had scarcely laid the first tier of the masonry when I discovered that the intoxication of Fortunato had in a great measure worn off. The earliest indication I had of this was a low moaning cry from the depth of the recess. It was *not* the cry of a drunken man. There was then a long and obstinate silence. I laid the second tier, and the third, and the fourth; and then I heard the furious vibrations of the chain. The noise lasted for several minutes, during which, that I might hearken to it with the more satisfaction, I ceased my labors and sat down upon the bones. When at last the clanking subsided, I resumed the trowel, and finished without interruption the fifth, the sixth, and the seventh tier. The wall was now nearly upon a level with my breast. I again paused, and holding the flambeaux over the mason-work, threw a few feeble rays upon the figure within.

77   A succession of loud and shrill screams, bursting suddenly from the throat of the chained form, seemed to thrust me violently back. For a brief moment I hesitated—I trembled. Unsheathing my rapier, I began to grope with it about the recess; but the thought of an instant reassured me. I placed my hand upon the solid fabric of the catacombs, and felt satisfied. I reapproached the wall. I replied to the yells of him who clamored. I re-echoed—I aided—I surpassed them in volume and in strength. I did this, and the clamorer grew still.

78   It was now midnight, and my task was drawing to a close. I had completed the eighth, the ninth, and the tenth tier. I had finished a portion of the last and the eleventh; there remained but a single stone to be fitted and plastered in. I struggled with its weight; I placed it par-

tially in its destined position. But now there came from out the niche a low laugh that erected the hairs upon my head. It was succeeded by a sad voice, which I had difficulty in recognizing as that of the noble Fortunato. The voice said—

79   "Ha! ha! ha!—he! he!—a very good joke indeed—an excellent jest. We will have many a rich laugh about it at the palazzo—he! he! he!—over our wine—he! he! he!"

80   "The Amontillado!" I said.

81   "He! he! he!—he! he! he!—yes, the Amontillado. But is it not getting late? Will not they be awaiting us at the palazzo, the Lady Fortunato and the rest? Let us be gone."

82   "Yes," I said, "let us be gone."

83   *"For the love of God, Montresor!"*

84   "Yes," I said, "for the love of God!"

85   But to these words I hearkened in vain for a reply. I grew impatient. I called aloud:

86   "Fortunato!"

87   No answer. I called again:

88   "Fortunato!"

89   No answer still. I thrust a torch through the remaining aperture and let it fall within. There came forth in return only a jingling of the bells. My heart grew sick—on account of the dampness of the catacombs. I hastened to make an end of my labor. I forced the last stone into its position; I plastered it up. Against the new masonry I re-erected the old rampart of bones. For half of a century no mortal has disturbed them. *In pace requiescat!*

The Cask of Amontillado
JOURNAL

1. MLA Works Cited

Using this model, record this reading here.

*Author's Last Name, First Name. "Title of the Story." <u>Title of the Book</u>. Ed.
First Last Name. City: Publisher, year. Pages of the story.*

2. Main Character(s)

*Describe each main character, and explain why you think each is a main
character.*

3. Supporting Characters

*Describe each supporting character, and explain why you think each is a
supporting character.*

4. Setting

*Describe the setting. Decide if this setting can be changed and, if so, to where
and when.*

5. **Sequence**

Relate the events of the story in order.

6. **Plot**

Tell the story in no more than three sentences.

7. **Conflicts**

Identify and explain the conflicts involved here.

8. **Significant Quotations**

Explain the importance of each of these quotations. Record the page number in the parentheses.

a. "I must not only punish, but punish with impunity" (   ).

b. "He [Fortunato] prided himself on his connoisseurship in wine" (   ).

c. " 'Amontillado!' "
   " 'As you are engaged, I am on my way to Luchesi' " (   ).

d. " 'It is this,' I answered, producing a trowel from beneath the folds of my *roquelaire*" (   ).

e. " 'Ha! ha! ha!—he! he!—a very good joke indeed—an excellent jest. We will have many a rich laugh about it at the palazzo—he! he! he!—over the wine—he! he! he!' " (   ).

9. **Foreshadowing.**
   Identify and explain the hints Poe gives to predict the actions.

FOLLOW-UP QUESTIONS

10 SHORT QUESTIONS

Select the <u>best</u> answer for each.

____ 1. Montresor looks on Fortunato as
   a. a friend.
   b. an enemy.
   c. a co-worker.

____ 2. Montresor
   a. is courteous to Fortunato.
   b. is discourteous to Fortunato.
   c. ignores Fortunato.

____ 3. Amontillado is
   a. a wine.
   b. a pipe.
   c. a person.

____ 4. Montresor probably
   a. is a mason for a living.
   b. knows little about masonry.
   c. comes from a family that made its wealth at masonry.

____ 5. Fortunato is
   a. jealous of Luchesi.
   b. friendly with Luchesi.
   c. does not know Luchesi.

____ 6. This story probably takes place in
   a. France.
   b. America.
   c. Italy.

____ 7. The bones probably indicate
   a. more murders.
   b. a burial place.
   c. many hungry dogs.

____ 8. Montresor uses Luchesi to
   a. scare Fortunato away.
   b. lure Fortunato on.
   c. help Fortunato.

____ 9. Montresor
   a. has planned well.
   b. has not planned well.
   c. has no plans.

____ 10. Montresor acts out of
   a. friendship.
   b. jealousy.
   c. revenge.

5 SIGNIFICANT QUOTATIONS

Explain the importance of each of these quotations.

1. "The thousand injuries of Fortunato I had borne as I best could; but when he ventured upon insult, I vowed revenge."

2. "He [Fortunato] prided himself on his connoisseurship in wine."

3. " 'Amontillado? A pipe? Impossible!' "

4. " 'Luchesi cannot tell Amontillado from Sherry.' "

5. "Against the new masonry I re-erected the old rampart of bones. For half a century no mortal has disturbed them."

2 COMPREHENSION ESSAY QUESTIONS

Use specific details and information from the story to answer these as completely as possible.

1. How does the title relate to the story? Explain the significance of the title using specific details and information from the story.

2. Poe plays with our sympathies for the protagonist and the antagonist. Using specific details and information from the story, explain whom you think the protagonist is and whom you think the antagonist is.

WRITING

Use each of these ideas for writing an essay.

1. We all have weaknesses (chocolate, being late, and so forth). Tell the story of a time one of your weaknesses got you into trouble.

2. Using specific details and information from this story, explain the shifting roles of protagonist and antagonist in the story

Further Writing

1. Compare and contrast Montresor with the narrator in Edgar Allan Poe's "The Tell-Tale Heart" (page 77).

2. Research today's use of the insanity plea in criminal actions, and use Poe's story as an insightful anecdote in this study.

To Build a Fire

JACK LONDON

PRE-READING VOCABULARY
CONTEXT

Use context clues to define these words before reading. Use a dictionary as needed.

1. The freezing winds whipped across the *Yukon* area of Alaska. *Yukon* means _____.

2. The Apache put the soft, leather *moccasins* on his feet. *Moccasin* means _____.

3. Men who use chewing tobacco spit out a brown-colored *spittle*. *Spittle* means _____.

4. If you put ice on a sore, the pain will go away, and the area will become *numb. Numb* means _____.

5. Large and furry *huskies* are often used in teams to pull dog sleds over the snow. *Husky* means _____.

6. Things we know how to do without ever being taught are called *instincts. Instinct* means _____.

7. When Barry awoke, the sunlight and birds chirping came into his *consciousness. Consciousness* means _____.

8. Jess was *apprehensive* that she would miss the plane because she woke up so late. *Apprehensive* means _____.

9. The freezing *arctic* winds came from of the North Pole and brought a large amount of snow and sleet. *Arctic* means _____.

10. Jack felt *compelled* to put money in the bank after he wrote a large check. *Compel* means _____.

11. Tom *obeyed* the speed limit sign and slowed down to 25 mph. *Obey* means _____.

12. Since Maureen had put the steak in the freezer, the steak had to *thaw out* before she could cook it. *Thaw out* means _____.

13. Mary Beth *singed* the cake when she left it in the oven for too long. *Singe* means _____.

14. We have *inherited* much of our size, shape, and intelligence from our ancestors who lived before us. *Inherited* means

_____.

15. Everyone got wet when the canoe *capsized* and dumped everyone in the water. *Capsized* means _____.

16. When the snow on the mountain became too heavy, the snow all came down in a loud *avalanche*. *Avalanche* means

_____.

17. With clumsy mittens on her hands, Martina *fumbled* the snowball and watched it fall to the ground. *Fumbled* means

_____.

18. The snow fell so heavily during the *blizzard* that Bernadette could not see two feet in front of her. *Blizzard* means _____.

19. Birds and worms were eating the *carcass* of the dead snake. *Carcass* means _____.

20. The clerks became *suspicious* of the new employee when money was missing and he was observed buying new clothes. *Suspicious* means

_____.

Pre-reading Vocabulary
Word Attack

Define these words by solving the parts. Use a dictionary as needed.

1. little-traveled
2. timberland
3. freeze-up
4. unbroken
5. hairline
6. spruce-covered
7. strangeness
8. undoubtedly
9. frailty
10. roundabout
11. immortality
12. mittened
13. warm-whiskered
14. gray-coated
15. crystaled
16. solidity
17. observant
18. candied
19. firewood
20. underbrush
21. old-timer
22. rapidity
23. lifeless
24. fire-provider
25. birchbark
26. faraway
27. food-provider

Pre-reading Questions

Try answering these questions as you read.

What is the setting?

Why is it important to build a fire?

Why can't the man build a fire?

What does the dog know?

What does the man know?

To Build a Fire

JACK LONDON

Jack London was born in San Francisco in 1876. London at first completed only elementary school as a result of his family's financial problems. He worked variously as a paperboy, a bowling alley pinsetter, a sailor (traveling as far as Japan), a hunter, and a hobo (traveling through mainland America, Canada, and Alaska). He became an avid reader, eventually completed high school, and then entered the University of California. He left after one semester and turned to writing. London died in Santa Rosa, California, in 1916.

Drawing from his travels and influenced by Marx, Nietzsche, and Darwin, London continually discusses instinct and base survival in his writing. The author of many stories, *The Call of the Wild* remains his master work.

D ay had broken cold and gray, exceedingly cold and gray, when the man turned aside from the main Yukon trail and climbed the high earth bank, where a dim and little-traveled trail led eastward through the fat spruce timberland. It was a steep bank, and he paused for breath at the top, excusing the act to himself by looking at his watch. It was nine o'clock. There was no sun nor hint of sun, though there was not a cloud in the sky. It was a clear day, and yet there seemed an intangible pall over the face of things, a subtle gloom that made the day dark, and that was due to the absence of sun. This fact did not worry the man. He was used to the lack of sun. It had been days since he had seen the sun, and he knew that a few more days must pass before that cheerful orb, due south, would just peep above the skyline and dip immediately from view.

2   The man flung a look back along the way he had come. The Yukon lay a mile wide and hidden under three feet of ice. On top of this ice were as many feet of snow. It was all pure white, rolling in gentle undulations where the ice jams of the freeze-up had formed. North and south, as far as his eye could see, it was unbroken white, save for a dark hairline that curved and twisted from around the spruce-covered island to the south, and that curved and twisted away into the north, where it disappeared behind another spruce-covered island. This dark hairline was the trail—the main trail—that led south five hundred miles to the Chilcoot Pass, Dyea, and salt water; and that led north seventy miles to Dawson, and still on to the north a thousand miles to Nulato, and finally to St. Michael on Bering Sea, a thousand miles and half a thousand more.

3   But all this—the mysterious, far-reaching hairline trail, the absence of sun from the sky, the tremendous cold, and the strangeness and weirdness of it all—made no impression on the man. It was not because he was long used to it. He was a newcomer in the land, a *chechaquo*, and this was his first winter. The trouble with him was that he was without imagination. He was quick and alert in the things of life, but only in the things, and not in the significances. Fifty degrees below zero meant eighty-odd degrees of frost. Such fact impressed him as being cold and uncomfortable, and that was all. It did not lead him to meditate upon his frailty as a creature of temperature, and upon man's frailty in general, able to live within certain narrow limits of heat and cold and from there on it did not lead him to the conjectural field of immortality and man's place in the universe. Fifty degrees below zero stood for a bite of frost that hurt and that must be guarded against by the use of mittens, ear flaps, warm moccasins, and thick socks. Fifty degrees below zero was to him just precisely fifty degrees

below zero. That there should be anything more to it than that was a thought that never entered his head.

4   As he turned to go on, he spat speculatively. There was a sharp, explosive crackle that startled him. He spat again. And again, in the air, before it could fall to the snow, the spittle crackled. He knew that at fifty below spittle crackled on the snow, but this spittle had crackled in the air. Undoubtedly it was colder than fifty below—how much colder he did not know. But the temperature did not matter. He was bound for the old claim on the left fork of Henderson Creek, where the boys were already. They had come over across the divide from the Indian Creek country, while he had come the roundabout way to take a look at the possibilities of getting out logs in the spring from the islands in the Yukon. He would be in to camp by six o'clock; a bit after dark, it was true, but the boys would be there, a fire would be going, and a hot supper would be ready. As for lunch, he passed his hand against the protruding bundle under his jacket. It was also under his shirt, wrapped up in a handkerchief and lying against the naked skin. It was the only way to keep the biscuits from freezing. He smiled agreeably to himself as he thought of those biscuits, each cut open and sopped in bacon grease, and each enclosing a generous slice of fried bacon.

5   He plunged in among the big spruce trees. The trail was faint. A foot of snow had fallen since the last sled had passed over, and he was glad he was without a sled, traveling light. In fact, he carried nothing but the lunch wrapped in the handkerchief. He was surprised, however, at the cold. It certainly was cold, he concluded, as he rubbed his numb nose and cheek bones with his mittened band. He was a warm-whiskered man, but the hair on his face did not protect the high cheek bones and the eager nose that thrust itself aggressively into the frosty air.

6   At the man's heels trotted a dog, a big native husky, the proper wolf dog, gray-coated and without any visible or temperamental difference from its brother, the wild wolf. The animal was depressed by the tremendous cold. It knew that it was no time for traveling. Its instinct told it a truer tale than was told to the man by the man's judgment. In reality, it was not merely colder than fifty below zero; it was colder than sixty below, than seventy below. It was seventy-five below zero. Since the freezing point is thirty-two above zero, it meant that one hundred and seven degrees of frost obtained. The dog did not know anything about thermometers. Possibly in the brain there was no sharp consciousness of a condition of very cold such as was in the man's brain. But the brute had its instinct. It experienced a vague but menac-

ing apprehension that subdued it and made it slink along at the man's heels, and that made it question eagerly every unwonted movement of the man, as if expecting him to go into camp or to seek shelter somewhere and build a fire. The dog had learned fire, and it wanted fire, or else to burrow under the snow and cuddle its warmth away from the air.

7   The frozen moisture of its breathing had settled on its fur in a fine powder of frost, and especially were its jowls, muzzle, and eyelashes whitened by its crystaled breath. The man's red beard and mustache were likewise frosted, but more solidly, the deposit taking the form of ice and increasing with every warm, moist breath he exhaled. Also the man was chewing tobacco, and the muzzle of ice held his lips so rigidly that he was unable to clean his chin when he expelled the juice. The result was that a crystal beard of the color and solidity of amber was increasing its length on his chin. If he fell down it would shatter itself, like glass, into brittle fragments. But he did not mind the appendage. It was the penalty all tobacco-chewers paid in that country, and he had been out before in two cold snaps. They had not been so cold as this, he knew, but by the spirit thermometer at Sixty Mile he knew they had been registered at fifty below and at fifty-five.

8   He held on through the level stretch of woods for several miles, crossed a wide flat of boulders, and dropped down a bank to the frozen bed of a small stream. This was Henderson Creek, and he knew he was ten miles from the forks. He looked at his watch. It was ten o'clock. He was making four miles an hour, and he calculated that he would arrive at the forks at half-past twelve. He decided to celebrate that event by eating his lunch there.

9   The dog dropped in again at his heels, with a tail drooping discouragement, as the man swung along the creek bed. The furrow of the old sled trail was plainly visible, but a dozen inches of snow covered the marks of the last runners. In a month no man had come up or down that silent creek. The man held steadily on. He was not much given to thinking, and just then particularly he had nothing to think about save that he would eat lunch at the forks and that at six o'clock he would be in camp with the boys. There was nobody to talk to; and, had there been, speech would have been impossible because of the ice muzzle on his mouth. So he continued monotonously to chew tobacco and to increase the length of his amber beard.

10   Once in a while the thought reiterated itself that it was very cold and that he had never experienced such cold. As he walked along he rubbed his cheek bones and nose with the back of his mittened hand. He did this automatically, now and again changing hands. But rub as he

would, the instant he stopped his cheek bones went numb, and the following instant the end of his nose went numb. He was sure to frost his cheeks; he knew that, and experienced a pang of regret that he had not devised a nose strap of the sort Bud wore in cold snaps. Such a strap passed across the cheeks, as well, and saved them. But it didn't matter much, after all. What were frosted cheeks? A bit painful, that was all; they were never serious.

11   Empty as the man's mind was of thoughts, he was keenly observant, and he noticed the changes in the creek, the curves and bends and timber jams, and always he sharply noted where he placed his feet. Once, coming around a bend, he shied abruptly, like a startled horse, curved away from the place where he had been walking, and retreated several paces back along the trail. The creek, he knew, was frozen clear to the bottom—no creek could contain water in that arctic winter—but he knew also that there were springs that bubbled out from the hillsides and ran along under the snow and on top of the ice of the creek. He knew that the coldest snaps never froze these springs, and he knew likewise their danger. They were traps. They hid pools of water under the snow that might be three inches deep, or three feet. Sometimes a skin of ice half an inch thick covered them, and in turn was covered by the snow. Sometimes there were alternate layers of water and ice skin, so that when one broke through he kept on breaking through for a while, sometimes wetting himself to the waist.

12   That was why he had shied in such panic. He had felt the give under his feet and heard the crackle of a snow-hidden ice skin. And to get his feet wet in such a temperature meant trouble and danger. At the very least it meant delay, for he would be forced to stop and build a fire, and under its protection to bare his feet while he dried his socks and moccasins. He stood and studied the creek bed and its banks, and decided that the flow of water came from the right. He reflected a while, rubbing his nose and cheeks, then skirted to the left, stepping gingerly and testing the footing for each step. Once clear of the danger, he took a fresh chew of tobacco and swung along at his four-mile gait.

13   In the course of the next two hours he came upon several similar traps. Usually the snow above the hidden pools had a sunken candied appearance that advertised the danger. Once again, however, he had a close call; and once, suspecting danger, he compelled the dog to go on in front. The dog did not want to go. It hung back until the man shoved it forward, and then it went quickly across the white, unbroken surface. Suddenly it broke through, floundered to one side, and got away to firmer footing. It had wet its forefeet and legs, and almost immediately the water that clung to it turned to ice. It made quick efforts to

lick the ice off its legs, then dropped down in the snow and began to bite out the ice that had formed between the toes. This was a matter of instinct. To permit the ice to remain there would mean sore feet. It did not know this. It merely obeyed the mysterious prompting that arose from the deep crypts of its being. But the man knew, having achieved a judgment on the subject, and he removed the mitten from his right hand and helped tear out the ice particles. He did not expose his fingers more than a minute, and was astonished at the swift numbness that smote them. It certainly was cold. He pulled on the mitten hastily, and beat the hand savagely across his chest.

14   At twelve o'clock the day was at its brightest. Yet the sun was too far south on its winter journey to clear the horizon. The bulge of the earth intervened between it and Henderson Creek, where the man walked under a clear sky at noon and cast no shadow. At half-past twelve, to the minute, he arrived at the forks of the creek. He was pleased at the speed he had made. If he kept it up, he would certainly be with the boys by six. He unbuttoned his jacket and shirt and drew forth his lunch. The action consumed no more than a quarter of a minute, yet in that brief moment the numbness laid hold of the exposed fingers. He did not put the mitten on, but, instead, struck the fingers a dozen sharp smashes against his leg. Then he sat down on a snow-covered log to eat. The sting that followed upon the striking of his fingers against his leg ceased so quickly that he was startled. He had had no chance to take a bite of biscuit. He struck the fingers repeatedly and returned them to the mitten, baring the other hand for the purpose of eating. He tried to take a mouthful, but the ice muzzle prevented. He had forgotten to build a fire and thaw out. He chuckled at his foolishness, and as he chuckled he noted the numbness creeping into the exposed fingers. Also he noted that the stinging which had first come to his toes when he sat down was already passing away. He wondered whether the toes were warm or numb. He moved them inside the moccasins and decided that they were numb.

15   He pulled the mitten on hurriedly and stood up. He was a bit frightened. He stamped up and down until the stinging returned into the feet. It certainly was cold, was his thought. That man from Sulphur Creek had spoken the truth when telling how cold it sometimes got in the country. And he had laughed at him at the time! That showed one must not be too sure of things.

16   There was no mistake about it, it *was* cold. He strode up and down, stamping his feet and threshing his arms, until reassured by the returning warmth. Then he got out matches and proceeded to make a fire. From the undergrowth, where high water of the previous spring had

lodged a supply of seasoned twigs, he got his firewood. Working care-fully from a small beginning, he soon had a roaring fire, over which he thawed the ice from his face and in the protection of which he ate his biscuits. For the moment the cold of space was outwitted. The dog took satisfaction in the fire, stretching out close enough for warmth and far enough away to escape being singed.

17   When the man had finished, he filled his pipe and took his com-fortable time over a smoke. Then he pulled on his mittens, settled the ear flaps of his cap firmly about his ears, and took the creek trail up the left fork. The dog was disappointed and yearned back toward the fire. The man did not know cold. Possibly all the generations of his ancestry had been ignorant of cold, of real cold, of cold one hundred and seven degrees below freezing point. But the dog knew; all its ancestry knew, and it had inherited the knowledge. And it knew that it was not good to walk abroad in such fearful cold. It was the time to lie snug in a hole in the snow and wait for a curtain of cloud to be drawn across the face of outer space whence this cold came. On the other hand, there was no keen intimacy between the dog and the man. The one was the toil-slave of the other, and the only caresses it had ever received were the caresses of the whiplash and of harsh and menacing throat sounds that threatened the whiplash. So the dog made no effort to communicate its apprehension to the man. It was not concerned in the welfare of the man; it was for its own sake that it yearned back toward the fire. But the man whistled, and spoke to it with the sound of whiplashes, and the dog swung in at the man's heels and followed after.

18   The man took a chew of tobacco and proceeded to start a new amber beard. Also, his moist breath quickly powdered with white his mustache, eyebrows, and lashes. There did not seem to be so many springs on the left fork of the Henderson, and for half an hour the man saw no signs of any. And then it happened. At a place where there were no signs, where the soft, unbroken snow seemed to advertise solidity beneath, the man broke through. It was not deep. He wet himself halfway to the knees before he floundered out to the firm crust.

19   He was angry, and cursed his luck aloud. He had hoped to get into camp with the boys at six o'clock, and this would delay him an hour, for he would have to build a fire and dry out his footgear. This was imperative at that low temperature—he knew that much; and he turned aside to the bank, which he climbed. On top, tangled in the underbrush about the trunks of several small spruce trees, was a high-water deposit of dry firewood—sticks and twigs, principally, but also larger portions of seasoned branches and fine, dry, last year's grasses. He threw down several large pieces on top of the snow. This served for

a foundation and prevented the young flame from drowning itself in the snow it otherwise would melt. The flame he got by touching a match to a small shred of birchbark that he took from his pocket. This burned even more readily than paper. Placing it on the foundation, he fed the young flame with wisps of dry grass and with the tiniest of dry twigs.

20   He worked slowly and carefully, keenly aware of his danger. Gradually, as the flame grew stronger, he increased the size of the twigs with which he fed it. He squatted in the snow, pulling the twigs out from their entanglement in the brush and feeding them directly to the flame. He knew there must be no failure. When it is seventy-five below zero, a man must not fail in his first attempt to build a fire—that is, if his feet are wet. If his feet are dry, and he fails, he can run along the trail for half a mile and restore his circulation. But the circulation of wet and freezing feet cannot be restored by running when it is seventy-five below. No matter how fast he runs, the wet feet will freeze the harder.

21   All this the man knew. The old-timer on Sulphur Creek had told him about it the previous fall, and now he was appreciating the advice. Already all sensation had gone out of his feet. To build a fire, he had been forced to remove his mittens, and the fingers had quickly gone numb. His pace of four miles an hour had kept his heart pumping blood to the surface of his body and to all the extremities. But the instant he stopped, the action of the pump eased down. The cold of space smote the unprotected tip of the planet, and he, being on that unprotected tip, received the full force of the blow. The blood of his body recoiled before it. The blood was alive, like the dog, and like the dog it wanted to hide away and cover itself up from the fearful cold. So long as he walked four miles an hour, he pumped that blood, willy-nilly, to the surface; but now it ebbed away and sank down into the recesses of his body. The extremities were the first to feel its absence. His wet feet froze the faster, and his exposed fingers numbed the faster, though they had not yet begun to freeze. Nose and cheeks were already freezing, while the skin of all his body chilled as it lost its blood.

22   But he was safe. Toes and nose and cheeks would be only touched by the frost, for the fire was beginning to burn with strength. He was feeding it with twigs the size of his finger. In another minute he would be able to feed it with branches the size of his wrist, and then he could remove his wet footgear, and, while it dried, he could keep his naked feet warm by the fire, rubbing them at first, of course, with snow. The fire was a success. He was safe. He remembered the advice of the old-timer on Sulphur Creek, and smiled. The old-timer had been very

serious in laying down the law that no man must travel alone in the Klondike after fifty below. Well, here he was; he had had the accident; he was alone; and he had saved himself. Those old-timers were rather womanish, some of them, he thought. All a man had to do was to keep his head, and he was all right. Any man who was a man could travel alone. But it was surprising the rapidity with which his cheeks and nose were freezing. And he had not thought his fingers could go lifeless in so short a time. Lifeless they were, for he could scarcely make them move together to grip a twig, and they seemed remote from his body and from him. When he touched a twig he had to look and see whether or not he had bold of it. The wires were pretty well down between him and his finger ends.

23   All of which counted for little. There was the fire, snapping and crackling and promising life with every dancing flame. He started to untie his moccasins. They were coated with ice; the thick German socks were like sheaths of iron halfway to the knees; and the moccasin strings were like rods of steel all twisted and knotted as by some conflagration. For a moment he tugged with his numb fingers, then, realizing the folly of it, he drew his sheath knife.

24   But before he could cut the strings, it happened. It was his own fault, or, rather, his mistake. He should not have built the fire under the spruce tree. He should have built it in the open. But it had been easier to pull the twigs from the brush and drop them directly on the fire. Now the tree under which he had done this carried a weight of snow on its boughs. No wind had blown for weeks, and each bough was fully freighted. Each time he had pulled a twig he had communicated a slight agitation to the tree—an imperceptible agitation, so far as he was concerned, but an agitation sufficient to bring about the disaster. High up in the tree one bough capsized its load of snow. This fell on the boughs beneath, capsizing them. This process continued, spreading out and involving the whole tree. It grew like an avalanche, and it descended without warning upon the man and the fire, and the fire was blotted out! Where it had burned was a mantle of fresh and disordered snow.

25   The man was shocked. It was as though he had just heard his own sentence of death. For a moment he sat and stared at the spot where the fire had been. Then he grew very calm. Perhaps the old-timer on Sulphur Creek was right. If he had only had a trail mate he would have been in no danger now. The trail mate could have built the fire. Well, it was up to him to build the fire over again, and this second time there must be no failure. Even if he succeeded, he would most likely lose some toes. His feet must be badly frozen by now, and there would be some time before the second fire was ready.

26   Such were his thoughts, but he did not sit and think them. He was busy all the time they were passing through his mind. He made a new foundation for a fire, this time in the open, where no treacherous tree could blot it out. Next he gathered dry grasses and tiny twigs from the high-water flotsam. He could not bring his fingers together to pull them out, but he was able to gather them by the handful. In this way he got many rotten twigs and bits of green moss that were undesirable, but it was the best he could do. He worked methodically, even collecting an armful of the larger branches to be used later when the fire gathered strength. And all the while the dog sat and watched him, a certain yearning wistfulness in its eyes, for it looked upon him as the fire-provider, and the fire was slow in coming.

27   When all was ready, the man reached in his pocket for a second piece of birchbark. He knew the bark was there, and, though he could not feel it with his fingers, he could hear its crisp rustling as he fumbled for it. Try as he would, he could not clutch hold of it. And all the time, in his consciousness, was the knowledge that each instant his feet were freezing. This thought tended to put him in a panic, but he fought against it and kept calm. He pulled on his mittens with his teeth, and threshed his arms back and forth, beating his hands with all his might against his sides. He did this sitting down, and he stood up to do it; and all the while the dog sat in the snow, its wolf brush of a tail curled around warmly over its forefeet, its sharp wolf ears pricked forward intently as it watched the man. And the man, as he beat and threshed his arms and hands, felt a great surge of envy as he regarded the creature that was warm and secure in its natural covering.

28   After a while he was aware of the first faraway signals of sensation in his beaten fingers. The faint tingling grew stronger till it evolved into a stinging ache that was excruciating, but which the man hailed with satisfaction. He stripped the mitten from his right hand and fetched forth the birchbark. The exposed fingers were quickly going numb again. Next he brought out his bunch of sulphur matches. But the tremendous cold had already driven the life out of his fingers. In his effort to separate one match from the others, the whole bunch fell in the snow. He tried to pick it up out of the snow, but failed. The dead fingers could neither touch nor clutch. He was very careful. He drove the thought of his freezing feet, and nose, and cheeks, out of his mind, devoting his whole soul to the matches. He watched, using the sense of vision in place of that of touch, and when he saw his fingers on each side the bunch, he closed them—that is, he willed to close them, for the wires were down, and the fingers did not obey. He pulled the mitten on the right hand, and beat it fiercely against his knee. Then, with

both mittened hands, he scooped the bunch of matches, along with much snow, into his lap. Yet he was no better off.

29   After some manipulation he managed to get the bunch between the heels of his mittened hands. In this fashion he carried it to his mouth. The ice crackled and snapped when by a violent effort he opened his mouth. He drew the lower jaw in, curled the upper lip out of the way, and scraped the bunch with his upper teeth in order to separate a match. He succeeded in getting one, which he dropped on his lap. He was no better off. He could not pick it up. Then he devised a way. He picked it up in his teeth and scratched it on his leg. Twenty times he scratched before he succeeded in lighting it. As it flamed he held it with his teeth to the birchbark. But the burning brimstone went up his nostrils and into his lungs, causing him to cough spasmodically. The match fell into the snow and went out.

30   The old-timer on Sulphur Creek was right, he thought in the moment of controlled despair that ensued: after fifty below, a man should travel with a partner. He beat his hands, but failed in exciting any sensation. Suddenly he bared both bands, removing the mittens with his teeth. He caught the whole bunch between the heels of his hands. His arm muscles, not being frozen, enabled him to press the hand heels tightly against the matches. Then he scratched the bunch along his leg. It flared into flame, seventy sulphur matches at once! There was no wind to blow them out. He kept his head to one side to escape the strangling fumes, and held the blazing bunch to the birchbark. As he so held it, he became aware of sensation in his hands. His flesh was burning. He could smell it. Deep down below the surface he could feel it. The sensation developed into pain that grew acute. And still he endured it, holding the flame of the matches clumsily to the bark that would not light readily because his own burning hands were in the way, absorbing most of the flame.

31   At last when he could endure no more, he jerked his hands apart. The blazing matches fell sizzling into the snow, but the birchbark was alight. He began laying dry grasses and the tiniest twigs on the flame. He could not pick and choose, for he had to lift the fuel between the heels of his hands. Small pieces of rotten wood and green moss clung to the twigs, and he bit them off as well as he could with his teeth. He cherished the flame carefully and awkwardly. It meant life, and it must not perish. The withdrawal of blood from the surface of his body now made him shiver, and he grew more awkward. A large piece of green moss fell squarely on the little fire. He tried to poke it out with his fingers, but his shivering frame made him poke too far, and he disrupted the nucleus of the little fire, the burning grasses and tiny twigs separat-

ing and scattering. He tried to poke them together again, but, in spite of the tenseness of the effort, his shivering got away with him, and the twigs were hopelessly scattered. Each twig gushed a puff of smoke and went out. The fire-provider had failed. As he looked apathetically about him, his eyes chanced on the dog, sitting across the ruins of the fire from him, in the snow, making restless, hunching movements, slightly lifting one forefoot and then the other, shifting its weight back and forth on them with wistful eagerness.

32   The sight of the dog put a wild idea into his head. He remembered the tale of the man, caught in a blizzard, who killed a steer and crawled inside the carcass, and so was saved. He would kill the dog and bury his hands in the warm body until the numbness went out of them. Then he could build another fire. He spoke to the dog, calling it to him; but in his voice was a strange note of fear that frightened the animal, who had never known the man to speak in such way before. Something was the matter, and its suspicious nature sensed danger—it knew not what danger, but somewhere, somehow, in its brain arose an apprehension of the man. It flattened its ears down at the sound of the man's voice, and its restless, hunching movements, and the liftings and shiftings of its forefeet became more pronounced; but it would not come to the man. He got on his hands and knees and crawled toward the dog. This unusual posture again excited suspicion, and the animal sidled mincingly away.

33   The man sat up in the snow for a moment and struggled for calmness. Then he pulled on his mittens, by means of his teeth, and got upon his feet. He glanced down at first in order to assure himself that he was really standing up, for the absence of sensation in his feet left him unrelated to the earth. His erect position in itself started to drive the webs of suspicion from the dog's mind; and when he spoke peremptorily with the sound of whiplashes in his voice, the dog rendered its customary allegiance and came to him. As it came within reaching distance, the man lost control. His arms flashed out to the dog, and he experienced genuine surprise when he discovered that his hands could not clutch, that there was neither bend nor feeling in the fingers. He had forgotten for the moment that they were frozen and that they were freezing more and more. All this happened quickly, and before the animal could get away, he encircled its body with his arms. He sat down in the snow, and in this fashion held the dog, while it snarled and whined and struggled.

34   But it was all he could do, hold its body encircled in his arms and sit there. He realized that he could not kill the dog. There was no way to do it. With his helpless hands he could neither draw nor hold his

sheath knife nor throttle the animal. He released it, and it plunged wildly away, with tail between its legs, and still snarling. It halted forty feet away and surveyed him curiously, with ears sharply pricked forward. The man looked down at his hands in order to locate them, and found them hanging on the ends of his arms. It struck him as curious that one should have to use his eyes in order to find out where his hands were. He began threshing his arms back and forth, beating the mittened hands against his sides. He did this for five minutes, violently, and his heart pumped enough blood up to the surface to put a stop to his shivering. But no sensation was aroused in the hands. He had an impression that they hung like weights on the ends of his arms, but when he tried to run the impression down, he could not find it.

35   A certain fear of death, dull and oppressive, came to him. This fear quickly became poignant as he realized that it was no longer a mere matter of freezing his fingers and toes, or of losing his hands and feet, but that it was a matter of life and death, with the chances against him. This threw him into a panic, and he turned and ran up the creek bed along the old dim trail. The dog joined in behind and kept up with him. He ran blindly, without intention, in fear such as he had never known in his life. Slowly, as he plowed and floundered through the snow, he began to see things again,—the banks of the creek, the old timber jams, the leafless aspens, and the sky. The running made him feel better. He did not shiver. Maybe, if he ran on, his feet would thaw out; and, anyway, if he ran far enough he would reach the camp and the boys. Without doubt he would lose some fingers and toes and some of his face; but the boys would take care of him, and save the rest of him when he got there. And at the same time there was another thought in his mind that said he would never get to the camp and the boys; that it was too many miles away, that the freezing had too great a start on him, and that he would soon be stiff and dead. This thought he kept in the background and refused to consider. Sometimes it pushed itself forward and demanded to be heard, and he thrust it back and strove to think of other things.

36   It struck him as curious that he could run at all on feet so frozen that he could not feel them when they struck the earth and took the weight of his body. He seemed to himself to skim along above the surface, and to have no connection with the earth. Somewhere he had once seen a winged Mercury, and he wondered if Mercury felt as he felt when skimming over the earth.

37   His theory of running until he reached camp and the boys had one flaw in it: he lacked the endurance. Several times he stumbled, and finally he tottered, crumpled up, and fell. When he tried to rise, he

failed. He must sit and rest, he decided, and next time he would merely walk and keep on going. As he sat and regained his breath, he noted that he was feeling quite warm and comfortable. He was not shivering, and it even seemed that a warm glow had come to his chest and trunk. And yet, when he touched his nose or cheeks, there was no sensation. Running would not thaw them out. Nor would it thaw out his hands and feet.

38   Then the thought came to him that the frozen portions of his body must be extending. He tried to keep this thought down, to forget it, to think of something else; he was aware of the panicky feeling that it caused, and he was afraid of the panic. But the thought asserted itself, and persisted, until it produced a vision of his body totally frozen. This was too much, and he made another wild run along the trail. Once he slowed down to a walk, but the thought of the freezing extending itself made him run again.

39   And all the time the dog ran with him, at his heels. When he fell down a second time, it curled its tail over its forefeet and sat in front of him, facing him, curiously eager and intent. The warmth and security of the animal angered him, and he cursed it till it flattened down its ears appeasingly. This time the shivering came more quickly upon the man. He was losing in his battle with the frost. It was creeping into his body from all sides. The thought of it drove him on, but he ran no more than a hundred feet, when he staggered and pitched headlong. It was his last panic. When he had recovered his breath and control, he sat up and entertained in his mind the conception of meeting death with dignity. However, the conception did not come to him in such terms. His idea of it was that he had been making a fool of himself, running around like a chicken with its head cut off—such was the simile that occurred to him. Well, he was bound to freeze anyway, and he might as well take it decently. With this new-found peace of mind came the first glimmerings of drowsiness. A good idea, he thought, to sleep off to death. It was like taking an anesthetic. Freezing was not so bad as people thought. There were lots worse ways to die.

40   He pictured the boys finding his body next day. Suddenly he found himself with them, coming along the trail and looking for himself. And, still with them, he came around a turn in the trail and found himself lying in the snow. He did not belong with himself any more, for even then he was out of himself, standing with the boys and looking at himself in the snow. It certainly was cold, was his thought. When he got back to the States, he could tell the folks what real cold was. He drifted on from this to a vision of the old-timer on Sulphur Creek. He could see him quite clearly, warm and comfortable, and smoking a pipe.

41   "You were right, old hoss; you were right," the man mumbled to
the old-timer of Sulphur Creek.

42   Then the man drowsed off into what seemed to him the most comfortable and satisfying sleep he had ever known. The dog sat facing him
and waiting. The brief day drew to a close in a long, slow twilight.
There were no signs of a fire to be made, and, besides, never in the dog's
experience had it known a man to sit like that in the snow and make
no fire. As the twilight drew on, its eager yearning for the fire mastered
it, and with a great lifting and shifting of forefeet, it whined softly, then
flattened its ears down in anticipation of being chidden by the man.
But the man remained silent. Later, the dog whined loudly. And still
later it crept close to the man and caught the scent of death. This made
the animal bristle and back away. A little longer it delayed, howling
under the stars that leaped and danced and shone brightly in the cold
sky. Then it turned and trotted up the trail in the direction of the camp
it knew, where were other food-providers and fire-providers.

To Build a Fire

JOURNAL

1. MLA Works Cited

Using this model, record this story here.

*Author's Last Name, First Name. "Title of the Story." <u>Title of the Book</u>. Ed.
First Last Name. City: Publisher, year. Pages of the story.*

2. Main Character(s)

*Describe each main character, and explain why you think each is a main
character.*

3. Supporting Characters

*Describe each supporting character, and explain why you think each is a
supporting character.*

4. Setting

*Describe the setting. Decide if the setting can be changed and, if so, to where
and when.*

5. Sequence

Relate the events of the story in order.

6. Plot

Tell the story in no more than three sentences.

7. Conflicts

Identify and explain the conflicts involved here.

8. Significant Quotations

Explain the importance of each of these quotations. Record the page number in the parentheses.

a. "Fifty degrees below zero was to him just precisely fifty degrees below zero. That there should be anything more to it than that was a thought that never entered his head" (   ).

b. "Its instinct told it a truer tale than was told to the man by the man's judgment" (   ).

c. "At a place where there were no signs, where the soft, unbroken snow seemed to advertise solidity beneath, the man broke through" (   ).

d. "Each time he had pulled a twig he had communicated a slight agitation to the tree—an imperceptible agitation, so far as he was concerned, but an agitation sufficient to bring about the disaster" (   ).

e. "And still later it crept close to the man and caught the scent of death" (   ).

9. Foreshadowing

Identify and explain the hints London gives along the way to predict events to come.

FOLLOW-UP QUESTIONS

10 SHORT QUESTIONS

Select the <u>best</u> answer for each.

____ 1. The story is set in
  a. eastern North America.
  b. northern North America.
  c. Africa.

____ 2. The man stays
  a. in the fields.
  b. away from the water.
  c. close to the water.

____ 3. The man is looking for
  a. logging routes.
  b. the creek.
  c. the path.

____ 4. The dog is
  a. happy to be out in this weather.
  b. unhappy to be out in this weather.
  c. unconcerned about being out in this weather.

____ 5. The dog is
  a. happy to leave the fire.
  b. unhappy to leave the fire.
  c. unconcerned about leaving the fire.

____ 6. The one who knows that it is too cold to be out in this weather is
  a. the dog.
  b. the man.
  c. the other campers.

____ 7. The man does
  a. not meet the old-timer.
  b. listen well to the old-timer.
  c. not listen well to the old-timer.

____ 8. The man builds the second fire
  a. too close to the spruce tree.
  b. far away from the spruce tree.
  c. too close to the creek.

____ 9. The man
  a. tries to help the dog.
  b. leaves the dog alone.
  c. wants to kill the dog.

____ 10. The one who probably makes it back to camp is
  a. the man.
  b. the dog.
  c. the old-timer.

5 SIGNIFICANT QUOTATIONS

Explain the importance of each of these quotations.

1. "It [fifty degrees below zero] did not lead him to meditate upon his frailty as a creature of temperature, and upon man's frailty in general [. . .]."

2. "The animal was depressed by the tremendous cold. It knew that it was no time for traveling."

3. "And then it happened. [. . .] He wet himself halfway to the knees before he floundered out to the firm crust."

4. "But before he could cut the strings, it happened. [. . .] He should not have built the fire under the spruce tree."

5. "Then it turned and trotted up the trail in the direction of the camp it knew [. . .]."

2 COMPREHENSION ESSAY QUESTIONS

Use specific details and information from the story to answer these as completely as possible.

1. How does the title relate to the story? Explain the significance of the title using specific details and information from the story.

2. London seems to respect the dog's natural knowledge more than the learned knowledge of the man. Explain this using specific details and information from the story.

WRITING

Use each of these ideas for writing an essay.

1. Write a narrative essay about a place in nature that has outwitted you or someone you know.

2. Write a narrative essay about a time that a pet or another animal has been wiser than you.

Further Writing

1. Read the *Tao Te Ching* (which can be found in a library) to learn about the Eastern view of harmony with nature. London's sense of harmony with nature is quite Eastern. Compare what you learned in this story with what you learn from the *Tao*.

2. Like London, Ray Bradbury questions the assumed intelligence of man's knowledge. Compare intelligence in this story with that in Bradbury's "There Will Come Soft Rains" (page 90).

Everyday Use

Alice Walker

PRE-READING VOCABULARY
CONTEXT

Use context clues to define these words before reading. Use a dictionary as needed.

1. The boy's leg became *lame* after he smashed his kneecap. *Lame* means _____.

2. Heather is a beautiful young woman, and no one would ever call her *homely*. *Homely* means _____.

3. Brian and Andy stood in *awe* of the beautiful woman and were so overcome that they did not say a word. *Awe* means _____.

4. Not to know is to be *ignorant*. *Ignorant* means _____.

5. The fire *blazed* white hot as they watched. *Blaze* means

   _____.

6. The characters in *Dumb and Dumber* act like *dimwits*. *Dimwit* means _____.

7. The cows lazily wandered the grassy *pasture*. *Pasture* means

   _____.

8. The hot water was *scalding* to the touch. *Scalding* means

   _____.

9. The *lye* Ben was boiling to make soap ate through the counter. *Lye* means _____.

10. The reds and oranges in her dress were so *loud* that they hurt my eyes. *Loud* means _____.

11. When the wind blew, the little leaves *trembled. Tremble* means _____.

12. The scared puppy was *cowering* in the corner. *Cower* means

_____.

13. When Anna cooked the pasta too long, the pasta became sticky and *limp. Limp* means _____.

14. The dictator forced his *oppressed* nation to follow his every rule. *Oppress* means _____.

15. After Karen put milk in the *butter churn*, the milk sat in the wooden pot waiting to be stirred into butter. *Butter churn* means

_____.

16. Dave used a sharp knife to *whittle* the little boat out of an old piece of wood. *Whittle* means _____.

17. Katherine went *rifling* through her dresser drawers looking for the ring she had lost. *Rifling* means _____.

18. A *quilt* is a large bed covering often made out of little pieces of material sewn together. *Quilt* means _____.

19. After Pia spilled the boiling water on her hand, she had bubbly *scars* all over her hand. *Scar* means _____.

20. The historical memory of a group or family is called its *heritage. Heritage* means _____.

PRE-READING VOCABULARY WORD ATTACK

Define these words by solving the parts. Use a dictionary as needed.

1. everyday
2. wavy
3. irregular
4. hopelessly
5. soft-seated
6. sporty
7. man-working
8. mercilessly
9. nightfall
10. uncooked
11. farthest
12. papery
13. make-believe
14. good-naturedly
15. rawhide
16. washday
17. faultfinding
18. salt-lick
19. artistic
20. priceless

PRE-READING QUESTIONS

Try answering these questions as you read.

What does the title mean?

Who are the main characters in the story? supporting characters?

How are the characters different?

Why are the quilts so important?

Everyday Use

ALICE WALKER

Alice Walker was born in rural Eatonton, Georgia, in 1944. She suffered an eye injury at the age of eight that was not surgically repaired until she was fourteen. Avoiding others because of her injury, Walker turned to writing poetry and to observing relationships among others. She later attended Spelman College in Atlanta and Sarah Lawrence College in New York City. She returned south to Mississippi as a teacher and became active in civil rights. Here she met Melvyn Leventhal, whom she married in 1967. Her writings present the often-heroic struggles of common African-American women, and her novel, *The Color Purple,* received the Pulitzer Prize for fiction and the American Book Award.

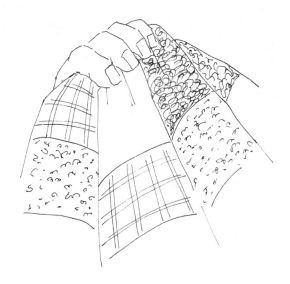

For your grandma

2   I will wait for her in the yard that Maggie and I made so clean and wavy yesterday afternoon. A yard like this is more comfortable than most people know. It is not just a yard. It is like an extended living room. When the hard clay is swept clean as a floor and the fine sand around the edges lined with tiny, irregular grooves, anyone can come and sit and look up into the elm tree and wait for the breezes that never come inside the house.

3   Maggie will be nervous until after her sister goes: she will stand hopelessly in corners homely and ashamed of the burn scars down her arms and legs, eyeing her sister with a mixture of envy and awe. She thinks her sister had held life always in the palm of one hand, that "no" is a word the world never learned to say to her.

4   You've no doubt seen those TV shows where the child who has "made it" is confronted, as a surprise, by her own mother and father, tottering in weakly from backstage. (A pleasant surprise, of course: What would they do if parent and child came on the show only to curse out and insult each other?) On TV mother and child embrace and smile into each other's faces. Sometimes the mother and father weep, the child wraps them in her arms and leans across the table to tell how she would not have made it without their help. I have seen these programs.

5   Sometimes I dream a dream in which Dee and I are suddenly brought together on a TV program of this sort. Out of a dark and soft-seated limousine I am ushered into a bright room filled with many people. There I meet a smiling, gray, sporty man like Johnny Carson who shakes my hand and tells me what a fine girl I have. Then we are on the stage and Dee is embracing me with tears in her eyes. She pins on my dress a large orchid, even though she has told me once that she thinks orchids are tacky flowers.

6   In real life I am a large, big-boned woman with rough, man-working hands. In the winter I wear flannel nightgowns to bed and overalls during the day. I can kill and clean a hog as mercilessly as a man. My fat keeps me hot in zero weather. I can work outside all day, breaking ice to get water for washing. I can eat pork liver cooked over the open fire minutes after it comes steaming from the hog. One winter I knocked a bull calf straight in the brain between the eyes with a sledge hammer and had the meat hung up to chill before nightfall. But of course all this does not show on television. I am the way my daughter would want me to be: a hundred pounds lighter, my skin like an uncooked barley pancake. My hair glistens in the hot bright lights.

Johnny Carson has much to do to keep up with my quick and witty tongue.

7   But that is a mistake. I know even before I wake up. Who ever knew a Johnson with a quick tongue? Who can even imagine me looking a strange white man in the eye? It seems to me I have talked to them always with one foot raised in flight, with my head turned in whichever way is farthest from them. Dee, though. She would always look anyone in the eye. Hesitation was no part of her nature.

8   "How do I look, Mama?" Maggie says, showing just enough of her thin body enveloped in pink skirt and red blouse for me to know she's there, almost hidden by the door.

9   "Come out into the yard," I say.

10   Have you ever seen a lame animal, perhaps a dog run over by some careless person rich enough to own a car, sidle up to someone who is ignorant enough to be kind to him? That is the way my Maggie walks. She has been like this, chin on chest, eyes on ground, feet in shuffle, ever since the fire that burned the other house to the ground.

11   Dee is lighter than Maggie, with nicer hair and a fuller figure. She's a woman now, though sometimes I forget. How long ago was it that the other house burned? Ten, twelve years? Sometimes I can still hear the flames and feel Maggie's arms sticking to me, her hair smoking and her dress falling off her in little black papery flakes. Her eyes seemed stretched open, blazed open by the flames reflected in them. And Dee. I see her standing off under the sweet gum tree she used to dig gum out of; a look of concentration on her face as she watched the last dingy gray board of the house fall in toward the red-hot brick chimney. Why don't you do a dance around the ashes? I'd wanted to ask her. She had hated the house that much.

12   I used to think she hated Maggie, too. But that was before we raised the money, the church and me, to send her to Augusta to school. She used to read to us without pity; forcing words, lies, other folks' habits, whole lives upon us two, sitting trapped and ignorant underneath her voice. She washed us in a river of make-believe, burned us with a lot of knowledge we didn't necessarily need to know. Pressed us to her with the serious way she read, to shove us away at just the moment, like dimwits, we seemed about to understand.

13   Dee wanted nice things. A yellow organdy dress to wear to her graduation from high school; black pumps to match a green suit she'd made from an old suit somebody gave me. She was determined to stare down any disaster in her efforts. Her eyelids would not flicker for

minutes at a time. Often I fought off the temptation to shake her. At sixteen she had a style of her own: and knew what style was.

14   I never had an education myself. After second grade the school was closed down. Don't ask me why: in 1927 colored asked fewer questions than they do now. Sometimes Maggie reads to me. She stumbles along good-naturedly but can't see well. She knows she is not bright. Like good looks and money, quickness passed her by. She will marry John Thomas (who has mossy teeth in an earnest face) and then I'll be free to sit here and I guess just sing church songs to myself. Although I never was a good singer. Never could carry a tune. I was always better at a man's job. I used to love to milk till I was hoofed in the side in '49. Cows are soothing and slow and don't bother you, unless you try to milk them the wrong way.

15   I have deliberately turned my back on the house. It is three rooms, just like the one that burned, except the roof is tin; they don't make shingle roofs any more. There are no real windows, just some holes cut in the sides, like the portholes in a ship, but not round and not square, with rawhide holding the shutters up on the outside. This house is in a pasture, too, like the other one. No doubt when Dee sees it she will want to tear it down. She wrote me once that no matter where we "choose" to live, she will manage to come see us. But she will never bring her friends. Maggie and I thought about this and Maggie asked me, "Mama, when did Dee ever *have* any friends?"

16   She had a few. Furtive boys in pink shirts hanging about on wash-day after school. Nervous girls who never laughed. Impressed with her they worshiped the well-turned phrase, the cute shape, the scalding humor that erupted like bubbles in lye. She read to them.

17   When she was courting Jimmy T she didn't have much time to pay to us, but turned all her faultfinding power on him. He *flew* to marry a cheap gal from a family of ignorant flashy people. She hardly had time to recompose herself.

18   When she comes I will meet—but there they are!

19   Maggie attempts to make a dash for the house, in her shuffling way; but I stay her with my hand. "Come back here," I say. And she stops and tries to dig a well in the sand with her toe.

20   It is hard to see them clearly through the strong sun. But even the first glimpse of leg out of the car tells me it is Dee. Her feet were always neat-looking, as if God himself had shaped them with a certain style. From the other side of the car comes a short, stocky man. Hair is all over his head a foot long and hanging from his chin like a kinky

mule tail. I hear Maggie suck in her breath. "Uhnnnh," is what it sounds like. Like when you see the wriggling end of a snake just in front of your foot on the road. "Uhnnnh."

21   Dee next. A dress down to the ground, in this hot weather. A dress so loud it hurts my eyes. There are yellows and oranges enough to throw back the light of the sun. I feel my whole face warming from the heat waves it throws out. Earrings, too, gold and hanging down to her shoulders. Bracelets dangling and making noises when she moves her arm up to shake the folds of the dress out of her armpits. The dress is loose and flows, and as she walks closer, I like it. I hear Maggie go "Uhnnnh" again. It is her sister's hair. It stands straight up like the wool on a sheep. It is black as night and around the edges are two long pigtails that rope about like small lizards disappearing behind her ears.

22   "Wa-su-zo-Tean-o!" she says, coming on in that gliding way the dress makes her move. The short stocky fellow with the hair to his navel is all grinning and he follows up with "Asalamalakim, my mother and sister!" He moves to hug Maggie but she falls back, right up against the back of my chair. I feel her trembling there and when I look up I see the perspiration falling off her chin.

23   "Don't get up," says Dee. Since I am stout it takes something of a push. You can see me trying to move a second or two before I make it. She turns, showing white heels through her sandals, and goes back to the car. Out she peeks next with a Polaroid. She stoops down quickly and lines up picture after picture of me sitting there in front of the house with Maggie cowering behind me. She never takes a shot without making sure the house is included. When a cow comes nibbling around the edge of the yard she snaps it and me and Maggie *and* the house. Then she puts the Polaroid in the back seat of the car, and comes up and kisses me on the forehead.

24   Meanwhile Asalamalakim is going through the motions with Maggie's hand. Maggie's hand is as limp as a fish, and probably as cold, despite the sweat, and she keeps trying to pull it back. It looks like Asalamalakim wants to shake hands but wants to do it fancy. Or maybe he don't know how people shake hands. Anyhow, he soon gives up on Maggie.

25   "Well," I say. "Dee."

26   "No, Mama," she says. "Not 'Dee,' Wangero Leewanika Kemanjo!"

27   "What happened to 'Dee'?" I wanted to know.

28   "She's dead," Wangero said. "I couldn't bear it any longer being named after the people who oppress me."

29   "You know as well as me you was named after your aunt Dicie," I said. Dicie is my sister. She named Dee. We called her "Big Dee" after Dee was born.

30   "But who was *she* named after?" asked Wangero.

31   "I guess after Grandma Dee," I said.

32   "And who was she named after?" asked Wangero.

33   "Her mother," I said, and saw Wangero was getting tired. "That's about as far back as I can trace it," I said. Though, in fact, I probably could have carried it back beyond the Civil War through the branches.

34   "Well," said Asalamalakim, "there you are."

35   "Uhnnnh," I heard Maggie say.

36   "There I was not," I said, "before 'Dicie' cropped up in our family, so why should I try to trace it that far back?"

37   He just stood there grinning, looking down on me like somebody inspecting a Model A car. Every once in a while he and Wangero sent eye signals over my head.

38   "How do you pronounce this name?" I asked.

39   "You don't have to call me by it if you don't want to," said Wangero.

40   "Why shouldn't I?" I asked. "If that's what you want us to call you, we'll call you."

41   "I know it might sound awkward at first," said Wangero.

42   "I'll get used to it," I said. "Ream it out again."

43   Well, soon we got the name out of the way. Asalamalakim had a name twice as long and three times as hard. After I tripped over it two or three times he told me to just call him Hakim-a-barber. I wanted to ask him was he a barber, but I didn't really think he was, so I didn't ask.

44   "You must belong to those beef-cattle peoples down the road," I said. They said "Asalamalakim" when they met you, too, but didn't shake hands. Always too busy: feeding the cattle, fixing the fences, putting up salt-lick shelters, throwing down hay. When the white folks poisoned some of the herd the men stayed up all night with rifles in their hands. I walked a mile and a half just to see the sight.

45   Hakim-a-barber said, "I accept some of their doctrines, but farming and raising cattle is not my style." (They didn't tell me, and I didn't ask, whether Wangero [Dee] had really gone and married him.)

46   We sat down to eat and right away he said he didn't eat collards and pork was unclean. Wangero, though, went on through the chitlins and corn bread, the greens and everything else. She talked a blue streak over the sweet potatoes. Everything delighted her. Even the fact that we still used the benches her daddy made for the table when we couldn't afford to buy chairs.

47   "Oh, Mama!" she cried. Then turned to Hakim-a-barber. "I never knew how lovely these benches are. You can feel the rump prints," she said, running her hands underneath her and along the bench. Then she gave a sigh and her hand closed over Grandma Dee's butter dish. "That's it!" she said. "I knew there was something I wanted to ask you if I could have." She jumped up from the table and went over in the corner where the churn stood, the milk in it clabber by now. She looked at the churn and looked at it.

48   "This churn top is what I need," she said. "Didn't Uncle Buddy whittle it out of a tree you all used to have?

49   "Yes," I said.

50   "Uh huh," she said happily. "And I want the dasher, too."

51   "Uncle Buddy whittle that, too?" asked the barber.

52   Dee (Wangero) looked up at me.

53   "Aunt Dee's first husband whittled the dash," said Maggie so low you almost couldn't hear her. "His name was Henry, but they called him Stash."

54   "Maggie's brain is like an elephant's," Wangero said, laughing. "I can use the churn top as a centerpiece for the alcove table," she said, sliding a plate over the churn, "and I'll think of something artistic to do with the dasher."

55   When she finished wrapping the dasher the handle stuck out. I took it for a moment in my hands. You didn't even have to look close to see where hands pushing the dasher up and down to make butter had left a kind of sink in the wood. In fact, there were a lot of small sinks; you could see where thumbs and fingers had sunk into the wood. It was beautiful light yellow wood, from a tree that grew in the yard where Big Dee and Stash had lived.

56   After dinner Dee (Wangero) went to the trunk at the foot of my bed and started rifling through it. Maggie hung back in the kitchen over the dishpan. Out came Wangero with two quilts. They had been pieced by Grandma Dee and then Big Dee and me had hung them on the quilt frames on the front porch and quilted them. One was in the Lone Star pattern. The other was Walk Around the Mountain. In both of them were scraps of dresses Grandma Dee had worn fifty and more years ago. Bits and pieces of Grandpa Jarrell's paisley shirts. And one teeny faded blue piece, about the piece of a penny matchbox, that was from Great Grandpa Ezra's uniform that he wore in the Civil War.

57   "Mama," Wangero said sweet as a bird. "Can I have these old quilts?"

58   I heard something fall in the kitchen, and a minute later the kitchen door slammed.

59   "Why don't you take one or two of the others?" I asked. "These old things was just done by me and Big Dee from some tops your grandma pieced before she died."

60   "No," said Wangero. "I don't want those. They are stitched around the borders by machine."

61   "That's make them last better," I said.

62   "That's not the point," said Wangero. "These are all pieces of dresses Grandma used to wear. She did all this stitching by hand. Imagine!" She held the quilts securely in her arms, stroking them.

63   "Some of the pieces, like those lavender ones, come from old clothes her mother handed down to her," I said, moving up to touch the quilts. Dee (Wangero) moved back just enough so that I couldn't reach the quilts. They already belonged to her.

64   "Imagine!" she breathed again, clutching them closely to her bosom.

65   "The truth is," I said, "I promised to give them quilts to Maggie, for when she marries John Thomas."

66   She gasped like a bee had stung her.

67   "Maggie can't appreciate these quilts!" she said. "She'd probably be backward enough to put them to everyday use."

68   "I reckon she would," I said. "God knows I been saving 'em for long enough with nobody using 'em. I hope she will!" I didn't want to bring up how I had offered Dee (Wangero) a quilt when she went away to college. Then she had told me they were old-fashioned, out of style.

69   "But they're *priceless!*" she was saying now, furiously; for she has a temper. "Maggie would put them on the bed and in five years they'd be in rags. Less than that!"

70   "She can always make some more," I said. "Maggie knows how to quilt."

71   Dee (Wangero) looked at me with hatred. "You just will not understand. The point is these quilts, *these* quilts!"

72   "Well," I said, stumped. "What would *you* do with them?"

73   "Hang them," she said. As if that was the only thing you *could* do with quilts.

74   Maggie by now was standing in the door. I could almost hear the sound her feet made as they scraped over each other.

75   "She can have them. Mama," she said, like somebody used to never winning anything, or having anything reserved for her. "I can 'member Grandma Dee without the quilts."

76   I looked at her hard. She had filled her bottom lip with checkerberry snuff and it gave her face a kind of dopey, hangdog look. It was

Grandma Dee and Big Dee who taught her how to quilt herself. She stood there with her scarred hands hidden in the folds of her skirt. She looked at her sister with something like fear but she wasn't mad at her. This was Maggie's portion. This was the way she knew God to work.

77   When I looked at her like that something hit me in the top of my head and ran down to the soles of my feet. Just like when I'm in church and the spirit of God touches me and I get happy and shout. I did something I never had done before: hugged Maggie to me, then dragged her on into the room, snatched the quilts out of Miss Wangero's hands and dumped them into Maggie's lap. Maggie just sat there on my bed with her mouth open.

78   "Take one or two of the others," I said to Dee.

79   But she turned without a word and went out to Hakim-a-barber.

80   "You just don't understand," she said, as Maggie and I came out to the car.

81   "What don't I understand?" I wanted to know.

82   "Your heritage," she said. And then she turned to Maggie, kissed her, and said, "You ought to try to make something of yourself, too, Maggie. It's really a new day for us. But from the way you and Mama still live you'd never know it."

83   She put on some sunglasses that hid everything above the tip of her nose and her chin.

84   Maggie smiled; maybe at the sunglasses. But a real smile, not scared. After we watched the car dust settle I asked Maggie to bring me a dip of snuff. And then the two of us sat there just enjoying, until it was time to go in the house and go to bed.

Everyday Use
JOURNAL

1. MLA Works Cited

Using this model, record this story here.

Author's Last Name, First Name. "Title of the Story." <u>Title of the Book</u>. Ed. First Last Name. City: Publisher, year. Pages of the story.

2. Main Character(s)

Describe each main character, and explain why you think each is a main character.

3. Supporting Characters

Describe each supporting character, and explain why you think each is a supporting character.

4. Setting

Describe the setting. Decide if the setting or the props can be changed and, if so, to where, when, or what.

5. Sequence

Relate the events of the story in order.

6. Plot

Tell the story in no more than two sentences.

7. Conflicts

Identify and explain the conflicts involved here.

8. Significant Quotations

Explain the importance of each of these quotations. Record the page number in the parentheses.

a. "Sometimes I can still hear the flames and feel Maggie's arms sticking to me, her hair smoking and her dress falling off her in little black papery flakes" (   ).

b. "At sixteen she had a style of her own: and knew what style was" (   ).

c. "Out she peeks next with a Polaroid. [. . .] She never takes a shot without making sure the house is included" (   ).

d. " 'I can use the churn top as a centerpiece for the alcove table,' she said, sliding a plate over the churn, 'and I'll think of something artistic to do with the dasher' " (   ).

e. " 'Maggie can't appreciate these quilts!' she said. 'She'd probably be backward enough to put them to everyday use' " (   ).

FOLLOW-UP QUESTIONS

10 SHORT QUESTIONS

Select the __best__ answer for each.

____ 1. Maggie is Dee's
   a. mother.
   b. cousin.
   c. sister.

____ 2. The narrator is Dee's
   a. mother.
   b. cousin.
   c. sister.

____ 3. The prettiest one is
   a. Maggie.
   b. Dee.
   c. the narrator.

____ 4. Dee
   a. did not care about the house she grew up in.
   b. liked the house she grew up in.
   c. disliked the house she grew up in.

____ 5. The one who was scarred in the fire was
   a. Maggie.
   b. Dee.
   c. the narrator.

____ 6. The one who is shy is
   a. Maggie.
   b. Dee.
   c. the narrator.

____ 7. Dee wants the quilts because
   a. she wants to use them.
   b. she likes the colors in them.
   c. she wants to show them off.

____ 8. Maggie wants the quilts because
   a. she wants to use them.
   b. she likes the colors.
   c. she wants to show them off.

____ 9. Dee's changed attitude is
   a. a sincere interest in her background.
   b. a sincere interest in the quilts.
   c. for show.

____ 10. The narrator is sympathetic to
   a. Dee.
   b. Maggie.
   c. the quilts.

5 SIGNIFICANT QUOTATIONS

Explain the importance of each of these quotations.

1. "Why don't you do a dance around the ashes? I'd wanted to ask her. She had hated the house that much."

2. "Impressed with her they worshipped the well-turned phrase, the cute shape, the scalding humor that erupted like bubbles in lye."

3. " 'No, Mama,' she said. 'Not "Dee," Wangero Leewanika Kemanjo!' "

4. " 'Mama,' Wangero said sweet as a bird. 'Can I have these old quilts?' "

5. "I did something I never had done before: hugged Maggie to me, then dragged her on into the room, snatched the quilts out of Miss Wangero's hands and dumped them into Maggie's lap."

2 COMPREHENSION ESSAY QUESTIONS

Use specific details and information from the story to answer these as completely as possible.

1. The quilts are central to the story. Explain the significance of the quilts using specific details and information from the story.

2. The mother and Maggie treat their heritage one way, while Dee treats it quite another. Contrast the difference in the way each treats her heritage, using specific details and information from the story.

WRITING

Use each of these ideas for writing an essay.

1. We all have special objects—a signed baseball, a good luck charm, a prom momento. Write an essay that narrates the story of your favorite special object.

2. We all know insincere people like Dee who put on airs to impress others. Write a narrative essay contrasting your sincerity with the insincerity of another.

Further Writing

1. Compare and contrast the characters in "Everyday Use" with the characters in Dorothy Parker's "The Wonderful Old Gentleman" (page 329).

2. Dee in this story and Tom Sawyer in the selection from Mark Twain (page 123) both use ruses or pretenses to try to get what they want. Compare and contrast their manipulations and their goals.

3

Plot and Foreshadowing

A story is based around a simple skeleton of events called a **plot.** Around this basic plot, a logical order of events or **sequence** occurs that builds tension or, in mysteries, suspense. In stories we call all the events in the sequence a **story line.**

Have you ever gone to the movies and watched the end credits roll while you were still waiting for the movie to get going? You looked at the person sitting next to you, felt cheated, and asked "What happened?" What happened is that somewhere along the line, the storyteller failed.

In a well-written story, one event logically leads to another event, and then to another, and so on, so that each word and action counts and builds tension that carries your interest. The tension peaks at the **climax** and then resolves in the **dénouement.** When any of these pieces is missing, poorly developed, or unbelievable, we are disappointed. (Movie sequels, in fact, purposely stop at the climax and before the dénouement so that we will return for the next episode.)

Each story in this chapter depends on the flow of events in the story. First, Frank Stockton plays with you and makes you very aware of the importance of resolution in "The Lady or the Tiger?" Then you are touched and even outraged by the unjust turns of events in "One Friday Morning," in "No Name Woman," and in "The Lottery." If "The Lottery" starts to give you a nasty taste, the actions that surround Hulga in "Good Country People" start to resemble evilness itself.

Foreshadowing is a technique some authors use to help explain or predict events to come. The author may sprinkle information or hints throughout the story to help predict actions that are yet to happen. Edgar Allan Poe is a master at foreshadowing. In his stories, there are hints along the way, although readers almost always miss the clues on the first reading and are astonished at the endings. After reading these stories in this chapter, look back and notice that each has hints along the way that help predict their unsettling endings.

The Lady or the Tiger?

FRANK STOCKTON

PRE-READING VOCABULARY
CONTEXT

Use context clues to define these words before reading. Use a dictionary as needed.

1. A person acting like a primitive beast is *barbaric. Barbaric* means

   _____ wild _____.

2. Carlos took a *fancy* to golf, and now he buys golf magazines and plays golf every chance he gets. *Fancy* means ____ liken ____.

3. Mothers have the *authority* to ground their children. *Authority* means ____ charge ____.

4. Steve shows great *valor* in standing up for what he believes, even when others disagree. *Valor* means ____ courage ____.

5. In Roman times, *gladiators* fought brave battles. *Gladiator* means

   _____ warriors _____.

6. The lecture will take place in the large *amphitheatre* that seats several thousand. *Amphitheatre* means ____ large auditorium ____.

7. *Virtue* and pureness of heart are qualities rarely found in a material world. *Virtue* means ____ good quality ____.

8. The judge was *impartial* to each person and never took sides unfairly. *Impartial* means ____ fairety ____.

9. The criminal was *accused* of robbing the bank after police saw his face on the bank video. *Accused* means ____ charged ____.

10. The actors took their show on the road and always played to large
    audiences. *Audience* means ___*Crowd*___ .

11. When Marna and Buzz decided to get married, they invited their
    favorite people to their *wedding*. *Wedding* means ___*marriage ceremony*___ .

12. The hungry children *devoured* the chocolate cake in minutes. *Devour*
    means ___*eat*___ .

13. Nala showed good *judgment* when she chose staying in school and
    not dropping out. *Judgment* means ___*decision*___ .

14. When Jay sued his neighbor, they ended having the lawsuit decided in
    a *trial*. *Trial* means ___*court*___ .

15. The young *courtiers* living in the king's castle enjoyed an easy life of
    hunting and feasting. *Courtier* means ___*servant*___ .

16. In America, everyone assumes that he or she can improve his
    or her *station* in life through hard work. *Station* means
    ___*Social position*___ .

17. The Seymours trimmed their double front *portals* in pine rope and
    twinkling lights. *Portal* means _____ .

18. The lovely *damsel* enjoyed arranging roses and setting lovely tea
    parties. *Damsel* means ___*young woman*___ .

19. Phyllis was overcome with *jealousy* when her neighbor's garden
    looked better than hers. *Jealousy* means ___*envy*___ .

20. Geri *anguished* over which carpet to chose, because she would have to
    live with it for a long time. *Anguished* means ___*pain*___ .

PRE-READING VOCABULARY
WORD ATTACK

Define these words by solving the parts. Use a dictionary as needed.

1. olden
2. progressive
3. irresistible
4. manly
5. beastly
6. encircling
7. incorruptible
8. idealism
9. aforementioned
10. fiercest
11. downcast
12. chorister
13. slightest
14. uncertainty
15. unfairness
16. humanity
17. fairness
18. exceedingly
19. relentless
20. admittance
21. possessed
22. curtained
23. unimportant
24. lookers-on
25. immovably
26. hot-blooded
27. oftener
28. recovered
29. futurity

PRE-READING QUESTIONS

Try answering these questions as you read.

What is the point of the amphitheatre?

What happens to the courtier?

How does the princess feel about the maiden?

What does the princess do?

The Lady or the Tiger?

FRANK STOCKTON

Frank Stockton was born in Philadelphia in 1834. After attending school in Philadelphia, he became a wood engraver. He wrote children's stories from 1867 until 1881, when he turned to writing adult stories. With a flair for fantasy and even for some primitive science fiction, "The Lady or the Tiger?" remains his most enduring piece. Stockton died in 1902.

In the very olden time, there lived a semi-barbaric king, whose ideas, though somewhat polished and sharpened by the progressiveness of distant Latin neighbors, were still large, florid, and untrammelled, as became the half of him which was barbaric. He was a man of exuberant fancy, and, withal, of an authority so irresistible that, at his will, he turned his varied fancies into facts. He was greatly given to self-communing; and, when he and himself agreed upon any thing, the thing was done. When every member of his domestic and political systems moved smoothly in its appointed course, his nature was bland and genial; but whenever there was a little hitch, and some of his orbs got out of their orbits, he was blander and more genial still, for nothing pleased him so much as to make the crooked straight, and crush down uneven places.

2   Among the borrowed notions by which his barbarism had become semified was that of the public arena, in which, by exhibitions of manly and beastly valor, the minds of his subjects were refined and cultured.

3   But even here the exuberant and barbaric fancy asserted itself. The arena of the king was built, not to give the people an opportunity of hearing the rhapsodies of dying gladiators, nor to enable them to view the inevitable conclusion of a conflict between religious opinions and hungry jaws, but for purposes far better adapted to widen and develop the mental energies of the people. This vast amphitheatre, with its encircling galleries, its mysterious vaults, and its unseen passages, was an agent of poetic justice, in which crime was punished, or virtue rewarded, by the decrees of an impartial and incorruptible chance.

4   When a subject was accused of a crime of sufficient importance to interest the king, public notice was given that on an appointed day the fate of the accused person would be decided in the king's arena—a structure which well deserved its name; for, although its form and plan were borrowed from afar, its purpose emanated solely from the brain of

this man, who, every barleycorn a king, knew no tradition to which he owed more allegiance than pleased his fancy, and who ingrafted on every adopted form of human thought and action the rich growth of his barbaric idealism.

5   When all the people had assembled in the galleries, and the king, surrounded by his court, sat high up on his throne of royal state on one side of the arena, he gave a signal, a door beneath him opened, and the accused subject stepped out into the amphitheatre. Directly opposite him, on the other side of the enclosed space, were two doors exactly alike and side by side. It was the duty and the privilege of the person on trial, to walk directly to these doors and open one of them. He could open either door he pleased: he was subject to no guidance or influence but that of the aforementioned impartial and incorruptible chance. If he opened the one, there came out of it a hungry tiger, the fiercest and most cruel that could be procured, which immediately sprang upon him, and tore him to pieces, as a punishment for his guilt. The moment that the case of the criminal was thus decided, doleful iron bells were clanged, great wails went up from the hired mourners posted on the outer rim of the arena, and the vast audience, with bowed heads and downcast hearts, wended slowly their homeward way, mourning greatly that one so young and fair, or so old and respected, should have merited so dire a fate.

6   But, if the accused person opened the other door, there came forth from it a lady, the most suitable to his years and station that his majesty could select among his fair subjects; and to this lady he was immediately married, as a reward of his innocence. It mattered not that he might already possess a wife and family, or that his affections might be engaged upon an object of his own selection: the king allowed no such subordinate arrangements to interfere with his great scheme of retribution and reward. The exercises, as in the other instance, took place immediately, and in the arena. Another door opened beneath the king, and a priest, followed by a band of choristers, and dancing maidens blowing joyous airs on golden horns and treading an epithalamic measure, advanced to where the pair stood, side by side; and the wedding was promptly and cheerily solemnized. Then the gay brass bells rang forth their merry peals, the people shouted glad hurrahs, and the innocent man, preceded by children strewing flowers on his path, led his bride to his home.

7   This was the king's semi-barbaric method of administering justice. Its perfect fairness is obvious. The criminal could not know out of which door would come the lady: he opened either he pleased, without having the slightest idea whether, in the next instant, he was to be

devoured or married. On some occasions the tiger came out of one door, and on some out of the other. The decisions of this tribunal were not only fair, they were positively determinate: the accused person was instantly punished if he found himself guilty; and, if innocent, he was rewarded on the spot, whether he liked it or not. There was no escape from the judgments of the king's arena.

8   The institution was a very popular one. When the people gathered together on one of the great trial days, they never knew whether they were to witness a bloody slaughter or a hilarious wedding. This element of uncertainty lent an interest to the occasion which it could not otherwise have attained. Thus, the masses were entertained and pleased, and the thinking part of the community could bring no charge of unfairness against this plan; for did not the accused person have the whole matter in his own hands?

9   This semi-barbaric king had a daughter as blooming as his most florid fancies, and with a soul as fervent and imperious as his own. As is usual in such cases, she was the apple of his eye, and was loved by him above all humanity. Among his courtiers was a young man of that fineness of blood and lowness of station common to the conventional heroes of romance who love royal maidens. This royal maiden was well satisfied with her lover, for he was handsome and brave to a degree unsurpassed in all this kingdom; and she loved him with an ardor that had enough of barbarism in it to make it exceedingly warm and strong. This love affair moved on happily for many months, until one day the king happened to discover its existence. He did not hesitate nor waver in regard to his duty in the premises. The youth was immediately cast into prison, and a day was appointed for his trial in the king's arena. This, of course, was an especially important occasion; and his majesty, as well as all the people, was greatly interested in the workings and development of this trial. Never before had such a case occurred; never before had a subject dared to love the daughter of a king. In after-years such things became commonplace enough; but then they were, in no slight degree, novel and startling.

10   The tiger-cages of the kingdom were searched for the most savage and relentless beasts, from which the fiercest monster might be selected for the arena; and the ranks of maiden youth and beauty throughout the land were carefully surveyed by competent judges, in order that the young man might have a fitting bride in case fate did not determine for him a different destiny. Of course, everybody knew that the deed with which the accused was charged had been done. He had loved the princess, and neither he, she, nor any one else thought of denying the fact; but the king would not think of allowing any fact of

this kind to interfere with the workings of the tribunal, in which he took such great delight and satisfaction. No matter how the affair turned out, the youth would be disposed of; and the king would take an aesthetic pleasure in watching the course of events, which would determine whether or not the young man had done wrong in allowing himself to love the princess.

11   The appointed day arrived. From far and near the people gathered, and thronged the great galleries of the arena; and crowds, unable to gain admittance, massed themselves against its outside walls. The king and his court were in their places, opposite the twin doors—those fateful portals, so terrible in their similarity.

12   All was ready. The signal was given. A door beneath the royal party opened, and the lover of the princess walked into the arena. Tall, beautiful, fair, his appearance was greeted with a low hum of admiration and anxiety. Half the audience had not known so grand a youth had lived among them. No wonder the princess loved him! What a terrible thing for him to be there!

13   As the youth advanced into the arena, he turned, as the custom was, to bow to the king: but he did not think at all of that royal personage; his eyes were fixed upon the princess, who sat to the right of her father. Had it not been for the moiety of barbarism in her nature, it is probable that lady would not have been there; but her intense and fervid soul would not allow her to be absent on an occasion in which she was so terribly interested. From the moment that the decree had gone forth, that her lover should decide his fate in the king's arena, she had thought of nothing, night or day, but this great event and the various subjects connected with it. Possessed of more power, influence, and force of character than any one who had ever before been interested in such a case, she had done what no other person had done—she had possessed herself of the secret of the doors. She knew in which of the two rooms, that lay behind those doors, stood the cage of the tiger, with its open front, and in which waited the lady. Through these thick doors, heavily curtained with skins on the inside, it was impossible that any noise or suggestion should come from within to the person who should approach to raise the latch of one of them; but gold, and the power of a woman's will, had brought the secret to the princess.

14   And not only did she know in which room stood the lady ready to emerge, all blushing and radiant, should her door be opened, but she knew who the lady was. It was one of the fairest and loveliest of the damsels of the court who had been selected as the reward of the accused youth, should he be proved innocent of the crime of aspiring to one so far above him; and the princess hated her. Often had she

seen, or imagined that she had seen, this fair creature throwing glances of admiration upon the person of her lover, and sometimes she thought these glances were perceived and even returned. Now and then she had seen them talking together; it was but for a moment or two, but much can be said in a brief space; it may have been on most unimportant topics, but how could she know that? The girl was lovely, but she had dared to raise her eyes to the loved one of the princess; and, with all the intensity of the savage blood transmitted to her through long lines of wholly barbaric ancestors, she hated the woman who blushed and trembled behind that silent door.

15   When her lover turned and looked at her, and his eye met hers as she sat there paler and whiter than any one in the vast ocean of anxious faces about her, he saw, by that power of quick perception which is given to those whose souls are one, that she knew behind which door crouched the tiger, and behind which stood the lady. He had expected her to know it. He understood her nature, and his soul was assured that she would never rest until she had made plain to herself this thing, hidden to all other lookers-on, even to the king. The only hope for the youth in which there was any element of certainty was based upon the success of the princess in discovering the mystery; and the moment he looked upon her, he saw she had succeeded, as in his soul he knew she would succeed.

16   Then it was that his quick and anxious glance asked the question: "Which?" It was as plain to her as if he shouted it from where he stood. There was not an instant to be lost. The question was asked in a flash; it must be answered in another.

17   Her right arm lay on the cushioned parapet before her. She raised her hand, and made a slight, quick movement toward the right. No one but her lover saw her. Every eye but his was fixed on the man in the arena.

18   He turned, and with a firm and rapid step he walked across the empty space. Every heart stopped beating, every breath was held, every eye was fixed immovably upon that man. Without the slightest hesitation, he went to the door on the right, and opened it.

19   Now, the point of the story is this: Did the tiger come out of that door, or did the lady?

20   The more we reflect upon this question, the harder it is to answer. It involves a study of the human heart which leads us through devious mazes of passion, out of which it is difficult to find our way. Think of it, fair reader, not as if the decision of the question depended upon yourself, but upon that hot-blooded, semi-barbaric princess, her soul at

a white heat beneath the combined fires of despair and jealousy. She had lost him, but who should have him?

21   How often, in her waking hours and in her dreams, had she started in wild horror, and covered her face with her hands as she thought of her lover opening the door on the other side of which waited the cruel fangs of the tiger!

22   But how much oftener had she seen him at the other door! How in her grievous reveries had she gnashed her teeth, and torn her hair, when she saw his start of rapturous delight as he opened the door of the lady! How her soul had burned in agony when she had seen him rush to meet that woman, with her flushing cheek and sparkling eye of triumph; when she had seen him lead her forth, his whole frame kindled with the joy of recovered life; when she had heard the glad shouts from the multitude, and the wild ringing of the happy bells; when she had seen the priest, with his joyous followers, advance to the couple, and make them man and wife before her very eyes; and when she had seen them walk away together upon their path of flowers, followed by the tremendous shouts of the hilarious multitude, in which her one despairing shriek was lost and drowned!

23   Would it not be better for him to die at once, and go to wait for her in the blessed regions of semi-barbaric futurity?

24   And yet, that awful tiger, those shrieks, that blood!

25   Her decision had been indicated in an instant, but it had been made after days and nights of anguished deliberation. She had known she would be asked, she had decided what she would answer, and, without the slightest hesitation, she had moved her hand to the right.

26   The question of her decision is one not to be lightly considered, and it is not for me to presume to set myself up as the one person able to answer it. And so I leave it with all of you: Which came out of the opened door—the lady, or the tiger?

The Lady or the Tiger?

JOURNAL

1. MLA Works Cited

Using this model, record this reading here.

Author's Last Name, First Name. "Title of the Story." Title of the Book*. Ed.*
First Name. City: Publisher, year. Pages of the story.

2. Main Character(s)

Describe each main character, and explain why you think each is a main
character.

3. Supporting Characters

Describe each supporting character, and explain why you think each is a
supporting character.

4. Setting

Describe the setting. Decide if this setting can be changed and, if so, to where
and when.

5. Sequence

Relate the events of the story in order.

6. Plot

Tell the story in no more than three sentences.

7. Conflicts

Identify and explain the conflicts involved here.

8. Significant Quotations

Explain the importance of each of these quotations. Record the page number in parentheses.

a. "Among the borrowed notions by which his barbarism had become semified was that of the public arena [. . .]" (   ).

b. "It was the duty and the privilege of the person on trial, to walk directly to these doors and open one on them" (   ).

c. "Among his courtiers was a young man of that fineness of blood and lowness of station common to the conventional heroes of romance who love royal maidens" (   ).

d. "The girl was lovely, but she had dared to raise her eyes to the loved one of the princess [. . .]" (   ).

e. "Then it was that his quick and anxious glance asked the question: 'Which?'" (   ).

Follow-up Questions

10 Short Questions

Select the best answer for each.

____ 1. The king seems
   a. brutal.
   b. kind.
   c. fair.

____ 2. The king feels the justice of the arena is
   a. kind.
   b. barbaric.
   c. fair.

____ 3. The princess is
   a. quiet.
   b. serene.
   c. passionate.

____ 4. The princess loves
   a. a royal man.
   b. a non-royal man.
   c. an acceptable man.

____ 5. The king is
   a. happy with the princess's choice.
   b. unconcerned about the princess's choice.
   c. outraged at the princess's choice.

____ 6. The king will
   a. let the princess marry the lover.
   b. not let the princess marry the lover.
   c. think about letting the princess marry the lover.

____ 7. The princess
   a. knows which door the maiden is behind.
   b. does not know which door the maiden is behind.
   c. does not know which door the tiger is behind.

____ 8. The princess probably learned what she does know about the doors
   a. through a teacher.
   b. through bribery.
   c. through the king.

____ 9. The princess
   a. is jealous of the maiden.
   b. is not jealous of the maiden.
   c. does not know of the maiden.

____ 10. The princess
   a. can bear to see her lover torn apart.
   b. cannot bear to see her lover torn apart.
   c. does not care if her lover is torn apart.

5 Significant Quotations

Explain the importance of each of these quotations.

1. "This vast amphitheatre [. . .] was an agent of poetic justice, in which crime was punished, or virtue rewarded, by the decrees of an impartial and incorruptible chance."

2. "If he opened one, there came out of it a hungry tiger, [. . .]
     "But, if the accused person opened the other door [. . .]."

3. "This royal maiden was well satisfied with her lover [. . .]."

4. "It was one of the fairest and loveliest damsels of the court [. . .] and the princess hated her."

5. "Without the slightest hesitation, he went to the door on the right, and opened it."

2 COMPREHENSION ESSAY QUESTIONS

Use specific details and information from the story to answer these as completely as possible.

1. Explain the king's justice system and how it relates to the courtier. Use specific details and information from the story to support your explanation.

2. Explain the maiden's role in the story. Use specific details and information from the story to support your explanation.

WRITING

Use each of these ideas for writing an essay.

1. Write an ending to "The Lady or the Tiger?" Explain your ending, and include references from the story to support your logic.

2. Tell the story of a difficult choice you have had to make. Explain the circumstances and consequences of your choice.

Further Writing

1. Read Hemingway's "The Short, Happy Life of Francis Macomber" (which can be found in a library), and compare Margot's choice with that of the princess in this story.

One Friday Morning

Langston Hughes

Pre-reading Vocabulary
Context

Use context clues to define these words before reading. Use a dictionary as needed.

1. Luis found it *thrilling* to finally get to the front of the line and buy the last concert tickets. *Thrilling* means _____.

2. Lauren was delighted to receive a *scholarship* for her studies in Italy; now she could afford to go. *Scholarship* means

   _____.

3. The honored guests were *feted* with a fabulous dinner party and dancing under the stars. *Fete* means _____.

4. Hughes refers to people of color as *colored* or *Negro*. *Colored* or *Negro* means _____.

5. At the family reunion, Rachel, her mother, and her grandmother represented three *generations*. *Generation* means _____.

6. A complex society that works together to achieve great things may be called a *civilization*. *Civilization* means _____.

7. The best player will win the Most Valuable Player *award*. *Award* means _____.

8. Ashley *beamed* and smiled from ear to ear when her mother bought her favorite toy. *Beam* means _____.

9. Nick takes great *pride* in the business he has put together from nothing. *Pride* means _____.

10. Jacob was *bursting* to tell everyone the good news about his report card. *Bursting* means _____.

11. Storekeepers may *discriminate* against teenagers because they feel the teens may steal from them. *Discriminate* means

    _____.

12. The school held a large pep *assembly* on Friday before the big game on Saturday. *Assembly* means _____.

13. The famous rock star was *acclaimed* throughout the country for his generosity. *Acclaimed* means _____.

14. Reid expressed his *gratitude* for his birthday gifts by writing everyone thank-you notes. *Gratitude* means _____.

15. The *poverty* in the neighborhood was so bad that people did not have enough money even to buy food. *Poverty* means

    _____.

16. The players gave their *allegiance* to each other, promising to support each other. *Allegiance* means _____.

17. There is usually a *pause* between each ring of the phone. *Pause* means

    _____.

18. Jodi was *ashamed* of herself after she called her best friend terrible names. *Ashamed* means _____.

19. The young artist with his natural *talent* could draw almost anything well. *Talent* means _____.

20. During the American Civil War, *Abolitionists* worked hard to abolish, or get rid of, slavery. *Abolitionist* means _____.

PRE-READING VOCABULARY
WORD ATTACK

Define these words by solving the parts. Use a dictionary as needed.

1. indirection
2. modernistic
3. basketball
4. velvety
5. red-haired
6. inked
7. copied
8. discovered
9. steadily
10. miraculous
11. leaflessly
12. lacy
13. airy
14. paper-white
15. halfway
16. familiarly
17. widened
18. tightened
19. unawares
20. acceptance
21. frightened
22. background
23. newspapers
24. fairness
25. friendship
26. football
27. happiness
28. breakfast
29. half-amused
30. unfortunately
31. sunlight
32. narrowness
33. outstretched

PRE-READING QUESTIONS

Try answering these questions as you read.

What is Nancy Lee's talent?

What does the scholarship mean to Nancy Lee?

What does the committee do?

What does Miss O'Shay do?

How does Nancy Lee react?

One Friday Morning

LANGSTON HUGHES

Langston Hughes was born in Joplin, Missouri, in 1902. After his parents' separation, he spent his early childhood with his grandmother in Laurence, Kansas. His grandmother gave him a positive outlook on his African-American heritage and on life through her stories filled with characters who triumphed over life's problems with zeal and determination. At twelve, he moved back with his mother and lived in Lincoln, Illinois. Later, he served as a crewman on freighters that traveled to Africa, Holland, and Paris. He returned to Washington, D.C., and then moved to New York City. Sharing the same patron as Zora Neale Hurston, he attended Columbia University and eventually became a central figure in the Harlem Renaissance. He died in 1967.

Hughes enjoyed a fruitful writing career. His writings reflect the rhythms of Harlem and the positive attitude of his grandmother. His poems and stories are available in several collections.

The thrilling news did not come directly to Nancy Lee, but it came in little indirections that finally added themselves up to one tremendous fact: she had won the prize! But being a calm and quiet young lady, she did not say anything, although the whole high school buzzed with rumors, guesses, reportedly authentic announcements on the part of students who had no right to be making announcements at all—since no student really knew yet who had won this year's art scholarship.

2   But Nancy Lee's drawing was so good, her lines so sure, her colors so bright and harmonious, that certainly no other student in the senior art class at George Washington High was thought to have very much of a chance. Yet you never could tell. Last year nobody had expected Joe Williams to win the Artist Club scholarship with that funny modernistic watercolor he had done of the high-level bridge. In fact, it was hard to make out there was a bridge until you had looked at the picture a long time. Still, Joe Williams got the prize, was feted by the community's leading painters, club women, and society folks at a big banquet at the Park-Rose Hotel, and was now an award student at the Art School—the city's only art school.

3   Nancy Lee Johnson was a colored girl, a few years out of the South. But seldom did her high-school classmates think of her as colored. She was smart, pretty, and brown, and fitted in well with the life of the school. She stood high in scholarship, played a swell game of basketball, had taken part in the senior musical in a soft, velvety voice, and

had never seemed to intrude or stand out except in pleasant ways, so it was seldom even mentioned—her color.

4   Nancy Lee sometimes forgot she was colored herself. She liked her classmates and her school. Particularly she liked her art teacher, Miss Dietrich, the tall red-haired woman who taught her law and order in doing things; and the beauty of working step by step until a job is done; a picture finished; a design created; or a block print carved out of nothing but an idea and a smooth square of linoleum, inked, proofs made, and finally put down on paper—clean, sharp, beautiful, individual, unlike any other in the world, thus making the paper have a meaning nobody else could give it except Nancy Lee. That was the wonderful thing about true creation. You made something nobody else on earth could make—but you.

5   Miss Dietrich was the kind of teacher who brought out the best in her students—but their own best, not anybody else's copied best. For anybody else's best, great though it might be, even Michelangelo's, wasn't enough to please Miss Dietrich, dealing with the creative impulses of young men and women living in an American city in the Middle West, and being American.

6   Nancy Lee was proud of being American, a Negro American with blood out of Africa a long time ago, too many generations back to count. But her parents had taught her the beauties of Africa, its strength, its song, its mighty rivers, its early smelting of iron, its building of the pyramids, and its ancient and important civilizations. And Miss Dietrich had discovered for her the sharp and humorous lines of African sculpture, Benin, Congo, Makonde. Nancy Lee's father was a mail carrier, her mother a social worker in a city settlement house. Both parents had been to Negro colleges in the South. And her mother had gotten a further degree in social work from a Northern university. Her parents were, like most Americans, simple ordinary people who had worked hard and steadily for their education. Now they were trying to make it easier for Nancy Lee to achieve learning than it had been for them. They would be very happy when they heard of the award to their daughter—yet Nancy did not tell them. To surprise them would be better. Besides, there had been a promise.

7   Casually, one day, Miss Dietrich asked Nancy Lee what color frame she thought would be best on her picture. That had been the first inkling.

8   "Blue," Nancy Lee said. Although the picture had been entered in the Artist Club contest a month ago, Nancy Lee did not hesitate in her choice of a color for the possible frame since she could still see her

picture clearly in her mind's eye—for that picture waiting for the blue frame had come out of her soul, her own life, and had bloomed into miraculous being with Miss Dietrich's help. It was, she knew, the best watercolor she had painted in her four years as a high-school art student, and she was glad she had made something Miss Dietrich liked well enough to permit her to enter in the contest before she graduated.

9   It was not a modernistic picture in the sense that you had to look at it a long time to understand what it meant. It was just a simple scene in the city park on a spring day with the trees still leaflessly lacy against the sky, the new grass fresh and green, a flag on a tall pole in the center, children playing, and an old Negro woman sitting on a bench with her head turned. A lot for one picture, to be sure, but it was not there in heavy and final detail like a calendar. Its charm was that everything was light and airy, happy like spring, with a lot of blue sky, paper-white clouds, and air showing through. You could tell that the old Negro woman was looking at the flag, and that the flag was proud in the spring breeze, and that the breeze helped to make the children's dresses billow as they played.

10   Miss Dietrich had taught Nancy Lee how to paint spring, people, and a breeze on what was only a plain white piece of paper from the supply closet. But Miss Dietrich had not said make it like any other spring-people-breeze ever seen before. She let it remain Nancy Lee's own. That is how the old Negro woman happened to be there looking at the flag—for in her mind the flag, the spring, and the woman formed a kind of triangle holding a dream Nancy Lee wanted to express. White stars on a blue field, spring, children, ever-growing life, and an old woman. Would the judges at the Artist Club like it?

11   One wet, rainy April afternoon Miss O'Shay, the girls' vice-principal, sent for Nancy Lee to stop by her office as school closed. Pupils without umbrellas or raincoats were clustered in doorways hoping to make it home between showers. Outside the skies were gray. Nancy Lee's thoughts were suddenly gray, too.

12   She did not think she had done anything wrong, yet that tight little knot came in her throat just the same as she approached Miss O'Shay's door. Perhaps she had banged her locker too often and too hard. Perhaps the note in French she had written to Sallie halfway across the study hall just for fun had never gotten to Sallie but into Miss O'Shay's hands instead. Or maybe she was failing in some subject and wouldn't be allowed to graduate. Chemistry! A pang went through the pit of her stomach.

13   She knocked on Miss O'Shay's door. That familiarly solid and competent voice said, "Come in."

14   Miss O'Shay had a way of making you feel welcome, even if you came to be expelled.

15   "Sit down, Nancy Lee Johnson," said Miss O'Shay. "I have something to tell you." Nancy Lee sat down. "But I must ask you to promise not to tell anyone yet."

16   "I won't, Miss O'Shay," Nancy Lee said, wondering what on earth the vice-principal had to say to her.

17   "You are about to graduate," Miss O'Shay said. "And we shall miss you. You have been an excellent student, Nancy, and you will not be without honors on the senior list, as I am sure you know."

18   At that point there was a light knock on the door. Miss O'Shay called out, "Come in," and Miss Dietrich entered. "May I be a part of this, too?" she asked, tall and smiling.

19   "Of course," Miss O'Shay said. "I was just telling Nancy Lee what we thought of her. But I hadn't gotten around to giving her the news. Perhaps, Miss Dietrich, you'd like to tell her yourself."

20   Miss Dietrich was always direct. "Nancy Lee," she said, "your picture has won the Artist Club scholarship."

21   The slender brown girl's eyes widened, her heart jumped, then her throat tightened again. She tried to smile, but instead tears came to her eyes.

22   "Dear Nancy Lee," Miss O'Shay said, "we are so happy for you." The elderly white woman took her hand and shook it warmly while Miss Dietrich beamed with pride.

23   Nancy Lee must have danced all the way home. She never remembered quite how she got there through the rain. She hoped she had been dignified. But certainly she hadn't stopped to tell anybody her secret on the way. Raindrops, smiles, and tears mingled on her brown cheeks. She hoped her mother hadn't yet gotten home and that the house was empty. She wanted to have time to calm down and look natural before she had to see anyone. She didn't want to be bursting with excitement—having a secret to contain.

24   Miss O'Shay's calling her to the office had been in the nature of a preparation and a warning. The kind, elderly vice-principal said she did not believe in catching young ladies unawares, even with honors, so she wished her to know about the coming award. In making acceptance speeches she wanted her to be calm, prepared, not nervous, overcome, and frightened. So Nancy Lee was asked to think what she would say when the scholarship was conferred upon her a few days

hence, both at the Friday morning high-school assembly hour when the announcement would be made, and at the evening banquet of the Artist Club. Nancy Lee promised the vice-principal to think calmly about what she would say.

25   Miss Dietrich had then asked for some facts about her parents, her background, and her life, since such material would probably be desired for the papers. Nancy Lee had told her how, six years before, they had come up from the Deep South, her father having been successful in achieving a transfer from the one post office to another, a thing he had long sought in order to give Nancy Lee a chance to go to school in the North. Now, they lived in a modest Negro neighborhood, went to see the best plays when they came to town, and had been saving to send Nancy Lee to art school, in case she were permitted to enter. But the scholarship would help a great deal, for they were not rich people.

26   "Now Mother can have a new coat next winter," Nancy Lee thought, "because my tuition will all be covered for the first year. And once in art school, there are other scholarships I can win."

27   Dreams began to dance through her head, plans and ambitions, beauties she would create for herself, her parents, and the Negro people—for Nancy Lee possessed a deep and reverent race pride. She could see the old woman in her picture (really her grandmother in the South) lifting her head to the bright stars on the flag in the distance. A Negro in America! Often hurt, discriminated against, sometimes lynched—but always there were the stars on the blue body of the flag. Was there any other flag in the world that had so many stars? Nancy Lee thought deeply but she could remember none in all the encyclopedias or geographies she had ever looked into.

28   "Hitch your wagon to a star," Nancy Lee thought, dancing home in the rain. "Who were our flag makers?"

29   Friday morning came, the morning when the world would know— her high-school world, the newspaper world, her mother and dad. Dad could not be there at the assembly to hear the announcement, nor see her prize picture displayed on the stage, nor listen to Nancy Lee's little speech of acceptance, but Mother would be able to come, although Mother was much puzzled as to why Nancy Lee was so insistent she be at school on that particular Friday morning.

30   When something is happening, something new and fine, something that will change your very life, it is hard to go to sleep at night for thinking about it, and hard to keep your heart from pounding, or a strange little knot of joy from gathering in your throat. Nancy Lee had taken her bath, brushed her hair until it glowed, and had gone to bed

thinking about the next day, the big day when, before three thousand students, she would be the one student honored, her painting the one painting to be acclaimed as the best of the year from all the art classes of the city. Her short speech of gratitude was ready. She went over it in her mind, not word for word (because she didn't want it to sound as if she had learned it by heart), but she let the thoughts flow simply and sincerely through her consciousness many times.

31   When the president of the Artist Club presented her with the medal and scroll of the scholarship award, she would say:

32   "Judges and members of the Artist Club. I want to thank you for this award that means so much to me personally and through me to my people, the colored people of this city who, sometimes, are discouraged and bewildered, thinking that color and poverty are against them. I accept this award with gratitude and pride, not for myself alone, but for my race that believes in American opportunity and American fairness—and the bright stars in our flag. I thank Miss Dietrich and the teachers who made it possible for me to have the knowledge and training that lie behind this honor you have conferred upon my painting. When I came here from the South a few years ago, I was not sure how you would receive me. You received me well. You have given me a chance and helped me along the road I wanted to follow. I suppose the judges know that every week here at assembly the students of this school pledge allegiance to the flag. I shall try to be worthy of that pledge, and of the help and friendship and understanding of my fellow citizens of whatever race or creed, and of our American dream of 'Liberty and justice for all!' "

33   That would be her response before the students in the morning. How proud and happy the Negro pupils would be, perhaps almost as proud as they were of the one colored star on the football team. Her mother would probably cry with happiness. Thus Nancy Lee went to sleep dreaming of a wonderful tomorrow.

34   The bright sunlight of an April morning woke her. There was breakfast with her parents—their half-amused and puzzled faces across the table, wondering what could be this secret that made her eyes so bright. The swift walk to school; the clock in the tower almost nine; hundreds of pupils streaming into the long, rambling old building that was the city's largest high school; the sudden quiet of the homeroom after the bell rang; then the teacher opening her record book to call the roll. But just before she began, she looked across the room until her eyes located Nancy Lee.

35   "Nancy," she said. "Miss O'Shay would like to see you in her office, please."

36   Nancy Lee rose and went out while the names were being called and the word *present* added its period to each name. Perhaps, Nancy Lee thought, the reporters from the papers had already come. Maybe they wanted to take her picture before assembly, which wasn't until ten o'clock. (Last year they had had the photograph of the winner of the award in the morning papers as soon as the announcement had been made.)

37   Nancy Lee knocked at Miss O'Shay's door.

38   "Come in."

39   The vice-principal stood at her desk. There was no one else in the room. It was very quiet.

40   "Sit down, Nancy Lee," she said. Miss O'Shay did not smile. There was a long pause. The seconds went by slowly. "I do not know how to tell you what I have to say," the elderly woman began, her eyes on the papers on her desk. "I am indignant and ashamed for myself and for this city." Then she lifted her eyes and looked at Nancy Lee in the neat blue dress sitting there before her. "You are not to receive the scholarship this morning."

41   Outside in the hall the electric bells announcing the first period rang, loud and interminably long. Miss O'Shay remained silent. To the brown girl there in the chair, the room grew suddenly smaller, smaller, smaller, and there was no air. She could not speak.

42   Miss O'Shay said, "When the committee learned that you were colored, they changed their plans."

43   Still Nancy Lee said nothing, for there was no air to give breath to her lungs.

44   "Here is the letter from the committee, Nancy Lee." Miss O'Shay picked it up and read the final paragraph to her.

45   "It seems to us wiser to arbitrarily rotate the award among the various high schools of the city from now on. And especially in this case since the student chosen happens to be colored, a circumstance which unfortunately, had we known, might have prevented this embarrassment. But there have never been any Negro students in the local art school, and the presence of one there might create difficulties for all concerned. We have high regard for the quality of Nancy Lee Johnson's talent, but we do not feel it would be fair to honor it with the Artist Club award." Miss O'Shay paused. She put the letter down.

46   "Nancy Lee, I am very sorry to have to give you this message."

47   "But my speech," Nancy Lee said, "was about . . ." The words stuck in her throat. ". . . about America . . ."

48   Miss O'Shay had risen, she turned her back and stood looking out the window at the spring tulips in the school yard.

49   "I thought, since the award would be made at assembly right after our oath of allegiance," the words tumbled almost hysterically from Nancy Lee's throat now, "I would put part of the flag salute in my speech. You know, Miss O'Shay, that part about 'liberty and justice for all.'"

50   "I know," said Miss O'Shay, slowly facing the room again. "But America is only what we who believe in it, make it. I am Irish. You may not know, Nancy Lee, but years ago we were called the dirty Irish, and mobs rioted against us in the big cities, and we were invited to go back where we came from. But we didn't go. And we didn't give up, because we believed in the American dream, and in our power to make that dream come true. Difficulties, yes. Mountains to climb, yes. Discouragements to face, yes. Democracy to make, yes. That is it, Nancy Lee! We still have in this world of ours democracy to *make*. You and I, Nancy Lee. But the premise and the base are here, the lines of the Declaration of Independence and the words of Lincoln are here, and the stars in our flag. Those who deny you this scholarship do not know the meaning of those stars, but it's up to us to make them know. As a teacher in the public schools of this city, I myself will go before the school board and ask them to remove from our system the offer of any prizes or awards denied to any student because of race or color."

51   Suddenly Miss O'Shay stopped speaking. Her clear, clear blue eyes looked into those of the girl before her. The woman's eyes were full of strength and courage. "Lift up your head, Nancy Lee, and smile at me."

52   Miss O'Shay stood against the open window with the green lawn and the tulips beyond, the sunlight tangled in her gray hair, her voice an electric flow of strength to the hurt spirit of Nancy Lee. The Abolitionists who believed in freedom when there was slavery must have been like that. The first white teachers who went into the Deep South to teach the freed slaves must have been like that. All those who stand against ignorance, narrowness, hate, and mud on stars must be like that.

53   Nancy Lee lifted her head and smiled. The bell for assembly rang. She went through the long hall filled with students toward the auditorium.

54   "There will be other awards," Nancy Lee thought. "There're schools in other cities. This won't keep me down. But when I'm a woman, I'll fight to see that these things don't happen to other girls as

this has happened to me. And men and women like Miss O'Shay will help me."

55   She took her seat among the seniors. The doors of the auditorium closed. As the principal came onto the platform, the students rose and turned their eyes to the flag on the stage.

56   One hand went to the heart, the other outstretched toward the flag. Three thousand voices spoke. Among them was the voice of a dark girl whose cheeks were suddenly wet with tears, ". . . one nation indivisible, with liberty and justice for all."

57   "That is the land we must make," she thought.

One Friday Morning

JOURNAL

1. MLA Works Cited

Using this model, record this story here.

Author's Last Name, First Name. "Title of the Story." <u>Title of the Book</u>. Ed.
First Last Name. City: Publisher, year. Pages of the story.

2. Main Character(s)

Describe each main character, and explain why you think each is a main character.

3. Supporting Characters

Describe each supporting character, and explain why you think each is a supporting character.

4. Setting

Describe the setting. Decide if the setting can be changed and, if so, to where and when.

5. Sequence

Relate the events of the story in order.

6. Plot

Tell the story in no more than two sentences.

7. Conflicts

Identify and explain the conflicts involved here.

8. Significant Quotations

Explain the importance of each of these quotations. Record the page number in the parentheses.

a. "For anybody else's best, great though it might be, even Michelangelo's, wasn't enough to please Miss Dietrich, dealing with the creative impulses of young men and women living in an American city in the Middle West, and being American" (   ).

b. "That is how the old Negro woman happened to be there looking at the flag—for in her [Nancy Lee's] mind the flag, the spring, and the woman formed a kind of triangle, holding a dream Nancy Lee wanted to express" (   ).

c. " 'But I hadn't gotten around to giving her the news. Perhaps, Miss Dietrich, you'd like to tell her yourself' " (   ).

d. " 'Sit down, Nancy Lee,' she said. Miss O'Shay did not smile. There was a long pause" (   ).

e. "Three thousand voices spoke. Among them was the voice of a dark girl whose cheeks were suddenly wet with tears, '. . . one nation indivisible, with liberty and justice for all' " (   ).

FOLLOW-UP QUESTIONS

10 SHORT QUESTIONS

Select the <u>best</u> answer for each.

_____ 1. Nancy Lee
- a. has artistic talent.
- b. has musical talent.
- c. does not have any special talent.

_____ 2. Miss Dietrich is
- a. a demanding and strict teacher.
- b. a kind and encouraging teacher.
- c. an uncaring teacher.

_____ 3. Miss Dietrich
- a. submits Nancy Lee's picture for competition.
- b. submits Nancy Lee's picture too late.
- c. does not submit Nancy Lee's picture for competition.

_____ 4. Nancy Lee is first called to Miss O'Shay's office because
- a. she is in trouble.
- b. she has failed chemistry.
- c. she has won the award.

_____ 5. Miss O'Shay
- a. is mad at Nancy Lee.
- b. reprimands Nancy Lee.
- c. is proud of Nancy Lee.

_____ 6. At this first meeting, Nancy Lee
- a. is upset and angry.
- b. is happy and proud.
- c. is unconcerned and unfeeling.

_____ 7. After this first meeting, Nancy Lee
- a. does not care about the award.
- b. does not plan on the award.
- c. is excited and plans her moment of accepting the award.

_____ 8. Nancy Lee's painting has been inspired by
- a. her mother.
- b. her father.
- c. her grandmother.

_____ 9. In the end, Nancy Lee
- a. wins the award.
- b. does not win the award.
- c. does not accept the award.

_____ 10. Nancy Lee's race
- a. influences the committee.
- b. does not influence the committee.
- c. is not considered by the committee.

5 SIGNIFICANT QUOTATIONS

Explain the importance of each of these quotations.

1. "Particularly she liked her art teacher, Miss Dietrich, the tall red-haired woman who taught her law and order in doing things; and the beauty of working step by step until a job is done [. . .]."

2. "You could tell that the old Negro woman was looking at the flag, and that the flag was proud in the spring breeze, and that the breeze helped make the children's dresses billow as they played."

3. "'Dear Nancy Lee,' Miss O'Shay said, 'we are so happy for you.'"

4. "The vice-principal stood at her desk. There was no one else in the room. It was very quiet."

5. "'That is the land we must make,' she thought."

2 COMPREHENSION ESSAY QUESTIONS

Use specific details and information from the story to answer these as completely as possible.

1. Explain the significance of the people and things in Nancy Lee's painting. Use specific details and information from the story to support your explanation.

2. Explain Nancy Lee's feelings during the assembly. Use specific details and information from the story to support your explanation.

WRITING

Use each of these ideas for writing an essay.

1. We have all suffered prejudice—not big enough for the team, too big for the team, not talented enough for the show, and so forth—for one reason or another. Write a narrative essay that tells about one experience you have had with prejudice.

2. We have all tried to succeed at something, only to be disappointed. Write an essay telling about one struggle and disappointment of your own.

Further Writing

1. Read Hughes's "Harlem" (which can be found in a library), and compare and contrast the message in "Harlem" with that in this story.

2. Compare Nancy Lee's determination with the determination of Old Phoenix in Eudora Welty's "A Worn Path" (page 26).

No Name Woman

MAXINE HONG KINGSTON

PRE-READING VOCABULARY
CONTEXT

Use context clues to define there words before reading. Use a dictionary as needed.

1. The water *well* had a wood frame around it and an umbrella-like wood cover over it. *Well* means _____.

2. Paula hoped she would have twins when she found out she was *pregnant*. *Pregnant* means _____.

3. The starving people *raided* the food trucks for any food they could find. *Raid* means _____.

4. The oil spill had *slaughtered* thousands of fish that washed up dead on the shore. *Slaughter* means _____.

5. Those influenced by Chinese culture greatly respect the relatives who have lived before them, their *ancestors*. *Ancestor* means

   _____.

6. The pigs live in the *pigsty* that is surrounded by a fence and filled with cooling mud. *Pigsty* means _____.

7. The leftover paper and garbage were *plugging up* the stopped-up sink. *Plugging up* means _____.

8. The team felt *humiliated* after the other team beat them 60–0. *Humiliated* means _____.

9. Hok Lu came to America as an *emigrant* from China. *Emigrant* means

   _____.

10. America has a very noisy and colorful *tradition* of shooting off firecrackers on July 4. *Tradition* means _____.

11. When Joel cheated on his wife by dating another woman, he committed *adultery*. *Adultery* means _____.

12. Linda felt very special when she was treated to the *extravagance* of getting a diamond necklace. *Extravagance* means _____.

13. The waiter was a *stranger* whom Bob had never seen or met before. *Stranger* means _____.

14. Since Michelle could not be at Alice's wedding to sign the license, Cheryl stood in for Michelle as *proxy*. *Proxy* means

    _____.

15. Charles chose to live apart, or *separate*, from his sister. *Separate* means _____.

16. The girl's drug abuse made her ugly and nasty, and she was a *disgrace* to her family. *Disgrace* means _____.

17. All the family will spend the holiday together so all the *kinsmen* can be together. *Kinsman* means _____.

18. The witch placed a *hex* on the old house, and ever since everyone has said it is haunted. *Hex* means _____.

19. Bobbie gets nervously *agoraphobic* in open fields and needs to come back inside. *Agoraphobic* means _____.

20. Carl had twitching muscle *spasms* in his arm after he held the paintbrush for too long. *Spasm* means _____.

Pre-reading Vocabulary
Word Attack

Define these words by solving the parts. Use a dictionary as needed.

1. hurry-up
2. encircled
3. searchlights
4. courtyard
5. overturned
6. earthenware
7. invisible
8. childhood
9. unspeakable
10. daughters-in-law
11. marketplace
12. drawn-out
13. lifetime
14. wrongdoers
15. deep-rooted
16. heart-catching
17. commonplace
18. loveliness
19. beloved
20. greatcoat
21. pigeon-toed
22. Chinese-feminine
23. silently
24. attentiveness
25. household
26. sisterliness
27. honorable
28. roundness
29. faithfully
30. shortsighted
31. predictably
32. fatalism
33. unprotected
34. pain-dealing
35. piglets
36. emptiness
37. kinspeople
38. crossroads

Pre-reading Questions

Try answering these questions as you read.

Who is the No Name Woman?

What does she do?

What happens to her?

Why does the narrator write about the No Name Woman?

No Name Woman

MAXINE HONG KINGSTON

Maxine Hong Kingston was born in Stockton, California, in 1940. Her father came first to America from China and then sent for her mother. Maxine is the oldest of six children and grew up around the family dry cleaning business, which became a magnet for Chinese immigrants who brought their many village stories. As she learned to speak English in school, her ideas mingled in Chinese and in English. She attended the University of California at Berkeley, married Earll Kingston, and later moved to Hawaii.

She became deeply impressed with gender disparities in Chinese culture, and her stories combine Chinese and American cultures—past and present—fact and fiction, and valiant female and male heroes. In 1976 she received the National Book Critics Circle recognition for *The Warrior Woman.*

You must not tell anyone," my mother said, "what I am about to tell you. In China your father had a sister who killed herself. She jumped into the family well. We say that your father has all brothers because it is as if she had never been born.

2   "In 1924 just a few days after our village celebrated seventeen hurry-up weddings—to make sure that every young man who went 'out on the road' would responsibly come home—your father and his brothers and your grandfather and his brothers and your aunt's new husband sailed for America, the Gold Mountain. It was your grandfather's last trip. Those lucky enough to get contracts waved goodbye from the decks. They fed and guarded the stowaways and helped them off in Cuba, New York, Bali, Hawaii. 'We'll meet in California next year,' they said. All of them sent money home.

3   "I remember looking at your aunt one day when she and I were dressing; I had not noticed before that she had such a protruding melon of a stomach. But I did not think, 'She's pregnant,' until she began to look like other pregnant women, her shirt pulling and the white tops of her black pants showing. She could not have been pregnant, you see, because her husband had been gone for years. No one said anything. We did not discuss it. In early summer she was ready to have the child, long after the time when it could have been possible.

4   "The village had also been counting. On the night the baby was to be born the villagers raided our house. Some were crying. Like a great saw, teeth strung with lights, files of people walked zigzag across our land, tearing the rice. Their lanterns doubled in the disturbed black

water, which drained away through the broken bunds. As the villagers closed in, we could see that some of them, probably men and women we knew well, wore white masks. The people with long hair hung it over their faces. Women with short hair made it stand up on end. Some had tied white bands around their foreheads, arms, and legs.

5   "At first they threw mud and rocks at the house. Then they threw eggs and began slaughtering our stock. We could hear the animals scream their deaths—the roosters, the pigs, a last great roar from the ox. Familiar wild heads flared in our night windows; the villagers encircled us. Some of the faces stopped to peer at us, their eyes rushing like searchlights. The hands flattened against the panes, framed heads, and left red prints.

6   "The villagers broke in the front and the back doors at the same time, even though we had not locked the doors against them. Their knives dripped with the blood of our animals. They smeared blood on the doors and walls. One woman swung a chicken, whose throat she had slit, splattering blood in red arcs about her. We stood together in the middle of our house, in the family hall with the pictures and tables of the ancestors around us, and looked straight ahead.

7   "At that time the house had only two wings. When the men came back, we would build two more to enclose our courtyard and a third one to begin a second courtyard. The villagers pushed through both wings, even your grandparents' rooms, to find your aunt's, which was also mine until the men returned. From this room a new wing for one of the younger families would grow. They ripped up her clothes and shoes and broke her combs, grinding them underfoot. They tore her work from the loom. They scattered the cooking fire and rolled the new weaving in it. We could hear them in the kitchen breaking our bowls and banging the pots. They overturned the great waist-high earthenware jugs; duck eggs, pickled fruits, vegetables burst out and mixed in acrid torrents. The old woman from the next field swept a broom through the air and loosed the spirits-of-the-broom over our heads. 'Pig.' 'Ghost.' 'Pig,' they sobbed and scolded while they ruined our house.

8   "When they left, they took sugar and oranges to bless themselves. They cut pieces from the dead animals. Some of them took bowls that were not broken and clothes that were not torn. Afterward we swept up the rice and sewed it back up into sacks. But the smells from the spilled preserves lasted. Your aunt gave birth in the pigsty that night. The next morning when I went for the water, I found her and the baby plugging up the family well.

9   "Don't let your father know that I told you. He denies her. Now that you have started to menstruate, what happened to her could

happen to you. Don't humiliate us. You wouldn't like to be forgotten as if you had never been born. The villagers are watchful."

10   Whenever she had to warn us about life, my mother told stories that ran like this one, a story to grow up on. She tested our strength to establish realities. Those in the emigrant generations who could not reassert brute survival died young and far from home. Those of us in the first American generations have had to figure out how the invisible world the emigrants built around our childhoods fits in solid America.

11   The emigrants confused the gods by diverting their curses, misleading them with crooked streets and false names. They must try to confuse their offspring as well, who, I suppose, threaten them in similar ways—always trying to get things straight, always trying to name the unspeakable. The Chinese I know hide their names; sojourners take new names when their lives change and guard their real names with silence.

12   Chinese-Americans, when you try to understand what things in you are Chinese, how do you separate what is peculiar to childhood, to poverty, insanities, one family, your mother who marked your growing with stories, from what is Chinese? What is Chinese tradition and what is the movies?

13   If I want to learn what clothes my aunt wore, whether flashy or ordinary, I would have to begin, "Remember Father's drowned-in-the-well sister?" I cannot ask that. My mother has told me once and for all the useful parts. She will add nothing unless powered by Necessity, a riverbank that guides her life. She plants vegetable gardens rather than lawns; she carries the odd-shaped tomatoes home from the fields and eats food left for the gods.

14   Whenever we did frivolous things, we used up energy; we flew high kites. We children came up off the ground over the melting cones our parents brought home from work and the American movie on New Year's Day—*Oh, You Beautiful Doll* with Betty Grable one year, and *She Wore a Yellow Ribbon* with John Wayne another year. After the one carnival ride each, we paid in guilt; our tired father counted his change on the dark walk home.

15   Adultery is extravagance. Could people who hatch their own chicks and eat the embryos and the heads for delicacies and boil the feet in vinegar for party food, leaving only the gravel, eating even the gizzard lining—could such people engender a prodigal aunt? To be a woman, to have a daughter in starvation time was a waste enough. My aunt could not have been the lone romantic who gave up everything for sex. Women in the old China did not choose. Some man had com-

manded her to lie with him and be his secret evil. I wonder whether he masked himself when he joined the raid on her family.

16   Perhaps she had encountered him in the fields or on the mountain where the daughters-in-law collected fuel. Or perhaps he first noticed her in the marketplace. He was not a stranger because the village housed no strangers. She had to have dealings with him other than sex. Perhaps he worked an adjoining field, or he sold her the cloth for the dress she sewed and wore. His demand must have surprised, then terrified her. She obeyed him; she always did as she was told.

17   When the family found a young man in the next village to be her husband, she had stood tractably beside the best rooster, his proxy, and promised before they met that she would be his forever. She was lucky that he was her age and she would be the first wife, an advantage secure now. The night she first saw him, he had sex with her. Then he left for America. She had almost forgotten what he looked like. When she tried to envision him, she only saw the black and white face in the group photograph the men had had taken before leaving.

18   The other man was not, after all, much different from her husband. They both gave orders: she followed. "If you tell your family, I'll beat you. I'll kill you. Be here again next week." No one talked sex, ever. And she might have separated the rapes from the rest of living if only she did not have to buy her oil from him or gather wood in the same forest. I want her fear to have lasted just as long as rape lasted so that the fear could have been contained. No drawnout fear. But women at sex hazarded birth and hence lifetimes. The fear did not stop but permeated everywhere. She told the man, "I think I'm pregnant." He organized the raid against her.

19   On nights when my mother and father talked about their life back home, sometimes they mentioned an "outcast table" whose business they still seemed to be settling, their voices tight. In a commensal tradition, where food is precious, the powerful older people made wrongdoers eat alone. Instead of letting them start separate new lives like the Japanese, who could become samurais and geishas, the Chinese family, faces averted but eyes glowering sideways, hung on to the offenders and fed them leftovers. My aunt must have lived in the same house as my parents and eaten at an outcast table. My mother spoke about the raid as if she had seen it, when she and my aunt, a daughter-in-law to a different household, should not have been living together at all. Daughters-in-law lived with their husbands' parents, not their own; a synonym for marriage in Chinese is "taking a daughter-in-law." Her husband's parents could have sold her, mortgaged her, stoned her. But

they had sent her back to her own mother and father, a mysterious act
hinting at disgraces not told me. Perhaps they had thrown her out to
deflect the avengers.

20   She was the only daughter; her four brothers went with her father,
husband, and uncles "out on the road" and for some years became
western men. When the goods were divided among the family, three of
the brothers took land, and the youngest, my father, chose an education. After my grandparents gave their daughter away to her husband's
family, they had dispensed all the adventure and all the property. They
expected her alone to keep the traditional ways, which her brothers,
now among the barbarians, could fumble without detection. The
heavy, deep-rooted women were to maintain the past against the flood,
safe for returning. But the rare urge west had fixed upon our family, and
so my aunt crossed boundaries not delineated in space.

21   The work of preservation demands that the feelings playing about
in one's guts not be turned into action. Just watch their passing like
cherry blossoms. But perhaps my aunt, my forerunner, caught in a slow
life, let dreams grow and fade and after some months or years went
toward what persisted. Fear at the enormities of the forbidden kept her
desires delicate, wire and bone. She looked at a man because she liked
the way the hair was tucked behind his ears, or she liked the question-
mark line of a long torso curving at the shoulder and straight at the hip.
For warm eyes or a soft voice or a slow walk—that's all—a few hairs, a
line, a brightness, a sound, a pace, she gave up family. She offered us up
for a charm that vanished with tiredness, a pigtail that didn't toss
when the wind died. Why, the wrong lighting could erase the dearest
thing about him.

22   It could very well have been, however, that my aunt did not take
subtle enjoyment of her friend, but, a wild woman, kept rollicking
company. Imagining her free with sex doesn't fit, though. I don't know
any women like that, or men either. Unless I see her life branching into
mine, she gives me no ancestral help.

23   To sustain her being in love, she often worked at herself in the mirror, guessing at the colors and shapes that would interest him, changing them frequently in order to hit on the right combination. She
wanted him to look back.

24   On a farm near the sea, a woman who tended her appearance
reaped a reputation for eccentricity. All the married women blunt-cut
their hair in flaps about their ears or pulled it back in tight buns. No
nonsense. Neither style blew easily into heart-catching tangles. And at
their weddings they displayed themselves in their long hair for the last

time. "It brushed the backs of my knees," my mother tells me. "It was braided, and even so, it brushed the backs of my knees."

25   At the mirror my aunt combed individuality into her bob. A bun could have been contrived to escape into black streamers blowing in the wind or in quiet wisps about her face, but only the older women in our picture album wear buns. She brushed her hair back from her forehead, tucking the flaps behind her ears. She looped a piece of thread, knotted into a circle between her index fingers and thumbs, and ran the double strand across her forehead. When she closed her fingers as if she were making a pair of shadow geese bite, the string twisted together catching the little hairs. Then she pulled the thread away from her skin, ripping the hairs out neatly, her eyes watering from the needles of pain. Opening her fingers, she cleaned the thread, then rolled it along her hairline and the tops of her eyebrows. My mother did the same to me and my sisters and herself. I used to believe that the expression "caught by the short hairs" meant a captive held with a depilatory string. It especially hurt at the temples, but my mother said we were lucky we didn't have to have our feet bound when we were seven. Sisters used to sit on their beds and cry together, she said, as their mothers or their slaves removed the bandages for a few minutes each night and let the blood gush back into their veins. I hope that the man my aunt loved appreciated a smooth brow, that he wasn't just a tits-and-ass man.

26   Once my aunt found a freckle on her chin, at a spot that the almanac said predestined her for unhappiness. She dug it out with a hot needle and washed the wound with peroxide.

27   More attention to her looks than these pullings of hairs and pickings at spots would have caused gossip among the villagers. They owned work clothes and good clothes, and they wore good clothes for feasting the new seasons. But since a woman combing her hair hexes beginnings, my aunt rarely found an occasion to look her best. Women looked like great sea snails—the corded wood, babies, and laundry they carried were the whorls on their backs. The Chinese did not admire a bent back; goddesses and warriors stood straight. Still there must have been a marvelous freeing of beauty when a worker laid down her burden and stretched and arched.

28   Such commonplace loveliness, however, was not enough for my aunt. She dreamed of a lover for the fifteen days of New Year's, the time for families to exchange visits, money, and food. She plied her secret comb. And sure enough she cursed the year, the family, the village, and herself.

29   Even as her hair lured her imminent lover, many other men looked at her. Uncles, cousins, nephews, brothers would have looked, too, had they been home between journeys. Perhaps they had already been restraining their curiosity, and they left, fearful that their glances, like a field of nesting birds, might be startled and caught. Poverty hurt, and that was their first reason for leaving. But another, final reason for leaving the crowded house was the never-said.

30   She may have been unusually beloved, the precious only daughter, spoiled and mirror gazing because of the affection the family lavished on her. When her husband left, they welcomed the chance to take her back from the in-laws; she could live like the little daughter for just a while longer. There are stories that my grandfather was different from other people, "crazy ever since the little Jap bayoneted him in the head." He used to put his naked penis on the dinner table, laughing. And one day he brought home a baby girl, wrapped up inside his brown western-style greatcoat. He had traded one of his sons, probably my father, the youngest, for her. My grandmother made him trade back. When he finally got a daughter of his own, he doted on her. They must have all loved her, except perhaps my father, the only brother who never went back to China, having once been traded for a girl.

31   Brothers and sisters, newly men and women, had to efface their sexual color and present plain miens. Disturbing hair and eyes, a smile like no other, threatened the ideal of five generations living under one roof. To focus blurs, people shouted face to face and yelled from room to room. The immigrants I know have loud voices, unmodulated to American tones even after years away from the village where they called their friendships out across the fields. I have not been able to stop my mother's screams in public libraries or over telephones. Walking erect (knees straight, toes pointed forward, not pigeon-toed, which is Chinese-feminine) and speaking in an inaudible voice, I have tried to turn myself American-feminine. Chinese communication was loud, public. Only sick people had to whisper. But at the dinner table, where the family members came nearest one another, no one could talk, not the outcasts nor any eaters. Every word that falls from the mouth is a coin lost. Silently they gave and accepted food with both hands. A preoccupied child who took his bowl with one hand got a sideways glare. A complete moment of total attention is due everyone alike. Children and lovers have no singularity here, but my aunt used a secret voice, a separate attentiveness.

32   She kept the man's name to herself throughout her labor and dying; she did not accuse him that he be punished with her. To save her inseminator's name she gave silent birth.

33   He may have been somebody in her own household, but inter-course with a man outside the family would have been no less abhor-rent. All the village were kinsmen, and the titles shouted in loud coun-try voices never let kinship be forgotten. Any man within visiting distance would have been neutralized as a lover—"brother," "younger brother," "older brother"—one hundred and fifteen relationship titles. Parents researched birth charts probably not so much to assure good fortune as to circumvent incest in a population that has but one hun-dred surnames. Everybody has eight million relatives. How useless then sexual mannerisms, how dangerous.

34   As if it came from an atavism deeper than fear, I used to add "brother" silently to boys' names. It hexed the boys, who would or would not ask me to dance, and made them less scary and as familiar and deserving of benevolence as girls.

35   But, of course, I hexed myself also—no dates. I should have stood up, both arms waving, and shouted out across libraries, "Hey, you! Love me back." I had no idea, though, how to make attraction selec-tive, how to control its direction and magnitude. If I made myself American-pretty so that the five or six Chinese boys in the class fell in love with me, everyone else—the Caucasian, Negro, and Japanese boys—would too. Sisterliness, dignified and honorable, made much more sense.

36   Attraction eludes control so stubbornly that whole societies designed to organize relationships among people cannot keep order, not even when they bind people to one another from childhood and raise them together. Among the very poor and the wealthy, brothers married their adopted sisters, like doves. Our family allowed some romance, paying adult brides' prices and providing dowries so that their sons and daughters could marry strangers. Marriage promises to turn strangers into friendly relatives—a nation of siblings.

37   In the village structure, spirits shimmered among the live crea-tures, balanced and held in equilibrium by time and land. But one human being flaring up into violence could open up a black hole, a maelstrom that pulled in the sky. The frightened villagers, who depended on one another to maintain the real, went to my aunt to show her a personal, physical representation of the break she had made in the "roundness." Misallying couples snapped off the future, which was to be embodied in true offspring. The villagers punished her for acting as if she could have a private life, secret and apart from them.

38   If my aunt had betrayed the family at a time of large grain yields and peace, when many boys were born, and wings were being built on many houses, perhaps she might have escaped such severe punishment. But

the men—hungry, greedy, tired of planting in dry soil—had been forced to leave the village in order to send food-money home. There were ghost plagues, bandit plagues, wars with the Japanese, floods. My Chinese brother and sister had died of an unknown sickness. Adultery, perhaps only a mistake during good times, became a crime when the village needed food.

39   The round moon cakes and round doorways, the round tables of graduated sizes that fit one roundness inside another, round windows and rice bowls—these talismans had lost their power to warn this family of the law: a family must be whole, faithfully keeping the descent line by having sons to feed the old and the dead, who in turn look after the family. The villagers came to show my aunt and her lover-in-hiding a broken house. The villagers were speeding up the circling of events because she was too shortsighted to see that her infidelity had already harmed the village, that waves of consequences would return unpredictably, sometimes in disguise, as now, to hurt her. This roundness had to be made coin-sized so that she would see its circumference: punish her at the birth of her baby. Awaken her to the inexorable. People who refused fatalism because they could invent small resources insisted on culpability. Deny accidents and wrest fault from the stars.

40   After the villagers left, their lanterns now scattering in various directions toward home, the family broke their silence and cursed her. "Aiaa, we're going to die. Death is coming. Death is coming. Look what you've done. You've killed us. Ghost! Dead ghost! Ghost! You've never been born." She ran out into the fields, far enough from the house so that she could no longer hear their voices, and pressed herself against the earth, her own land no more. When she felt the birth coming, she thought that she had been hurt. Her body seized together. "They've hurt me too much," she thought. "This is gall, and it will kill me." With forehead and knees against the earth, her body convulsed and then relaxed. She turned on her back, lay on the ground. The black well of sky and stars went out and out and out forever; her body and her complexity seemed to disappear. She was one of the stars, a bright dot in blackness, without home, without a companion, in eternal cold and silence. An agoraphobia rose in her, speeding higher and higher, bigger and bigger; she would not be able to contain it; there would no end to fear.

41   Flayed, unprotected against space, she felt pain return, focusing her body. This pain chilled her—a cold, steady kind of surface pain. Inside, spasmodically, the other pain, the pain of the child, heated her. For hours she lay on the ground, alternately body and space. Sometimes a vision of normal comfort obliterated reality: she saw the family in the

evening gambling at the dinner table, the young people massaging their elders' backs. She saw them congratulating one another, high joy on the mornings the rice shoots came up. When these pictures burst, the stars drew yet further apart. Black space opened.

42   She got to her feet to fight better and remembered that old-fashioned women gave birth in their pigsties to fool the jealous, pain-dealing gods, who do not snatch piglets. Before the next spasms could stop her, she ran to the pigsty, each step a rushing out into emptiness. She climbed over the fence and knelt in the dirt. It was good to have a fence enclosing her, a tribal person alone.

43   Laboring, this woman who had carried her child as a foreign growth that sickened her every day, expelled it at last. She reached down to touch the hot, wet, moving mass, surely smaller than any-thing human, and could feel that it was human after all—fingers, toes, nails, nose. She pulled it up on to her belly, and it lay curled there, butt in the air, feet precisely tucked one under the other. She opened her loose shirt and buttoned the child inside. After resting, it squirmed and thrashed and she pushed it up to her breast. It turned its head this way and that until it found her nipple. There, it made little snuffling noises. She clenched her teeth at its preciousness, lovely as a young calf, a piglet, a little dog.

44   She may have gone to the pigsty as a last act of responsibility: she would protect this child as she had protected its father. It would look after her soul, leaving supplies on her grave. But how would this tiny child without family find her grave when there would be no marker for her anywhere, neither in the earth nor the family hall? No one would give her a family hall name. She had taken the child with her into the wastes. At its birth the two of them had felt the same raw pain of sepa-ration, a wound that only the family pressing tight could close. A child with no descent line would not soften her life but only trail after her, ghostlike, begging her to give it purpose. At dawn the villagers on their way to the fields would stand around the fence and look.

45   Full of milk, the little ghost slept. When it awoke, she hardened her breasts against the milk that crying loosens. Toward morning she picked up the baby and walked to the well.

46   Carrying the baby to the well shows loving. Otherwise abandon it. Turn its face into the mud. Mothers who love their children take them along. It was probably a girl; there is some hope of forgiveness for boys.

47   "Don't tell anyone you had an aunt. Your father does not want to hear her name. She has never been born." I have believed that sex was unspeakable and words so strong and fathers so frail that "aunt" would

do my father mysterious harm. I have thought that my family, having settled among immigrants who had also been their neighbors in the ancestral land, needed to clean their name, and a wrong word would incite the kinspeople even here. But there is more to this silence: they want me to participate in her punishment. And I have.

48   In the twenty years since I heard this story I have not asked for details nor said my aunt's name; I do not know it. People who can comfort the dead can also chase after them to hurt them further—a reverse ancestor worship. The real punishment was not the raid swiftly inflicted by the villagers, but the family's deliberately forgetting her. Her betrayal so maddened them, they saw to it that she would suffer forever, even after death. Always hungry, always needing, she would have to beg food from other ghosts, snatch and steal it from those whose living descendants give them gifts. She would have to fight the ghosts massed at crossroads for the buns a few thoughtful citizens leave to decoy her away from village and home so that the ancestral spirits could feast unharassed. At peace, they could act like gods, not ghosts, their descent lines providing them with paper suits and dresses, spirit money, paper houses, paper automobiles, chicken, meat, and rice into eternity—essences delivered up in smoke and flames, steam and incense rising from each rice bowl. In an attempt to make the Chinese care for people outside the family, Chairman Mao encourages us now to give our paper replicas to the spirits of outstanding soldiers and workers, no matter whose ancestors they may be. My aunt remains forever hungry. Goods are not distributed evenly among the dead.

49   My aunt haunts me—her ghost drawn to me because now, after fifty years of neglect, I alone devote pages of paper to her, though not origamied into houses and clothes. I do not think she always means me well. I am telling on her, and she was a spite suicide, drowning herself in the drinking water. The Chinese are always very frightened of the drowned one, whose weeping ghost, wet hair hanging and skin bloated, waits silently by the water to pull down a substitute.

No Name Woman

JOURNAL

1. MLA Works Cited

Using this model, record this story here.

Author's Last Name, First Name. "Title of the Story." <u>Title of the Book</u>. Ed. First Last Name. City: Publisher, year. Pages of the story.

2. Main Character(s)

Describe each main character, and explain why you think each is a main character.

3. Supporting Characters

Describe each supporting character, and explain why you think each is a supporting character.

4. Setting

Describe the setting. Decide if the setting can be changed and, if so, to where and when.

5. Sequence

Relate the events of the story in order.

6. Plot

Tell the story in no more than three sentences.

7. Conflicts

Identify and explain the conflicts involved here.

8. Significant Quotations

Explain the importance of each of these quotations. Record the page number in the parentheses.

a. " 'No one said anything. [. . .] In early summer she was ready to have the child, long after the time when it could have been possible' " (   ).

b. " 'Pig.' 'Ghost.' 'Pig,' they sobbed and scolded while they ruined our house" (   ).

c. "Perhaps she had encountered him in the fields or on the mountain where the daughters-in-law collected fuel" (   ).

d. "To save her inseminator's name she gave silent birth" (   ).

e. "It was probably a girl; there is some hope of forgiveness for boys" (   ).

9. Foreshadowing

Identify and explain the hints you are given about the story's ending.

FOLLOW-UP QUESTIONS

10 SHORT QUESTIONS

Select the <u>best</u> answer for each.

____ 1. The narrator lives in
   a. Japan.
   b. China.
   c. America.

____ 2. The narrator's father
   a. has lived in China.
   b. has not lived in China.
   c. has never lived in China.

____ 3. The aunt
   a. is married to the baby's father.
   b. is not married to the baby's father.
   c. does not know the baby's father.

____ 4. The villagers
   a. attack the house.
   b. attack the aunt.
   c. kill the aunt.

____ 5. The No Name Woman probably
   a. knows the father of her baby.
   b. does not know the father of her baby.
   c. has never seen the father of her baby before.

____ 6. We
   a. are sure that the aunt was raped.
   b. are not sure that the aunt was raped.
   c. are clearly told that the aunt was raped.

____ 7. We
   a. are sure that the aunt lured the baby's father.
   b. are not sure that the aunt lured the baby's father.
   c. are clearly told that the aunt lured the baby's father.

____ 8. The aunt
   a. thinks that the villagers approve of her.
   b. cares if the villagers approve of her.
   c. does not care if the villagers approve of her.

____ 9. The aunt
   a. hates the baby.
   b. does not care for the baby.
   c. cares for the baby.

____ 10. The aunt
   a. is killed.
   b. commits suicide.
   c. kills herself and her baby.

5 SIGNIFICANT QUOTATIONS

Explain the importance of each of these quotations.

1. " 'She jumped into the family well.' "

2. " 'The villagers broke in the front and the back doors at the same time, even though we had not locked the doors against them.' "

3. "He was not a stranger because the village housed no strangers."

4. "She kept the man's name to herself throughout her labor and dying; she did not accuse him that he be punished with her."

5. "Full of milk, the little ghost slept."

2 COMPREHENSION ESSAY QUESTIONS

Use specific details and information from the story to answer these as completely as possible.

1. How does the woman come to be called the "No Name Woman"? Use specific details and information from the story to support your explanation.

2. Explain the role of discrimination in this story. Use specific details and information from the story to support your explanation.

WRITING

Use each of these ideas for writing an essay.

1. Here we see the severe cruelty of ostracism, but we have all felt left out at one time or another. Write an essay telling about a time you were left out.

2. Families and/or communities often treat males and females differently. Write an essay about one time you or someone you know was treated differently, based on sex.

Further Writing

1. Compare and contrast the No Name Woman in this story with Tessie Hutchinson in Shirley Jackson's "The Lottery" (page 243).

2. Compare and contrast the No Name Woman in this story with Nancy Lee in Langston Hughes's "One Friday Morning" (page 207).

The Lottery

Shirley Jackson

Pre-reading Vocabulary
Context

Use context clues to define these words before reading. Use a dictionary as needed.

1. The stores, the churches, and all the activity centered around the *village square. Village square* means *the center of a village*

2. Taking a chance on winning a million, Margaret bought a *lottery* ticket. *Lottery* means *a contest of chance.*

3. The students all *assembled* in the gym for the basketball game. *Assemble* means *come together* .

4. The loud children were so *boisterous* that the neighbors called the police to keep them quiet. *Boisterous* means *loud, noisy* .

5. Ted takes *civic* pride in being a resident of Sea Girt, a town he truly loves. *Civic* means *citizenship* .

6. Fearing it would be bad news, Ahmed *hesitated* and did not answer the phone right away. *Hesitate* means *reluctant* .

7. Maria collected the wrapping paper, ribbons, boxes, and all the *paraphernalia* she needed for the gifts. *Paraphernalia* means *articles; personal belonging* .

8. Decorating a tree and giving gifts at Christmas are Christian traditions. *Tradition* means *passing down from Gen to Gen* .

9. The sisters will *represent* their relatives who can't come to the wedding. *Represent* means *to stand for; symbolize* .

10. With the paint peeling and the siding falling off, the little old house looked *shabby*. *Shabby* means ___worn down, falling about___

11. Grandmother, mother, and daughter represent three *generations*. *Generation* means ___offspring from a common ancestor___

12. Neal faced the problem seriously and *soberly*. *Soberly* means ___solemn___.

13. We often go through daily routines *perfunctorily*, carrying them out without thinking or caring. *Perfunctory* means ___routine___.

14. The lecturer seemed to go on *interminably* and to speak for hours when he only spoke for minutes. *Interminably* means ___long time___.

15. Roger will try to *duck out* of cleaning the pool by not going home until late. *Duck out* means ___get out___.

16. Bonnie was *defiant* and refused to pay the entry fee. *Defiant* means ___resistance. Not willing to. opposing___

17. When Tricia opened the gift card, it was *blank* with no writing on it; as a result, she did not know who sent the gift. *Blank* means ___nothing on it; empty___.

18. When David bought everyone new cars, it caused quite a *stir* in the family. *Stir* means ___upset; confusing___.

19. After swimming underwater for quite awhile, Bill came up *gasping* for air. *Gasping* means ___out of breath___.

20. The criminal wanted *desperately* to escape the electric chair. *Desperately* means ___nearly hopeless; last resort___.

PRE-READING VOCABULARY
WORD ATTACK

Define these words by solving the parts. Use a dictionary as needed.

1. full-summer
2. uneasily
3. menfolk
4. round-faced
5. underfoot
6. household
7. swearing-in
8. carelessly
9. hurriedly
10. good-humoredly
11. cheerfully
12. regretfully
13. nervously
14. humorlessly
15. breathless
16. willingly
17. wonderingly
18. heavily

PRE-READING QUESTIONS

Try answering these questions as you read.

What has to be done for the lottery?

Who are the characters in the story?

How does the lottery change?

What clues does Jackson give you to predict the end?

The Lottery

SHIRLEY JACKSON

Shirley Jackson was born in 1919 in San Francisco and raised in California. She later attended Syracuse University. Eight years after marrying literary critic Stanley Edgar Hyman, she published *The Road Through the Wall*. She enjoyed early recognition, and "The Lottery" remains typical of her fascination with combining fantasy with terror. Other works include *Life Among the Savages* and *Raising Demons*. Jackson died in 1965 in Bennington, Vermont.

The morning of June 27th was clear and sunny, with the fresh warmth of a full-summer day; the flowers were blossoming profusely and the grass was richly, green. The people of the village began to gather in the square, between the post office and the bank, around ten o'clock; in some towns there were so many people that the lottery took two days and had to be started on June 26th, but in this village, where there were only about three hundred people, the whole lottery took less than two hours, so it could begin at ten o'clock in the morning and still be through in time to allow the villagers to get home for noon dinner.

2   The children assembled first, of course. School was recently over for the summer, and the feeling of liberty sat uneasily on most of them; they tended to gather together quietly for a while before they broke into boisterous play, and their talk was still of the classroom and the teacher, of books and reprimands. Bobby Martin had already stuffed his pockets full of stones, and the other boys soon followed his example, selecting the smoothest and roundest stones; Bobby and Harry Jones and Dickie Delacroix—the villagers pronounced this name "Dellacroy"—eventually made a great pile of stones in one corner of the square and guarded it against the raids of the other boys. The girls stood aside, talking among themselves, looking over their shoulders at the boys, and the very small children rolled in the dust or clung to the hands of their older brothers or sisters.

3   Soon the men began to gather, surveying their own children, speaking of planting and rain, tractors and taxes. They stood together, away from the pile of stones in the corner, and their jokes were quiet and they smiled rather than laughed. The women, wearing faded house dresses and sweaters, came shortly after their menfolk. They greeted one another and exchanged bits of gossip as they went to join their husbands. Soon the women, standing by their husbands, began to call to

their children, and the children came reluctantly, having to be called four or five times. Bobby Martin ducked under his mother's grasping hand and ran, laughing, back to the pile of stones. His father spoke up sharply, and Bobby came quickly and took his place between his father and his oldest brother.

4   The lottery was conducted—as were the square dances, the teenage club, the Halloween program—by Mr. Summers, who had time and energy to devote to civic activities. He was a round-faced, jovial man and he ran the coal business, and people were sorry for him, because he had no children and his wife was a scold. When he arrived in the square, carrying the black wooden box, there was a murmur of conversation among the villagers and he waved and called, "Little late today, folks." The postmaster, Mr. Graves, followed him, carrying a three-legged stool, and the stool was put in the center of the square and Mr. Summers set the black box down on it. The villagers kept their distance, leaving a space between themselves and the stool, and when Mr. Summers said, "Some of you fellows want to give me a hand?" there was a hesitation before two men, Mr. Martin and his oldest son, Baxter, came forward to hold the box steady on the stool while Mr. Summers stirred up the papers inside it.

5   The original paraphernalia for the lottery had been lost long ago, and the black box now resting on the stool had been put into use even before Old Man Warner, the oldest man in town, was born. Mr. Summers spoke frequently to the villagers about making a new box, but no one liked to upset even as much tradition as was represented by the black box. There was a story that the present box had been made with some pieces of the box that had preceded it, the one that had been constructed when the first people settled down to make a village here. Every year, after the lottery, Mr. Summers began talking again about a new box, but every year the subject was allowed to fade off without anything's being done. The black box grew shabbier each year; by now it was no longer completely black but splintered badly along one side to show the original wood color, and in some places faded or stained.

6   Mr. Martin and his oldest son, Baxter, held the black box securely on the stool until Mr. Summers had stirred the papers thoroughly with his hand. Because so much of the ritual had been forgotten or discarded, Mr. Summers had been successful in having slips of paper substituted for the chips of wood that had been used for generations. Chips of wood, Mr. Summers had argued, had been all very well when the village was tiny, but now that the population was more than three hundred and likely to keep on growing, it was necessary to use something that would fit more easily into the black box. The night before the lot-

tery, Mr. Summers and Mr. Graves made up the slips of paper and put them in the box, and it was then taken to the safe of Mr. Summers's coal company and locked up until Mr. Summers was ready to take it to the square next morning. The rest of the year, the box was put away, sometimes one place, sometimes another; it had spent one year in Mr. Graves's barn and another year underfoot in the post office, and sometimes it was set on a shelf in the Martin grocery and left there.

7   There was a great deal of fussing to be done before Mr. Summers declared the lottery open. There were lists to make up—of heads of families, heads of households in each family, members of each household in each family. There was the proper swearing-in of Mr. Summers by the postmaster, as the official of the lottery; at one time, some people remembered, there had been a recital of some sort, performed by the official of the lottery, a perfunctory, tuneless chant that had been rattled off duly each year; some people believed that the official of the lottery used to stand just so when he said or sang it, others believed that he was supposed to walk among the people, but years and years ago this part of the ritual had been allowed to lapse. There had been, also, a ritual salute, which the official of the lottery had had to use in addressing each person who came up to draw from the box, but this also had changed with time, until now it was felt necessary only for the official to speak to each person approaching. Mr. Summers was very good at all this; in his clean white shirt and blue jeans, with one hand resting carelessly on the black box, he seemed very proper and important as he talked interminably to Mr. Graves and the Martins.

8   Just as Mr. Summers finally left off talking and turned to the assembled villagers, Mrs. Hutchinson came hurriedly along the path to the square, her sweater thrown over her shoulders, and slid into place in the back of the crowd. "Clean forgot what day it was," she said to Mrs. Delacroix, who stood next to her, and they both laughed softly. "Thought my old man was out back stacking wood," Mrs. Hutchinson went on, "and then I looked out the window and the kids were gone, and then I remembered it was the twenty-seventh and came a-running." She dried her hands on her apron, and Mrs. Delacroix said, "You're in time, though. They're still talking away up there."

9   Mrs. Hutchinson craned her neck to see through the crowd and found her husband and children standing near the front. She tapped Mrs. Delacroix on the arm as a farewell and began to make her way through the crowd. The people separated good-humoredly to let her through; two or three people said, in voices just loud enough to be heard across the crowd, "Here comes your Missus, Hutchinson," and "Bill, she made it after all." Mrs. Hutchinson reached her husband, and

Mr. Summers, who had been waiting, said cheerfully, "Thought we were going to have to get on without you, Tessie." Mrs. Hutchinson said, grinning, "Wouldn't have me leave m'dishes in the sink, now would you, Joe?" and soft laughter ran through the crowd as the people stirred back into position after Mrs. Hutchinson's arrival.

10   "Well, now," Mr. Summers said, soberly, "guess we better get started, get this over with, so's we can go back to work. Anybody ain't here?"

11   "Dunbar," several people said. "Dunbar, Dunbar."

12   Mr. Summers consulted his list. "Clyde Dunbar," he said. "That's right. He's broke his leg, hasn't he? Who's drawing for him?"

13   "Me, I guess," a woman said, and Mr. Summers turned to look at her. "Wife draws for her husband," Mr. Summers said. "Don't you have a grown boy to do it for you, Janey?" Although Mr. Summers and everyone else in the village knew the answer perfectly well, it was the business of the official of the lottery to ask such questions formally. Mr. Summers waited with an expression of polite interest while Mrs. Dunbar answered.

14   "Horace's not but sixteen yet," Mrs. Dunbar said regretfully. "Guess I gotta fill in for the old man this year."

15   "Right," Mr. Summers said. He made a note on the list he was holding. Then he asked, "Watson boy drawing this year?"

16   A tall boy in the crowd raised his hand. "Here," he said. "I'm drawing for m'mother and me." He blinked his eyes nervously and ducked his head as several voices in the crowd said things like "Good fellow, Jack," and "Glad to see your mother's got a man to do it."

17   "Well," Mr. Summers said, "guess that's everyone. Old Man Warner make it?"

18   "Here," a voice said, and Mr. Summers nodded.

19   A sudden hush fell on the crowd as Mr. Summers cleared his throat and looked at the list. "All ready?" he called. "Now, I'll read the names—heads of families first—and the men come up and take a paper out of the box. Keep the paper folded in your hand without looking at it until everyone has had a turn. Everything clear?"

20   The people had done it so many times that they only half listened to the directions, most of them were quiet, wetting their lips, not looking around. Then Mr. Summers raised one hand high and said, "Adams." A man disengaged himself from the crowd and came forward. "Hi, Steve," Mr. Summers said, and Mr. Adams said, "Hi, Joe." They grinned at one another humorlessly and nervously. Then Mr. Adams reached into the black box and took out a folded paper. He held it firmly by one corner as he turned and went hastily back to his place

in the crowd, where he stood a little apart from his family, not looking down at his hand.

21   "Allen," Mr. Summers said. "Anderson. . . . Bentham."

22   "Seems like there's no time at all between lotteries any more," Mrs. Delacroix said to Mrs. Graves in the back row. "Seems like we got through with the last one only last week."

23   "Time sure goes fast," Mrs. Graves said.

24   "Clark. . . . Delacroix."

25   "There goes my old man," Mrs. Delacroix said. She held her breath while her husband went forward.

26   "Dunbar," Mr. Summers said, and Mrs. Dunbar went steadily to the box while one of the women said, "Go on, Janey," and another said, "There she goes."

27   "We're next," Mrs. Graves said. She watched while Mr. Graves came around from the side of the box, greeted Mr. Summers gravely, and selected a slip of paper from the box. By now, all through the crowd there were men holding the small folded papers in their large hands, turning them over and over nervously. Mrs. Dunbar and her two sons stood together, Mrs. Dunbar holding the slip of paper.

28   "Harburt. . . . Hutchinson."

29   "Get up there, Bill," Mrs. Hutchinson said, and the people near her laughed.

30   "Jones."

31   "They do say," Mr. Adams said to Old Man Warner, who stood next to him, "that over in the north village they're talking of giving up the lottery."

32   Old Man Warner snorted, "Pack of crazy fools," he said. "Listening to the young folks, nothing's good enough for *them*. Next thing you know, they'll be wanting to go back to living in caves, nobody work any more, live *that* way for a while. Used to be a saying about 'Lottery in June, corn be heavy soon.' First thing you know, we'd all be eating stewed chickweed and acorns. There's *always* been a lottery," he added petulantly. "Bad enough to see young Joe Summers up there joking with everybody."

33   "Some places have already quit lotteries," Mrs. Adams said.

34   "Nothing but trouble in *that*," Old Man Warner said stoutly. "Pack young fools."

35   "Martin." And Bobby Martin watched his father go forward. "Overdyke. . . . Percy."

36   "I wish they'd hurry," Mrs. Dunbar said to her older son. "I wish they'd hurry."

37   "They're almost through" her son said.

38   "You get ready to run tell Dad," Mrs. Dunbar said.

39   Mr. Summers called his own name and then stepped forward precisely and selected a slip from the box. Then he called, "Warner."

40   "Seventy-seventh year I been in the lottery," Old Man Warner said as he went through the crowd. "Seventy-seventh time."

41   "Watson." The tall boy came awkwardly through the crowd. Someone said, "Don't be nervous, Jack," and Mr. Summers said, "Take your time, son."

42   "Zanini."

43   After that, there was a long pause, a breathless pause, until Mr. Summers, holding his slip of paper in the air, said, "All right, fellows." For a minute, no one moved, and then all the slips of paper were opened. Suddenly, all women began to speak at once, saying, "Who is it?," "Who's got it?," "Is it the Dunbars?," "Is it the Watsons?" Then the voices began to say, "It's Hutchinson. It's Bill." "Bill Hutchinson's got it."

44   "Go tell your father," Mrs. Dunbar said to her older son.

45   People began to look around to see the Hutchinsons. Bill Hutchinson was standing quiet, staring down at the paper in his hand. Suddenly, Tessie Hutchinson shouted to Mr. Summers, "You didn't give him time enough to take any paper he wanted. I saw you. It wasn't fair!"

46   "Be a good sport, Tessie." Mrs. Delacroix called, and Mrs. Graves said, "All of us took the same chance."

47   "Shut up, Tessie," Bill Hutchinson said.

48   "Well, everyone," Mr. Summers said, "that was done pretty fast, and now we've got to be hurrying a little more to get it done in time." He consulted his next list. "Bill," he said, "you draw for the Hutchinson family. You got any other households in the Hutchinsons?"

49   "There's Don and Eva," Mrs. Hutchinson yelled. "Make *them* take their chance!"

50   "Daughters draw with their husbands' families, Tessie," Mr. Summers said gently. "You know that as well as anyone else."

51   "It wasn't fair," Tessie said.

52   "I guess not, Joe," Bill Hutchinson said regretfully. "My daughter draws with her husband's family, that's only fair. And I've got no other family except the kids."

53   "Then, as far as drawing for families is concerned, it's you," Mr. Summers said in explanation, "and as far as drawing for households is concerned, that's you, too. Right?"

54   "Right," Bill Hutchinson said.

55   "How many kids, Bill?" Mr. Summers asked formally.

56   "Three," Bill Hutchinson said. "There's Bill, Jr., and Nancy, and little Dave. And Tessie and me."

57   "All right, then," Mr. Summers said. "Harry, you got their tickets back?"

58   Mr. Graves nodded and held up the slips of paper. "Put them in the box, then," Mr. Summers directed. "Take Bill's and put it in."

59   "I think we ought to start over," Mrs. Hutchinson said, as quietly as she could. "I tell you it wasn't *fair*. You didn't give him time enough to choose. *Everybody* saw that."

60   Mr. Graves had selected the five slips and put them in the box, and he dropped all the papers but those onto the ground, where the breeze caught them and lifted them off.

61   "Listen, everybody," Mrs. Hutchinson was saying to the people around her.

62   "Ready, Bill?" Mr. Summers asked, and Bill Hutchinson, with one quick glance around at his wife and children, nodded.

63   "Remember," Mr. Summers said, "take the slips and keep them folded until each person has taken one. Harry, you help little Dave." Mr. Graves took the hand of the little boy, who came willingly with him up to the box. "Take a paper out of the box, Davy," Mr. Summers said. Davy put his hand into the box and laughed. "Take just *one* paper," Mr. Summers said. "Harry, you hold it for him." Mr. Graves took the child's hand and removed the folded paper from the tight fist and held it while little Dave stood next to him and looked up at him wonderingly.

64   "Nancy next," Mr. Summers said. Nancy was twelve, and her school friends breathed heavily as she went forward, switching her skirt, and took a slip daintily from the box. "Bill, Jr.," Mr. Summers said, and Billy, his face red and his feet over-large, nearly knocked the box over as he got a paper out. "Tessie," Mr. Summers said. She hesitated for a minute, looking around defiantly, and then set her lips and went up to the box. She snatched a paper out and held it behind her.

65   "Bill," Mr. Summers said, and Bill Hutchinson reached into the box and felt around, bringing his hand out at last with the slip of paper in it.

66   The crowd was quiet. A girl whispered, "I hope it's not Nancy," and the sound of the whisper reached the edges of the crowd.

67   "It's not the way it used to be," Old Man Warner said clearly. "People ain't the way they used to be."

68   "All right," Mr. Summers said. "Open the papers. Harry, you open little Dave's."

69   Mr. Graves opened the slip of paper and there was a general sigh through the crowd as he held it up and everyone could see that it was blank. Nancy and Bill, Jr., opened theirs at the same time, and both beamed and laughed, turning around to the crowd and holding their slips of paper above their heads.

70   "Tessie," Mr. Summers, said. There was a pause, and then Mr. Summers looked at Bill Hutchinson, and Bill unfolded his paper and showed it. It was blank.

71   "It's Tessie," Mr. Summers said, and his voice was hushed. "Show us her paper, Bill."

72   Bill Hutchinson went over to his wife and forced the slip of paper out of her hand. It had a black spot on it, the black spot Mr. Summers had made the night before with the heavy pencil in the coal-company office. Bill Hutchinson held it up, and there was a stir in the crowd.

73   "All right, folks," Mr. Summers said, "let's finish quickly."

74   Although the villagers had forgotten the ritual and lost the original black box, they still remembered to use stones. The pile of stones the boys had made earlier was ready; there were stones on the ground with the blowing scraps of paper that had come out of the box. Mrs. Delacroix selected a stone so large she had to pick it up with both hands and turned to Mrs. Dunbar. "Come on," she said. "Hurry up."

75   Mrs. Dunbar had small stones in both hands, and she said, gasping for breath, "I can't run at all. You'll have to go ahead and I'll catch up with you."

76   The children had stones already, and someone gave little Davy Hutchinson a few pebbles.

77   Tessie Hutchinson was in the center of a cleared space by now, and she held her hands out desperately as the villagers moved in on her. "It isn't fair," she said. A stone hit her on the side of the head.

78   Old Man Warner was saying, "Come on, come on, everyone." Steve Adams was in the front of the crowd of villagers, with Mrs. Graves beside him.

79   "It isn't fair, it isn't right," Mrs. Hutchinson screamed, and then they were upon her.

The Lottery

JOURNAL

1. MLA Works Cited

Using this model, record this story here.

Author's Last Name, First Name. "Title of the Story." <u>Title of the Book</u>. Ed. First Last Name. City: Publisher, year. Pages of the story.

Jackson, Shirley "The Lottery"
<u>american 24-Karat Gold</u> Yvonne Elliaud Sisko

2. Main Character(s)

Describe each main character, and explain why you think each is a main character.

Mr Summers
Mr. Graves
Bill + Tessie Hutchinson
Mr. warner
Mr + mrs. Delacroix
Mr + mrs. Dunbar

3. Supporting Characters

Describe each supporting character, and explain why you think each is a supporting character.

4. Setting

Describe the setting. Decide if the setting can be changed and, if so, to where and when.

The Story takes place in a small old village.

5. Sequence

Relate the events of the story in order.

6. Plot

Tell the story in no more than three sentences.

7. Conflicts

Identify and explain the conflicts involved here.

8. Significant Quotations

Explain the importance of each of these quotations. Record the page number in the parentheses.

a. "Bobby Martin had already stuffed his pockets full of stones, and the other boys soon followed his example, selecting the smoothest and roundest stones [. . .]" (   ).

b. "There has been, also, a ritual salute, which the official of the lottery had had to use in addressing each person who came up to draw from the box, but this also had changed with time [. . .]" (   ).

c. "The people separated goodhumoredly to let her through [. . .]" (   ).

d. "Bill Hutchinson went over to his wife and forced the slip of paper out of her hand" (   ).

e. "It isn't fair,' she said. A stone hit her on the side of the head" (   ).

9. Foreshadowing

Identify and explain the clues Jackson plants to predict the forthcoming events.

FOLLOW-UP QUESTIONS

10 SHORT QUESTIONS

Select the best answer for each.

_____ 1. While piling the stones, the boys seem to be
a. upset to have to do this.
b. unhappy to do this chore.
c. having fun.

_____ 2. The word "lottery" implies
a. a happy event.
b. a lonely event.
c. a sad event.

_____ 3. The townspeople seem to gather
a. at any time they like.
b. willingly.
c. unwillingly.

_____ 4. Mr. Summers is
a. for the lottery.
b. against the lottery.
c. undecided about the lottery.

_____ 5. Mr. Graves is
a. for the lottery.
b. against the lottery.
c. undecided about the lottery.

_____ 6. The town
a. remembers where the lottery came from.
b. does not remember where the lottery came from.
c. just started the lottery.

_____ 7. Old Man Warner is
a. for the lottery.
b. against the lottery.
c. unconcerned about the lottery.

_____ 8. Tessie Hutchinson thinks the drawing is
a. wise.
b. fair.
c. unfair.

_____ 9. The children are
a. removed from the lottery.
b. not involved in the lottery.
c. involved in the lottery.

_____ 10. Tessie is
a. happy.
b. alive.
c. stoned to death.

5 SIGNIFICANT QUOTATIONS

Explain the importance of each of these quotations.

1. "The children assembled first, of course. [. . . and] eventually made a great pile of stones [. . .]."

2. "There was a great deal of fussing to be done before Mr. Summers declared the lottery open."

3. " 'They do say,' Mr. Adams said to Old Man Warner, who stood next to him, 'that over in the north village they're talking of giving up the lottery.'
   "Old Man Warner snorted, 'Pack of crazy fools,' he said."

4. "For a minute, no one moved, and then all the slips of paper were opened."

5. "The children had stones already, and someone gave little Davy Hutchinson a few pebbles."

2 COMPREHENSION ESSAY QUESTIONS

Use specific details and information from the story to answer these as completely as possible.

1. How does the title relate to story? Explain the significance of the title using specific details and information from the story.

2. Explain what happens to Mrs. Hutchinson. Use specific details and information from the story in your explanation.

WRITING

Use each of these ideas for writing an essay.

1. Write a narrative essay on a pointless or even harmful tradition in your family, neighborhood, or culture.

2. Write a narrative essay about a time you have had great hope and been greatly disappointed.

Further Writing

1. Compare the questioning of cultural dictates in Maxine Hong Kingston's "No Name Woman" (page 224) and Jackson's theme of questioning cultural dictates in this story.

2. Compare the questioning of cultural dictates in Alice Walker's "Everyday Use" (page 175) and Jackson's theme of questioning cultural dictates in this story.

3. Read O.Henry's "Two Thanksgiving Day Gentlemen" (which can be found in a library), and use O'Henry's story in a discussion of Jackson's theme of questioning cultural dictates in this story.

4. Read Richard Wright's "The Man Who Lived Underground" (which can be found in a library), and use Wright's story in a discussion of Jackson's theme of questioning cultural dictates in this story.

Good Country People

Flannery O'Connor

Pre-reading Vocabulary
Context

Use context clues to define these words before reading. Use a dictionary as needed.

1. When Jules had to have a leg removed, the vet supplied an *artificial* leg so the dog could walk. *Artificial* means _____.

2. The erasure *obliterated* all the assignments that had just been written on the board. *Obliterate* means _____.

3. Jennifer could not take her eyes off the rock star and just *stared* and *stared*. *Stare* means _____.

4. Abdul had a *tenant* living in the apartment over his garage. *Tenant* means _____.

5. If you eat too much ice cream, you may end up round and *stout*. *Stout* means _____.

6. Zach enjoys his *privacy* and lives in a house with high bushes and guards so no one can see him. *Privacy* means _____.

7. When Julia won the award, she was so nervous that all she could speak was *gibberish,* and no one understood her. *Gibberish* means

_____.

8. *Vulcan*, the ugly Roman god of metal-working and fire, was married to Venus, the beautiful goddess of love. *Vulcan* means

_____.

9. Christians read the selections in the *Bible* for spiritual guidance. *Bible* means _____.

10. After Mark injured his knee, he wore a *brace* around his knee to help support it. *Brace* means _____.

11. Aunt Alice needed to pack for her trip to Florida and looked for her *satchel* or *valise*. *Satchel* and *valise* mean

_____.

12. Close friends often totally trust each other and tell each other their *intimate* secrets. *Intimate* means _____.

13. Joan decided to become a *missionary* so that she could carry the word of God to others. *Missionary* means _____.

14. The winning team crossed the field *triumphantly*. *Triumphantly* means _____.

15. The lovely woman brought the handsome man up to her room and *seduced* him. *Seduce* means _____.

16. Magicians often use smoke and mirrors to create their *illusions*. *Illusion* means _____.

17. Little children who trust easily and who have not learned to do bad things have a pure *innocence*. *Innocence* means _____.

18. When you do something that you feel is wrong, you may have feelings of *shame*. *Shame* means _____.

19. Hatomen *lunged* and almost fell over the railing when he tried to catch the Yankee's home run ball. *Lunge* means _____.

20. John became entranced and *mesmerized* watching waves rolling one after another on the beach. *Mesmerize* means _____.

PRE-READING VOCABULARY
WORD ATTACK

Define these words by solving the parts. Use a dictionary as needed.

1. indistinguishable
2. godsend
3. nosiest
4. beforehand
5. legally
6. ugliest
7. mechanical
8. steel-pointed
9. deformities
10. incurable
11. scarecrow
12. idiotic
13. squint-eyed
14. stupidity
15. afresh
16. hatless
17. nowadays
18. recognizable
19. roundabout
20. stonily
21. feverishly
22. awestricken
23. jointure

PRE-READING QUESTIONS

Try answering these questions as you read.

Who is Hulga?

Who is Manley Pointer?

What does Hulga think Manley Pointer wants?

What does Manley Pointer really want?

Good Country People

FLANNERY O'CONNOR

> **Mary Flannery O'Connor** was born in 1925 in Georgia. She was the only child of a comfortable Roman Catholic family. She studied at Georgia State College for Women and Iowa State University and lived in New York state, New York City, and Connecticut. Already an established writer but starting her battle with lupus, she returned home to her mother's farm where she died in 1964.
>
> Raised amid southern Protestantism, she became determined in her Catholicism, and it fairly explodes in her writing that often violently confronts good and evil. She was posthumously named to the Phi Kappa Phi National Honor Society and received three O. Henry awards. Her short stories are available in several collections.

Besides the neutral expression that she wore when she was alone, Mrs. Freeman had two others, forward and reverse, that she used for all her human dealings. Her forward expression was steady and driving like the advance of a heavy truck. Her eyes never swerved to left or right but turned as the story turned as if they followed a yellow line down the center of it. She seldom used the other expression because it was not often necessary for her to retract a statement, but when she did, her face came to a complete stop, there was an almost imperceptible movement of her black eyes, during which they seemed to be receding, and then the observer would see that Mrs. Freeman, though she might stand there as real as several grain sacks thrown on top of each other, was no longer there in spirit. As for getting anything across to her when this was the case, Mrs. Hopewell had given it up. She might talk her head off. Mrs. Freeman could never be brought to admit herself wrong on any point. She would stand there and if she could be brought to say anything, it was something like, "Well, I wouldn't of said it was and I wouldn't of said it wasn't," or letting her gaze range over the top kitchen shelf where there was an assortment of dusty bottles, she might remark, "I see you ain't ate many of them figs you put up last summer."

2   They carried on their most important business in the kitchen at breakfast. Every morning Mrs. Hopewell got up at seven o'clock and lit her gas heater and Joy's. Joy was her daughter, a large blonde girl who had an artificial leg. Mrs. Hopewell thought of her as a child though she was thirty-two years old and highly educated. Joy would get up while her mother was eating and lumber into the bathroom and slam the door, and before long, Mrs. Freeman would arrive at the back door.

Joy would hear her mother call, "Come on in," and then they would talk a while in low voices that were indistinguishable in the bathroom. By the time Joy came in, they had usually finished the weather report and were on one or the other of Mrs. Freeman's daughters, Glynese or Carramae, Joy called them Glycerin and Caramel. Glynese, a redhead, was eighteen and had many admirers; Carramae, a blonde, was only fifteen but already married and pregnant. She could not keep anything on her stomach. Every morning Mrs. Freeman told Mrs. Hopewell how many times she had vomited since the last report.

3   Mrs. Hopewell liked to tell people that Glynese and Carramae were two of the finest girls she knew and that Mrs. Freeman was a *lady* and that she was never ashamed to take her anywhere or introduce her to anybody they might meet. Then she would tell how she had happened to hire the Freemans in the first place and how they were a godsend to her and how she had had them four years. The reason for her keeping them so long was that they were not trash. They were good country people. She had telephoned the man whose name they had given as a reference and he had told her that Mr. Freeman was a good farmer but that his wife was the nosiest woman ever to walk the earth. "She's got to be into everything," the man said. "If she don't get there before the dust settles, you can bet she's dead, that's all. She'll want to know all your business. I can stand him real good," he had said, "but me nor my wife neither could have stood that woman one more minute on this place." That had put Mrs. Hopewell off for a few days.

4   She had hired them in the end because there were no other applicants but she had made up her mind beforehand exactly how she would handle the woman. Since she was the type who had to be into everything, then, Mrs. Hopewell had decided, she would not only let her be into everything, she would *see to it* that she was into everything—she would give her the responsibility of everything, she would put her in charge. Mrs. Hopewell had no bad qualities of her own but she was able to use other people's in such a constructive way that she never felt the lack. She had hired the Freemans and she had kept them four years.

5   Nothing is perfect. This was one of Mrs. Hopewell's favorite sayings. Another was: that is life! And still another, the most important, was: well, other people have their opinions too. She would make these statements, usually at the table, in a tone of gentle insistence as if no one held them but her, and the large hulking Joy, whose constant outrage had obliterated every expression from her face, would stare just a little to the side of her, her eyes icy blue, with the look of someone who has achieved blindness by an act of will and means to keep it.

6   When Mrs. Hopewell said to Mrs. Freeman that life was like that, Mrs. Freeman would say, "I always said so myself." Nothing had been arrived at by anyone that had not first been arrived at by her. She was quicker than Mr. Freeman. When Mrs. Hopewell said to her after they had been on the place a while, "You know, you're the wheel behind the wheel," and winked, Mrs. Freeman had said, "I know it. I've always been quick. It's some that are quicker than others."

7   "Everybody is different," Mrs. Hopewell said.

8   "Yes, most people is," Mrs. Freeman said.

9   "It takes all kinds to make the world."

10   "I always said it did myself."

11   The girl was used to this kind of dialogue for breakfast and more of it for dinner; sometimes they had it for supper too. When they had no guest they ate in the kitchen because that was easier. Mrs. Freeman always managed to arrive at some point during the meal and to watch them finish it. She would stand in the doorway if it were summer but in the winter she would stand with one elbow on top of the refrigerator and look down on them, or she would stand by the gas heater, lifting the back of her skirt slightly. Occasionally she would stand against the wall and roll her head from side to side. At no time was she in any hurry to leave. All this was very trying on Mrs. Hopewell but she was a woman of great patience. She realized that nothing is perfect and that in the Freemans she had good country people and that if, in this day and age, you get good country people, you had better hang onto them.

12   She had had plenty of experience with trash. Before the Freemans she had averaged one tenant family a year. The wives of these farmers were not the kind you would want to be around you for very long. Mrs. Hopewell, who had divorced her husband long ago, needed someone to walk over the fields with her; and when Joy had to be impressed for these services, her remarks were usually so ugly and her face so glum that Mrs. Hopewell would say, "If you can't come pleasantly, I don't want you at all," to which the girl, standing square and rigid-shouldered with her neck thrust slightly forward, would reply, "If you want me, here I am—LIKE I AM."

13   Mrs. Hopewell excused this attitude because of the leg (which had been shot off in a hunting accident when Joy was ten). It was hard for Mrs. Hopewell to realize that her child was thirty-two now and that for more than twenty years she had had only one leg. She thought of her still as a child because it tore her heart to think instead of the poor stout girl in her thirties who had never danced a step or had any *normal* good times. Her name was really Joy but as soon as she was twenty-one

and away from home, she had had it legally changed. Mrs. Hopewell was certain that she had thought and thought until she had hit upon the ugliest name in any language. Then she had gone and had the beautiful name, Joy, changed without telling her mother until after she had done it. Her legal name was Hulga.

14   When Mrs. Hopewell thought the name Hulga, she thought of the broad blank hull of a battleship. She would not use it. She continued to call her Joy to which the girl responded but in a purely mechanical way.

15   Hulga had learned to tolerate Mrs. Freeman who saved her from taking walks with her mother. Even Glynese and Carramae were useful when they occupied attention that might otherwise have been directed at her. At first she had thought she could not stand Mrs. Freeman for she had found that it was not possible to be rude to her. Mrs. Freeman would take on strange resentments and for days together she would be sullen but the source of her displeasure was always obscure; a direct attack, a positive leer, blatant ugliness to her face—these never touched her. And without warning one day, she began calling her Hulga.

16   She did not call her that in front of Mrs. Hopewell who would have been incensed but when she and the girl happened to be out of the house together, she would say something and add the name Hulga to the end of it, and the big spectacled Joy-Hulga would scowl and redden as if her privacy had been intruded upon. She considered the name her personal affair. She had arrived at it first purely on the basis of its ugly sound and then the full genius of its fitness had struck her. She had a vision of the name working like the ugly sweating Vulcan who stayed in the furnace and to whom, presumably, the goddess had to come when called. She saw it as the name of her highest creative act. One of her major triumphs was that her mother had not been able to turn her dust into Joy, but the greater one was that she had been able to turn it herself into Hulga. However, Mrs. Freeman's relish for using the name only irritated her. It was as if Mrs. Freeman's beady steel-pointed eyes had penetrated far enough behind her face to reach some secret fact. Something about her seemed to fascinate Mrs. Freeman and then one day Hulga realized that it was the artificial leg. Mrs. Freeman had a special fondness for the details of secret infections, hidden deformities, assaults upon children. Of diseases, she preferred the lingering or incurable. Hulga had heard Mrs. Hopewell give her the details of the hunting accident, how the leg had been literally blasted off, how she had never lost consciousness. Mrs. Freeman could listen to it any time as if it had happened an hour ago.

17   When Hulga stumped into the kitchen in the morning (she could walk without making the awful noise but she made it—Mrs. Hopewell was certain—because it was ugly-sounding), she glanced at them and did not speak. Mrs. Hopewell would be in her red kimono with her hair tied around her head in rags. She would be sitting at the table, finishing her breakfast and Mrs. Freeman would be hanging by her elbow outward from the refrigerator, looking down at the table. Hulga always put her eggs on the stove to boil and then stood over them with her arms folded, and Mrs. Hopewell would look at her—a kind of indirect gaze divided between her and Mrs. Freeman—and would think that if she would only keep herself up a little, she wouldn't be so bad looking. There was nothing wrong with her face that a pleasant expression wouldn't help. Mrs. Hopewell said that people who looked on the bright side of things would be beautiful even if they were not.

18   Whenever she looked at Joy this way, she could not help but feel that it would have been better if the child had not taken the Ph.D. It had certainly not brought her out any and now that she had it, there was no more excuse for her to go to school again. Mrs. Hopewell thought it was nice for girls to go to school to have a good time but Joy had "gone through." Anyhow, she would not have been strong enough to go again. The doctors had told Mrs. Hopewell that with the best of care, Joy might see forty-five. She had a weak heart. Joy had made it plain that if it had not been for this condition, she would be far from these red hills and good country people. She would be in a university lecturing to people who knew what she was talking about. And Mrs. Hopewell could very well picture her there, looking like a scarecrow and lecturing to more of the same. Here she went about all day in a six-year-old skirt and a yellow sweat shirt with a faded cowboy on a horse embossed on it. She thought this was funny; Mrs. Hopewell thought it was idiotic and showed simply that she was still a child. She was brilliant but she didn't have a grain of sense. It seemed to Mrs. Hopewell that every year she grew less like other people and more like herself—bloated, rude, and squint-eyed. And she said such strange things! To her own mother she had said—without warning, without excuse, standing up in the middle of a meal with her face purple and her mouth half full—"Woman! do you ever look inside? Do you ever look inside and see what you are *not*? God!" she had cried sinking down again and staring at her plate, "Malebranche was right: we are not our own light. We are not our own light!" Mrs. Hopewell had no idea to this day what brought that on. She had only made the remark, hoping Joy would take it in, that a smile never hurt anyone.

19   The girl had taken the Ph.D. in philosophy and this left Mrs. Hopewell at a complete loss. You could say, "My daughter is a nurse," or "My daughter is a schoolteacher," or even, "My daughter is a chemical engineer." You could not say, "My daughter is a philosopher." That was something that had ended with the Greeks and Romans. All day Joy sat on her neck in a deep chair, reading. Sometimes she went for walks but she didn't like dogs or cats or birds or flowers or nature or nice young men. She looked at nice young men as if she could smell their stupidity.

20   One day Mrs. Hopewell had picked up one of the books the girl had just put down and opening it at random, she read, "Science, on the other hand, has to assert its soberness and seriousness afresh and declare that it is concerned solely with what-is. Nothing—how can it be for science anything but a horror and a phantasm? If science is right, then one thing stands firm: science wishes to know nothing of nothing. Such is after all the strictly scientific approach to Nothing. We know it by wishing to know nothing of Nothing." These words had been underlined with a blue pencil and they worked on Mrs. Hopewell like some evil incantation in gibberish. She shut the book quickly and went out of the room as if she were having a chill.

21   This morning when the girl came in, Mrs. Freeman was on Carramae. "She thrown up four times after supper," she said, "and was up twict in the night after three o'clock. Yesterday she didn't do nothing but ramble in the bureau drawer. All she did. Stand up there and see what she could run up on."

22   "She's got to eat," Mrs. Hopewell muttered, sipping her coffee, while she watched Joy's back at the stove. She was wondering what the child had said to the Bible salesman. She could not imagine what kind of a conversation she could possibly have had with him.

23   He was a tall gaunt hatless youth who had called yesterday to sell them a Bible. He had appeared at the door, carrying a large black suitcase that weighted him so heavily on one side that he had to brace himself against the door facing. He seemed on the point of collapse but he said in a cheerful voice, "Good morning, Mrs. Cedars!" and set the suitcase down on the mat. He was not a bad-looking young man though he had on a bright blue suit and yellow socks that were not pulled up far enough. He had prominent face bones and a streak of sticky-looking brown hair falling across his forehead.

24   "I'm Mrs. Hopewell," she said.

25   "Oh!" he said, pretending to look puzzled but with his eyes sparkling, "I saw it said 'The Cedars' on the mailbox so I thought you was Mrs. Cedars!" and he burst out in a pleasant laugh. He picked up

the satchel and under cover of a pant, he fell forward into her hall. It was rather as if the suitcase had moved first, jerking him after it. "Mrs. Hopewell!" he said and grabbed her hand. "I hope you are well!" and he laughed again and then all at once his face sobered completely. He paused and gave her a straight earnest look and said, "Lady, I've come to speak of serious things."

26   "Well, come in," she muttered, none too pleased because her dinner was almost ready. He came into the parlor and sat down on the edge of a straight chair and put the suitcase between his feet and glanced around the room as if he were sizing her up by it. Her silver gleamed on the two sideboards; she decided he had never been in a room as elegant as this.

27   "Mrs. Hopewell," he began, using her name in a way that sounded almost intimate, "I know you believe in Chrustian service."

28   "Well yes," she murmured.

29   "I know," he said and paused, looking very wise with his head cocked on one side, "that you're a good woman. Friends have told me."

30   Mrs. Hopewell never liked to be taken for a fool. "What are you selling?" she asked.

31   "Bibles," the young man said and his eye raced around the room before he added, "I see you have no family Bible in your parlor, I see that is the one lack you got!"

32   Mrs. Hopewell could not say, "My daughter is an atheist and won't let me keep the Bible in the parlor." She said, stiffening slightly, "I keep my Bible by my bedside." This was not the truth. It was in the attic somewhere.

33   "Lady," he said, "the word of God ought to be in the parlor."

34   "Well, I think that's a matter of taste," she began. "I think . . ."

35   "Lady," he said, "for a Chrustian, the word of God ought to be in every room in the house besides in his heart. I know, you're a Chrustian because I can see it in every line of your face."

36   She stood up and said, "Well, young man, I don't want to buy a Bible and I smell my dinner burning."

37   He didn't get up. He began to twist his hands and looking down at them he said softly, "Well lady, I'll tell you the truth—not many people want to buy one nowadays and besides, I know I'm real simple. I don't know how to say a thing but to say it. I'm just a country boy." He glanced up into her unfriendly face. "People like you don't like to fool with country people like me!"

38   "Why!" she cried, "good country people are the salt of the earth! Besides, we all have different ways of doing, it takes all kinds to make the world go 'round. That's life!"

39   "You said a mouthful," he said.

40   "Why, I think there aren't enough good country people in the world!" she said, stirred. "I think that's what's wrong with it!"

41   His face had brightened. "I didn't inraduce myself," he said. "I'm Manley Pointer from out in the country around Willohobie, not even from a place, just from near a place."

42   "You wait a minute," she said. "I have to see about my dinner." She went out to the kitchen and found Joy standing near the door where she had been listening.

43   "Get rid of the salt of the earth," she said, "and let's eat."

44   Mrs. Hopewell gave her a pained look and turned the heat down under the vegetables. "*I* can't be rude to anybody," she murmured and went back into the parlor.

45   He had opened the suitcase and was sitting with a Bible on each knee.

46   "You might as well put those up," she told him. "I don't want one."

47   "I appreciate your honesty," he said. "You don't see any more real honest people unless you go way out in the country."

48   "I know," she said, "real genuine folks!" Through the crack in the door she heard a groan.

49   "I guess a lot of boys come telling you they're working their way through college," he said, "but I'm not going to tell you that. Some-how," he said, "I don't want to go to college. I want to devote my life to Chrustian service. See," he said, lowering his voice, "I got this heart condition. I may not live long. When you know it's something wrong with you and you may not live long, well then, lady . . ." He paused, with his mouth open, and stared at her.

50   He and Joy had the same condition! She knew that her eyes were filling with tears but she collected herself quickly and murmured, "Won't you stay for dinner? We'd love to have you!" and was sorry the instant she heard herself say it.

51   "Yes mam," he said in an abashed voice, "I would sher love to do that!"

52   Joy had given him one look on being introduced to him and then throughout the meal had not glanced at him again. He had addressed several remarks to her, which she had pretended not to hear. Mrs. Hopewell could not understand deliberate rudeness, although she lived with it, and she felt she had always to overflow with hospitality to make up for Joy's lack of courtesy. She urged him to talk about himself and he did. He said he was the seventh child of twelve and that his father had been crushed under a tree when he himself was eight years old. He had been crushed very badly, in fact, almost cut in two and was

practically not recognizable. His mother had got along the best she could by hard working and she had always seen that her children went to Sunday School and that they read the Bible every evening. He was now nineteen years old and he had been selling Bibles for four months. In that time he had sold seventy-seven Bibles and had the promise of two more sales. He wanted to become a missionary because he thought that was the way you could do most for people. "He who losest his life shall find it," he said simply and he was so sincere, so genuine and earnest that Mrs. Hopewell would not for the world have smiled. He prevented his peas from sliding onto the table by blocking them with a piece of bread which he later cleaned his plate with. She could see Joy observing sidewise how he handled his knife and fork and she saw too that every few minutes, the boy would dart a keen appraising glance at the girl as if he were trying to attract her attention.

53   After dinner Joy cleared the dishes off the table and disappeared and Mrs. Hopewell was left to talk with him. He told her again about his childhood and his father's accident and about various things that had happened to him. Every five minutes or so she would stifle a yawn. He sat for two hours until finally she told him she must go because she had an appointment in town. He packed his Bibles and thanked her and prepared to leave, but in the doorway he stopped and wrung her hand and said that not on any of his trips had he met a lady as nice as her and he asked if he could come again. She had said she would always be happy to see him.

54   Joy had been standing in the road, apparently looking at something in the distance, when he came down the steps toward her, bent to the side with his heavy valise. He stopped where she was standing and confronted her directly. Mrs. Hopewell could not hear what he said but she trembled to think what Joy would say to him. She could see that after a minute Joy said something and that then the boy began to speak again, making an excited gesture with his free hand. After a minute Joy said something else at which the boy began to speak once more. Then to her amazement, Mrs. Hopewell saw the two of them walk off together, toward the gate. Joy had walked all the way to the gate with him and Mrs. Hopewell could not imagine what they had said to each other, and she had not yet dared to ask.

55   Mrs. Freeman was insisting upon her attention. She had moved from the refrigerator to the heater so that Mrs. Hopewell had to turn and face her in order to seem to be listening. "Glynese gone out with Harvey Hill again last night," she said. "She had this sty."

56   "Hill," Mrs. Hopewell said absently, "is that the one who works in the garage?"

57   "Nome, he's the one that goes to chiropracter school," Mrs. Freeman said. "She had this sty. Been had it two days. So she says when he brought her in the other night he says, 'Lemme get rid of that sty for you,' and she says, 'How?' and he says, 'You just lay yourself down acrost the seat of that car and I'll show you.' So she done it and he popped her neck. Kept on a-popping it several times until she made him quit. This morning," Mrs. Freeman said, "she ain't got no sty. She ain't got no traces of a sty."

58   "I never heard of that before," Mrs. Hopewell said.

59   "He ast her to marry him before the Ordinary," Mrs. Freeman went on, "and she told him she wasn't going to be married in no *office*."

60   "Well, Glynese is a fine girl," Mrs. Hopewell said. "Glynese and Carramae are both fine girls."

61   "Carramae said when her and Lyman was married Lyman said it sure felt sacred to him. She said he said he wouldn't take five hundred dollars for being married by a preacher."

62   "How much would he take?" the girl asked from the stove.

63   "He said he wouldn't take five hundred dollars," Mrs. Freeman repeated.

64   "Well we all have work to do," Mrs. Hopewell said.

65   "Lyman said it just felt more sacred to him," Mrs. Freeman said. "The doctor wants Carramae to eat prunes. Says instead of medicine. Says them cramps is coming from pressure. You know where I think it is?"

66   "She'll be better in a few weeks," Mrs. Hopewell said.

67   "In the tube," Mrs. Freeman said. "Else she wouldn't be as sick as she is."

68   Hulga had cracked her two eggs into a saucer and was bringing them to the table along with a cup of coffee that she had filled too full. She sat down carefully and began to eat, meaning to keep Mrs. Freeman there by questions if for any reason she showed an inclination to leave. She could perceive her mother's eye on her. The first round-about question would be about the Bible salesman and she did not wish to bring it on. "How did he pop her neck?" she asked.

69   Mrs. Freeman went into a description of how he had popped her neck. She said he owned a '55 Mercury but that Glynese said she would rather marry a man with only a '36 Plymouth who would be married by a preacher. The girl asked what if he had a '32 Plymouth and Mrs. Freeman said what Glynese had said was a '36 Plymouth.

70   Mrs. Hopewell said there were not many girls with Glynese's common sense. She said what she admired in those girls was their common

sense. She said that reminded her that they had had a nice visitor yesterday, a young man selling Bibles. "Lord," she said, "he bored me to death but he was so sincere and genuine I couldn't be rude to him. He was just good country people, you know," she said, "—just the salt of the earth."

71   "I seen him walk up," Mrs. Freeman said, "and then later—I seen him walk off," and Hulga could feel the slight shift in her voice, the slight insinuation, that he had not walked off alone, had he? Her face remained expressionless but the color rose into her neck and she seemed to swallow it down with the next spoonful of egg. Mrs. Freeman was looking at her as if they had a secret together.

72   "Well, it takes all kinds of people to make the world go 'round," Mrs. Hopewell said. "It's very good we aren't all alike."

73   "Some people are more alike than others," Mrs. Freeman said.

74   Hulga got up and stumped, with about twice the noise that was necessary, into her room and locked the door. She was to meet the Bible salesman at ten o'clock at the gate. She had thought about it half the night. She had started thinking of it as a great joke and then she had begun to see profound implications in it. She had lain in bed imagining dialogues for them that were insane on the surface but that reached below to depths that no Bible salesman would be aware of. Their conversation yesterday had been of this kind.

75   He had stopped in front of her and had simply stood there. His face was bony and sweaty and bright, with a little pointed nose in the center of it, and his look was different from what it had been at the dinner table. He was gazing at her with open curiosity, with fascination, like a child watching a new fantastic animal at the zoo, and he was breathing as if he had run a great distance to reach her. His gaze seemed somehow familiar but she could not think where she had been regarded with it before. For almost a minute he didn't say anything. Then on what seemed an insuck of breath, he whispered, "You ever ate a chicken that was two days old?"

76   The girl looked at him stonily. He might have just put this question up for consideration at the meeting of a philosophical association. "Yes," she presently replied as if she had considered it from all angles.

77   "It must have been mighty small!" he said triumphantly and shook all over with little nervous giggles, getting very red in the face, and subsiding finally into his gaze of complete admiration, while the girl's expression remained exactly the same.

78   "How old are you?" he asked softly.

79   She waited some time before she answered. Then in a flat voice she said, "Seventeen."

80   His smiles came in succession like waves breaking on the surface of a little lake. "I see you got a wooden leg," he said. "I think you're brave. I think you're real sweet."

81   The girl stood blank and solid and silent.

82   "Walk to the gate with me," he said. "You're a brave sweet little thing and I liked you the minute I seen you walk in the door."

83   Hulga began to move forward.

84   "What's your name?" he asked, smiling down on the top of her head.

85   "Hulga," she said.

86   "Hulga," he murmured, "Hulga. Hulga. I never heard of anybody name Hulga before. You're shy, aren't you, Hulga?" he asked.

87   She nodded, watching his large red hand on the handle of the giant valise.

88   "I like girls that wear glasses," he said. "I think a lot. I'm not like these people that a serious thought don't ever enter their heads. It's because I may die."

89   "I may die too," she said suddenly and looked up at him. His eyes were very small and brown, glittering feverishly.

90   "Listen," he said, "don't you think some people was meant to meet on account of what all they got in common and all? Like they both think serious thoughts and all?" He shifted the valise to his other hand so that the hand nearest her was free. He caught hold of her elbow and shook it a little. "I don't work on Saturday," he said. "I like to walk in the woods and see what Mother Nature is wearing. O'er the hills and far away. Pic-nics and things. Couldn't we go on a pic-nic tomorrow? Say yes, Hulga," he said and gave her a dying look as if he felt his insides about to drop out of him. He had even seemed to sway slightly toward her.

91   During the night she had imagined that she seduced him. She imagined that the two of them walked on the place until they came to the storage barn beyond the two back fields and there, she imagined, that things came to such a pass that she very easily seduced him and that then, of course, she had to reckon with his remorse. True genius can get an idea across even to an inferior mind. She imagined that she took his remorse in hand and changed it into a deeper understanding of life. She took all his shame away and turned it into something useful.

92   She set off for the gate at exactly ten o'clock, escaping without drawing Mrs. Hopewell's attention. She didn't take anything to eat, forgetting that food is usually taken on a pic-nic. She wore a pair of slacks and a dirty white shirt, and as an afterthought, she had put some

Vapex on the collar of it since she did not own any perfume. When she reached the gate no one was there.

93   She looked up and down the empty highway and had the furious feeling that she had been tricked, that he had only meant to make her walk to the gate after the idea of him. Then suddenly he stood up, very tall, from behind a bush on the opposite embankment. Smiling, he lifted his hat which was new and wide-brimmed. He had not worn it yesterday and she wondered if he had bought it for the occasion. It was toast-colored with a red and white band around it and was slightly too large for him. He stepped from behind the bush still carrying the black valise. He had on the same suit and the same yellow socks sucked down in his shoes from walking. He crossed the highway and said, "I knew you'd come!"

94   The girl wondered acidly how he had known this. She pointed to the valise and asked, "Why did you bring your Bibles?"

95   He took her elbow, smiling down on her as if he could not stop. "You can never tell when you'll need the word of God, Hulga," he said. She had a moment in which she doubted that this was actually happening and then they began to climb the embankment. They went down into the pasture toward the woods. The boy walked lightly by her side, bouncing on his toes. The valise did not seem to be heavy today; he even swung it. They crossed half the pasture without saying anything and then, putting his hand easily on the small of her back, he asked softly, "Where does your wooden leg join on?"

96   She turned an ugly red and glared at him and for an instant the boy looked abashed. "I didn't mean you no harm," he said. "I only meant you're so brave and all. I guess God takes care of you."

97   "No," she said, looking forward and walking fast, "I don't even believe in God."

98   At this he stopped and whistled. "No!" he exclaimed as if he were too astonished to say anything else.

99   She walked on and in a second he was bouncing at her side, fanning with his hat. "That's very unusual for a girl," he remarked, watching her out of the corner of his eye. When they reached the edge of the wood, he put his hand on her back again and drew her against him without a word and kissed her heavily.

100   The kiss, which had more pressure than feeling behind it, produced that extra surge of adrenalin in the girl that enables one to carry a packed trunk out of a burning house, but in her, the power went at once to the brain. Even before he released her, her mind, clear and detached and ironic anyway, was regarding him from a great distance, with amusement but with pity. She had never been kissed before and

she was pleased to discover that it was an unexceptional experience and all a matter of the mind's control. Some people might enjoy drain water if they were told it was vodka. When the boy, looking expectant but uncertain, pushed her gently away, she turned and walked on, saying nothing as if such business, for her, were common enough.

101   He came along panting at her side, trying to help her when he saw a root that she might trip over. He caught and held back the long swaying blades of thorn vine until she had passed beyond them. She led the way and he came breathing heavily behind her. Then they came out on a sunlit hillside, sloping softly into another one a little smaller. Beyond, they could see the rusted top of the old barn where the extra hay was stored.

102   The hill was sprinkled with small pink weeds. "Then you ain't saved?" he asked suddenly, stopping.

103   The girl smiled. It was the first time she had smiled at him at all. "In my economy," she said, "I'm saved and you are damned but I told you I didn't believe in God."

104   Nothing seemed to destroy the boy's look of admiration. He gazed at her now as if the fantastic animal at the zoo had put its paw through the bars and given him a loving poke. She thought he looked as if he wanted to kiss her again and she walked on before he had the chance.

105   "Ain't there somewheres we can sit down sometime?" he murmured, his voice softening toward the end of the sentence.

106   "In that barn," she said.

107   They made for it rapidly as if it might slide away like a train. It was a large two-story barn, cool and dark inside. The boy pointed up the ladder that led into the loft and said, "It's too bad we can't go up there."

108   "Why can't we?" she asked.

109   "Yer leg," he said reverently.

110   The girl gave him a contemptuous look and putting both hands on the ladder, she climbed it while he stood below, apparently awestruck. She pulled herself expertly through the opening and then looked down at him and said, "Well, come on if you're coming," and he began to climb the ladder, awkwardly bringing the suitcase with him.

111   "We won't need the Bible," she observed.

112   "You never can tell," he said, panting. After he had got into the loft, he was a few seconds catching his breath. She had sat down in a pile of straw. A wide sheath of sunlight, filled with dust particles, slanted over her. She lay back against a bale, her face turned away, looking out the front opening of the barn where hay was thrown from a wagon into the loft. The two pinkspeckled hillsides lay back against a dark ridge of woods. The sky was cloudless and cold blue. The boy

dropped down by her side and put one arm under her and the other over her and began methodically kissing her face, making little noises like a fish. He did not remove his hat but it was pushed far enough back not to interfere. When her glasses got in his way, he took them off of her and slipped them into his pocket.

113   The girl at first did not return any of the kisses but presently she began to and after she had put several on his cheek, she reached his lips and remained there, kissing him again and again as if she were trying to draw all the breath out of him. His breath was clear and sweet like a child's and the kisses were sticky like a child's. He mumbled about loving her and about knowing when he first seen her that he loved her, but the mumbling was like the sleepy fretting of a child being put to sleep by his mother. Her mind, throughout this, never stopped or lost itself for a second to her feelings. "You ain't said you loved me none," he whispered finally, pulling back from her. "You got to say that."

114   She looked away from him off into the hollow sky and then down at a black ridge and then down farther into what appeared to be two green swelling lakes. She didn't realize he had taken her glasses but this landscape could not seem exceptional to her for she seldom paid any close attention to her surroundings.

115   "You got to say it," he repeated. "You got to say you love me."

116   She was always careful how she committed herself. "In a sense," she began, "if you use the word loosely, you might say that. But it's not a word I use. I don't have illusions. I'm one of those people who see *through* to nothing."

117   The boy was frowning. "You got to say it. I said it and you got to say it," he said.

118   The girl looked at him almost tenderly. "You poor baby," she murmured. "It's just as well you don't understand," and she pulled him by the neck, facedown, against her. "We are all damned," she said, "but some of us have taken off our blindfolds and see that there's nothing to see. It's a kind of salvation."

119   The boy's astonished eyes looked blankly through the ends of her hair. "Okay," he almost whined, "but do you love me or don'tcher?"

120   "Yes," she said and added, "in a sense. But I must tell you something. There mustn't be anything dishonest between us." She lifted his head and looked him in the eye. "I am thirty years old," she said. "I have a number of degrees."

121   The boy's look was irritated but dogged. "I don't care," he said. "I don't care a thing about what all you done. I just want to know if you love me or don'tcher?" and he caught her to him and wildly planted her face with kisses until she said, "Yes, yes."

122   "Okay then," he said, letting her go. "Prove it."

123   She smiled, looking dreamily out on the shifty landscape. She had
seduced him without even making up her mind to try. "How?" she
asked, feeling that he should be delayed a little.

124   He leaned over and put his lips to her ear. "Show me where your
wooden leg joins on," he whispered.

125   The girl uttered a sharp little cry and her face instantly drained of
color. The obscenity of the suggestion was not what shocked her. As a
child she had sometimes been subject to feelings of shame but education had removed the last traces of that as a good surgeon scrapes for
cancer; she would no more have felt it over what he was asking than
she would have believed in his Bible. But she was as sensitive about the
artificial leg as a peacock about his tail. No one ever touched it but her.
She took care of it as someone else would his soul, in private and
almost with her own eyes turned away. "No," she said.

126   "I known it," he muttered, sitting up. "You're just playing me for a
sucker."

127   "Oh no no!" she cried. "It joins on at the knee. Only at the knee.
Why do you want to see it?"

128   The boy gave her a long penetrating look. "Because," he said, "it's
what makes you different. You ain't like anybody else."

129   She sat staring at him. There was nothing about her face or her
round freezing-blue eyes to indicate that this had moved her; but she
felt as if her heart had stopped and left her mind to pump her blood. She
decided that for the first time in her life she was face to face with real
innocence. This boy, with an instinct that came from beyond wisdom,
had touched the truth about her. When after a minute, she said in a
hoarse high voice, "All right," it was like surrendering to him completely. It was like losing her own life and finding it again, miracu-
lously, in his.

130   Very gently he began to roll the slack leg up. The artificial limb, in
a white sock and brown flat shoe, was bound in a heavy material like
canvas and ended in an ugly jointure where it was attached to the
stump. The boy's face and his voice were entirely reverent as he uncovered it and said, "Now show me how to take it off and on."

131   She took it off for him and put it back on again and then he took it
off himself, handling it as tenderly as if it were a real one. "See!" he
said with a delighted child's face. "Now I can do it myself!"

132   "Put it back on," she said. She was thinking that she would run
away with him and that every night he would take the leg off and every
morning put it back on again. "Put it back on," she said.

133   "Not yet," he murmured, setting it on its foot out of her reach. "Leave it off for a while. You got me instead."

134   She gave a little cry of alarm but he pushed her down and began to kiss her again. Without the leg she felt entirely dependent on him. Her brain seemed to have stopped thinking altogether and to be about some other function that it was not very good at. Different expressions raced back and forth over her face. Every now and then the boy, his eyes like two steel spikes, would glance behind him where the leg stood. Finally she pushed him off and said, "Put it back on me now."

135   "Wait," he said. He leaned the other way and pulled the valise toward him and opened it. It had a pale blue spotted lining and there were only two Bibles in it. He took one of these out and opened the cover of it. It was hollow and contained a pocket flask of whiskey, a pack of cards, and a small blue box with printing on it. He laid these out in front of her one at a time in an evenly-spaced row, like one presenting offerings at the shrine of a goddess. He put the blue box in her hand. THIS PRODUCT TO BE USED ONLY FOR THE PREVENTION OF DISEASE, she read, and dropped it. The boy was unscrewing the top of the flask. He stopped and pointed, with a smile, to the deck of cards. It was not an ordinary deck but one with an obscene picture on the back of each card. "Take a swig," he said, offering her the bottle first. He held it in front of her, but like one mesmerized, she did not move.

136   Her voice when she spoke had an almost pleading sound. "Aren't you," she murmured, "aren't you just good country people?"

137   The boy cocked his head. He looked as if he were just beginning to understand that she might be trying to insult him. "Yeah," he said, curling his lip slightly, "but it ain't held me back none. I'm as good as you any day in the week."

138   "Give me my leg," she said.

139   He pushed it farther away with his foot. "Come on now, let's begin to have us a good time," he said coaxingly. "We ain't got to know one another good yet."

140   "Give me my leg!" she screamed and tried to lunge for it but he pushed her down easily.

141   "What's the matter with you all of a sudden?" he asked, frowning as he screwed the top on the flask and put it quickly back inside the Bible. "You just a while ago said you didn't believe in nothing. I thought you was some girl!"

142   Her face was almost purple. "You're a Christian!" she hissed. "You're a fine Christian! You're just like them all—say one thing and do another. You're a perfect Christian, you're . . ."

143   The boy's mouth was set angrily. "I hope you don't think," he said in a lofty indignant tone, "that I believe in that crap! I may sell Bibles but I know which end is up and I wasn't born yesterday and I know where I'm going!"

144   "Give me my leg!" she screeched. He jumped up so quickly that she barely saw him sweep the cards and the blue box into the Bible and throw the Bible into the valise. She saw him grab the leg and then she saw it for an instant slanted forlornly across the inside of the suitcase with a Bible at either side of its opposite ends. He slammed the lid shut and snatched up the valise and swung it down the hole and then stepped through himself.

145   When all of him had passed but his head, he turned and regarded her with a look that no longer had any admiration in it. "I've gotten a lot of interesting things," he said. "One time I got a woman's glass eye this way. And you needn't to think you'll catch me because Pointer ain't really my name. I use a different name at every house I call at and don't stay nowhere long. And I'll tell you another thing, Hulga," he said, using the name as if he didn't think much of it, "you ain't so smart. I been believing in nothing ever since I was born!" and then the toast-colored hat disappeared down the hole and the girl was left, sitting on the straw in the dusty sunlight. When she turned her churning face toward the opening, she saw his blue figure struggling successfully over the green speckled lake.

146   Mrs. Hopewell and Mrs. Freeman, who were in the back pasture, digging up onions, saw him emerge a little later from the woods and head across the meadow toward the highway. "Why, that looks like that nice dull young man that tried to sell me a Bible yesterday," Mrs. Hopewell said, squinting. "He must have been selling them to the Negroes back in there. He was so simple," she said, "but I guess the world would be better off if we were all that simple."

147   Mrs. Freeman's gaze drove forward and just touched him before he disappeared under the hill. Then she returned her attention to the evil-smelling onion shoot she was lifting from the ground. "Some can't be that simple," she said. "I know I never could."

Good Country People

Journal

1. MLA Works Cited

Using this model, record this story here.

Author's Last Name, First Name. "Title of the Story." <u>Title of the Book</u>. Ed. First Last Name. City: Publisher, year. Pages of the story.

2. Main Character(s)

Describe each main character, and explain why you think each is a main character.

3. Supporting Characters

Describe each supporting character, and explain why you think each is a supporting character.

4. Setting

Describe the setting. Decide if the setting can be changed and, if so, to where and when.

5. Sequence

Relate the events of the story in order.

6. Plot

Tell the story in no more than three sentences.

7. Conflicts

Identify and explain the conflicts involved here.

8. Significant Quotations

Explain the importance of each of these quotations. Record the page number in the parentheses.

a. "Mrs. Hopewell excused this attitude because of the leg [. . .]" (   ).

b. " 'Why, I think there aren't enough good country people in the world!' she said, stirred" (   ).

c. "She imagined that the two of them walked on the place until they came to the storage barn beyond the two back fields and there, she imagined, that things came to such a pass that she very easily seduced him and that then, of course, she had to reckon with his remorse" (   ).

d. " 'It joins on at the knee. Only at the knee. Why do you want to see it?' " (   ).

e. " 'Aren't you,' she murmured, 'aren't you just good country people?' " (   ).

9. **Foreshadowing**

Identify and explain the hints O'Connor gives to suggest the ending.

FOLLOW-UP QUESTIONS

10 SHORT QUESTIONS

Select the best answer for each.

____ 1. Mrs. Freeman's daughters are
   a. like Hulga.
   b. unlike Hulga.
   c. unknown to Hulga.

____ 2. Mrs. Hopewell is Mrs. Freeman's
   a. relative.
   b. landlord.
   c. close friend.

____ 3. Mrs. Hopewell uses the term "good country people" as
   a. a positive term.
   b. a negative term.
   c. a neutral term.

____ 4. For the name change,
   a. Mrs. Hopewell changes Joy's name to Hulga.
   b. Mrs. Freeman changes Joy's name to Hulga.
   c. Joy changes Joy's name to Hulga.

____ 5. When Mrs. Freeman calls Joy "Hulga," Joy seems to feel
   a. satisfied.
   b. invaded.
   c. comfortable.

____ 6. Hulga seems to
   a. not know Mrs. Freeman.
   b. like Mrs. Freeman.
   c. dislike Mrs. Freeman.

____ 7. Hulga is
   a. well educated.
   b. a middle school dropout.
   c. a high school dropout.

____ 8. Manley Pointer is selling
   a. gadgets.
   b. tools.
   c. Bibles.

____ 9. Hulga
   a. thinks she has control over Pointer.
   b. does not think she has control over Pointer.
   c. is not interested in Pointer.

____ 10. In the end,
   a. Pointer controls the situation.
   b. Hulga controls the situation.
   c. Mrs. Freeman controls the situation.

5 SIGNIFICANT QUOTATIONS

Explain the importance of each of these quotations.

1. "When Mrs. Hopewell thought the name Hulga, she thought of the broad blank hull of a battleship."

2. " 'I'm just a country boy. [. . .] People like you don't like to fool with country people like me!' "

3. "During the night she had imagined that she seduced him."

4. "He leaned over and put his lips to her ear. 'Show me where your wooden leg joins on,' he whispered."

5. " ' And I'll tell you another thing, Hulga,' he said, using the name as if he didn't think much of it, 'you ain't so smart. I been believing in nothing ever since I was born!' "

2 COMPREHENSION ESSAY QUESTIONS

Use specific details and information from the story to answer these as completely as possible.

1. Explain Hulga's misunderstandings of Pointer. Use specific details and information from the story to support your explanation.

2. How does the title relate to Pointer? Explain the significance of the title using specific details and information from the story.

WRITING

Use each of these ideas for writing an essay.

1. We have all been disappointed in others. Write an essay about one person you know, contrasting how you thought they were with how they really are.

2. We have all had high expectations for events or situations. Write an essay about an event or incident that turned out badly, contrasting how wonderful you thought it would be with how it turned out.

Further Writing

1. Read Joyce Carol Oates's "Where Are You Going, Where Have You Been?" (which can be found in a library), and compare this writing with "Good Country People."

2. Compare Manley Pointer in this story with Montresor in Edgar Allan Poe's "The Cask of Amontillado" (page 137).

4

Irony

Irony is found in the difference between what *is* and what *should be.* Irony may be bitter—you work and work, and someone new, who has done nothing, arrives at your job and gets the promotion you deserve. Irony may be humorous—you wake up late and race around knowing you will be late for class, only to get to school and find out that your class has been canceled. Irony may even be providential—you sleep in and miss your bus, only to find out that the bus was in an accident and you are still safe at home. Think of ironies as unexpected twists in time, places, or events.

A story by O. Henry is a good example of irony. In the story a gentleman treats a poor man to a Thanksgiving feast. In the end, both men end up in the hospital. The reader finds out that the poor man has had a big dinner before this second feast and is overfed. Meanwhile, the proud gentleman has spent his money on feeding this poor man who does not need more food, and the gentleman is underfed. The irony, of course, is that the man who does not need the food is fed, while the man who does need the food goes without food.

The stories in this chapter focus on irony. First, Kate Chopin's "The Story of an Hour" turns marital assumptions upside down. Then the American master, O. Henry, presents touching and even bittersweet irony in "Gifts of the Magi" and humorous inversion in "The Ransom of Red Chief." Next, Dorothy Parker infuriates the reader in "The Wonderful Old Gentleman." And last, but certainly not least, Zora Neale Hurston's ironic twist satisfies the reader's sense of justice in "Sweat."

Enjoy the twists here, and reflect on the ironies you have read in other stories—and on those you have experienced in your own life.

The Story of an Hour

KATE CHOPIN

PRE-READING VOCABULARY
CONTEXT

Use context clues to define these words before reading. Use a dictionary as needed.

1. Kara was *afflicted* with a need to shop at the mall every weekend.
   Afflicted means _____.

2. The horrible earthquake caused major *disasters,* such as gas explosions and buildings collapsing, that resulted in injuries and deaths. *Disaster* means _____.

3. Before there were telephones, Sung Yu had to go to an office and send a *telegram* with news. *Telegram* means _____.

4. Vernie tried to *hasten* Stephanie so that she could get to school on time. *Hasten* means _____.

5. After the children lost their beloved dog, they suffered much *grief* and cried for days. *Grief* means _____.

6. The little leaves were all *aquiver* as the breeze blew through the tree. *Aquiver* means _____.

7. Some people are never allowed to laugh; they suffer severe *repression* when they see something funny. *Repression* means

   _____.

8. When Dottie did not understand the directions, her face became *vacant* with no expression. *Vacant* means _____.

9. The puppy had a *keen* sense of smell and could scent a hamburger a mile away. *Keen* means _____.

10. Blood *pulses* through our veins with a steady beat. *Pulse* means

    _____.

11. The king held the most *exalted* position in the kingdom. *Exalted*

    means _____.

12. In the Macy's *procession*, colorful floats followed one after another

    after another. *Procession* means _____.

13. The host opened the door and warmly *welcomed* each guest as he or

    she arrived. *Welcome* means _____.

14. Without thinking about it, Daren followed his *impulse* and suddenly

    bet all his chips on red. *Impulse* means _____.

15. When Todd thinks he is right, he answers with enough confidence

    and *self-assertion* to convince others he is right. *Self-assertion* means

    _____.

16. Nancy was *imploring* the builder to start her deck as soon as possible

    before the rains came. *Implore* means _____.

17. A substance that can change all into gold, that can make one live

    forever, or that allows one to taste the very best of life is called an

    elixir. Elixir _____.

18. Robbie *shuddered* at the thought of having to take another algebra

    test. *Shudder* means _____.

19. The Cougars yelled, screamed, and jumped in *triumph* when they won

    the game. *Triumph* means _____.

20. Margaret was absolutely *amazed* when she won the ten-million-dollar

    lottery. *Amazed* means _____.

Pre-reading Vocabulary
Word Attack

Define these words by solving the parts. Use a dictionary as needed.

1. inability
2. bespoke
3. fearfully
4. powerless
5. fellow-creatures
6. illumination
7. keyhole
8. feverish
9. latchkey
10. travel-stained

Pre-reading Questions

Try answering these questions as you read.

What happens to Mr. Mallard?

How does Mrs. Mallard feel?

What happens to Mrs. Mallard?

What is ironic in the story?

The Story of an Hour

KATE CHOPIN

> **Kate O'Flaherty Chopin** was born in St. Louis, Missouri, in 1851 to an affluent family. Although her father died when she was young, her widowed mother gave young Kate a taste of female independence. In 1870 Kate married Oscar Chopin and moved to New Orleans and then to Natchitoches Parish. Here she met the Creoles, Acadians, and southern African Americans she would later write about. Oscar died in 1882, and by 1884 she sold the plantation, gathered her five children, and returned home to St. Louis where she began to write and where her works were published in popular women's magazines. Influenced noticeably by de Maupassant's sense of irony and Ibsen's social comment, Chopin wrote stories, often touched with rich symbols and images of nature, that question societal assumptions and dictates. *The Awakening* remains her master work, although stories such as "Desiree's Baby" and "The Kiss" offer Chopin at her most terse. Chopin died in 1904.

Knowing that Mrs. Mallard was afflicted with a heart trouble, great care was taken to break to her as gently as possible the news of her husband's death.

2   It was her sister Josephine who told her, in broken sentences; veiled hints that revealed in half concealing. Her husband's friend Richards was there, too, near her. It was he who had been in the newspaper office when intelligence of the railroad disaster was received, with Brently Mallard's name leading the list of "killed." He had only taken the time to assure himself of its truth by a second telegram, and had hastened to forestall any less careful, less tender friend in bearing the sad message.

3   She did not hear the story as many women have heard the same, with a paralyzed inability to accept its significance. She wept at once, with sudden, wild abandonment, in her sister's arms. When the storm of grief had spent itself she went away to her room alone. She would have no one follow her.

4   There stood, facing the open window, a comfortable, roomy armchair. Into this she sank, pressed down by a physical exhaustion that haunted her body and seemed to reach into her soul.

5   She could see in the open square before her house the tops of trees that were all aquiver with the new spring life. The delicious breath of rain was in the air. In the street below a peddler was crying his wares. The notes of a distant song which some one was singing reached her faintly, and countless sparrows were twittering in the caves.

6   There were patches of blue sky showing here and there through the clouds that had met and piled one above the other in the west facing her window.

7   She sat with her head thrown back upon the cushion of the chair, quite motionless, except when a sob came up into her throat and shook her, as a child who has cried itself to sleep continues to sob in its dreams.

8   She was young, with a fair, calm face, whose lines bespoke repression and even a certain strength. But now there was a dull stare in her eyes, whose gaze was fixed away off yonder on one of those patches of blue sky. It was not a glance of reflection, but rather indicated a suspension of intelligent thought.

9   There was something coming to her and she was waiting for it, fearfully. What was it? She did not know; it was too subtle and elusive to name. But she felt it, creeping out of the sky, reaching toward her through the sounds, the scents, the color that filled the air.

10   Now her bosom rose and fell tumultuously. She was beginning to recognize this thing that was approaching to possess her, and she was striving to beat it back with her will—as powerless as her two white slender hands would have been.

11   When she abandoned herself a little whispered word escaped her slightly parted lips. She said it over and over under her breath: "free, free, free!" The vacant stare and the look of terror that had followed it went from her eyes. They stayed keen and bright. Her pulses beat fast, and the coursing blood warmed and relaxed every inch of her body.

12   She did not stop to ask if it were or were not a monstrous joy that held her. A clear and exalted perception enabled her to dismiss the suggestion as trivial.

13   She knew that she would weep again when she saw the kind, tender hands folded in death; the face that had never looked save with love upon her, fixed and gray and dead. But she saw beyond that bitter moment a long procession of years to come that would belong to her absolutely. And she opened and spread her arms out to them in welcome.

14   There would be no one to live for her during those coming years; she would live for herself There would be no powerful will bending hers in that blind persistence with which men and women believe they have a right to impose a private will upon a fellow-creature. A kind intention or a cruel intention made the act seem no less a crime as she looked upon it in that brief moment of illumination.

15   And yet she had loved him—sometimes. Often she had not. What did it matter! What could love, the unsolved mystery, count for in face

of this possession of self-assertion which she suddenly recognized as the strongest impulse of her being!

16   "Free! Body and soul free!" she kept whispering.

17   Josephine was kneeling before the closed door with her lips to the keyhole, imploring for admission. "Louise, open the door! I beg; open the door—you will make yourself ill. What are you doing, Louise? For heaven's sake open the door."

18   "Go away. I am not making myself ill." No; she was drinking in a very elixir of life through that open window.

19   Her fancy was running riot along those days ahead of her. Spring days, and summer days, and all sorts of days that would be her own. She breathed a quick prayer that life might be long. It was only yesterday she had thought with a shudder that life might be long.

20   She arose at length and opened the door to her sister's importunities. There was a feverish triumph in her eyes, and she carried herself unwittingly like a goddess of Victory. She clasped her sister's waist, and together they descended the stairs. Richards stood waiting for them at the bottom.

21   Some one was opening the front door with a latchkey. It was Brently Mallard who entered, a little travel-stained, composedly carrying his grip-sack and umbrella. He had been far from the scene of accident, and did not even know there had been one. He stood amazed at Josephine's piercing cry; at Richards' quick motion to screen him from the view of his wife.

22   But Richards was too late.

23   When the doctors came they said she had died of heart disease—of joy that kills.

The Story of an Hour

JOURNAL

1. MLA Works Cited

Using this model, record this reading here.

Author's Last Name, First Name. "Title of the Story." <u>Title of the Book</u>. Ed.
*   First Last Name. City: Publisher, year. Pages of the story.*

2. Main Character(s)

Describe each main character, and explain why you think each is a main
character.

3. Supporting Characters

Describe each supporting character, and explain why you think each is a
supporting character.

4. Setting

Describe the setting. Decide if this setting can be changed and, if so, to where
and when.

5. Sequence

Relate the events of the story in order.

6. Plot

Tell the story in no more than two sentences.

7. Conflict

Identify and explain the conflicts involved here.

8. Significant Quotations

Explain the importance of each of these quotations. Record the page number in the parentheses.

a. "Knowing that Mrs. Mallard was afflicted with a heart trouble, great care was taken to break to her as gently as possible the news of her husband's death" (   ).

b. "When the storm of grief had spent itself she went away to her room alone" (   ).

c. "She could see in the open square before her house the tops of trees that were all aquiver with the new spring life" (   ).

d. "When she abandoned herself a little whispered word escaped her slightly parted lips. She said it over and over under her breath: 'free, free, free!' " (   ).

e. "Some one was opening the door with a latchkey" (   ).

9. Irony

Identify and explain the irony in this story.

Follow-up Questions

10 Short Questions

Select the <u>best</u> answer for each.

____ 1. The person to first hear the news of the accident is
    a. Mrs. Mallard.
    b. Josephine.
    c. Richards.

____ 2. S/he hears the news
    a. at the railroad station.
    b. from the newspaper.
    c. at home.

____ 3. Josephine and Richards are at the Mallard house
    a. to awaken Mrs. Mallard.
    b. to have lunch with Mrs. Mallard.
    c. to tell Mrs. Mallard about the accident.

____ 4. Mrs. Mallard is immediately
    a. overwhelmed.
    b. overjoyed.
    c. unimpressed.

____ 5. Mrs. Mallard
    a. goes to her room.
    b. stays with her sister.
    c. makes lunch.

____ 6. Mrs. Mallard slowly
    a. cries.
    b. faints.
    c. whispers "free."

____ 7. Mrs. Mallard
    a. always loved Brently Mallard.
    b. did not always love Brently Mallard.
    c. was looking forward to Brently Mallard's return.

____ 8. Brently
    a. was at home all the time.
    b. was in the accident.
    c. was not in the accident.

____ 9. Brently
    a. does come home.
    b. does not come home.
    c. is dead.

____ 10. Mrs. Mallard is
    a. delighted by his return.
    b. unmoved by his return.
    c. destroyed by his return.

5 Significant Quotations

Explain the importance of each of these quotations.

1. "Knowing that Mrs. Mallard was afflicted with a heart condition, great care was taken to break to her as gently as possible the news of her husband's death."

2. "She wept at once, with sudden, wild abandonment, in her sister's arms."

3. "There was something coming to her and she was waiting for it, fearfully."

4. "She breathed a quick prayer that life might be long. It was only yesterday she had thought with a shudder that life might be long."

5. "When the doctors came they said she had died of heart disease—of joy that kills."

2 COMPREHENSION ESSAY QUESTIONS

Use specific details and information from the story to answer these as completely as possible.

1. How does the title relate to the story? Explain the significance of the title using specific details and information from the story.

2. Explain the phrase "of joy that kills." Use specific details and information from the story in your explanation.

WRITING

Use each of these ideas for writing an essay.

1. We have all tried to cover up our feelings at one time or another. Tell the story of a time you or someone you know used pleasure or sorrow to cover up real feelings about a situation or event. Pay special attention in your narrative to the reactions of others.

2. We have all made mistakes about how we think others feel. Sometimes these misunderstandings are quite humorous. Describe a time when you or someone you know assumed the wrong thing about someone else's feelings.

Further Writing

1. Discuss the similarities between Mrs. Mallard in this story and Calixta in Kate Chopin's "The Storm" (which can be found in a library).

2. Discuss the similarities between Mrs. Mallard in this story and Nathalie in Kate Chopin's "The Kiss" (which can be found in a library).

3. Discuss the similarities between Mrs. Mallard in this story and Mrs. Alving in Henrik Ibsen's *Ghosts* (which can be found in a library).

Gifts of the Magi

O. Henry

Pre-reading Vocabulary
Context

Use context clues to define these words before reading. Use a dictionary as needed.

1. Sam was always cheap and never paid for anything he didn't have to, as a result of his *parsimony. Parsimony* means _____.

2. Rajan would never live in a *shabby* little shack and always demands the best in life. *Shabby* means _____.

3. Patricia owns and maintains her home and is truly the *mistress* of her home. *Mistress* means _____.

4. Laura liked only the very fine and beautiful—the most *sterling*— things in life. *Sterling* means _____.

5. Baby Ashley had many *possessions,* including toys, dolls, beautiful clothes, and a sun-filled room. *Possession* means _____.

6. At Niagara Falls, the water comes *cascading* down the falls at the rate of thousands of gallons each minute. *Cascading* means

   _____.

7. Kirk went *ransacking* through his closet trying to find his favorite fraternity T-shirt that was lost. *Ransack* means _____.

8. Ted attached a *fob chain* to his pocket watch so that it would hang out of his vest pocket for all to see. *Fob chain* means

   _____.

9. The town suffered the *ravages* of war with burned-down buildings and blown-apart streets. *Ravage* means _____.

10. In past times, being a dancer in a line as a *chorus girl* was looked on as a lowly job only for loose women. *Chorus girl* means

    _____.

11. Alex was *terrified* of snakes and would faint at the sight of one. *Terrified* means _____.

12. Patty has the most *peculiar* laugh and is the only person in the world who can laugh the way she does. *Peculiar* means _____.

13. The men who came to visit baby Jesus and who brought precious gifts were considered to be wise and were called the *Magi*. *Magi* means

    _____.

14. George was *ecstatic* when his name was called as the winner of the lottery. *Ecstatic* means _____.

15. Sue became *hysterical* and had to be calmed down when she learned her cat had suddenly died. *Hysterical* means _____.

16. After Stu took the medicine, his headache *vanished,* and he felt fine. *Vanish* means _____.

17. Missy loves hot fudge sundaes and absolutely *craves* one when she hasn't had one in a long time. *Crave* means _____.

18. Bernice had wonderfully thick hair, and she took very special care of her beautiful *tresses. Tress* means _____.

19. The newborn Jesus may be referred to as the *Babe in the manger.* *Babe in the manger* means _____.

20. Ethan *sacrificed* his free time to help teach the students how to write poetry. *Sacrifice* means _____.

PRE-READING VOCABULARY
WORD ATTACK

Define these words by solving the parts. Use a dictionary as needed.

1. bulldozing
2. predominating
3. subsiding
4. furnished
5. blurred
6. airshaft
7. rippling
8. nervously
9. ornamentation
10. close-lying
11. critically
12. overcoat
13. immovable
14. fixedly
15. laboriously
16. mathematician
17. illumination
18. necessitating
19. lamely

PRE-READING QUESTIONS

Try answering these questions as you read.

What does Della sell?

What does Della buy?

What does Jim sell?

What does Jim buy?

What is ironic in the story?

Gifts of the Magi

O. Henry

> **William Sydney Porter** was born in 1862 to an educated and comfortable family living in Greensboro, North Carolina, in the Reconstruction South. As a result of his mother's early death and his father's alcoholism, he was raised by his aunt, who gave him a love for narration. Like his father, he became a pharmacist's apprentice, and although he did not like the work, his uncle's drugstore provided him with a good vantage point from which to observe the townspeople. In 1882 he married Athol Estes Roach, settled into work at the National Bank of Texas, and bought a printing press to publish his stories in the short-lived *The Rolling Stone*. He was charged and cleared of embezzlement—a charge he consistently denied. Later, faced with retrial, he fled to New Orleans and then to Honduras, all the while observing others. Returning to Texas because of his wife's ailing health and subsequent death, he was retried and sent to the Ohio state penitentiary where he served three years of a five-year sentence. Although it was a dark period in his life, he was again observing and, perhaps, gained his compassion for the underdog, as well as the pen name "O. Henry." In 1902 he moved to New York City to produce weekly stories for *The New York Sunday World*, and at the turn of the century and amid the streets of New York that were largely filled with immigrants, he found endless stock for his stories. O. Henry died in 1910.
>
> His stories are marked by concise characterizations, concern for working women and the poor, adroit wit, and succinct irony. His many stories and selected sketches are largely based on kernels from his real-life observations and are available in many collections.

One dollar and eighty-seven cents. That was all. And 60 cents of it was in pennies. Pennies saved one and two at a time by bulldozing the grocer and the vegetable man and the butcher until one's cheeks burned with the silent imputation of parsimony that such close dealing implied. Three times Della counted it. One dollar and eighty-seven cents. And the next day would be Christmas.

2   There was clearly nothing to do but flop down on the shabby little couch and howl. So Della did it. Which instigates the moral reflection that life is made up of sobs, sniffles and smiles, with sniffles predominating.

3   While the mistress of the home is gradually subsiding from the first stage to the second take a look at the home. A furnished flat at $8 per week. It did not exactly beggar description, but it certainly had that word on the lookout for the mendicancy squad.

4   In the vestibule below belonged to this flat a letter-box into which no letter would go, and an electric button from which no mortal finger

could coax a ring. Also appertaining thereunto was a card bearing the name "Mr. James Dillingham Young."

5   The "Dillingham" had been flung to the breeze during a former period of prosperity when its possessor was being paid $30 per week. Now, when the income was shrunk to $20, the letters of "Dillingham" looked blurred, as though they were thinking seriously of contracting to a modest and unassuming D. But whenever Mr. James Dillingham Young came home and reached his flat above he was called "Jim" and greatly hugged by Mrs. James Dillingham Young, already introduced to you as Della. Which is all very good.

6   Della finished her cry and attended to her cheeks with the powder rag. She stood by the window and looked out dully at a gray cat walking a gray fence in a gray backyard. Tomorrow would be Christmas Day, and she had only $1.87 with which to buy Jim a present. She had been saving every penny she could for months, with this result. Twenty dollars a week doesn't go far. Expenses had been greater than she had calculated. They always are. Only $1.87 to buy a present for Jim. Her Jim. Many a happy hour she had spent planning for something nice for him. Something fine and rare and sterling— something just a little bit near to being worthy of the honor of being owned by Jim.

7   There was a pier-glass between the windows of the room. Perhaps you have seen a pier-glass in an $8 flat. A very thin and very agile person may, by observing his reflection in a rapid sequence of longitudinal strips, obtain a fairly accurate conception of his looks. Della, being slender, had mastered the art.

8   Suddenly she whirled from the window and stood before the glass. Her eyes were shining brilliantly, but her face had lost its color within twenty seconds. Rapidly she pulled down her hair and let it fall to its full length.

9   Now, there were two possessions of the James Dillingham Youngs in which they both took a mighty pride. One was Jim's gold watch that had been his father's and his grandfather's. The other was Della's hair. Had the Queen of Sheba lived in the flat across the airshaft Della would have let her hair hang out the window some day to dry and mocked at Her Majesty's jewels and gifts. Had King Solomon been the janitor, with all his treasures piled up in the basement, Jim would have pulled out his watch every time he passed, just to see him pluck at his beard from envy.

10   So now Della's beautiful hair fell about her, rippling and shining like a cascade of brown waters. It reached below her knee and made itself almost a garment for her. And then she did it up again nervously

and quickly. Once she faltered for a minute and stood still while a tear or two splashed on the worn red carpet.

11   On went her old brown jacket; on went her old brown hat. With a whirl of skirts and with the brilliant sparkle still in her eyes, she fluttered out the door and down the stairs to the street.

12   Where she stopped the sign read: "Mme. Sofronie. Hair Goods of All Kinds." One flight up Della ran, and collected herself, panting, before Madame, large, too white, chilly and hardly looking the "Sofronie."

13   "Will you buy my hair?" asked Della.

14   "I buy hair," said Madame. "Take yer hat off and let's have a sight at the looks of it."

15   Down rippled the brown cascade.

16   "Twenty dollars," said Madame, lifting the mass with a practised hand.

17   "Give it to me quick," said Della.

18   Oh, and the next two hours tripped by on rosy wings. Forget the hashed metaphor. She was ransacking the stores for Jim's present.

19   She found it at last. It surely had been made for Jim and no one else. There was none other like it in any of the stores, and she had turned all of them inside out. It was a platinum fob chain simple and chaste in design, properly proclaiming its value by substance alone and not by meretricious ornamentation—as all good things should do. It was even worthy of The Watch. As soon as she saw it she knew that it must be Jim's. It was like him. Quietness and value—the description applied to both. Twenty-one dollars they took from her for it, and she hurried home with the 87 cents. With that chain on his watch Jim might be properly anxious about the time in any company. Grand as the watch was, he sometimes looked at it on the sly on account of the old leather strap that he used in place of a chain.

20   When Della reached home her intoxication gave way a little to prudence and reason. She got out her curling irons and lighted the gas and went to work repairing the ravages made by generosity added to love. Which is always a tremendous task, dear friends—a mammoth task.

21   Within forty minutes her head was covered with tiny, close-lying curls that made her look wonderfully like a truant schoolboy. She looked at her reflection in the mirror long, carefully and critically.

22   "If Jim doesn't kill me," she said to herself, "before he takes a second look at me, he'll say I look like a Coney Island chorus girl. But what could I do—oh, what could I do with a dollar and eighty-seven cents!""

23   At 7 o'clock the coffee was made and the frying pan was on the back of the stove hot and ready to cook the chops.

24   Jim was never late. Della doubled the fob chain in her hand and sat on the corner of the table near the door that he always entered. Then she heard his step on the stair away down on the first flight, and she turned white for just a moment. She had a habit of saying little silent prayers about the simplest everyday things, and now she whispered: "Please, God, make him think I am still pretty."

25   The door opened and Jim stepped in and closed it. He looked thin and very serious. Poor fellow, he was only twenty-two—and to be burdened with a family! He needed a new overcoat and he was without gloves.

26   Jim stopped inside the door, as immovable as a setter at the scent of quail. His eyes were fixed upon Della, and there was an expression in them that she could not read, and it terrified her. It was not anger, nor surprise, nor disapproval, nor horror, nor any of the sentiments that she had been prepared for. He simply stared at her fixedly with that peculiar expression on his face.

27   Della wriggled off the table and went for him.

28   "Jim, darling," she cried, "don't look at me that way. I had my hair cut off and sold it because I couldn't have lived through Christmas without giving you a present. It'll grow again—you won't mind, will you? I just had to do it. My hair grows awfully fast. Say 'Merry Christmas!' Jim, and let's be happy. You don't know what a nice— what a beautiful, nice gift I've got for you."

29   "You've cut off your hair?" asked Jim, laboriously, as if he had not arrived at that patent fact yet even after the hardest mental labor.

30   "Cut it off and sold it," said Della. "Don't you like me just as well, anyhow? I'm me without my hair, ain't I?"

31   Jim looked about the room curiously.

32   "You say your hair is gone?" he said, with an air almost of idiocy.

33   "You needn't look for it," said Della. "It's sold, I tell you—sold and gone too. It's Christmas Eve, boy. Be good to me, for it went for you. Maybe the hairs of my head were numbered," she went on with a sudden serious sweetness, "but nobody could ever count my love for you. Shall I put the chops on, Jim?"

34   Out of his trance Jim seemed to quickly wake. He enfolded his Della. For ten seconds let us regard with discreet scrutiny some inconsequential object in the other direction. Eight dollars a week or a million a year—what is the difference? A mathematician or a wit would give you the wrong answer. The magi brought valuable gifts, but that was not among them. This dark assertion will be illuminated later on.

35   Jim drew a package from his overcoat pocket and threw it upon the table.

36   "Don't make any mistake, Dell," he said, "about me. I don't think there's anything in the way of a haircut or a shave or a shampoo that could make me like my girl any less. But if you'll unwrap that package you may see why you had me going awhile at first."

37   White fingers and nimble tore at the string and paper. And then an ecstatic scream of joy; and then, alas! a quick feminine change to hysterical tears and wails, necessitating the immediate employment of all the comforting powers of the lord of the flat.

38   For there lay The Combs—the set of combs, side and back, that Della had worshipped for long in a Broadway window. Beautiful combs, pure tortoise shell, with jewelled rims—just the shade to wear in the beautiful vanished hair. They were expensive combs, she knew, and her heart had simply craved and yearned over them without the least hope of possession. And now, they were hers, but the tresses that should have adorned the coveted adornments were gone.

39   But she hugged them to her bosom, and at length she was able to look up with dim eyes and a smile and say: "My hair grows so fast, Jim!"

40   And then Della leaped up like a little singed cat and cried, "Oh, oh!"

41   Jim had not yet seen his beautiful present. She held it out to him eagerly upon her open palm. The dull, precious metal seemed to flash with a reflection of her bright and ardent spirit.

42   "Isn't it a dandy, Jim? I hunted all over town to find it. You'll have to look at the time a hundred times a day now. Give me your watch. I want to see how it looks on it."

43   Instead of obeying, Jim tumbled down on the couch and put his hands under the back of his head and smiled.

44   "Dell," said he, "let's put our Christmas presents away and keep 'em a while. They're too nice to use just at present. I sold the watch to get the money to buy your combs. And now suppose you put the chops on."

45   The magi, as you know, were wise men—wonderfully wise men—who brought gifts to the Babe in the manger. They invented the art of giving Christmas gifts. Being wise, their gifts were no doubt wise ones, possibly bearing the privilege of exchange in case of duplication. And here I have lamely related to you the uneventful chronicle of two foolish children in a flat who most unwisely sacrificed for each other the greatest treasures of their house. But in a last word to the wise of these days let it be said that of all who give gifts these two were of the wisest. Of all who give and receive gifts, such as they are the wisest. Everywhere they are the wisest. They are the magi.

Gifts of the Magi

Journal

1. MLA Works Cited

Using this model, record this reading here.

Author's Last Name, First Name. "Title of the Story." <u>Title of the Book</u>. Ed. First Last Name. City: Publisher, year. Pages of the story.

2. Main Character(s)

Describe each main character, and explain why you think each is a main character.

3. Supporting Characters

Describe each supporting character, and explain why you think each is a supporting character.

4. Setting

Describe the setting. Decide if this setting can be changed and, if so, to where and when.

5. **Sequence**

   Relate the events of the story in order.

6. **Plot**

   Tell the story in no more than two sentences.

7. **Conflict.**

   Identify and explain the conflicts involved here.

8. **Significant Quotations**

   Explain the importance of each of these quotations. Record the page number in the parentheses.

   a. "Tomorrow would be Christmas Day, and she had only $1.87 with which to buy Jim a present" (   ).

b. "One was Jim's gold watch that had been his father's and his grandfather's. The other was Della's hair" (   ).

c. " 'Will you buy my hair?' asked Della" (   ).

d. "For there lay The Combs—the set of combs, side and back, that Della had worshipped for long in a Broadway window" (   ).

e. " 'Dell,' he said, 'let's put our Christmas presents away and keep 'em for a while' " (   ).

9. Irony

Identify and explain the irony in this story.

Follow-up Questions

10 Short Questions

*Select the **best** answer for each.*

____ 1. This story is set in
   a. Boston.
   b. Dallas.
   c. New York.

____ 2. The Youngs are
   a. rich.
   b. poor.
   c. middle class.

____ 3. Della's most prized possession is her
   a. apartment.
   b. hair.
   c. watch.

____ 4. Jim's most prized possession is his
   a. apartment.
   b. hair.
   c. watch.

____ 5. Della wants to
   a. sell her hair.
   b. pawn Jim's watch.
   c. purchase the combs.

____ 6. Della wants to
   a. buy the combs.
   b. buy Jim's watch.
   c. buy Jim a fob chain.

____ 7. Jim wants to
   a. sell Della's hair.
   b. pawn his watch.
   c. purchase the fob chain.

____ 8. Jim wants to
   a. buy the combs.
   b. buy the watch.
   c. buy the fob chain.

____ 9. The gifts are for
   a. Della's birthday.
   b. Jim's birthday.
   c. Christmas.

____ 10. Their celebration
   a. is ruined because of the gifts.
   b. is not ruined because of the gifts.
   c. is ruined by their losses.

5 Significant Quotations

Explain the importance of each of these quotations.

1. "One dollar and eighty-seven cents. That was all."

2. "Now, there were two possessions of the James Dillingham Youngs in which they both took a mighty pride."

3. " 'I buy hair,' said Madame."

4. "And now, they were hers, but the tresses that should have adorned the coveted adornments were gone."

5. " 'Dell,' he said, 'let's put our Christmas presents away and keep 'em a while.' "

2 Comprehension Essay Questions

Use specific details and information from the story to answer these as completely as possible.

1. Explain the ironies in this story, using specific details and information from the story.

2. "Magi" has come to imply "wise." Explain the irony in this title, using specific details and information from the story.

Writing

Use each of these ideas for writing an essay.

1. Tell the story of a purchase that you or someone you know worked or saved long and hard for and that turned out not to be worth the effort.

2. Tell the story of an ironic twist in your life or in the life of someone you know.

Further Writing

1. "Gifts of the Magi" is classic O. Henry. Compare the irony in this story to the irony centered on an object in Guy de Maupassant's "The Necklace" (which can be found in a library).

2. Compare the irony of these gifts with the irony of the inheritance in Dorothy Parker's "The Wonderful Old Gentleman" (page 329).

The Ransom of Red Chief

O. HENRY

PRE-READING VOCABULARY
CONTEXT

Use context clues to define these words before reading. Use a dictionary as needed.

1. *Kidnapping,* or the taking of someone against his or her will, is a federal offense. *Kidnapping* means _____.

2. When Kristin climbed to the very top of the hill, she had reached the *summit. Summit* means _____.

3. Miguel is a very honest person and refuses to be part of anything that is *fraudulent. Fraudulent* means _____.

4. Vernie had a *scheme* to make a fortune; she would buy old houses, fix them up, and sell them for a profit. *Scheme* means _____.

5. Nancy is a *prominent* citizen who has served as mayor, senator, and governor. *Prominent* means _____.

6. In order to get back his rare bird that was that stolen, José had to pay a *ransom* of five hundred dollars. *Ransom* means _____.

7. Janet decided to drive across the flat fields of Ohio and Illinois, which are part of the American *plains. Plains* means _____.

8. When Ajay had his head shaved, he looked as if the top of his head was gone and he had been *scalped. Scalped* means _____.

9. When Steve bought a new boat, he *christened* it *Weekends* and had this name painted on the back. *Christen* means _____.

10. When Purvi lost her wallet with all her money in it, she was *desperate* to get it back. *Desperate* means _____.

11. After getting lost, Artie had to get out the map and *reconnoiter* to figure out where he was. *Reconnoiter* means _____.

12. Evelyn loved the many trees that were around her home and that gave her a rich, *sylvan* view. *Sylvan* means _____.

13. Joyce *complies* with the law and always obeys the speed limit. *Comply* means _____.

14. Warren looked at Michael *suspiciously* when Michael's face was covered with chocolate and the new cake was missing. *Suspicious* means _____.

15. Old cowboys in the West sometimes referred to a horse as a *"hoss."* *Hoss* means _____.

16. Carrie thought Reid was trying to cheat her, but then she decided he was being fair and *square.* *Square* means _____.

17. Mark offered a thousand dollars for the car, but the seller offered a *counter-proposition* of two thousand dollars. *Counter-proposition* means _____.

18. The people who live around you are called your *neighbors. Neighbor* means _____.

19. Betsy was so *liberal* in spreading the jelly that the bread fell apart because of the sheer weight of the jelly. *Liberal* means

_____.

20. After walking on the old wooden boardwalk, Missy had to *abstract* a splinter from her foot. *Abstract* means _____.

Pre-reading Vocabulary
Word Attack

Define these words by solving the parts. Use a dictionary as needed.

 1. self-satisfied
 2. semi-rural
 3. bloodhound
 4. fancier
 5. forecloser
 6. welter-weight
 7. tail-feathers
 8. magic-lantern
 9. warpath
10. during-dinner
11. war-whoop
12. outlaw
13. indecent
14. terrifying
15. sun-up

16. sleepiness
17. lambkin
18. disappearance
19. earthquake
20. skyrocket
21. parental
22. wildcat
23. hereinafter
24. fence-post
25. postmaster
26. mail-carrier
27. self-defense
28. mad-house
29. counterplot
30. spend-thrift

Pre-reading Questions

Try answering these questions as you read.

What is the plan?

How does the boy react?

What goes wrong?

What is the irony in the story?

The Ransom of Red Chief

O. HENRY

William Sydney Porter was born in 1862 to an educated and comfortable family living in Greensboro, North Carolina, in the Reconstruction South. As a result of his mother's early death and his father's alcoholism, he was raised by his aunt, who gave him a love for narration. Like his father, he became a pharmacist's apprentice, and although he did not like the work, his uncle's drugstore provided him with a good vantage point from which to observe the townspeople. In 1882 he married Athol Estes Roach, settled into work at the National Bank of Texas, and bought a printing press to publish his stories in the short-lived *The Rolling Stone.* He was charged and cleared of embezzlement—a charge he consistently denied. Later, faced with retrial, he fled to New Orleans and then to Honduras, all the while observing others. Returning to Texas because of his wife's ailing health and subsequent death, he was retried and sent to the Ohio state penitentiary where he served three years of a five-year sentence. Although it was a dark period in his life, he was again observing and, perhaps, gained his compassion for the underdog, as well as the pen name "O. Henry." In 1902 he moved to New York City to produce weekly stories for *The New York Sunday World,* and at the turn of the century and amid the streets of New York that were largely filled with immigrants, he found endless stock for his stories. O. Henry died in 1910.

His stories are marked by concise characterizations, concern for working women and the poor, adroit wit, and succinct irony. His many stories and selected sketches are largely based on kernels from his real-life observations and are available in many collections.

It looked like a good thing: but wait till I tell you. We were down South, in Alabama—Bill Driscoll and myself—when this kidnapping idea struck us. It was, as Bill afterward expressed it, "during a moment of temporary mental apparition"; but we didn't find that out till later.

2   There was a town down there, as flat as a flannel-cake, and called Summit, of course. It contained inhabitants of as undeleterious and self-satisfied a class of peasantry as ever clustered around a Maypole.

3   Bill and me had a joint capital of about six hundred dollars, and we needed just two thousand dollars more to pull off a fraudulent town-lot scheme in Western Illinois with. We talked it over on the front steps of the hotel. Philoprogenitoveness, says we, is strong in semi-rural communities; therefore, and for other reasons, a kidnapping project ought to do better there than in the radius of newspapers that send reporters

out in plain clothes to stir up talk about such things. We knew that Summit couldn't get after us with anything stronger than constables and, maybe, some lackadaisical bloodhounds and a diatribe or two in the *Weekly Farmers' Budget*. So, it looked good.

4   We selected for our victim the only child of a prominent citizen named Ebenezer Dorset. The father was respectable and tight, a mortgage fancier and a stern, upright collection-plate passer and forecloser. The kid was a boy of ten, with bas-relief freckles, and hair the color of the cover of the magazine you buy at the news-stand when you want to catch a train. Bill and me figured that Ebenezer would melt down for a ransom of two thousand dollars to a cent. But wait till I tell you.

5   About two miles from Summit was a little mountain, covered with a dense cedar brake. On the rear elevation of this mountain was a cave. There we stored provisions.

6   One evening after sundown, we drove in a buggy past old Dorset's house. The kid was in the street, throwing rocks at a kitten on the opposite fence.

7   "Hey, little boy!" says Bill, "would you like to have a bag of candy and a nice ride?"

8   The boy catches Bill neatly in the eye with a piece of brick.

9   "That will cost the old man an extra five hundred dollars," says Bill, climbing over the wheel.

10   That boy put up a fight like a welter-weight cinnamon bear; but, at last, we got him down in the bottom of the buggy and drove away. We took him up to the cave, and I hitched the horse in the cedar brake. After dark I drove the buggy to the little village, three miles away, where we had hired it, and walked back to the mountain.

11   Bill was pasting court-plaster over the scratches and bruises on his features. There was a fire burning behind the big rock at the entrance of the cave, and the boy was watching a pot of boiling coffee, with two buzzard tail-feathers stuck in his red hair. He points a stick at me when I come up, and says:

12   "Ha! cursed paleface, do you dare to enter the camp of Red Chief, the terror of the plains?"

13   "He's all right now," says Bill, rolling up his trousers and examining some bruises on his shins. "We're playing Indian. We're making Buffalo Bill's show look like magic-lantern views of Palestine in the town hall. I'm Old Hank, the Trapper, Red Chief's captive, and I'm to be scalped at daybreak. By Geronimo! that kid can kick hard."

14   Yes, sir, that boy seemed to be having the time of his life. The fun of camping out in a cave had made him forget that he was a captive

himself. He immediately christened me Snake-eye, the Spy, and announced that, when his braves returned from the warpath, I was to be broiled at the stake at the rising of the sun.

15   Then we had supper; and he filled his mouth full of bacon and bread and gravy, and began to talk. He made a during-dinner speech something like this:

16   "I like this fine. I never camped out before; but I had a pet 'possum once, and I was nine last birthday. I hate to go to school. Rats ate up sixteen of Jimmy Talbot's aunt's speckled hen's eggs. Are there any real Indians in these woods? I want some more gravy. Does the trees moving make the wind blow? We had five puppies. What makes your nose so red, Hank? My father has lots of money. Are the stars hot? I whipped Ed Walker twice, Saturday. I don't like girls. You dassent catch toads unless with a string. Do oxen make any noise? Why are oranges round? Have you got beds to sleep on in this cave? Amos Murray has got six toes. A parrot can talk, but a monkey or a fish can't. How many does it take to make twelve?"

17   Every few minutes he would remember that he was a pesky redskin, and pick up his stick rifle and tiptoe to the mouth of the cave to rubber for the scouts of the hated paleface. Now and then he would let out a war-whoop that made Old Hank the Trapper shiver. That boy had Bill terrorized from the start.

18   "Red Chief," says I to the kid, "would you like to go home?"

19   "Aw, what for?" says he. "I don't have any fun at home. I hate to go to school. I like to camp out. You won't take me back home again, Snake-eye, will you?"

20   "Not right away," says I. "We'll stay here in the cave awhile."

21   "All right!" says he. "That'll be fine. I never had such fun in all my life."

22   We went to bed about eleven o'clock. We spread down some wide blankets and quilts and put Red Chief between us. We weren't afraid he'd run away. He kept us awake for three hours, jumping up and reaching for his rifle and screeching: "Hist! pard," in mine and Bill's ears, as the fancied crackle of a twig or the rustle of a leaf revealed to his young imagination the stealthy approach of the outlaw band. At last, I fell into a troubled sleep, and dreamed that I had been kidnapped and chained to a tree by a ferocious pirate with red hair.

23   Just at daybreak, I was awakened by a series of awful screams from Bill. They weren't yells, or howls, or shouts, or whoops, or yawps, such as you'd expect from a manly set of vocal organs—they were simply indecent, terrifying, humiliating screams, such as women emit when

they see ghosts or caterpillars. It's an awful thing to hear a strong, desperate, fat man scream incontinently in a cave at daybreak.

24   I jumped up to see what the matter was. Red Chief was sitting on Bill's chest, with one hand twined in Bill's hair. In the other he had the sharp case-knife we used for slicing bacon; and he was industriously and realistically trying to take Bill's scalp, according to the sentence that had been pronounced upon him the evening before.

25   I got the knife away from the kid and made him lie down again. But, from that moment, Bill's spirit was broken. He laid down on his side of the bed, but he never closed an eye again in sleep as long as that boy was with us. I dozed off for a while, but along toward sun-up I remembered that Red Chief had said I was to be burned at the stake at the rising of the sun. I wasn't nervous or afraid; but I sat up and lit my pipe and leaned against a rock.

26   "What you getting up so soon for, Sam?" asked Bill.

27   "Me?" says I. "Oh, I got a kind of pain in my shoulder. I thought sitting up would rest it."

28   "You're a liar!" says Bill. "You're afraid. You was to be burned at sunrise, and you was afraid he'd do it. And he would, too, if he could find a match. Ain't it awful, Sam? Do you think anybody will pay out money to get a little imp like that back home?"

29   "Sure," said I. "A rowdy kid like that is just the kind that parents dote on. Now, you and the Chief get up and cook breakfast, while I go up on the top of this mountain and reconnoitre."

30   I went up on the peak of the little mountain and ran my eye over the contiguous vicinity. Over towards Summit I expected to see the sturdy yeomanry of the village armed with scythes and pitchforks beating the countryside for the dastardly kidnappers. But what I saw was a peaceful landscape dotted with one man ploughing with a dun mule. Nobody was dragging the creek; no couriers dashed hither and yon, bringing tidings of no news to the distracted parents. There was a sylvan attitude of somnolent sleepiness pervading that section of the external outward surface of Alabama that lay exposed to my view. "Perhaps," says I to myself, "it has not yet been discovered that the wolves have borne away the tender lambkin from the fold. Heaven help the wolves!" says I, and I went down the mountain to breakfast.

31   When I got to the cave I found Bill backed up against the side of it, breathing hard, and the boy threatening to smash him with a rock half as big as a cocoanut.

32   "He put a red-hot boiled potato down my back," explained Bill, "and then mashed it with his foot; and I boxed his ears. Have you got a gun about you, Sam?"

33   I took the rock away from the boy and kind of patched up the argument. "I'll fix you," says the kid to Bill. "No man ever yet struck the Red Chief but he got paid for it. You better beware!"

34   After breakfast the kid takes a piece of leather with strings wrapped around it out of his pocket and goes outside the cave unwinding it.

35   "What's he up to now?" says Bill, anxiously. "You don't think he'll run away, do you, Sam?"

36   "No fear of it," says I. "He don't seem to be much of a home body. But we've got to fix up some plan about the ransom. There don't seem to be much excitement around Summit on account of his disappearance; but maybe they haven't realized yet that he's gone. His folks may think he's spending the night with Aunt Jane or one of the neighbors. Anyhow, he'll be missed to-day. To-night we must get a message to his father demanding the two thousand dollars for his return."

37   Just then we heard a kind of war-whoop, such as David might have emitted when he knocked out the champion Goliath. It was a sling that Red Chief had pulled out of his pocket, and he was whirling it around his head.

38   I dodged, and heard a heavy thud and a kind of a sigh from Bill, like a horse gives out when you take his saddle off. A n——head rock the size of an egg had caught Bill just behind his left ear. He loosened himself all over and fell in the fire across the frying pan of hot water for washing the dishes. I dragged him out and poured cold water on his head for half an hour.

39   By and by, Bill sits up and feels behind his ear and says: "Sam, do you know who my favorite Biblical character is?"

40   "Take it easy," says I. "You'll come to your senses presently."

41   "King Herod," says he. "You won't go away and leave me here alone, will you, Sam?"

42   I went out and caught that boy and shook him until his freckles rattled.

43   "If you don't behave," says I, "I'll take you straight home. Now, are you going to be good, or not?"

44   "I was only funning," says he, sullenly. "I didn't mean to hurt Old Hank. But what did he hit me for? I'll behave, Snake-eye, if you won't send me home, and if you'll let me play the Black Scout to-day."

45   "I don't know the game," says I. "That's for you and Mr. Bill to decide. He's your playmate for the day. I'm going away for a while, on business. Now, you come in and make friends with him and say you are sorry for hurting him, or home you go, at once."

46   I made him and Bill shake hands, and then I took Bill aside and told him I was going to Poplar Grove, a little village three miles from the

cave, and find out what I could about how the kidnapping had been regarded in Summit. Also, I thought it best to send a peremptory letter to old man Dorset that day, demanding the ransom and dictating how it should be paid.

47   "You know, Sam," says Bill, "I've stood by you without batting an eye in earthquakes, fire and flood—in poker games, dynamite outrages, police raids, train robberies, and cyclones. I never lost my nerve yet till we kidnapped that two-legged skyrocket of a kid. He's got me going. You won't leave me long with him, will you, Sam?"

48   "I'll be back some time this afternoon," says I. "You must keep the boy amused and quiet till I return. And now we'll write the letter to old Dorset."

49   Bill and I got paper and pencil and worked on the letter while Red Chief, with a blanket wrapped around him, strutted up and down, guarding the mouth of the cave. Bill begged me tearfully to make the ransom fifteen hundred dollars instead of two thousand. "I ain't attempting," says he, "to decry the celebrated moral aspect of parental affection, but we're dealing with humans, and it ain't human for anybody to give up two thousand dollars for that forty-pound chunk of freckled wildcat. I'm willing to take a chance at fifteen hundred dollars. You can charge the difference up to me."

50   So, to relieve Bill, I acceded, and we collaborated a letter that ran this way:

51   Ebenezer Dorset, Esq.:

52   We have your boy concealed in a place far from Summit. It is useless for you or the most skilful detectives to attempt to find him. Absolutely, the only terms on which you can have him restored to you are these: We demand fifteen hundred dollars in large bills for his return; the money to be left at midnight to-night at the same spot and in the same box as your reply—as hereinafter described. If you agree to these terms, send your answer in writing by a solitary messenger to-night at half-past eight o'clock. After crossing Owl Creek on the road to Poplar Grove, there are three large trees about a hundred yards apart, close to the fence of the wheat field on the right-hand side. At the bottom of the fence-post, opposite the third tree, will be found a small pasteboard box.

53   The messenger will place the answer in this box and return immediately to Summit.

54   If you attempt any treachery or fail to comply with our demand as stated, you will never see your boy again.

55   If you pay the money as demanded, he will be returned to you safe and well within three hours. These terms are final, and if you do not accede to them no further communication will be attempted.

56   Two Desperate Men

57   I addressed this letter to Dorset, and put it in my pocket. As I was about to start, the kid comes up to me and says:

58   "Aw, Snake-eye, you said I could play the Black Scout while you was gone."

59   "Play it, of course," says I. "Mr. Bill will play with you. What kind of a game is it?"

60   "I'm the Black Scout," says Red Chief, "and I have to ride to the stockade to warn the settlers that the Indians are coming. I'm tired of playing Indian myself. I want to be the Black Scout."

61   "All right," says I. "It sounds harmless to me. I guess Mr. Bill will help you foil the pesky savages."

62   "What am I to do?" asks Bill, looking at the kid suspiciously.

63   "You are the hoss," says Black Scout. "Get down on your hands and knees. How can I ride to the stockade without a hoss?"

64   "You'd better keep him interested," said I, "till we get the scheme going. Loosen up."

65   Bill gets down on his all fours, and a look comes in his eye like a rabbit's when you catch it in a trap.

66   "How far is it to the stockade, kid?" he asks, in a husky manner of voice.

67   "Ninety miles," says the Black Scout. "And you have to hump yourself to get there on time. Whoa, now!"

68   The Black Scout jumps on Bill's back and digs his heels in his side.

69   "For Heaven's sake," says Bill, "hurry back, Sam, as soon as you can. I wish we hadn't made the ransom more than a thousand. Say, you quit kicking me or I'll get up and warm you good."

70   I walked over to Poplar Grove and sat around the post-office and store, talking with the chaw-bacons that came in to trade. One whiskerando says that he hears Summit is all upset on account of Elder Ebenezer Dorset's boy having been lost or stolen. That was all I wanted to know. I bought some smoking tobacco, referred casually to the price of blackeyed peas, posted my letter surreptitiously, and came away. The postmaster said the mail-carrier would come by in an hour to take the mail to Summit.

71   When I got back to the cave Bill and the boy were not to be found. I explored the vicinity of the cave, and risked a yodel or two, but there was no response.

72   So I lighted my pipe and sat down on a mossy bank to await developments.

73   In about half an hour I heard the bushes rustle, and Bill wabbled out into the little glade in front of the cave. Behind him was the kid,

stepping softly like a scout, with a broad grin on his face. Bill stopped, took off his hat, and wiped his face with a red handkerchief. The kid stopped about eight feet behind him.

74   "Sam," says Bill, "I suppose you'll think I'm a renegade, but I couldn't help it. I'm a grown person with masculine proclivities and habits of self-defense, but there is a time when all systems of egotism and predominance fall. The boy is gone. I sent him home. All is off. There was martyrs in old times," goes on Bill, "that suffered death rather than give up the particular graft they enjoyed. None of 'em ever was subjugated to such supernatural tortures as I have been. I tried to be faithful to our articles of depredation; but there came a limit."

75   "What's the trouble, Bill?" I asks him.

76   "I was rode," says Bill, "the ninety miles to the stockade, not barring an inch. Then, when the settlers was rescued, I was given oats. Sand ain't a palatable substitute. And then, for an hour I had to try to explain to him why there was nothin' in holes, how a road can run both ways, and what makes the grass green. I tell you, Sam, a human can only stand so much. I takes him by the neck of his clothes and drags him down the mountain. On the way he kicks my legs black and blue from the knees down; and I've got to have two or three bites on my thumb and hand cauterized.

77   "But he's gone"—continues Bill—"gone home. I showed him the road to Summit and kicked him about eight feet nearer there at one kick. I'm sorry we lose the ransom; but it was either that or Bill Driscoll to the madhouse."

78   Bill is puffing and blowing, but there is a look of ineffable peace and growing content on his rose-pink features.

79   "Bill," says I, "there isn't any heart disease in your family, is there?"

80   "No," says Bill, "nothing chronic except malaria and accidents. Why?"

81   "Then you might turn around," says I, "and have a look behind you."

82   Bill turns and sees the boy, and loses his complexion and sits down plump on the ground and begins to pluck aimlessly at grass and little sticks. For an hour I was afraid of his mind. And then I told him that my scheme was to put the whole job through immediately and that we would get the ransom and be off with it by midnight if old Dorset fell in with our proposition. So Bill braced up enough to give the kid a weak sort of a smile and a promise to play the Russian in a Japanese war with him as soon as he felt a little better.

83   I had a scheme for collecting that ransom without danger of being caught by counterplots that ought to commend itself to professional

kidnappers. The tree under which the answer was to be left—and the money later on—was close to the road fence with big, bare fields on all sides. If a gang of constables should be watching for any one to come for the note, they could see him a long way off crossing the fields or in the road. But no, sirree! At half-past eight I was up in that tree as well hidden as a tree toad, waiting for the messenger to arrive.

84   Exactly on time, a half-grown boy rides up the road on a bicycle, locates the pasteboard box at the foot of the fence-post, slips a folded piece of paper into it, and pedals away again back toward Summit.

85   I waited an hour and then concluded the thing was square. I slid down the tree, got the note, slipped along the fence till I struck the woods, and was back at the cave in another half an hour. I opened the note, got near the lantern, and read it to Bill. It was written with a pen in a crabbed hand, and the sum and substance of it was this:

86   Two Desperate Men.

87   Gentlemen: I received your letter to-day by post, in regard to the ransom you ask for the return of my son. I think you are a little high in your demands, and I hereby make you a counter-proposition, which I am inclined to believe you will accept. You bring Johnny home and pay me two hundred and fifty dollars in cash, and I agree to take him off your hands. You had better come at night, for the neighbors believe he is lost, and I couldn't be responsible for what they would do to anybody they saw bringing him back. Very respectfully,

88   Ebenezer Dorset

89   "Great pirates of Penzance," says I; "of all the impudent—"

90   But I glanced at Bill, and hesitated. He had the most appealing look in his eyes I ever saw on the face of a dumb or a talking brute.

91   "Sam," says he, "what's two hundred and fifty dollars, after all? We've got the money. One more night of this kid will send me to a bed in Bedlam. Besides being a thorough gentleman, I think Mr. Dorset is a spendthrift for making us such a liberal offer. You ain't going to let the chance go, are you?"

92   "Tell you the truth, Bill," says I, "this little he ewe lamb has somewhat got on my nerves too. We'll take him home, pay the ransom, and make our getaway."

93   We took him home that night. We got him to go to telling him that his father had bought a silver-mounted rifle and a pair of moccasins for him, and we were to hunt bears the next day.

94   It was just twelve o'clock when we knocked at Ebenezer's front door. Just at the moment when I should have been abstracting the fifteen hundred dollars from the box under the tree, according to the

original proposition, Bill was counting out two hundred and fifty dollars into Dorset's hand.

95   When the kid found out we were going to leave him at home he started up a howl like a calliope and fastened himself as tight as a leech to Bill's leg. His father peeled him away gradually, like a porous plaster.

96   "How long can you hold him?" asks Bill.

97   "I'm not as strong as I used to be," says old Dorset, "but I think I can promise you ten minutes."

98   "Enough," says Bill. "In ten minutes I shall cross the Central, Southern, and Middle Western States, and be legging it trippingly for the Canadian border."

99   And, as dark as it was, and as fat as Bill was, and as good a runner as I am, he was a good mile and a half out of Summit before I could catch up with him.

The Ransom of Red Chief

JOURNAL

1. MLA Works Cited

Using this model, record this reading here.

Author's Last Name, First Name. "Title of the Story." <u>Title of the Book</u>. Ed. First Last Name. City: Publisher, year. Pages of the story.

2. Main Character(s)

Describe each main character, and explain why you think each is a main character.

3. Supporting Characters

Describe each supporting character, and explain why you think each is a supporting character.

4. Setting

Describe the setting. Decide if this setting can be changed and, if so, to where and when.

5. **Sequence**

   Relate the events of the story in order.

6. **Plot**

   Tell the story in no more than two sentences.

7. **Conflict.**

   Identify and explain the conflicts involved here.

8. **Significant Quotations**

   Explain the importance of each of these quotations. Record the page number in the parentheses.

   a. "Bill and me had a joint capital of about six hundred dollars, and we needed just two thousand dollars more to pull off a fraudulent town-lot scheme in Western Illinois with" (   ).

b. " 'For Heaven's sake,' says Bill, 'hurry back, Sam, as soon as you can. I wish we hadn't made the ransom more than a thousand' " (   ).

c. " 'Then you might turn around,' says I, 'and have a look behind you' " (   ).

d. " 'You bring Johnny home and pay me two hundred and fifty dollars in cash, and I agree to take him off your hands' " (   ).

e. "[. . .] Bill was counting out two hundred and fifty dollars into Dorset's hand" (   ).

9. Irony.
Identify and explain the irony in this story.

FOLLOW-UP QUESTIONS

10 SHORT QUESTIONS

*Select the **best** answer for each.*

_____ 1. Bill and Sam probably
   a. are rich.
   b. are comfortable.
   c. need money.

_____ 2. Johnny Dorset
   a. leaves easily.
   b. has to be forced to leave.
   c. decides to stay home.

_____ 3. When Johnny is with Bill and Sam, he feels
   a. that he is suffering.
   b. as if he is out camping.
   c. homesick.

_____ 4. Bill
   a. pays no attention to Johnny.
   b. enjoys playing with Johnny.
   c. does not enjoy playing with Johnny.

_____ 5. The one who seems to plan the scheme is
   a. Sam.
   b. Bill.
   c. Johnny.

_____ 6. When Sam goes to Poplar Grove, he thinks Summit
   a. is happy or, at least, relieved.
   b. is deeply concerned and upset.
   c. has not heard the news yet.

_____ 7. In fact, Summit probably
   a. is happy or, at least, relieved.
   b. is deeply concerned and upset.
   c. has not heard the news yet.

_____ 8. Bill and Sam ask for a ransom of
   a. $2,000.
   b. $1,500.
   c. $250.

_____ 9. Ebenezer Dorset
   a. rapidly pays the ransom.
   b. sends out the sheriff.
   c. sends a counter-proposition.

_____ 10. In the end, Bill and Sam
   a. gain $2,000.
   b. gain $1,500.
   c. pay out $250.

5 SIGNIFICANT QUOTATIONS

Explain the importance of each of these quotations.

1. "We selected for our our victim the only child of a prominent citizen named Ebenezer Dorset."

2. " 'You're a liar!' says Bill. '[. . .] You was to be burned at sunrise, and you was afraid he'd do it.' "

3. " 'We demand fifteen hundred dollars in large bills for his return [. . .].' "

4. "One whiskerando says that he hears Summit is all upset on account of Elder Ebenezer Dorset's boy having been lost or stolen."

5. " 'I think you are a little high in your demands, and I hereby make you a counter-proposition, which I am inclined to believe you will accept.' "

2 COMPREHENSION ESSAY QUESTIONS

Use specific details and information from the story to answer these as completely as possible.

1. Explain the irony in this story. Use specific details and information from the story to support your explanation.

2. Explain Sam and Bill's mistakes. Use specific details and information from the story to support your explanation.

WRITING

Use each of these ideas for writing an essay.

1. The irony here is based on a series of misunderstandings and wrong assumptions. Write about a time that you or someone you know had problems because of misunderstandings or wrong assumptions.

2. The irony in this story is a series of humorous twists. Write about a humorous twist in your life or in the life of someone you know.

Further Writing

1. Compare and contrast Johnny Dorset in this story with Tom Sawyer in the selection by Mark Twain (page 123).

2. Compare and contrast the society in the stories of Mark Twain and O. Henry, which are set in simpler times, with American society of today.

The Wonderful Old Gentleman

DOROTHY PARKER

PRE-READING VOCABULARY
CONTEXT

Use context clues to define these words before reading. Use a dictionary as needed.

1. The children put everything scary they could think of into the haunted house so that it would be a *chamber of horrors. Chamber of horrors* means _____.

2. Carmen wanted to see the beautiful paintings in person, so she went to the *museum. Museum* means _____.

3. The hungry tiger was *savage* as it attacked the raw meat thrown to it. *Savage* means _____.

4. The ugly statue, with its hanging tongue and ragged claws, was *grotesque. Grotesque* means _____.

5. Carrie *married well* when she married the multimillionaire who offered her a life of ease and comfort. *Married well* means

   _____.

6. When the clerk left to find a new job, her boss Pam wrote her a very nice *reference. Reference* means _____.

7. Terry took the white cotton *handkerchief* trimmed in lace from her purse to wipe her tears. *Handkerchief* means

   _____.

8. Elaine wore the beautiful *crepe de Chine* gown with her topaz and amethyst jewelry. *Crepe de Chine* means _____.

9. Theo's coat was all *rumpled* and wrinkled after he slept in it all night on the train. *Rumpled* means _____.

10. Eli was absolutely *distraught* when he found out that his favorite team, the Tigers, had lost the championship. *Distraught* means

_____.

11. Shahin bought a very expensive *Persian rug* to lay in the middle of the foyer floor. *Persian rug* means _____.

12. Kelly needed to hire several *servants* to cook and clean when she bought the forty-room mansion. *Servant* means _____.

13. When Tim went away to school, he had to pay five hundred dollars a month *board* money for his room and food. *Board* means

_____.

14. When Renee was kinder to one child than to the other, she was definitely showing her *favoritism. Favoritism* means _____.

15. Yvette chose to ride in the limousine with the c*hauffeur* driving rather than take her own car. *Chauffeur* means _____.

16. When the company was hiring typists and filers, Jess found a *clerical,* summer job. *Clerical* means _____.

17. After spending all of his mom's money and then going to jail for robbery, Paul became the *black sheep* of the family. *Black sheep* means _____.

18. Bob stated clearly in his *will* that all his money would go to his children when he died. *Will* means _____.

19. Lisa found all the noise and confusion around her very *disturbing. Disturbing* means _____.

20. The family *passionately* loved their little dog and were beside themselves when she died. *Passionate* means _____.

Pre-reading Vocabulary
Word Attack

Define these words by solving the parts. Use a dictionary as needed.

1. living-room
2. discomfort
3. wedding-present
4. transforming
5. high-ceilinged
6. woodwork
7. unavoidable
8. eyeless
9. earthy
10. center-table
11. blameless
12. shoulder-muscles
13. bronze-colored
14. curly-headed
15. realistically
16. steel-engraving
17. chariot-race
18. maddened
19. grave-like
20. hopelessly
21. casualness
22. upright
23. ash-receiver
24. nervousness
25. unconscious
26. necessitating
27. untidiness
28. painstakingly
29. forefinger
30. storm-window
31. light-fixture
32. guest-room
33. fair-mindedness
34. lovelier
35. liveliness
36. seaman
37. housekeeper
38. kindliest
39. shakily

Pre-reading Questions

Try answering these questions as you read.

Who is the Old Gentleman?

What is Mrs. Bain like? Mrs. Whittaker?

What does the Old Gentleman do to Mrs. Bain? Mrs. Whittaker?

Who really cares about the Old Gentleman?

What is ironic in this story?

The Wonderful Old Gentleman

DOROTHY PARKER

Dorothy Rothschild Parker was born in 1893 to a well-to-do Jewish father and a Protestant mother. She grew up in New York City. With her mother dying shortly after Parker was born, Parker grew to resent her strict father and what she perceived as her mixed heritage. She was part of the Manhattan scene, first as a writer for *Vogue,* then as a critic for *Vanity Fair,* and then as a writer for the *New Yorker.* With her second husband, Alan Campbell, she moved to California and wrote the script for the 1937 film, *A Star is Born.* Holding long-time family resentments, developing cynical views on relationships, and having an interest in liberal politics, Parker led a rather unsettled life. Her writing offers concise and often bitterly ironic support for sincere women, while it often abrades superficial women and men in general. Her many short stories appear in several collections. Parker died in 1967.

If the Bains had striven for years, they could have been no more successful in making their living-room into a small but admirably complete museum of objects suggesting strain, discomfort, or the tomb. Yet they had never even tried for the effect. Some of the articles that the room contained were wedding-presents; some had been put in from time to time as substitutes as their predecessors succumbed to age and wear; a few had been brought along by the Old Gentleman when he had come to make his home with the Bains some five years before.

2   It was curious how perfectly they all fitted into the general scheme. It was as if they had all been selected by a single enthusiast to whom time was but little object, so long as he could achieve the eventual result of transforming the Bain living-room into a home chamber of horrors, modified a bit for family use.

3   It was a high-ceilinged room, with heavy, dark old woodwork, that brought long and unavoidable thoughts of silver handles and weaving worms. The paper was the color of stale mustard. Its design, once a dashing affair of a darker tone splashed with twinkling gold, had faded into lines and smears that resolved themselves, before the eyes of the sensitive, into hordes of battered heads and tortured profiles, some eyeless, some with clotted gashes for mouths.

4   The furniture was dark and cumbersome and subject to painful creakings—sudden, sharp creaks that seemed to be wrung from its brave silence only when it could bear no more. A close, earthy smell came from its dulled tapestry cushions, and try as Mrs. Bain might, furry gray dust accumulated in the crevices.

5   The center-table was upheld by the perpetually strained arms of three carved figures, insistently female to the waist, then trailing discreetly off into a confusion of scrolls and scales. Upon it rested a row of blameless books, kept in place at the ends by the straining shoulder-muscles of two bronze-colored plaster elephants, forever pushing at their tedious toil.

6   On the heavily carved mantel was a gayly colored figure of a curly-headed peasant boy, ingeniously made so that he sat on the shelf and dangled one leg over. He was in the eternal act of removing a thorn from his chubby foot, his round face realistically wrinkled with the cruel pain. Just above him hung a steel-engraving of a chariot-race, the dust flying, the chariots careening wildly, the drivers ferociously lashing their maddened horses, the horses themselves caught by the artist the moment before their hearts burst, and they dropped in their traces.

7   The opposite wall was devoted to the religious in art; a steel-engraving of the Crucifixion, lavish of ghastly detail; a sepia-print of the martyrdom of Saint Sebastian, the cords cutting deep into the arms

writhing from the stake, arrows bristling in the thick, soft-looking body; a water-color copy of a "Mother of Sorrows," the agonized eyes raised to a cold heaven, great, bitter tears forever on the wan cheeks, paler for the grave-like draperies that wrapped the head.

8   Beneath the windows hung a painting in oil of two lost sheep, huddled hopelessly together in the midst of a wild blizzard. This was one of the Old Gentleman's contributions to the room. Mrs. Bain was wont to observe of it that the frame was worth she didn't know how much.

9   The wall-space beside the door was reserved for a bit of modern art that had once caught Mr. Bain's eye in a stationer's window—a colored print, showing a railroad-crossing, with a train flying relentlessly toward it, and a low, red automobile trying to dash across the track before the iron terror shattered it into eternity. Nervous visitors who were given chairs facing this scene usually made opportunity to change their seats before they could give their whole minds to the conversation.

10   The ornaments, placed with careful casualness on the table and the upright piano, included a small gilt lion of Lucerne, a little, chipped, plaster Laocoön, and a savage china kitten eternally about to pounce upon a plump and helpless china mouse. This last had been one of the Old Gentleman's own wedding-gifts. Mrs. Bain explained, in tones low with awe, that it was very old.

11   The ash-receivers, of Oriental manufacture, were in the form of grotesque heads, tufted with bits of gray human hair, and given bulging, dead, glassy eyes and mouths stretched into great gapes, into which those who had the heart for it might flick their ashes. Thus the smallest details of the room kept loyally to the spirit of the thing, and carried on the effect.

12   But the three people now sitting in the Bains' living-room were not in the least oppressed by the decorative scheme. Two of them, Mr. and Mrs. Bain, not only had had twenty-eight years of the room to accustom themselves to it, but had been stanch admirers of it from the first. And no surroundings, however morbid, could close in on the aristocratic calm of Mrs. Bain's sister, Mrs. Whittaker.

13   She graciously patronized the very chair she now sat in, smiled kindly on the glass of cider she held in her hand. The Bains were poor, and Mrs. Whittaker had, as it is ingenuously called, married well, and none of them ever lost sight of these facts.

14   But Mrs. Whittaker's attitude of kindly tolerance was not confined to her less fortunate relatives. It extended to friends of her youth, working people, the arts, politics, the United States in general, and God, Who had always supplied her with the best of service. She could have given Him an excellent reference at any time.

15   The three people sat with a comfortable look of spending the evening. There was an air of expectancy about them, a not unpleasant little nervousness, as of those who wait for a curtain to rise. Mrs. Bain had brought in cider in the best tumblers, and had served some of her nut cookies in the plate painted by hand with clusters of cherries—the plate she had used for sandwiches when, several years ago, her card club had met at her house.

16   She had thought it over a little tonight, before she lifted out the cherry plate, then quickly decided and resolutely heaped it with cookies. After all, it was an occasion—formal, perhaps, but still an occasion. The Old Gentleman was dying upstairs. At five o'clock that afternoon the doctor had said that it would be a surprise to him if the Old Gentleman lasted till the middle of the night—a big surprise, he had augmented.

17   There was no need for them to gather at the Old Gentleman's bedside. He would not have known any of them. In fact, he had not known them for almost a year, addressing them by wrong names and asking them grave, courteous questions about the health of husbands or wives or children who belonged to other branches of the family. And he was quite unconscious now.

18   Miss Chester, the nurse who had been with him since "this last stroke," as Mrs. Bain importantly called it, was entirely competent to attend and watch him. She had promised to call them if, in her tactful words, she saw any signs.

19   So the Old Gentleman's daughters and son-in-law waited in the warm living-room, and sipped their cider, and conversed in low, polite tones.

20   Mrs. Bain cried a little in pauses in the conversation. She had always cried easily and often. Yet, in spite of her years of practice, she did not do it well. Her eyelids grew pink and sticky, and her nose gave her no little trouble, necessitating almost constant sniffling. She sniffled loudly and conscientiously, and frequently removed her pince-nez to wipe her eyes with a crumpled handkerchief, gray with damp.

21   Mrs. Whittaker, too, bore a handkerchief, but she appeared to be holding it in waiting. She was dressed, in compliment to the occasion, in her black crepe de Chine, and she had left her lapis-lazuli pin, her olivine bracelet, and her topaz and amethyst rings at home in her bureau drawer, retaining only her lorgnette on its gold chain, in case there should be any reading to be done.

22   Mrs. Whittaker's dress was always studiously suited to its occasion; thus, her bearing had always that calm that only the correctly attired may enjoy. She was an authority on where to place monograms

on linen, how to instruct working folk, and what to say in letters of condolence. The word "lady" figured largely in her conversation. Blood, she often predicted, would tell.

23   Mrs. Bain wore a rumpled white shirt-waist and the old blue skirt she saved for "around the kitchen." There had been time to change, after she had telephoned the doctor's verdict to her sister, but she had not been quite sure whether it was the thing to do. She had thought that Mrs. Whittaker might expect her to display a little distraught untidiness at a time like this; might even go in for it in a mild way herself.

24   Now Mrs. Bain looked at her sister's elaborately curled, painstakingly brown coiffure, and, nervously patted her own straggling hair, gray at the front, with strands of almost lime-color in the little twist at the back. Her eyelids grew wet and sticky again, and she hung her glasses over one forefinger while she applied the damp handkerchief. After all, she reminded herself and the others, it was her poor father.

25   Oh, but it was really the best thing. Mrs. Whittaker explained in her gentle, patient voice.

26   "You wouldn't want to see father go on like this," she pointed out. Mr. Bain echoed her, as if struck with the idea. Mrs. Bain had nothing to reply to them. No, she wouldn't want to see the Old Gentleman go on like this.

27   Five years before, Mrs. Whittaker had decided that the Old Gentleman was getting too old to live alone with only old Annie to cook for him and look after him. It was only a question of a little time before it "wouldn't have looked right," his living alone, when he had his children to take care of him. Mrs. Whittaker always stopped things before they got to the stage where they didn't look right. So he had come to live with the Bains.

28   Some of his furniture had been sold; a few things, such as his silver, his tall clock, and the Persian rug he had bought at the Exposition, Mrs. Whittaker had found room for in her own house; and some he brought with him to the Bains'.

29   Mrs. Whittaker's house was much larger than her sister's, and she had three servants and no children. But, as she told her friends, she had held back and let Allie and Lewis have the Old Gentleman.

30   "You see," she explained, dropping her voice to the tones reserved for not very pretty subjects, "Allie and Lewis are—well, they haven't a great deal."

31   So it was gathered that the Old Gentleman would do big things for the Bains when he came to live with them. Not exactly by paying board—it is a little too much to ask your father to pay for his food and

lodging, as if he were a stranger. But, as Mrs. Whittaker suggested, he could do a great deal in the way of buying needed things for the house and keeping everything going.

32   And the Old Gentleman did contribute to the Bain household. He bought an electric heater and an electric fan, new curtains, storm-windows, and light-fixtures, all for his bedroom; and had a nice little bathroom for his personal use made out of the small guest-room adjoining it.

33   He shopped for days until he found a coffee-cup large enough for his taste; he bought several large ash-trays, and a dozen extra-size bath-towels, that Mrs. Bain marked with his initials. And every Christmas and birthday he gave Mrs. Bain a round, new, shining ten-dollar gold piece. Of course, he presented gold pieces to Mrs. Whittaker, too, on like appropriate occasions. The Old Gentleman prided himself always on his fair-mindedness. He often said that he was not one to show any favoritism.

34   Mrs. Whittaker was Cordelia-like to her father during his declining years. She came to see him several times a month, bringing him jelly or potted hyacinths. Sometimes she sent her car and chauffeur for him, so that he might take an easy drive through the town, and Mrs. Bain might be afforded a chance to drop her cooking and accompany him. When Mrs. Whittaker was away on trips with her husband, she almost never neglected to send her father picture post-cards of various points of interest.

35   The Old Gentleman appreciated her affection, and took pride in her. He enjoyed being told that she was like him.

36   "That Hattie," he used to tell Mrs. Bain, "she's a fine woman—a fine woman."

37   As soon as she had heard that the Old Gentleman was dying Mrs. Whittaker had come right over, stopping only to change her dress and have her dinner. Her husband was away in the woods with some men, fishing. She explained to the Bains that there was no use in disturbing him—it would have been impossible for him to get back that night. As soon as—well, if anything happened she would telegraph him, and he could return in time for the funeral.

38   Mrs. Bain was sorry that he was away. She liked her ruddy, jovial, loud-voiced brother-in-law.

39   "It's too bad that Clint couldn't be here," she said, as she had said several times before. "He's so fond of cider," she added.

40   "Father," said Mrs. Whittaker, "was always very fond of Clint." Already the Old Gentleman had slipped into the past tense.

41   "Everybody likes Clint," Mr. Bain stated.

42   He was included in the "everybody." The last time he had failed in business, Clint had given him the clerical position he had since held over at the brush works. It was pretty generally understood that this had been brought about through Mrs. Whittaker's intervention, but still they were Clint's brush works, and it was Clint who paid him his salary. And forty dollars a week is indubitably forty dollars a week.

43   "I hope he'll be sure and be here in time for the funeral," said Mrs. Bain. "It will be Wednesday morning, I suppose, Hat?"

44   Mrs. Whittaker nodded.

45   "Or perhaps around two o'clock Wednesday afternoon," she amended. "I always think that's a nice time. Father has his frock coat, Allie?"

46   "Oh, yes," Mrs. Bain said eagerly. "And it's all clean and lovely. He has everything. Hattie, I noticed the other day at Mr. Newton's funeral they had more of a blue necktie on him, so I suppose they're wearing them—Mollie Newton always has everything just so. But I don't know—"

47   "I think," said Mrs. Whittaker firmly, "that there is nothing lovelier than black for an old gentleman."

48   "Poor Old Gentleman," said Mr. Bain, shaking his head. "He would have been eighty-five if he just could have lived till next September. Well, I suppose it's all for the best."

49   He took a small draft of cider and another cooky.

50   "A wonderful, wonderful life," summarized Mrs. Whittaker. "And a wonderful, wonderful old gentleman.

51   "Well, I should say so," said Mrs. Bain. "Why, up to the last year he was as interested in everything! It was, 'Allie, how much do you have to give for your eggs now?' and 'Allie, why don't you change your butcher? —this one's robbing you,' and 'Allie, who was that you were talking to on the telephone?' all day long! Everybody used to speak of it."

52   "And he used to come to the table right up to this stroke," Mr. Bain related, chuckling reminiscently. "My, he used to raise Cain when Allie didn't cut up his meat fast enough to suit him. Always had a temper, *I'll* you, the Old Gentleman did. Wouldn't stand for us having anybody in to meals—he didn't like that worth a cent. Eighty-four years old, and sitting right up there at the table with us!"

53   They vied in telling instances of the Old Gentleman's intelligence and liveliness, as parents cap one another's anecdotes of precocious children.

54   "It's only the past year that he had to be helped up- and down-stairs," said Mrs. Bain. "Walked up-stairs all by himself, and more than eighty years old!"

55   Mrs. Whittaker was amused.

56   "I remember you said that once when Clint was here," she remarked, "and Clint said, 'Well, if you can't walk up-stairs by the time you're eighty, when are you going to learn?'"

57   Mrs. Bain smiled politely, because her brother-in-law had said it. Otherwise she would have been shocked and wounded.

58   "Yes, sir," said Mr. Bain. "Wonderful."

59   "The only thing I could have wished," Mrs. Bain said, after a pause—"I could have wished he'd been a little different about Paul. Somehow I've never felt quite right since Paul went into the navy."

60   Mrs. Whittaker's voice fell into the key used for the subject that has been gone over and over and over again.

61   "Now, Allie," she said, "you know yourself that was the best thing that could have happened. Father told you that himself, often and often. Paul was young, and he wanted to have all his young friends running in and out of the house, banging doors and making all sorts of racket, and it would have been a terrible nuisance for father. You must realize that father was more than eighty years old, Allie."

62   "Yes, I know," Mrs. Bain said. Her eyes went to the photograph of her son in his seaman's uniform, and she sighed.

63   "And besides," Mrs. Whittaker pointed out triumphantly, "now that Miss Chester's here in Paul's room, there wouldn't have been any room for him. So you see!"

64   There was rather a long pause. Then Mrs. Bain edged toward the other thing that had been weighing upon her.

65   "Hattie," she said, "I suppose—I suppose we'd ought to let Matt know?"

66   "I shouldn't," said Mrs. Whittaker composedly. She always took great pains with her "shall's" and "will's." "I only hope that he doesn't see it in the papers in time to come on for the funeral. If you want to have your brother turn up drunk at the services, Allie, *I* don't."

67   "But I thought he'd straightened up," said Mr. Bain. "Thought he was all right since he got married."

68   "Yes, I know, I know, Lewis," Mrs. Whittaker said wearily. "I've heard all about that. All I say is, *I* know what Matt is."

69   "John Loomis was telling me," reported Mr. Bain, "he was going through Akron, and he stopped off to see Matt. Said they had a nice little place, and he seemed to be getting along fine. Said she seemed like a crackerjack housekeeper."

70   Mrs. Whittaker smiled.

71   "Yes," she said, "John Loomis and Matt were always two of a kind—you couldn't believe a word either of them said. Probably she did seem to be a good housekeeper. I've no doubt she acted the part very well. Matt never made any bones of the fact that she was on the stage once, for almost a year. Excuse me from having that woman come to father's funeral. If you want to know what *I* think, *I* think that Matt marrying a woman like that had a good deal to do with hastening father's death."

72   The Bains sat in awe.

73   "And after all father did for Matt, too," added Mrs. Whittaker, her voice shaken.

74   "Well, I should think so," Mr. Bain was glad to agree.

75   "I remember how the Old Gentleman used to try and help Matt get along. He'd go down, like it was to Mr. Fuller, that time Matt was working at the bank, and he'd explain to him, 'Now, Mr. Fuller,' he'd say, 'I don't know whether you know it, but this son of mine has always been what you might call the black sheep of the family. He's been kind of a drinker,' he'd say, 'and he's got himself into trouble a couple of times, and if you'd just keep an eye on him, so's to see he keeps straight, it'd be a favor to me.'

76   "Mr. Fuller told me about it himself. Said it was wonderful the way the Old Gentleman came right out and talked just as frankly to him. Said *he'd* never had any idea Matt was that way—wanted to hear all about it."

77   Mrs. Whittaker nodded sadly.

78   "Oh, I know," she said. "Time and again father would do that. And then, as like as not, Matt would get one of sulky fits, and not turn up at his work."

79   "And when Matt would be out of work," Mrs. Bain said, "the way father'd hand him out his car-fare, and I don't know what all! When Matt was a grown man, going on thirty years old, father would take him down to Newins & Malley's and buy him a whole new outfit—pick out everything himself. He always used to say Matt was the kind that would get cheated out of his eye-teeth if he went into a store alone."

80   "My, father hated to see anybody make a fool of themselves about money," Mrs. Whittaker commented. "Remember how he always used to say, 'Anybody can make money, but it takes a wise man to keep it'?"

81   "I suppose he must be a pretty rich man," Mr. Bain said, abruptly restoring the Old Gentleman to the present.

82   "Oh—rich!" Mrs. Whittaker's smile was at its kindliest. "But he managed his affairs very well, father did, right up to the last. Everything is in splendid shape, Clint says."

83   "He showed you the will, didn't he, Hat?" asked Mrs. Bain, forming bits of her sleeve into little plaits between her thin, hard fingers.

84   "Yes," said her sister. "Yes, he did. He showed me the will. A little over a year ago, I think it was, wasn't it? You know, just before he started to fail, that time."

85   She took a small bite of cooky.

86   "*Awfully* good," she said. She broke into a little bubbly laugh, the laugh she used at teas and wedding receptions and fairly formal dinners. "You know," she went on, as one sharing a good story, "he's gone and left all that old money to me. 'Why, Father!' I said, as soon as I'd read that part. But it seems he'd gotten some sort of idea in his head that Clint and I would be able to take care of it better than anybody else, and you know what father was, once he made up that mind of his. You can just imagine how *I* felt. I couldn't say a thing."

87   She laughed again, shaking her head in amused bewilderment.

88   "Oh, and Allie," she said, "he's left you all the furniture he brought here with him, and all the things he bought since he came. And Lewis is to have his set of Thackeray. And that money he lent Lewis, to try and tide him over in the hardware business that time—that's to be regarded as a gift."

89   She sat back and looked at them, smiling.

90   "Lewis paid back most all of that money father lent him that time," Mrs. Bain said. "There was only about two hundred dollars more, and then he would have had it all paid up."

91   "That's to be regarded as a gift," insisted Mrs. Whittaker. She leaned over and patted her brother-in-law's arm. "Father always liked you, Lewis," she said softly.

92   "Poor Old Gentleman," murmured Mr. Bain.

93   "Did it—did it say anything about Matt?" asked Mrs. Bain.

94   "Oh, Allie!" Mrs. Whittaker gently reproved her. "When you think of all the money father spent and spent on Matt, it seems to me he did more than enough—more than enough. And then when Matt went way off there to live, and married that woman, and never a word about it—father hearing it all through strangers—well, I don't think any of us realize how it hurt father. He never said much about it, but I don't think he ever got over it. I'm always so thankful that poor dear mother didn't live to see how Matt turned out."

95   "Poor mother," said Mrs. Bain shakily, and brought the grayish handkerchief into action once more. "I can hear her now, just as plain. 'Now, children,' she used to say, 'do for goodness' sake let's all try and keep your father in a good humor.' If I've heard her say it once, I've heard her say it a hundred times. Remember, Hat?"

96   "Do I remember!" said Mrs. Whittaker. "And do you remember how they used to play whist, and how furious father used to get when he lost?"

97   "Yes," Mrs. Bain cried excitedly, "and how mother used to have to cheat, so as to be sure and not win from him? She got so she used to be able to do it just as well!"

98   They laughed softly, filled with memories of the gone days. A pleasant, thoughtful silence fell around them.

99   Mrs. Bain patted a yawn to extinction, and looked at the clock.

100   "Ten minutes to eleven," she said. "Goodness, I had no idea it was anywhere near so late. I wish—" She stopped just in time, crimson at what her wish would have been.

101   "You see, Lew and I have got in the way of going to bed early," she explained. "Father slept so light, we couldn't have people in like we used to before he came here, to play a little bridge or anything, on account of disturbing him. And if we wanted to go to the movies or anywhere, he'd go on so about being left alone that we just kind of gave up going."

102   "Oh, the Old Gentleman always let you know what he wanted," said Mr. Bain, smiling. "He was a wonder, *I'll* tell you. Nearly eighty-five years old!"

103   "Think of it," said Mrs. Whittaker.

104   A door clicked open above them, and feet ran quickly and not lightly down the stairs. Miss Chester burst into the room.

105   "Oh, Mrs. Bain!" she cried. "Oh, the Old Gentleman! Oh, he's gone! I noticed him kind of stirring and whimpering a little, and he seemed to be trying to make motions at his warm milk, like as if he wanted some. So I put the cup up to his mouth, and he sort of fell over, and just like that he was gone, and the milk all over him."

106   Mrs. Bain instantly collapsed into passionate weeping. Her husband put his arm tenderly about her, and murmured a series of "Now-now's."

107   Mrs. Whittaker rose, set her cider-glass carefully on the table, shook out her handkerchief, and moved toward the door.

108   "A lovely death," she pronounced. "A wonderful, wonderful life, and now a beautiful, peaceful death. Oh, it's the best thing, Allie; it's the best thing."

109   "Oh, it is, Mrs. Bain; it's the best thing," Miss Chester said earnestly. "It's really a blessing. That's what it is."

110   Among them they got Mrs. Bain up the stairs.

The Wonderful Old Gentleman

JOURNAL

1. MLA Works Cited

Using this model, record this reading here.

Author's Last Name, First Name. "Title of the Story." <u>Title of the Book</u>. Ed. First Last Name. City: Publisher, year. Pages of the story.

2. Main Character(s)

Describe each main character, and explain why you think each is a main character.

3. Supporting Characters

Describe each supporting character, and explain why you think each is a supporting character.

4. Setting

Describe the setting. Decide if this setting can be changed and, if so, to where and when.

5. **Sequence**

Relate the events of the story in order.

6. **Plot**

Tell the story in no more than two sentences.

7. **Conflict.**

Identify and explain the conflicts involved here.

8. **Significant Quotations**

Explain the importance of each of these quotations. Record the page number in the parentheses.

a. "Mrs. Whittaker, too, bore a handkerchief, but she appeared to be holding it in waiting" (   ).

b. "Mrs. Whittaker's house was much larger than her sister's, and she had three servants and no children. But, as she told her friends, she had held back and let Allie and Lewis have the Old Gentleman" (   ).

c. " 'And besides,' Mrs. Whittaker pointed out triumphantly, 'now that Miss Chester's here in Paul's room, there wouldn't be any room for him' " (   ).

d. " 'Mr. Fuller told me about it himself. [. . .] Said *he'd* never had any idea Matt was that way—wanted to hear all about it' " (   ).

e. " 'You know,' she went on, as one sharing a good story, 'he's gone and left all that old money to me' " (   ).

9. Irony.

Identify and explain the irony in this story.

FOLLOW-UP QUESTIONS

10 SHORT QUESTIONS

Select the <u>best</u> answer for each.

_____ 1. The Bains are
   a. richer than the Whittakers.
   b. poorer than the Whittakers.
   c. the same as the Whittakers.

_____ 2. The Whittakers are
   a. richer than the Bains.
   b. poorer than the Bains.
   c. the same as the Bains.

_____ 3. The Old Gentleman is father to
   a. Mrs. Bain.
   b. Mrs Whittaker.
   c. both Mrs. Bain and Mrs. Whittaker.

_____ 4. The Old Gentleman lives
   a. with the Bains.
   b. with the Whittakers.
   c. by himself.

_____ 5. The Old Gentleman
   a. enjoys his grandson, Paul.
   b. welcomes his grandson, Paul.
   c. drives away his grandson, Paul.

_____ 6. Mrs. Bain is
   a. upset that Paul is gone.
   b. happy that Paul is gone.
   c. unconcerned about Paul being gone.

_____ 7. The Old Gentleman has
   a. regular meetings with his son, Matt.
   b. been good to his son, Matt.
   c. undermined his son, Matt.

_____ 8. The person who sincerely cares about the Old Gentleman is
   a. Mrs. Bain.
   b. Mrs. Whittaker.
   c. Matt.

_____ 9. The Old Gentleman will leave his wealth to
   a. Mrs. Bain.
   b. Mrs. Whittaker.
   c. Matt.

_____ 10. The Old Gentleman
   a. treats all his children equally.
   b. plays favorites among his children.
   c. is fair to all his children.

5 SIGNIFICANT QUOTATIONS

Explain the importance of each of these quotations.

1. "She sniffed loudly and conscientiously, and frequently removed her pince-nez to wipe her eyes with a crumpled handkerchief, gray with damp."

2. "Five years before, Mrs. Whittaker had decided that the Old Gentleman was getting too old to live alone [. . .]. So he had come to live with the Bains."

3. " 'The only thing I could have wished,' Mrs. Bain said, after a pause—'I could have wished he'd been a little different about Paul.' "

4. " 'Hattie,' she said, 'I suppose—I suppose we'd ought to let Matt know?' "

5. " 'He showed you the will, didn't he, Hat?' asked Mrs. Bain [. . .].' "

2 COMPREHENSION ESSAY QUESTIONS

Use specific details and information from the story to answer these as completely as possible.

1. Explain the irony in this story. Use specific details and information from the story to support your explanation.

2. Discuss who should have inherited the Old Gentleman's wealth and why. Use specific details and information from the story to support your discussion.

WRITING

Use each of these ideas for writing an essay.

1. We all have, or know of someone who has, worked hard only to have the reward for that hard work given to another. Write an essay contrasting the worker with the receiver.

2. Many families treat one member differently from another. Write a narrative essay telling about one instance of different treatment in your own family or in a family you know.

Further Writing

1. Compare this story with Alice Walker's "Everyday Use" (page 175).

2. Read and compare Dorothy Parker's "A Telephone Call" with Parker's "New York to Detroit" (both of which can be found in a library).

Sweat

ZORA NEALE HURSTON

PRE-READING VOCABULARY
CONTEXT

Use context clues to define these words before reading. Use a dictionary as needed.

1. John *soiled* his hands when he was digging in the garden and moving dirt around. *Soiled* means _____.

2. Tom hitched up the horse, put his vegetables in the *buckboard,* and drove the *buckboard* to town. *Buckboard* means _____.

3. Ernie used a chair and a long leather *whip* to train the tigers. *Whip* means _____.

4. Sam *truculently* denied the charges, loudly claiming he was innocent. *Truculently* means _____.

5. The wind blew the leaves *helter-skelter,* and it took hours to rake them up. *Helter-skelter* means _____.

6. Alice found, much to her *dismay,* that the jacket she planned to save money on was no longer on sale. *Dismay* means _____.

7. Jacob grew into a strong, *strapping* young man who lettered in football and track. *Strapping* means _____.

8. Akim loved eating and sat down at the dinner table prepared to eat his *vittles. Vittles* means _____.

9. The bunny backed up into the protective woods, *cowed* by the large dog's barking. *Cowed* means _____.

10. After the wind storm, Theodora cleared all the broken twigs, leaves, and *debris* that the storm had brought down. *Debris* means

_____.

11. Farmers *sow* seeds and *reap* what grows. *Sow* means _____, and *reap* means _____.

12. Robert was completely *indifferent* and did not care one way or the other if he went to the party. *Indifferent* means _____.

13. Allison *abominates* washing dishes and always refuses to wash them. *Abominate* means _____.

14. Josette was in a *fury* when the tax assessor overrated her home by a hundred percent. *Fury* means _____.

15. Much to Michelle's *amazement,* her son surprised her with a totally unexpected party. *Amazement* means _____.

16. The escaped tarantula struck *horror* and *terror* into Chris's heart when he found the spider under the chair. *Horror* and *terror* mean

_____.

17. Zach *crouched* under the stairs so his friends would not find him and he could surprise them. *Crouch* means _____.

18. Reid is such a good *ventriloquist* that he can make it seem like his dog is talking while Reid's lips don't move. *Ventriloquist* means

_____.

19. Teresa was so nervous when she won the award that she spoke *gibberish,* and no one could understand her. *Gibberish* means

_____.

20. When the fire flared up, the firemen came with water and *extinguished* the fire. *Extinguish* means _____.

Pre-reading Vocabulary
Word Attack

Define these words by solving the parts. Use a dictionary as needed.

1. washwoman
2. mournful
3. washbench
4. scornfully
5. habitual
6. knuckly
7. numerous
8. penniless
9. knotty
10. earthworks
11. biggety
12. swellest
13. work-worn
14. friendliness
15. bloodier
16. underfoot
17. maddened

Pre-reading Questions

Try answering these questions as you read.

What is Delia like?

What is Sykes like?

What does Sykes do?

What is ironic in the story?

Sweat

ZORA NEALE HURSTON

Zora Neale Hurston was born in 1901 in Eatonville, Florida, the first African-American–incorporated town in America. Although her mother died when Hurston was young and she was shifted from relative to relative, Hurston enjoyed a childhood relatively free of the discrimination found elsewhere. Marked by creativity and determination throughout her life, she managed to secure scholarships at the Morgan Academy, Howard University, and Barnard College, where she studied under Franz Boaz, the renown anthropologist. Securing support from the same patron who supported Langston Hughes, Hurston returned to Eatonville to study its stories, melodies, and folkways. She thoroughly believed that the African-American experience was both unique and positive, and these small town ways and speech fairly sing through her writing. Her female characters, especially, emerge as intelligent, thoughtful, resourceful, and surviving. However, in presenting too much of the positive and too little of the anger in the African-American experience, she was heavily criticized, although today many consider her a forerunner in African-American self-recognition. A part of the Harlem Renaissance in the 1920s and a thoughtful writer in the 1930s, she was devoted to recreating the Eatonville experience—a devotion that continued throughout her writing. *Their Eyes Were Watching God* is her master work. Hurston died in 1960 in Saint Lucie, Florida, of continuing gastrointestinal problems.

Ⅰt was eleven o'clock of a Spring night in Florida. It was Sunday. Any other night, Delia Jones would have been in bed for two hours by this time. But she was a washwoman, and Monday morning meant a great deal to her. So she collected the soiled clothes on Saturday when she returned the clean things. Sunday night after church, she sorted them and put the white things to soak. It saved her almost a half day's start. A great hamper in the bedroom held the clothes that she brought home. It was so much neater than a number of bundles lying around.

2   She squatted in the kitchen floor beside the great pile of clothes, sorting them into small heaps according to color, and humming a song in a mournful key, but wondering through it all where Sykes, her husband, had gone with her horse and buckboard.

3   Just then something long, round, limp, and black fell upon her shoulders and slithered to the floor beside her. A great terror took hold of her. It softened her knees and dried her mouth so that it was a full minute before she could cry out or move. Then she saw that it was the big bull whip her husband liked to carry when he drove.

4   She lifted her eyes to the door and saw him standing there bent over with laughter at her fright. She screamed at him.

5   "Sykes, what you throw dat whip on me like dat? You know it would skeer me—looks just like a snake, an' you knows how skeered Ah is of snakes."

6   "Course Ah knowed it! That's how come Ah done it." He slapped his leg with his hand and almost rolled on the ground in his mirth. "If you such a big fool dat you got to have a fit over a earth worm or a string, Ah don't keer how bad Ah skeer you."

7   "You aint got no business doing it. Gawd knows it's a sin. Some day Ah'm gointuh drop dead from some of yo' foolishness. 'Nother thing, where you been wid mah rig? Ah feeds dat pony. He aint fuh you to be drivin' wid no bull whip."

8   "Yo sho is one aggravatin' n—— woman!" he declared and stepped into the room. She resumed her work and did not answer him at once. "Ah done tole you time and again to keep them white folks' clothes outa dis house."

9   He picked up the whip and glared down at her. Delia went on with her work. She went out into the yard and returned with a galvanized tub and set it on the washbench. She saw that Sykes had kicked all of the clothes together again, and now stood in her way truculently, his whole manner hoping, praying, for an argument. But she walked calmly around him and commenced to re-sort the things.

10   "Next time, Ah'm gointer to kick 'em outdoors," he threatened as he struck a match along the leg of his corduroy breeches.

11   Delia never looked up from her work, and her thin, stooped shoulders sagged further.

12   "Ah aint for no fuss t'night Sykes. Ah just come from taking sacrament at the church house."

13   He snorted scornfully. "Yeah, you just come from de church house on a Sunday night, but heah you is gone to work on them clothes. You aint nothing but a hypocrite. One of them amen-corner Christians—sing, whoop, shout, then come home and wash white folks clothes on the Sabbath."

14   He stepped roughly upon the whitest pile of things, kicking them helter-skelter as he crossed the room. His wife gave a little scream of dismay, and quickly gathered them together again.

15   "Sykes, you quit grindin' dirt into these clothes! How can Ah git through by Sat'day if Ah don't start on Sunday?"

16   "Ah don't keer if you never git through. Anyhow, Ah done promised Gawd and a couple of other men, Ah aint gointer have it in mah house. Don't gimme no lip neither, else Ah'll throw 'em out and put mah fist up side yo' head to boot."

17   Delia's habitual meekness seemed to slip from her shoulders like a blown scarf. She was on her feet; her poor little body, her bare knuckly hands bravely defying the strapping hulk before her.

18   "Looka heah, Sykes, you done gone too fur. Ah been married to you fur fifteen years, and Ah been takin' in washin' for fifteen years. Sweat, sweat, sweat! Work and sweat, cry and sweat, pray and sweat!"

19   "What's that go to do with me?" he asked brutally.

20   "What's it got to do with you, Sykes? Mah tub of suds is filled yo' belly with vittles more times than yo' hands is filled it. Mah sweat is done paid for this house and Ah reckon Ah kin keep on sweatin' in it."

21   She seized the iron skillet from the stove and struck a defensive pose, which act surprised him greatly, coming from her. It cowed him and he did not strike her as he usually did.

22   "Naw you won't," she panted, "that ole snaggle-toothed black woman you runnin' with aint comin' heah to pile up on *mah* sweat and blood. You aint paid for nothin' on this place, and Ah'm gointer stay right heah till Ah'm toted out foot foremost."

23   "Well, you better quit gittin' me riled up, else they'll be totin' you out sooner than you expect. Ah'm so tired of you Ah don't know whut to do. Gawd! how Ah hates skinny wimmen!"

24   A little awed by this new Delia, he sidled out of the door and slammed the back gate after him. He did not say where he had gone, but she knew too well. She knew very well that he would not return

until nearly daybreak also. Her work over, she went on to bed but not to sleep at once. Things had come to a pretty pass!

25   She lay awake, gazing upon the debris that cluttered their matrimonial trail. Not an image left standing along the way. Anything like flowers had long ago been drowned in the salty stream that had been pressed from her heart. Her tears, her sweat, her blood. She had brought love to the union and he had brought a longing for the flesh. Two months after the wedding, he had given her the first brutal beating. She had the memory of numerous trips to Orlando with all of his wages when he had returned to her penniless, even before the first year had passed. She was young and soft then, but now she thought of her knotty, muscled limbs, her harsh knuckly hands, and drew herself up into an unhappy little ball in the middle of the big feather bed. Too late now to hope for love, even if it were not Bertha it would be someone else. This case differed from the others only in that she was bolder than the others. Too late for everything except her little home. She had built it for her old days, and planted one by one the trees and flowers there. It was lovely to her, lovely.

26   Somehow before sleep came, she found herself saying aloud: "Oh well, whatever goes over the Devil's back, is got to come under his belly. Sometime or ruther, Sykes, like everybody else, is gointer reap his sowing." After that she was able to build a spiritual earthworks against her husband. His shells could no longer reach her. *Amen.* She went to sleep and slept until he announced his presence in bed by kicking her feet and rudely snatching the cover away.

27   "Gimme some kivah heah, an' git yo' damn foots over on yo' own side! Ah oughter mash you in yo' mouf fuh drawing dat skillet on me."

28   Delia went clear to the rail without answering him. A triumphant indifference to all that he was or did.

29   The week was as full of work for Delia as all other weeks, and Saturday found her behind her little pony, collecting and delivering clothes.

30   It was a hot, hot day near the end of July. The village men on Joe Clarke's porch even chewed cane listlessly. They did not hurl the cane-knots as usual. They let them dribble over the edge of the porch. Even conversation had collapsed under the heat.

31   "Heah comes Delia Jones," Jim Merchant said, as the shaggy pony came 'round the bend of the road toward them. The rusty buckboard was heaped with baskets of crisp, clean laundry.

32   "Yep," Joe Lindsay agreed. "Hot or col', rain or shine, jes ez reg'lar ez de weeks roll roun' Delia carries 'em an' fetches 'em on Sat'day."

33   "She better if she wanter eat," said Moss. "Syke Jones aint wuth de shot an' powder hit would tek tuh kill 'em. Not to *bub* he aint."

34   "He sho' aint," Walter Thomas chimed in. "It's too bad, too, cause she wuz a right pritty lil trick when he got huh. Ah'd uh mah'ied huh mahseff if he hadnter beat me to it."

35   Delia nodded briefly at the men as she drove past.

36   "Too much knockin' will ruin *any* 'oman. He done beat huh 'nough tuh kill three women, let 'lone change they looks," said Elijah Mosely. "How Syke kin stommuck dat big black greasy Mogul he's layin' roun' wid, gits me. Ah swear dat eight-rock couldn't kiss a sardine can Ah done thowed out de back do' 'way las' yeah."

37   "Aw, she's fat, thass how come. He's allus been crazy 'bout fat women," put in Merchant. "He'd a' been tied up wid one long time ago if he could a' found one tuh have him. Did Ah tell yuh 'bout him come sidlin' roun *mah* wife—bringin' her a basket uh pee-cans outa his yard fuh a present? Yes-sir, mah wife! She tol' him tuh take 'em right straight back home, cause Delia works so hard ovah dat washtub she reckon everything en de place taste lak sweat an' soapsuds. Ah jus' wisht Ah'd a' caught 'im 'roun' dere! Ah'd a' made his hips ketch on fiah down dat shell road."

38   "Ah know he done it, too. Ah sees 'im grinnin' at every 'oman dat passes," Walter Thomas said. "But even so, he useter eat some mighty big hunks uh humble pie tuh git dat lil' 'oman he got. She wuz *ez pritty ez* a speckled pup! Dat wuz fifteen yeahs ago. He useter be so skeered uh losin' huh, she could make him do some parts of a husband's duty. Dey never wuz de same in de mind."

39   "There oughter be a law about him," said Lindsay. "He aint fit tuh carry guts tuh a bear."

40   Clarke spoke for the first time. "Taint no law on earth dat kin make a man be decent if it aint in 'im. There's plenty men dat takes a wife lak dey do a joint uh sugar-cane. It's round, juicy an' sweet when dey gits it. But dey squeeze an' grind, squeeze an' grind an' wring tell dey wring every drop uh pleasure dat's in 'em out. When dey's satisfied dat dey is wrung dry, dey treats 'em jes lak dey do a cane-chew. Dey thows 'em away. Dey knows whut dey is doin' while dey is at it, an' hates theirselves fuh it but they keeps on hangin' after huh tell she's empty. Den dey hates huh fuh bein' a cane-chew an' in de way."

41   "We oughter take Syke an' dat stray 'oman uh his'n down in Lake Howell swamp an' lay on de rawhide till they cain't say 'Lawd a' mussy.' He allus wuz uh ovahbearin' n——, but since dat white 'oman from up north done teached 'im how to run a automobile, he done got too biggety to live—an' we oughter kill 'im," Old Man Anderson advised.

42   A grunt of approval went around the porch. But the heat was melting their civic virtue and Elijah Moseley began to bait Joe Clarke.

43   "Come on, Joe, git a melon outa dere an' slice it up for yo' customers. We'se all sufferin' wid de heat. De bear's done got *me!*"

44   "Thass right, Joe, a watermelon is jes' whut Ah needs tuh cure de eppizudicks," Walter Thomas joined forces with Moseley. "Come on dere, Joe. We all is steady customers an' you aint set us up in a long time. Ah chooses dat long, bowlegged Floridy favorite."

45   "A god, an' be dough. You all gimme twenty cents and slice away," Clarke retorted. "Ah needs a col' slice m'self. Heah, everybody chip in. Ah'll lend y'll mah meat knife."

46   The money was quickly subscribed and the huge melon brought forth. At that moment, Sykes and Bertha arrived. A determined silence fell on the porch and the melon was put away again.

47   Merchant snapped down the blade of his jackknife and moved toward the store door.

48   "Come on in, Joe, an' gimme a slab uh sow belly an' uh pound uh coffee—almost fuhgot 'twas Sat'day. Got to git on home." Most of the men left also.

49   Just then Delia drove past on her way home, as Sykes was ordering magnificently for Bertha. It pleased him for Delia to see.

50   "Git whutsoever yo' heart desires, Honey. Wait a minute, Joe. Give huh two bottles uh strawberry soda-water, uh quart uh parched groundpeas, an' a block uh chewin' gum."

51   With all this they left the store, with Sykes reminding Bertha that this was his town and she could have it if she wanted it.

52   The men returned soon after they left, and held their watermelon feast. "Where did Syke Jones git dat 'oman from nohow?" Lindsay asked.

53   "Ovah Apopka. Guess dey musta been cleanin' out de town when she lef'. She don't look lak a thing but a hunk uh liver wid hair on it."

54   "Well, she sho' kin squall," Dave Carter contributed. "When she gits ready tuh laff, she jes' opens huh mouf an' latches it back tuh de las' notch. No ole grandpa alligator down in Lake Bell aint got nothin' on huh."

55   Bertha had been in town three months now. Sykes was still paying her room rent at Della Lewis'—the only house in town that would have taken her in. Sykes took her frequently to Winter Park to "stomps." He still assured her that he was the swellest man in the state.

56   "Sho! you kin have dat lil' ole house soon's Ah kin git dat 'oman outa dere. Everything b'longs tuh me an' you sho' kin have it. Ah sho'

'bominates uh skinny 'oman. Lawdy, you sho' is got one portly shape on you! You kin git *anything* you wants. Dis is *mah* town an' you sho' kin have it.

57   Delia's work-worn knees crawled over the earth in Gethsemane and on the rocks of Calvary many, many times during these months. She avoided the villagers and meeting places in her efforts to be blind and deaf. But Bertha nullified this to a degree, by coming to Delia's house to call Sykes out to her at the gate.

58   Delia and Sykes fought all the time now with no peaceful interludes. They slept and ate in silence. Two or three times Delia had attempted a timid friendliness, but she was repulsed each time. It was plain that the breaches must remain agape.

59   The sun had burned July to August. The heat streamed down like a million hot arrows, smiting all things living upon the earth. Grass withered, leaves browned, snakes went blind in shedding and men and dogs went mad. Dog days!

60   Delia came home one day and found Sykes there before her. She wondered, but started to go on into the house without speaking, even though he was standing in the kitchen door and she must either stoop under his arm or ask him to move. He made no room for her. She noticed a soap box beside the steps, but paid no particular attention to it, knowing that he must have brought it there. As she was stooping to pass under his outstretched arm, he suddenly pushed her backward, laughingly.

61   "Look in de box dere Delia, Ah done brung yuh somethin'!"

62   She nearly fell upon the box in her stumbling, and when she saw what it held, she all but fainted outright.

63   "Syke! Syke, mah Gawd! You take dat rattlesnake 'way from heah! You *gottuh*. Oh, Jesus, have mussy!"

64   "Ah aint gut tuh do nuthin' uh de kin'—fact is Ah aint got tuh do nothin' but die. Taint no use uh you puttin' on airs makin' out lak you sceered uh dat snake—he's gointer stay right heah tell he die. He wouldn't bite me cause Ah knows how tuh handle 'im. Nohow he wouldn't risk breakin' out his fangs 'gin yo' skinny laigs."

65   "Naw, now Syke, don't keep dat thing 'roun' heah tuh skeer me tuh death. You knows Ah'm even feared uh earth worms. Thass de biggest snake Ah evah did see. Kill 'im Syke, please."

66   "Doan ast me tuh do nothin' fuh yuh. Goin' 'roun' tryin' to be so damn asterperious. Naw, Ah aint gonna kill it. Ah think uh damn sight mo' uh him dan you! Dat's a nice snake an' anybody doan lak 'im kin jes' hit de grit."

67   The village soon heard that Sykes had the snake, and came to see and ask questions.

68   "How de hen-fire did you ketch dat six-foot rattler, Syke?" Thomas asked.

69   "He's full uh frogs so he caint hardly move, thass how Ah eased up on 'm. But Ah'm a snake charmer an' knows how tuh handle 'em. Shux, dat aint nothin'. Ah could ketch one eve'y day if Ah so wanted tuh."

70   "Whut he needs is a heavy hick'ry club leaned real heavy on his head. Dat's de bes' way tuh charm a rattlesnake."

71   "Naw, Walt, y'll jes' don't understand dese diamon' backs lak Ah do," said Sykes in a superior tone of voice.

72   The village agreed with Walter, but the snake stayed on. His box remained by the kitchen door with its screen wire covering. Two or three days later it had digested its meal of frogs and literally came to life. It rattled at every movement in the kitchen or the yard. One day as Delia came down the kitchen steps she saw his chalky-white fangs curved like scimitars hung in the wire meshes. This time she did not run away with averted eyes as usual. She stood for a long time in the doorway in a red fury that grew bloodier for every second that she regarded the creature that was her torment.

73   That night she broached the subject as soon as Sykes sat down to the table.

74   "Syke, Ah wants you tuh take dat snake 'way fum heah. You done starved me an' Ah put up widcher, you done beat me an' Ah took dat, but you done kilt all mah insides bringin' dat varmint heah."

75   Sykes poured out a saucer full of coffee and drank it deliberately before he answered her.

76   "A whole lot Ah keer 'bout how you feels inside uh out. Dat snake aint goin' no damn wheah till Ah gits ready fuh 'im tuh go. So fur as beatin' is concerned, yuh aint took near all dat you gointer take ef yuh stay 'roun' *me.*"

77   Delia pushed back her plate and got up from the table, "Ah hates you, Sykes," she said calmly. "Ah hates you tuh de same degree dat Ah useter love yuh. Ah done took an' took till mah belly is full up tuh mah neck. Dat's de reason Ah got mah letter fum de church an' moved mah membership tuh Woodbridge—so Ah don't haftuh take no sacrament wid yuh. Ah don't wantuh see yuh, 'roun' me atall. Lay 'roun' wid dat 'oman all yuh wants tuh, but gwan 'way fum me an' mah house. Ah hates yuh lak uh suck-egg dog."

78   Sykes almost let the huge wad of corn bread and collard greens he was chewing fall out of his mouth in amazement. He had a hard time whipping himself to the proper fury to try to answer Delia.

78   "Well, Ah'm glad you does hate me. Ah'm sho' tiahed uh you hangin' ontuh me. Ah don't want yuh. Look at yuh stringey ole neck! Yo' raw-bony laigs an' arms is enough tuh cut uh man tuh death. You looks jes' lak de devvul's doll-baby tuh *me*. You cain't hate me no worse dan Ah hates you. Ah been hatin' *you* fuh years."

79   "Yo' ole black hide don't look lak nothin' tuh me, but uh passle uh wrinkled up rubber, wid yo' big ole yeahs flappin' on each side lak up paih uh buzzard wings. Don't think Ah'm gointuh be run 'way fum mah house neither. Ah'm goin' tuh de white folks about *you*, mah young man, de very nex' time you lay yo' han's on me. Mah cup is done run ovah." Delia said this with no signs of fear and Sykes departed from the house, threatening her, but made not the slightest move to carry out any of them.

80   That night he did not return at all, and the next day being Sunday, Delia was glad that she did not have to quarrel before she hitched up her pony and drove the four miles to Woodbridge.

81   She stayed to the night service—"love feast"—which was very warm and full of spirit. In the emotional winds her domestic trials were borne far and wide so that she sang as she drove homeward,

82   "Jurden water, black an' col'
83   Chills de body, not de soul
84   An' Ah wantah cross Jurden in uh calm time."

85   She came from the barn to the kitchen door and stopped.

86   "Whut's de mattah, ol' satan, you aint kickin' up yo' racket?" She addressed the snake's box. Complete silence. She went on into the house with a new hope in its birth struggles. Perhaps her threat to go to the white folks had frightened Sykes! Perhaps he was sorry! Fifteen years of misery and suppression had brought Delia to the place where she would hope *anything* that looked towards a way over or through her wall of inhibitions.

87   She felt in the match safe behind the stove at once for a match. There was only one there.

88   "Dat n—— wouldn't fetch nothin heah tuh save his rotten neck, but he kin run thew whut Ah brings quick enough. Now he done toted off nigh on tuh haff uh box uh matches. He done had dat 'oman heah in mah house, too."

89   Nobody but a woman could tell how she knew this even before she struck the match. But she did and it put her into a new fury.

90   Presently she brought in the tubs to put the white things to soak. This time she decided she need not bring the hamper out of the bed-

room; she would go in there and do the sorting. She picked up the pot-bellied lamp and went in. The room was small and the hamper stood hard by the foot of the white iron bed. She could sit and reach through the bedposts—resting as she worked.

91   "Ah wantah cross Jurden in uh calm time." She was singing again. The mood of the "love feast" had returned. She threw back the lid of the basket almost gaily. Then, moved by both horror and terror, she sprang back toward the door. *There lay the snake in the basket!* He moved sluggishly at first, but even as she turned round and round, jumped up and down in an insanity of fear, he began to stir vigorously. She saw him pouring his awful beauty from the basket upon the bed, then she seized the lamp and ran as fast as she could to the kitchen. The wind from the open door blew out the light and the darkness added to her terror. She sped to the darkness of the yard, slamming the door after her before she thought to set down the lamp. She did not feel safe even on the ground, so she climbed up in the hay barn.

92   There for an hour or more she lay sprawled upon the hay a gibbering wreck.

93   Finally she grew quiet, and after that, coherent thought. With this, stalked through her a cold, bloody rage. Hours of this. A period of introspection, a space of retrospection, then a mixture of both. Out of this an awful calm.

94   "Well, Ah done de bes' Ah could. If things aint right, Gawd knows taint mah fault."

95   She went to sleep—a twitchy sleep—and woke up to a faint gray sky. There was a loud hollow sound below. She peered out. Sykes was at the wood-pile, demolishing a wire-covered box.

96   He hurried to the kitchen door, but hung outside there some minutes before he entered, and stood some minutes more inside before he closed it after him.

97   The gray in the sky was spreading. Delia descended without fear now, and crouched beneath the low bedroom window. The drawn shade shut out the dawn, shut in the night. But the thin walls held back no sound.

98   "Dat ol' scratch is woke up now!" She mused at the tremendous whirr inside, which every woodsman knows, is one of the sound illusions. The rattler is a ventriloquist. His whirr sounds to the right, to the left, straight ahead, behind, close under foot—everywhere but where it is. Woe to him who guesses wrong unless he is prepared to hold up his end of the argument! Sometimes he strikes without rattling at all.

99   Inside, Sykes heard nothing until he knocked a pot lid off the stove while trying to reach the match safe in the dark. He had emptied his pockets at Bertha's.

100   The snake seemed to wake up under the stove and Sykes made a quick leap into the bedroom. In spite of the gin he had had, his head was clearing now.

101   "Mah Gawd!" he chattered, "ef Ah could on'y strack uh light!"

102   The rattling ceased for a moment as he stood paralyzed. He waited. It seemed that the snake waited also.

103   "Oh, fuh de light! Ah thought he'd be too sick"—Sykes was muttering to himself when the whirr began again, closer, right underfoot this time. Long before this, Sykes' ability to think had been flattened down to primitive instinct and he leaped—onto the bed.

104   Outside Delia heard a cry that might have come from a maddened chimpanzee, a stricken gorilla. All the terror, all the horror, all the rage that man possibly could express, without a recognizable human sound.

105   A tremendous stir inside there, another series of animal screams, the intermittent whirr of the reptile. The shade torn violently down from the window, letting in the red dawn, a huge brown hand seizing the window stick, great dull blows upon the wooden floor punctuating the gibberish of sound long after the rattle of the snake had abruptly subsided. All this Delia could see and hear from her place beneath the window, and it made her ill. She crept over to the four-o'clocks and stretched herself on the cool earth to recover.

106   She lay there. "Delia, Delia!" She could hear Sykes calling in a most despairing tone as one who expected no answer. The sun crept on up, and he called. Delia could not move—her legs were gone flabby. She never moved, he called, and the sun kept rising.

107   "Mah Gawd!" She heard him moan, "Mah Gawd fum Heben!" She heard him stumbling about and got up from her flower-bed. The sun was growing warm. As she approached the door she heard him call out hopefully, "Delia, is dat you Ah heah?"

108   She saw him on his hands and knees as soon as she reached the door. He crept an inch or two toward her—all that he was able, and she saw his horribly swollen neck and his one open eye shining with hope. A surge of pity too strong to support bore her away from that eye that must, could not, fail to see the tubs. He would see the lamp. Orlando with its doctors was too far. She could scarcely reach the Chinaberry tree, where she waited in the growing heat while inside she knew the cold river was creeping up and up to extinguish that eye which must know by now that she knew.

Sweat

JOURNAL

1. MLA Works Cited

Using this model, record this reading here.

*Author's Last Name, First Name. "Title of the Story." Title of the Book. Ed.
First Last Name. City: Publisher, year. Pages of the story.*

2. Main Character(s)

*Describe each main character, and explain why you think each is a main
character.*

3. Supporting Characters

*Describe each supporting character, and explain why you think each is a
supporting character.*

4. Setting

*Describe the setting. Decide if this setting can be changed and, if so, to where
and when.*

5. Sequence

Relate the events of the story in order.

6. Plot

Tell the story in no more than two sentences.

7. Conflict.

Identify and explain the conflicts involved here.

8. Significant Quotations

Explain the importance of each of these quotations. Record the page number in the parentheses.

a. " 'Mah sweat is done paid for this house and Ah reckon Ah kin keep on sweatin' in it' " (   ).

b. "She had brought love to the union and he had brought a longing after the flesh" (   ).

c. " 'Taint no use uh you puttin' on airs makin' out lak you skeered uh dat snake—he's gointer stay right heah tell he die. He wouldn't bite me cause Ah knows how tuh handle 'im' " (   ).

d. " 'Whut's de mattah, ol' satan, you aint kickin' up yo' racket?' She addressed the snake's box. Complete silence" (   ).

e. "She lay there. 'Delia, Delia!' She could hear Sykes calling [. . . but] She never moved, he called, and the sun kept rising" (   ).

8. Irony

Identify and explain the irony in this story.

FOLLOW-UP QUESTIONS

10 SHORT QUESTIONS

Select the <u>best</u> answer for each.

____ 1. Delia
   a. works hard.
   b. seems to have no job.
   c. seems to be up to no good.

____ 2. Sykes
   a. works hard.
   b. is faithful.
   c. has another woman.

____ 3. Sykes
   a. is kind to Delia.
   b. has beaten Delia.
   c. has not beaten Delia.

____ 4. The town
   a. thinks highly of Sykes.
   b. does not think highly of Sykes.
   c. does not know Sykes.

____ 5. Delia
   a. wants a pet snake.
   b. is afraid of snakes.
   c. is not afraid of snakes.

____ 6. Sykes feels he
   a. can handle a rattlesnake.
   b. cannot handle a rattle-snake.
   c. does not want a rattle-snake.

____ 7. Sykes uses the snake because
   a. he likes animals.
   b. he wants Delia to stay.
   c. he wants Delia to leave.

____ 8. Delia plans
   a. to stay.
   b. to leave.
   c. to kill Sykes.

____ 9. When Sykes calls for help, Delia
   a. goes to help him.
   b. does not hear him.
   c. does not help him.

____ 10. In the end, Sykes
   a. lives and leaves Delia.
   b. dies.
   c. lives and pushes Delia out.

5 SIGNIFICANT QUOTATIONS

Explain the importance of each of these quotations.

1. " 'Ah been married to you fur fifteen years, and Ah been takin' in washin' fur fifteen years. Sweat, sweat, sweat! Work and sweat, cry and sweat, pray and sweat!' "

2. "Oh well, whatever goes over the Devil's back, is got to come under his belly. Sometime or ruther, Sykes, like everybody else, is gointer reap his sowing.' "

3. " 'Syke! Syke, mah Gawd! You take dat rattlesnake 'way from heah! You *gottuh*. Oh, Jesus, have mussy!' "

4. " 'But Ah'm a snake charmer an' knows how tuh handle 'em' "

5. "Delia could not move—her legs were gone flabby. She never moved, he called, and the sun kept rising."

2 COMPREHENSION ESSAY QUESTIONS

Use specific details and information from the story to answer these as completely as possible.

1. Explain the irony in this story. Use specific details and information from the story to support your explanation.

2. Create another title for this story. Use specific details and information from the story to explain your choice.

WRITING

Use each of these ideas for writing an essay.

1. Whether younger or older, one often has to face something feared. Write an essay telling the story of something you or someone you know has feared and has had to face.

2. Many of us have found ourselves locked in bad relationships. Describe a poor relationship you or someone you know has been in, and describe how you or your friend got out of it.

Further Writing

1. Compare Hurston's storytelling with that of Roberta Fernandez in "Zulema" (page 42).

2. Compare Hurston's irony with that in Dorothy Parker's "The Wonderful Old Gentleman" (page 329).

3. Research spousal abuse, and use Delia's story to offer insight into the question, "Why don't they leave?"

5

Extended Short Story Study

The stories in this chapter, each longer and more complex than the others you have read, combine the elements that you have studied. Each offers the opportunity for you to study the thoughts and actions of stirring characters, significant settings and props, well-developed plots and story lines, and ironic twists. Further, each study offers you the opportunity to study complex conflicts.

Nathaniel Hawthorne introduces us to American Gothic in this tale told with a light touch of humor. In a dark and foreboding setting, we watch as Dr. Heidegger offers his guests magic from the Fountain of Youth. Read to see how well the guests use the magic they are offered.

William Faulkner's "A Rose for Emily" presents several of Faulkner's wonderfully strange characters in a tale steeped in a decaying South. Much as Faulkner denied it, literary symbols seem to appear almost everywhere. **Symbols** are objects or characters that represent something beyond their face value. For instance, an American flag is really nothing more than pieces of cloth sewn together, but an American flag represents the pride and glory and industry of America. By looking beyond the surface, you will find many symbols in literature.

With Edgar Allan Poe and Herman Melville, we enter the world of the supernatural. In "The Masque of the Red Death," Poe offers many hints that foreshadow events as we come face-to-face with evil, complete with a cryptic figure. In reading the "The Bell-Tower," you should know that a person arrogantly placing himself or herself above the gods or God is called **hubris,** a term used by the ancient Greeks. You will see that Melville offers biblical references to explain the demonic actions and horrible irony of this story.

Look for the conflicts, and study the rich details as you read each of these stories.

Dr. Heidegger's Experiment

Nathaniel Hawthorne

Pre-reading Vocabulary
Context

Use context clues to define these words before reading. Use a dictionary as needed.

1. The learned wisdom and great dignity of the judge made him a *venerable* person. *Venerable* means _____.

2. After becoming a lieutenant, a captain, and then a major, Juan was made a *colonel* in the Army. *Colonel* means _____.

3. The grape *withered* into a wrinkled little raisin as it sat in the sun. *Withered* means _____.

4. After his father died, Don went to visit his mother who now had become a *widow*. *Widow* means _____.

5. With her store selling merchandise valued in the millions, Debbie has become the most successful *merchant* in town. *Merchant* means

_____.

6. After losing everything, Chuck became a mere *mendicant*, begging in the streets. *Mendicant* means _____.

7. There are many little-known, *obscure* artists trying to sell their work. *Obscure* means _____.

8. When everyone learned about the politician cheating on his wife, everyone looked on him as *scandalous*. *Scandalous* means

_____.

9. When Mary Beth moved into a large home in the country, she became part of the wealthy, landed *gentry*. *Gentry* means _____.

10. Mukendi lost his check records, and his checking account became a *woful* mess. *Woful* means _____.

11. The children loved to listen when Purvi read them a wonderful *fable* about a turtle and a rabbit. *Fable* means _____.

12. The museum had *busts,* or statues of the heads and shoulders, of Hippocrates, Plato, and Socrates. *Bust* means _____.

13. Alice looked into the *looking-glass* to see if she needed to fix her hair. *Looking-glass* means _____.

14. Laura's *magnificent* gown was made of bright and sparkling colors and was not at all faded or dull. *Magnificent* means _____.

15. Laurie decided to hang elegant and heavy satin *brocade* and *damask* drapes. *Brocade* and *damask* mean _____.

16. Scott had the *visage* of a happy man as his eyes sparkled, his lips were curved into a smile, and his steps were light. *Visage* means

_____.

17. Isabelle had a great *curiosity* about her neighbors and decided to spy on them to learn more. *Curiosity* means _____.

18. The heavy book with its many folios was a sizable *volume* to try to place on the shelf. *Volume* means _____.

19. The adults dressed up as *ghastly* creatures and tried to win the Most Scary prize at the party. *Ghastly* means _____.

20. Zoltan decorated the top of the drapes with a heavy, braided *festoon.* *Festoon* means _____.

21. On New Year's eve, many drink a bottle of expensive *champagne* to celebrate the evening. *Champagne* means _____.

22. Artie waited for the tomatoes to ripen and turn bright *crimson* before he picked them. *Crimson* means _____.

23. Jay is a master of *deception* and seems to be able to lie about everything and to get away with it. *Deception* means _____.

24. When Janet had a cold, the doctor told her to rest and to drink a lot of *fluids*. *Fluid* means _____.

25. Scientists are looking for *rejuvenescent* creams that will make the wrinkles of old age disappear. *Rejuvenescent* means _____.

26. Mary felt very *repentant* after she broke her mother's vase, and she went everywhere to try to buy a new vase. *Repentant* means

_____.

27. After he drank far too much coffee, Hal's *palsied* hands shook uncontrollably. *Palsied* means _____.

28. Donnie and Marie *bestowed* the crown *upon* the new Miss America. *Bestow upon* means _____.

29. The elderly man was old and *decrepit* and could hardly walk without assistance. *Decrepit* means _____.

30. Ann has to have a lot of *patience* to work so long and hard at sewing on beading. *Patience* means _____.

31. Yolanda was under the *delusion* that she had lost the contest, only to find out later that she had won. *Delusion* means _____.

32. At twenty-two, Theo is in the *prime* of his life and enjoys perfect health and lots of energy. *Prime* means _____.

33. Loyalty to one's country is called *patriotism*. *Patriotism* means

_____.

34. The poor student was whining and *simpering* over her failing grades instead of studying. *Simpering* means _____.

35. Sandy's cake completely *vanished,* and not even a crumb was left after the hungry children came home from school. *Vanished* means

    _____.

36. The nasty woman made fun of and *mocked* the older woman who moved so slowly. *Mocked* means _____.

37. When Eileen wears her judge's robes and elegantly enters the courtroom, she moves with great *dignity. Dignity* means

    _____.

38. Amy and Caitlin shared a great *rivalship* when each competed with the other to be prom queen. *Rivalship* means _____.

39. The young man was absolutely *bewitched* by the young girl's charm and beauty. *Bewitched* means _____.

40. Gloria flirted in playful *coquetry* with every young man she met. *Coquetry* means _____.

41. Tom and Teddy *grappled* with facts and figures as they tried to develop a sales proposal. *Grapple* means _____.

42. The unhappy residents *protested* the new taxes they felt they should not have to pay. *Protest* means _____.

43. Paul mistakenly hit the delicate vase and *dashed* it to the floor. *Dash* means _____.

44. The balloon *shriveled* up after Victoria poked it with a pin and let the air out of it. *Shrivel* means _____.

45. Worry caused deep *furrows* in the old woman's forehead. *Furrow* means _____.

46. Childhood is only a *transient* state, because it disappears in a relatively short time. *Transient* means _____.

47. High fever can cause *delirium,* resulting in one seeing and hearing things that are not really there. *Delirium* means _____.

48. The wealthy woman *lavished* all her wealth on a man who later left her with nothing. *Lavished* means _____.

49. The religious people made a *pilgrimage* to the visit the places that they considered to be holy. *Pilgrimage* means _____.

50. The football players took deep *quaffs* of water to satisfy their thirst in the hot sun. *Quaff* means _____.

Pre-reading Vocabulary
Word Attack

Define these words by solving the parts. Use a dictionary as needed.

1. white-bearded	23. reviving
2. gentlewoman	24. deathlike
3. unfortunate	25. animated
4. misfortune	26. improvement
5. sinful	27. corpse-like
6. ruined	28. brimful
7. infamous	29. duskier
8. unfrequently	30. joyously
9. recollections	31. successive
10. desirous	32. new-created
11. old-fashioned	33. maddened
12. besprinkled	34. frolicsomeness
13. oaken	35. gayety
14. obscurest	36. mischievous
15. ornamented	37. merriment
16. chambermaid	38. pessimistic
17. workmanship	39. disengage
18. ashen	40. livelier
19. exceedingly	41. threatening
20. withered	42. overturned
21. blossomed	43. chillness
22. faded	44. deepening

Pre-reading Questions

Try answering these questions as you read.

What does Dr. Heidegger have?

What characteristics do Dr. Heidegger's guests have?

How do they change?

How do they stay the same?

Dr. Heidegger's Experiment

NATHANIEL HAWTHORNE

Nathaniel Hawthorne was born in 1804. He came from a family of long standing in Salem, Massachusetts. Hawthorne was related to wealthy merchants on his father's side and to working transporters on his mother's side. Hawthorne's family saved money to send him to Bowdoin College in Maine. There he roomed with Franklin Pierce, who would become the fourteenth president of the United States, and met Henry Wadsworth Longfellow. Wishing to become a writer but realizing that writers do not make much money, Hawthorne turned to work in the Boston customhouse and later married Sophia Peabody. Eventually, he returned to Salem and to writing. He later served as President Pierce's consul in Liverpool, England. Hawthorne died of a debilitating disease in 1860.

A friend of Longfellow and of Ralph Waldo Emerson and esteemed by Herman Melville, who dedicated *Moby Dick* to him, Hawthorne raised questions about the human condition. *The Scarlet Letter* and *The House of Seven Gables* remain his masterworks. This story is taken from *Twice-Told Tales*.

The home that inspired *The House of Seven Gables* is open to the public, and a visit there offers insight into the mysterious, Gothic, and often eerie world that appears in Hawthorne's writings.

That very singular man, old Dr. Heidegger, once invited four venerable friends to meet him in his study. There were three white-bearded gentlemen, Mr. Medbourne, Colonel Killigrew, and Mr. Gascoigne, and a withered gentlewoman, whose name was the Widow Wycherly. They were all melancholy old creatures, who had been unfortunate in life, and whose greatest misfortune it was that they were not long ago in their graves. Mr. Medbourne, in the vigor of his age, had been a prosperous merchant, but had lost his all by a frantic speculation, and was now little better than a mendicant. Colonel Killigrew had wasted his best years, and his health and substance, in the pursuit of sinful pleasures, which had given birth to a brood of pains, such as the gout, and divers other torments of soul and body. Mr. Gascoigne was a ruined politician, a man of evil fame, or at least had been so till time had buried him from the knowledge of the present generation, and made him obscure instead of infamous. As for the Widow Wycherly, tradition tells us that she was a great beauty in her day; but, for a long while past, she had lived in deep seclusion, on account of certain scandalous stories which had prejudiced the gentry of the town against her. It is a circumstance worth mentioning that each of these three old gentlemen, Mr. Medbourne, Colonel Killigrew, and Mr. Gascoigne, were early lovers of the Widow Wycherly, and had once been on the point of cutting each other's throats for her sake. And, before proceeding further, I will merely hint that Dr. Heidegger and all his four guests were sometimes thought to be a little beside themselves—as is not unfrequently the case with old people, when worried either by present troubles or woful recollections.

2   "My dear old friends," said Dr. Heidegger, motioning them to be seated, "I am desirous of your assistance in one of those little experiments with which I amuse myself here in my study."

3   If all stories were true, Dr. Heidegger's study must have been a very curious place. It was a dim, old-fashioned chamber, festooned with cobwebs, and besprinkled with antique dust. Around the walls stood several oaken bookcases, the lower shelves of which were filled with rows of gigantic folios and black-letter quartos, and the upper with little parchment-covered duodecimos. Over the central bookcase was a bronze bust of Hippocrates, with which, according to some authorities, Dr. Heidegger was accustomed to hold consultations in all difficult cases of his practice. In the obscurest corner of the room stood a tall and narrow oaken closet, with its door ajar, within which doubtfully appeared a skeleton. Between two of the bookcases hung a looking-glass, presenting its high and dusty plate within a tarnished gilt frame. Among many wonderful stories related of this mirror, it was fabled that the spirits of all the doctor's deceased patients dwelt within its verge, and would stare him in the face whenever he looked thitherward. The opposite side of the chamber was ornamented with the full-length portrait of a young lady, arrayed in the faded magnificence of silk, satin, and brocade, and with a visage as faded as her dress. Above half a century ago, Dr. Heidegger had been on the point of marriage with this young lady; but, being affected with some slight disorder, she had swallowed one of her lover's prescriptions, and died on the bridal evening. The greatest curiosity of the study remains to be mentioned; it was a ponderous folio volume, bound in black leather, with massive silver clasps. There were no letters on the back, and nobody could tell the title of the book. But it was well known to be a book of magic; and once, when a chambermaid had lifted it, merely to brush away the dust, the skeleton had rattled in its closet, the picture of the young lady had stepped one foot upon the floor, and several ghastly faces had peeped forth from the mirror; while the brazen head of Hippocrates frowned, and said—"Forbear!"

4   Such was Dr. Heidegger's study. On the summer afternoon of our tale a small round table, as black as ebony, stood in the centre of the

room, sustaining a cut-glass vase of beautiful form and elaborate work-manship. The sunshine came through the window, between the heavy festoons of two faded damask curtains, and fell directly across this vase; so that a mild splendor was reflected from it on the ashen visages of the five old people who sat around. Four champagne glasses were also on the table.

5   "My dear old friends," repeated Dr. Heidegger, "may I reckon on your aid in performing an exceedingly curious experiment?"

6   Now Dr. Heidegger was a very strange old gentleman, whose eccentricity had become the nucleus for a thousand fantastic stories. Some of these fables, to my shame be it spoken, might possibly be traced back to my own veracious self; and if any passages of the present tale should startle the reader's faith, I must be content to bear the stigma of a fiction monger.

7   When the doctor's four guests heard him talk of his proposed experiment, they anticipated nothing more wonderful than the murder of a mouse in an air pump, or the examination of a cobweb by the microscope, or some similar nonsense, with which he was constantly in the habit of pestering his intimates. But without waiting for a reply, Dr. Heidegger hobbled across the chamber, and returned with the same ponderous folio, bound in black leather, which common report affirmed to be a book of magic. Undoing the silver clasps, he opened the volume, and took from among its black-letter pages a rose, or what was once a rose, though now the green leaves and crimson petals had assumed one brownish hue, and the ancient flower seemed ready to crumble to dust in the doctor's hands.

8   "This rose," said Dr. Heidegger, with a sigh, "this same withered and crumbling flower, blossomed five and fifty years ago. It was given me by Sylvia Ward, whose portrait hangs yonder; and I meant to wear it in my bosom at our wedding. Five and fifty years it has been treasured between the leaves of this old volume. Now, would you deem it possi-ble that this rose of half a century could ever bloom again?"

9   "Nonsense!" said the Widow Wycherly, with a peevish toss of her head. "You might as well ask whether an old woman's wrinkled face could ever bloom again."

10   "See!" answered Dr. Heidegger.

11   He uncovered the vase, and threw the faded rose into the water which it contained. At first, it lay lightly on the surface of the fluid, appearing to imbibe none of its moisture. Soon, however, a singular change began to be visible. The crushed and dried petals stirred, and assumed a deepening tinge of crimson as if the flower were reviving

from a deathlike slumber; the slender stalk and twigs of foliage became green; and there was the rose of half a century, looking as fresh as when Sylvia Ward had first given it to her lover. It was scarcely full blown; for some of its delicate red leaves curled modestly around its moist bosom, within which two or three dewdrops were sparkling.

12   "That is certainly a very pretty deception," said the doctor's friends; carelessly, however, for they had witnessed greater miracles at a conjurer's show; "pray how was it effected?"

13   "Did you never hear of the 'Fountain of Youth'?" asked Dr. Heidegger, "which Ponce de Leon, the Spanish adventurer, went in search of two or three centuries ago?"

14   "But did Ponce de Leon ever find it?" said the Widow Wycherly.

15   "No," answered Dr. Heidegger, "for he never sought it in the right place. The famous Fountain of Youth, if I am rightly informed, is situated in the southern part of the Floridian peninsula, not far from Lake Macaco. Its source is overshadowed by several gigantic magnolias, which, though numberless centuries old, have been kept as fresh as violets by the virtues of this wonderful water. An acquaintance of mine, knowing my curiosity in such matters, has sent me what you see in the vase."

16   "Ahem!" said Colonel Killigrew, who believed not a word of the doctor's story: "and what may be the effect of this fluid on the human frame?"

17   "You shall judge for yourself, my dear colonel," replied Dr. Heidegger; "and all of you, my respected friends, are welcome to so much of this admirable fluid as may restore to you the bloom of youth. For my own part, having had much trouble in growing old, I am in no hurry to grow young again. With your permission, therefore, I will merely watch the progress of the experiment."

18   While he spoke, Dr. Heidegger had been filling the four champagne glasses with the water of the Fountain of Youth. It was apparently impregnated with an effervescent gas, for little bubbles were continually ascending from the depths of the glasses, and bursting in silvery spray at the surface. As the liquor diffused a pleasant perfume, the old people doubted not that it possessed cordial and comfortable properties; and though utter sceptics as to its rejuvenescent power, they were inclined to swallow it at once. But Dr. Heidegger besought them to stay a moment.

19   "Before you drink, my respectable, old friends," said he, "it would be well that, with the experience of a lifetime to direct you, you should draw up a few general rules for your guidance, in passing a second time

through the perils of youth. Think what a sin and shame it would be, if, with your peculiar advantages, you should not become patterns of virtue and wisdom to all the young people of the age!"

20   The doctor's four venerable friends made him no answer, except by a feeble and tremulous laugh; so very ridiculous was the idea that, knowing how closely repentance treads behind the steps of error, they should ever go astray again.

21   "Drink, then," said the doctor, bowing: "I rejoice that I have so well selected the subjects of my experiment."

22   With palsied hands, they raised the glasses to their lips. The liquor, if it really possessed such virtues as Dr. Heidegger imputed to it, could not have been bestowed on four human beings who needed it more wofully. They looked as if they had never known what youth or pleasure was, but had been the offspring of Nature's dotage, and always the gray, decrepit, sapless, miserable creatures, who now sat stooping round the doctor's table, without life enough in their souls or bodies to be animated even by the prospect of growing young again. They drank off the water, and replaced their glasses on the table.

23   Assuredly there was an almost immediate improvement in the aspect of the party, not unlike what might have been produced by a glass of generous wine, together with a sudden glow of cheerful sunshine brightening over all their visages at once. There was a healthful suffusion on their cheeks, instead of the ashen hue that had made them look so corpse-like. They gazed at one another, and fancied that some magic power had really begun to smooth away the deep and sad inscriptions which Father Time had been so long engraving on their brows. The Widow Wycherly adjusted her cap, for she felt almost like a woman again.

24   "Give us more of this wondrous water!" cried they, eagerly. "We are younger—but we are still too old! Quick—give us more!"

25   "Patience, patience!" quoth Dr. Heidegger, who sat watching the experiment with philosophic coolness. "You have been a long time growing old. Surely, you might be content to grow young in half an hour! But the water is at your service."

26   Again he filled their glasses with the liquor of youth, enough of which still remained in the vase to turn half the old people in the city to the age of their own grandchildren. While the bubbles were yet sparkling on the brim, the doctor's four guests snatched their glasses from the table, and swallowed the contents at a single gulp. Was it delusion? even while the draught was passing down their throats, it

seemed to have wrought a change on their whole systems. Their eyes grew clear and bright; a dark shade deepened among their silvery locks, they sat around the table, three gentlemen of middle age, and a woman, hardly beyond her buxom prime.

27   "My dear widow, you are charming!" cried Colonel Killigrew, whose eyes had been fixed upon her face, while the shadows of age were flitting from it like darkness from the crimson daybreak.

28   The fair widow knew, of old, that Colonel Killigrew's compliments were not always measured by sober truth; so she started up and ran to the mirror, still dreading that the ugly visage of an old woman would meet her gaze. Meanwhile, the three gentlemen behaved in such a manner as proved that the water of the Fountain of Youth possessed some intoxicating qualities; unless, indeed, their exhilaration of spirits were merely a lightsome dizziness caused by the sudden removal of the weight of years. Mr. Gascoigne's mind seemed to run on political topics, but whether relating to the past, present, or future could not easily be determined, since the same ideas and phrases have been in vogue these fifty years. Now he rattled forth full-throated sentences about patriotism, national glory, and the people's right; now he muttered some perilous stuff or other, in a sly and doubtful whisper, so cautiously that even his own conscience could scarcely catch the secret; and now, again, he spoke in measured accents, and a deeply deferential tone, as if a royal ear were listening to his well-turned periods. Colonel Killigrew all this time had been trolling forth a jolly bottle song, and ringing his glass in symphony with the chorus, while his eyes wandered toward the buxom figure of the Widow Wycherly. On the other side of the table, Mr. Medbourne was involved in a calculation of dollars and cents, with which was strangely intermingled a project for supplying the East Indies with ice, by harnessing a team of whales to the polar icebergs.

29   As for the Widow Wycherly, she stood before the mirror courtesying and simpering to her own image, and greeting it as the friend whom she loved better than all the world beside. She thrust her face close to the glass, to see whether some long-remembered wrinkle or crow's foot had indeed vanished. She examined whether the snow had so entirely melted from her hair that the venerable cap could be safely thrown aside. At last, turning briskly away, she came with a sort of dancing step to the table.

30   "My dear old doctor," cried she, "pray favor me with another, glass!"

31   "Certainly, my dear madam, certainly!" replied the complaisant doctor; "see! I have already filled the glasses."

32   There, in fact, stood the four glasses, brimful of this wonderful water, the delicate spray of which, as it effervesced from the surface, resembled the tremulous glitter of diamonds. It was now so nearly sunset that the chamber had grown duskier than ever; but a mild and moonlike splendor gleamed from within the vase, and rested alike on the four guests and on the doctor's venerable figure. He sat in a high-backed, elaborately-carved, oaken arm-chair, with a gray dignity of aspect that might have well befitted that very Father Time, whose power had never been disputed, save by this fortunate company. Even while quaffing the third draught of the Fountain of Youth, they were almost awed by the expression of his mysterious visage.

33   But, the next moment, the exhilarating gush of young life shot through their veins. They were now in the happy prime of youth. Age, with its miserable train of cares and sorrows and diseases, was remembered only as the trouble of a dream, from which they had joyously awoke. The fresh gloss of the soul, so early lost, and without which the world's successive scenes had been but a gallery of faded pictures, again threw its enchantment over all their prospects. They felt like new-created beings in a new-created universe.

34   "We are young! We are young!" they cried exultingly.

35   Youth, like the extremity of age, had effaced the strongly-marked characteristics of middle life, and mutually assimilated them all. They were a group of merry youngsters, almost maddened with the exuberant frolicsomeness of their years. The most singular effect of their gayety was an impulse to mock the infirmity and decrepitude of which they had so lately been the victims. They laughed loudly at their old-fashioned attire, the wide-skirted coats and flapped waistcoats of the young men, and the ancient cap and gown of the blooming girl. One limped across the floor like a gouty grandfather; one set a pair of spectacles astride of his nose, and pretended to pore over the black-letter pages of the book of magic; a third seated himself in an arm-chair, and strove to imitate the venerable dignity of Dr. Heidegger. Then all shouted mirthfully, and leaped about the room. The Widow Wycherly—if so fresh a damsel could be called a widow—tripped up to the doctor's chair, with a mischievous merriment in her rosy face.

36   "Doctor, you dear old soul," cried she, "get up and dance with me!" And then the four young people laughed louder than ever, to think what a queer figure the poor old doctor would cut.

37   "Pray excuse me," answered the doctor quietly. "I am old and rheumatic, and my dancing days were over long ago. But either of these gay young gentlemen will be glad of so pretty a partner."

38   "Dance with me, Clara!" cried Colonel Killigrew.

39   "No, no, I will be her partner!" shouted Mr. Gascoigne.

40   "She promised me her hand, fifty years ago!" exclaimed Mr. Medbourne.

41   They all gathered round her. One caught both her hands in his passionate grasp—another threw his arm about her waist—the third buried his hand among the glossy curls that clustered beneath the widow's cap. Blushing, panting, struggling, chiding, laughing, her warm breath fanning each of their faces by turns, she strove to disengage herself, yet still remained in their triple embrace. Never was there a livelier picture of youthful rivalship, with bewitching beauty for the prize. Yet, by a strange deception, owing to the duskiness of the chamber, and the antique dresses which they still wore, the tall mirror is said to have reflected the figures of the three old, gray, withered grandsires, ridiculously contending for the skinny ugliness of a shrivelled grandam.

42   But they were young: their burning passions proved them so. Inflamed to madness by the coquetry of the girl-widow, who neither granted nor quite withheld her favors, the three rivals began to interchange threatening glances. Still keeping hold of the fair prize, they grappled fiercely at one another's throats. As they struggled to and fro, the table was overturned, and the vase dashed into a thousand fragments. The precious Water of Youth flowed in a bright stream across the floor, moistening the wings of a butterfly, which, grown old in the decline of summer, had alighted there to die. The insect fluttered lightly through the chamber, and settled on the snowy head of Dr. Heidegger.

43   "Come, come, gentlemen! come, Madam Wycherly," exclaimed the doctor, "I really must protest against this riot."

44   They stood still and shivered; for it seemed as if gray Time were calling them back from their sunny youth, far down into the chill and darksome vale of years. They looked at old Dr. Heidegger, who sat in his carved arm-chair, holding the rose of half a century, which he had rescued from among the fragments of the shattered vase. At the motion of his hand, the four rioters resumed their seats; the more readily, because their violent exertions had wearied them, youthful though they were.

45   "My poor Sylvia's rose!" ejaculated Dr. Heidegger, holding it in the light of the sunset clouds; "it appears to be fading again."

46   And so it was. Even while the party were looking at it, the flower continued to shrivel up, till it became as dry and fragile as when the doctor had first thrown it into the vase. He shook off the few drops of moisture which clung to its petals.

47   "I love it as well thus as in its dewy freshness," observed he, pressing the withered rose to his withered lips. While he spoke, the butterfly fluttered down from the doctor's snowy head, and fell upon the floor.

48   His guests shivered again. A strange chillness, whether of the body or spirit they could not tell, was creeping gradually over them all. They gazed at one another, and fancied that each fleeting moment snatched away a charm, and left a deepening furrow where none had been before. Was it an illusion? Had the changes of a lifetime been crowded into so brief a space, and were they now four aged people, sitting with their old friend, Dr. Heidegger?

49   "Are we grown old again, so soon?" cried they, dolefully.

50   In truth they had. The Water of Youth possessed merely a virtue more transient than that of wine. The delirium which it created had effervesced away. Yes! they were old again. With a shuddering impulse, that showed her a woman still, the widow clasped her skinny hands before her face, and wished that the coffin lid were over it, since it could be no longer beautiful.

51   "Yes, friends, ye are old again," said Dr. Heidegger, "and lo! the Water of Youth is all lavished on the ground. Well—I bemoan it not; for if the fountain gushed at my very doorstep, I would not stoop to bathe my lips in it—no, though its delirium were for years instead of moments. Such is the lesson ye have taught me!"

52   But the doctor's four friends had taught no such lesson to themselves. They resolved forthwith to make a pilgrimage to Florida, and quaff at morning, noon, and night, from the Fountain of Youth.

Note: In an English review, not long since, I have been accused of plagiarizing the idea of this story from a chapter in one of the novels of Alexandre Dumas. There has undoubtedly been a plagiarism on one side or the other; but as my story was written a good deal more than twenty years ago, and as the novel is of considerably more recent date, I take pleasure in thinking that M. Dumas has done me the honor to appropriate one of the fanciful conceptions of my earlier days. He is heartily welcome to it; nor is it the only instance, by many, in which the great French romancer has exercised the privilege of commanding genius by confiscating the intellectual property of less famous people to his own use and behoof.

September, 1860.

Dr. Heidegger's Experiment

JOURNAL

1. MLA Works Cited

Using this model, record this story.

Author's Last Name, First Name. "Title of the Story." <u>Title of the Book</u>. Ed. First Last Name. City: Publisher, year. Pages of the story.

2. Main Character(s)

Describe each main character, and explain why you think each is a main character.

3. Supporting Characters

Describe each supporting character, and explain why you think each is a supporting character.

4. Setting

Describe the setting. Decide if the setting can be changed and, if so, to where or when.

5. **Sequence**

   Relate the events of the story in order.

6. **Plot**

   Tell the story in no more than three sentences.

7. **Conflicts**

   Identify and explain the conflicts involved here.

8. **Significant Quotations**

   Explain the importance of each of these quotations. Record the page number in the parentheses.

   a. "But it was well known to a be a book of magic [. . .]" (   ).

b. " 'My dear old friends,' repeated Dr. Heidegger, 'may I reckon on your aid in performing an exceedingly curious experiment?' " (   ).

c. "The crushed and dried petals stirred, and assumed a deepening tinge of crimson, as if the flower were reviving from a deathlike slumber [. . .]" (   ).

d. "But they were young: their burning passions proved them so" (   ).

e. "But the doctor's four friends had taught no such lesson to themselves" (   ).

9. Irony

Identify and explain the irony in this story.

FOLLOW-UP QUESTIONS

10 SHORT QUESTIONS

Select the <u>best</u> answer for each.

____ 1. Dr. Heidegger is probably
   a. a doctor of philosophy.
   b. a doctor of medicine.
   c. a doctor of education.

____ 2. Mr. Medbourne was probably
   a. a serious businessman.
   b. an honest businessman.
   c. a dishonest businessman.

____ 3. Colonel Killigrew was probably
   a. a virtuous man.
   b. a minister.
   c. a lady's man.

____ 4. Mr. Gascoigne was probably
   a. an honest politician.
   b. a deceitful politician.
   c. a devoted public servant.

____ 5. Widow Wycherly was probably
   a. a virtuous young woman.
   b. a sincere and serious young woman.
   c. a flirtatious young woman.

____ 6. The mirror seems to
   a. be magical.
   b. reflect reality.
   c. be cracked and useless.

____ 7. The water seems to
   a. be magical.
   b. be infected.
   c. be of no use.

____ 8. The rose that is fifty-five years old is
   a. not kept in the book.
   b. not a reminder of Dr. Heidegger's fiancée.
   c. dried and then becomes fresh again.

____ 9. The four drink the water and
   a. become young again.
   b. become young forever.
   c. become wiser in their youth.

____ 10. The four do not
   a. behave like young fools.
   b. learn from their experiences.
   c. set off to find the Fountain of Youth.

5 SIGNIFICANT QUOTATIONS

Explain the importance of each of these quotations.

1. " 'My dear old friends,' said Dr. Heidegger, motioning them to be seated, 'I am desirous of your assistance in one of those little experiments with which I amuse myself here in my study.' "

2. "The greatest curiosity of the study remains to be mentioned; it was a ponderous folio volume [. . .]."

3. "He uncovered the vase, and threw the faded rose into the water which it contained."

4. "Inflamed to madness by the coquetry of the girl-widow, who neither granted nor quite withheld her favors, the three rivals began to interchange threatening glances."

5. "They resolved forthwith to make a pilgrimage to Florida, and quaff at morning, noon, and night, from the Fountain of Youth."

2 COMPREHENSION ESSAY QUESTIONS

Use specific details and information from the story to answer these as completely as possible.

1. How does the title relate to the story? Explain the significance of the title using specific details and information from the story.

2. Explain the characters' actions. Use specific details and information from the story to support your explanations.

WRITING

Use each of these ideas for writing an essay.

1. Dr. Heidegger takes his characters back to their youth. Describe an age or a moment to which you would like to return.

2. If you had the chance to go back and change something or sometime in your life, what would it be? Describe the situation and how you would change it.

Further Writing

1. Read Herman Melville's "The Bell-Tower" (page 426), and contrast, both as scientists and as men, Dr. Heidegger with Bannadonna.

2. Read Nathaniel Hawthorne's "Lady Eleanor's Mantle" (which can be found in a library), and compare this story with Edgar Allan Poe's "The Masque of the Red Death" (page 409).

A Rose for Emily

William Faulkner

PRE-READING VOCABULARY
CONTEXT

Use context clues to define these words before reading. Use a dictionary as needed.

1. *Necro–* means "death" and *–philia* means "love of" or "to love."
   Necrophilia means _____.

2. Juanita caught the first flight after her grandmother died, so that she could attend the *funeral. Funeral* means _____.

3. Carrie's *curiosity* got the best of her, and she secretly listened to overhear what her friends said. *Curiosity* means _____.

4. Olympic athletes are a very *select* group of the best athletes. *Select* means _____.

5. Ben bought machinery called a *cotton gin* to separate the cotton balls from the seeds inside. *Cotton gin* means _____.

6. When Caesar ruled over most of the known world by himself, he held a most *august* position. *August* means _____.

7. The dead, rotting snake began to smell as it *decayed* by the side of the road. *Decay* means _____.

8. The old tires and rusty cars that Karl left in the yard around his house were an *eyesore* to the neighborhood. *Eyesore* means

   _____.

9. Since Libby had offered to buy lunch, she accepted her *obligation* and paid the bill. *Obligation* means _____.

10. When the Smiths did not have money, their landlord gave them a *dispensation,* and they did not have to pay rent for the month. *Dispensation* means _____ .

11. JoAnne always saves money so that when she receives her *tax notice,* she can pay her taxes right away. *Tax notice* means

_____ .

12. For years, the United *Negro* College Fund has gotten money for African-American students to attend college. *Negro* means

_____ .

13. The elderly woman used a slender *cane* made out of oak to help support her as she walked. *Cane* means _____ .

14. *Ebony* is a fine hardwood that grows in Africa and turns black when stained. *Ebony* means _____ .

15. Teddy brought his car to a rapid *halt* when traffic stopped in front of him. *Halt* means _____ .

16. Vernie married her high school *sweetheart* whom she had dated all through high school. *Sweetheart* means _____ .

17. When the alarm went off, the criminals fled quickly and *deserted* the scene of the crime. *Desert* means _____ .

18. Nancy bought a bag full of *lime* powder to sprinkle on the soil when her garden started to smell. *Lime* means _____ .

19. *Insanity* occurs when someone can no longer tell fact from fantasy. *Insanity* means _____ .

20. The children felt great *grief* and sadness when both of their parents died in a crash. *Grief* means _____ .

21. Gary had to drive all over town to get to the recycle station
    so he could *dispose* of his empty paint cans. *Dispose* means

    _____.

22. When Susan decided to go horseback riding, she chose to ride the *bay*-
    colored horse. *Bay* means _____.

23. Construction workers who are paid by the hour are considered to be
    day laborers. Day laborer means _____.

24. When a person becomes very rich, some believe he or she has a duty
    to do good things for the community; this duty is called *noblesse
    oblige. Noblesse oblige* means _____.

25. Since Deidre wanted to get rid of rats, she bought *arsenic* to put on
    food for them to kill them. *Arsenic* means _____.

26. Ed knew the cleaning fluid was poisonous because it had the sign of
    the *skull and bones* on it. *Skull and bones* means _____.

27. When Laura was getting married, her friends organized a *bridal* party
    for her. *Bridal* means _____.

28. When Judy and Mike had been separated for a month and were
    reunited, they hugged each other at the airport gate in a warm
    embrace. Embrace means _____.

29. When Joe's car was struck from behind, the other car left a large
    indentation in the trunk. *Indentation* means _____.

30. The rotting trees in the swamp gave off a sharp, *acrid* smell. *Acrid*
    means _____.

PRE-READING VOCABULARY
WORD ATTACK

Define these words by solving the parts. Use a dictionary as needed.

1. respectful
2. man-servant
3. gardener
4. squarish
5. scrolled
6. repaying
7. dissatisfaction
8. china-painting
9. disuse
10. leather-covered
11. plumpness
12. spokesman
13. invisible
14. graybeards
15. outbuildings
16. foreground
17. horsewhip
18. humanized
19. machinery
20. foreman
21. day laborer
22. kinfolk
23. earthiness
24. druggist
25. eyesockets
26. marrying
27. disgrace
28. blood-kin
29. iron-gray
30. regularity
31. backbone
32. inescapable
33. bottle-neck
34. fleshless

PRE-READING QUESTIONS

Try answering these as you read.

Who is Miss Emily?

What do the townspeople see?

What do the townspeople think?

Who is Homer Barron?

What happens to Homer Barron?

A Rose for Emily

WILLIAM FAULKNER

William Faulkner, the great grandson of a Confederate colonel, was born in New Albany, Mississippi, in 1897. In 1902 Faulkner's family moved to Oxford, Mississippi, in Lafayette County. In addition to being the home of the University of Mississippi and a place Faulkner would continually return to, Oxford and Lafayette County would inspire the fictional Jefferson and Yoknapatawpha County in Faulkner's writing. Faulkner left school after tenth grade, volunteered for the United States Army, and eventually entered the Canadian Royal Air Force during World War I. He then returned home to attend the University of Mississippi, but he did not finish his first year. He became interested in writing, moved to New York City and then to New Orleans, and then toured Europe. He returned to Oxford in 1929 and married Estelle Oldham. Shortly thereafter, he began a writing career marked by spurts and lapses. From 1929 to 1936 he wrote his major works—works that include *The Sound and the Fury* and *Light in August.* From 1936 to 1948 he produced little writing, and then in 1949 his writing increased again. Faulkner died in Oxford in 1962.

His complex writing reflects his interests in family relationships, in history, and in the South itself. Often portraying the decay of the old South, Faulkner's writing is as rich as it is shocking. He is credited with developing the narrative technique called flashback, wherein a character's present story "flashes back" to a story or stories from his or her past.

When Miss Emily Grierson died, our whole town went to her funeral: the men through a sort of respectful affection for a fallen monument, the women mostly out of curiosity to see the inside of her house, which no one save an old man-servant—a combined gardener and cook—had seen in at least ten years.

2   It was a big, squarish frame house that had once been white, decorated with cupolas and spires and scrolled balconies in the heavily lightsome style of the seventies, set on what had once been our most select street. But garages and cotton gins had encroached and obliterated even the august names of that neighborhood; only Miss Emily's house was left, lifting its stubborn and coquettish decay above the cotton wagons and the gasoline pumps—an eyesore among eyesores. And now Miss Emily had gone to join the representatives of those august names where they lay in the cedar-bemused cemetery among the ranked and anonymous graves of Union and Confederate soldiers who fell at the battle of Jefferson.

3   Alive, Miss Emily had been a tradition, a duty, and a care; a sort of hereditary obligation upon the town, dating from that day in 1894 when Colonel Sartoris, the mayor—he who fathered the edict that no Negro woman should appear on the streets without an apron—remitted her taxes, the dispensation dating from the death of her father on into perpetuity. Not that Miss Emily would have accepted charity. Colonel Sartoris invented an involved tale to the effect that Miss Emily's father had loaned money to the town, which the town, as a matter of business, preferred this way of repaying. Only a man of Colonel Sartoris' generation and thought could have invented it, and only a woman could have believed it.

4   When the next generation, with its more modem ideas, became mayors and aldermen, this arrangement created some little dissatisfaction. On the first of the year they mailed her a tax notice. February came, and there was no reply. They wrote her a formal letter, asking her to call at the sheriff's office at her convenience. A week later the mayor wrote her himself, offering to call or to send his car for her, and received in reply a note on paper of an archaic shape, in a thin, flowing calligraphy in faded ink, to the effect that she no longer went out at all. The tax notice was also enclosed, without comment.

5   They called a special meeting of the Board of Aldermen. A deputation waited upon her, knocked at the door through which no visitor had passed since she ceased giving china-painting lessons eight or ten years earlier. They were admitted by the old Negro into a dim hall from which a stairway mounted into still more shadow. It smelled of dust and disuse—a close, dank smell. The Negro led them into the parlor. It was furnished in heavy, leather-covered furniture. When the Negro opened the blinds of one window, they could see that the leather was cracked; and when they sat down, a faint dust rose sluggishly about their thighs, spinning with slow motes in the single sun-ray. On a tarnished gilt easel before the fireplace stood a crayon portrait of Miss Emily's father.

6   They rose when she entered—a small, fat woman in black, with a thin gold chain descending to her waist and vanishing into her belt, leaning on an ebony cane with a tarnished gold head. Her skeleton was small and spare; perhaps that was why what would have been merely plumpness in another was obesity in her. She looked bloated, like a body long submerged in motionless water, and of that pallid hue. Her eyes, lost in the fatty ridges of her face, looked like two small pieces of coal pressed into a lump of dough as they moved from one face to another while the visitors stated their errand.

7   She did not ask them to sit. She just stood in the door and listened quietly until the spokesman came to a stumbling halt. Then they could hear the invisible watch ticking at the end of the gold chain.

8   Her voice was dry and cold. "I have no taxes in Jefferson. Colonel Sartoris explained it to me. Perhaps one of you can gain access to the city records and satisfy yourselves."

9   "But we have. We are the city authorities, Miss Emily. Didn't you get a notice from the sheriff, signed by him?"

10   "I received a paper, yes," Miss Emily said. "Perhaps he considers himself the sheriff . . . I have no taxes in Jefferson."

11   "But there is nothing on the books to show that, you see. We must go by the—"

12   "See Colonel Sartoris. I have no taxes in Jefferson."

13   "But, Miss Emily—"

14   "See Colonel Sartoris." (Colonel Sartoris had been dead almost ten years.) "I have no taxes in Jeff Jefferson. Tobe!" The Negro appeared. "Show these gentlemen out."

II

15   So she vanquished them, horse and foot, just as she had vanquished their fathers thirty years before about the smell. That was two years after her father's death and a short time after her sweetheart—the one we believed would marry her—had deserted her. After her father's death she went out very little; after her sweetheart went away, people hardly saw her at all. A few of the ladies had the temerity to call, but were not received, and the only sign of life about the place was the Negro man—a young man then—going in and out with a market basket.

16   "Just as if a man—any man—could keep a kitchen properly," the ladies said; so they were not surprised when the smell developed. It was another link between the gross, teeming world and the high and mighty Griersons.

17   A neighbor, a woman, complained to the mayor, Judge Stevens, eighty years old.

18   "But what will you have me do about it, madam?" he said.

19   "Why, send her word to stop it," the woman said. "Isn't there a law?"

20   "I'm sure that won't be necessary," Judge Stevens said. "It's probably just a snake or a rat that n—— of hers killed in the yard. I'll speak to him about it."

21   The next day he received two more complaints, one from a man who came in diffident deprecation. "We really must do something

about it, Judge. I'd be the last one in the world to bother Miss Emily, but we've got to do something." That night the Board of Aldermen met—three graybeards and one younger man, a member of the rising generation.

22   "It's simple enough," he said. "Send her word to have her place cleaned up. Give her a certain time to do it in, and if she don't . . ."

23   "Dammit, sir," Judge Stevens said, "will you accuse a lady to her face of smelling bad?"

24   So the next night, after midnight, four men crossed Miss Emily's lawn and slunk about the house like burglars, sniffing along the base of the brickwork and at the cellar openings while one of them performed a regular sowing motion with his hand out of a sack slung from his shoulder. They broke open the cellar door and sprinkled lime there, and in all the outbuildings. As they recrossed the lawn, a window that had been dark was lighted and Miss Emily sat in it, the light behind her, and her upright torso motionless as that of an idol. They crept quietly across the lawn and into the shadow of the locusts that lined the street. After a week or two the smell went away.

25   That was when people had begun to feel really sorry for her. People in our town, remembering how old lady Wyatt, her great-aunt, had gone completely crazy at last, believed that the Griersons held themselves a little too high for what they really were. None of the young men were quite good enough for Miss Emily and such. We had long thought of them as a tableau, Miss Emily a slender figure in white in the background, her father a spraddled silhouette in the foreground, his back to her and clutching a horsewhip, the two of them framed by the back-flung front door. So when she got to be thirty and was still single, we were not pleased exactly, but vindicated; even with insanity in the family she wouldn't have turned down all of her chances if they had really materialized.

26   When her father died, it got about that the house was all that was left to her; and in a way, people were glad. At last they could pity Miss Emily. Being left alone, and a pauper, she had become humanized. Now she too would know the old thrill and the old despair of a penny more or less.

27   The day after his death all the ladies prepared to call at the house and offer condolence and aid, as is our custom. Miss Emily met them at the door, dressed as usual and with no trace of grief on her face. She told them that her father was not dead. She did that for three days, with the ministers calling on her, and the doctors, trying to persuade her to let them dispose of the body. Just as they were about to resort to law and force, she broke down, and they buried her father quickly.

28   We did not say she was crazy then. We believed she had to do that. We remembered all the young men her father had driven away, and we knew that with nothing left, she would have to cling to that which had robbed her, as people will.

III

29   She was sick for a long time. When we saw her again her hair was cut short, making her look like a girl, with a vague resemblance to those angels in colored church windows—sort of tragic and serene.

30   The town had just let the contracts for paving the sidewalks, and in the summer after her father's death they began the work. The construction company came with n——s and mules and machinery, and a foreman named Homer Barron, a Yankee—a big, dark, ready man, with a big voice and eyes lighter than his face. The little boys would follow in groups to hear him cuss the n——s, and the n——s singing in time to the rise and fall of picks. Pretty soon he knew everybody in town. Whenever you heard a lot of laughing anywhere about the square, Homer Barron would be in the center of the group. Presently we began to see him and Miss Emily on Sunday afternoons driving in the yellow-wheeled buggy and the matched team of bays from the livery stable.

31   At first we were glad that Miss Emily would have an interest, because the ladies all said, "Of course a Grierson would not think seriously of a Northerner, a day laborer." But there were still others, older people, who said that even grief could not cause a real lady to forget *noblesse oblige*—without calling it *noblesse oblige*. They just said, "Poor Emily. Her kinsfolk should come to her." She had some kin in Alabama; but years ago her father had fallen out with them over the estate of old lady Wyatt, the crazy woman, and there was no communication between the two families. They had not even been represented at the funeral.

32   And as soon as the old people said, "Poor Emily," the whispering began. "Do you suppose it's really so?" they said to one another. "Of course it is. What else could . . ." This behind their hands; rustling of craned silk and satin behind jalousies closed upon the sun of Sunday afternoon as the thin, swift clop-clop-clop of the matched team passed: "Poor Emily."

33   She carried her head high enough—even when we believed that she was fallen. It was as if she demanded more than ever the recognition of her dignity as the last Grierson; as if it had wanted that touch of earthiness to reaffirm her imperviousness. Like when she bought the rat poi-

son, the arsenic. That was over a year after they had begun to say "Poor Emily," and while the two female cousins were visiting her.

34   "I want some poison," she said to the druggist. She was over thirty then, still a slight woman, though thinner than usual, with cold, haughty black eyes in a face the flesh of which was strained across the temples and about the eyesockets as you imagine a lighthousekeeper's face ought to look. "I want some poison," she said.

35   "Yes, Miss Emily. What kind? For rats and such? I'd recom—"

36   "I want the best you have. I don't care what kind."

37   The druggist named several. "They'll kill anything up to an elephant. But what you want is—"

38   "Arsenic," Miss Emily said. "Is that a good one?"

39   "Is . . . arsenic? Yes, ma'am. But what you want—"

40   "I want arsenic."

41   The druggist looked down at her. She looked back at him, erect, her face like a strained flag. "Why, of course," the druggist said. "If that's what you want. But the law requires you to tell what you are going to use it for."

42   Miss Emily just stared at him, her head tilted back in order to look him eye for eye, until he looked away and went and got the arsenic and wrapped it up. The Negro delivery boy brought her the package; the druggist didn't come back. When she opened the package at home there was written on the box, under the skull and bones: "For rats."

IV

43 So the next day we all said, "She will kill herself"; and we said it would be the best thing. When she had first begun to be seen with Homer Barron, we had said, "She will marry him." Then we said, "She will persuade him yet," because Homer himself had remarked—he liked men, and it was known that he drank with the younger men in the Elks' Club—that he was not a marrying man. Later we said, "Poor Emily" behind the jalousies as they passed on Sunday afternoon in the glittering buggy, Miss Emily with her head high and Homer Barron with his hat cocked and a cigar in his teeth, reins and whip in a yellow glove.

44   Then some of the ladies began to say that it was a disgrace to the town and a bad example to the young people. The men did not want to interfere, but at last the ladies forced the Baptist minister—Miss Emily's people were Episcopal—to call upon her. He would never divulge what happened during that interview, but he refused to go back again. The next Sunday they again drove about the streets, and the

following day the minister's wife wrote to Miss Emily's relations in Alabama.

45   So she had blood-kin under her roof again and we sat back to watch developments. At first nothing happened. Then we were sure that they were to be married. We learned that Miss Emily had been to the jeweler's and ordered a man's toilet set in silver, with the letters H. B. on each piece. Two days later we learned that she had bought a complete outfit of men's clothing, including a nightshirt, and we said, "They are married." We were really glad. We were glad because the two female cousins were even more Grierson than Miss Emily had ever been.

46   So we were not surprised when Homer Barron—the streets had been finished some time since—was gone. We were a little disappointed that there was not a public blowing-off, but we believed that he had gone on to prepare for Miss Emily's coming, or to give her a chance to get rid of the cousins. (By that time it was a cabal, and we were all Miss Emily's allies to help circumvent the cousins.) Sure enough, after another week they departed. And, as we had expected all along, within three days Homer Barron was back in town. A neighbor saw the Negro man admit him at the kitchen door at dusk one evening.

47   And that was the last we saw of Homer Barron. And of Miss Emily for some time. The Negro man went in and out with the market basket, but the front door remained closed. Now and then we would see her at a window for a moment, as the men did that night when they sprinkled the lime, but for almost six months she did not appear on the streets. Then we knew that this was to be expected too; as if that quality of her father which had thwarted her woman's life so many times had been too virulent and too furious to die.

48   When we next saw Miss Emily, she had grown fat and her hair was turning gray. During the next few years it grew grayer and grayer until it attained an even pepper-and-salt iron-gray, when it ceased turning. Up to the day of her death at seventy-four it was still that vigorous iron-gray, like the hair of an active man.

49   From that time on her front door remained closed, save for a period of six or seven years, when she was about forty, during which she gave lessons in chinapainting. She fitted up a studio in one of the downstairs rooms, where the daughters and granddaughters of Colonel Sartoris' contemporaries were sent to her with the same regularity and in the same spirit that they were sent to church on Sundays with a twenty-five-cent piece for the collection plate. Meanwhile her taxes had been remitted.

50   Then the newer generation became the backbone and the spirit of the town, and the painting pupils grew up and fell away and did not send

their children to her with boxes of color and tedious brushes and pictures cut from the ladies' magazines. The front door closed upon the last one and remained closed for good. When the town got free postal delivery, Miss Emily alone refused to let them fasten the metal numbers above her door and attach a mailbox to it. She would not listen to them.

51   Daily, monthly, yearly we watched the Negro grow grayer and more stooped, going in and out with the market basket. Each December we sent her a tax notice, which would be returned by the post office a week later, unclaimed. Now and then we would see her in one of the downstairs windows—she had evidently shut up the top floor of the house—like the carven torso of an idol in a niche, looking or not looking at us, we could never tell which. Thus she passed from generation to generation—dear, inescapable, impervious, tranquil, and perverse.

52   And so she died. Fell ill in the house filled with dust and shadows, with only a doddering Negro man to wait on her. We did not even know she was sick; we had long since given up trying to get any information from the Negro. He talked to no one, probably not even to her, for his voice had grown harsh and rusty, as if from disuse.

53   She died in one of the downstairs rooms, in a heavy walnut bed with a curtain, her gray head propped on a pillow yellow and moldy with age and lack of sunlight.

V

54 The Negro met the first of the ladies at the front door and let them in, with their hushed, sibilant voices and their quick, curious glances, and then he disappeared. He walked right through the house and out the back and was not seen again.

55   The two female cousins came at once. They held the funeral on the second day, with the town coming to look at Miss Emily beneath a mass of bought flowers, with the crayon face of her father musing profoundly above the bier and the ladies sibilant and macabre; and the very old men—some in their brushed Confederate uniforms—on the porch and the lawn, talking of Miss Emily as if she had been a contemporary of theirs, believing that they had danced with her and courted her perhaps, confusing time with its mathematical progression, as the old do, to whom all the past is not a diminishing road but, instead, a huge meadow which no winter ever quite touches, divided from them now by the narrow bottle-neck of the most recent decade of years.

56   Already we knew that there was one room in that region above stairs which no one had seen in forty years, and which would have to

be forced. They waited until Miss Emily was decently in the ground before they opened it.

57   The violence of breaking down the door seemed to fill this room with pervading dust. A thin, acrid pall as of the tomb seemed to lie everywhere upon this room decked and furnished as for a bridal: upon the valance curtains of faded rose color, upon the rose-shaded lights, upon the dressing table, upon the delicate array of crystal and the man's toilet things backed with tarnished silver, silver so tarnished that the monogram was obscured. Among them lay a collar and tie, as if they had just been removed, which, lifted, left upon the surface a pale crescent in the dust. Upon a chair hung the suit, carefully folded; beneath it the two mute shoes and the discarded socks.

58   The man himself lay in the bed.

59   For a long while we just stood there, looking down at the profound and fleshless grin. The body had apparently once lain in the attitude of an embrace, but now the long sleep that outlasts love, that conquers even the grimace of love, had cuckolded him. What was left of him, rotted beneath what was left of the night-shirt, had become inextricable from the bed in which he lay; and upon him and upon the pillow beside him lay that even coating of the patient and biding dust.

60   Then we noticed that in the second pillow was the indentation of a head. One of us lifted something from it, and leaning forward, that faint and invisible dust dry and acrid in the nostrils, we saw a long strand of iron-gray hair.

A Rose for Emily

Journal

1. MLA Works Cited

Using this model, record this story here.

Author's Last Name, First Name. "Title of the Story." <u>Title of the Book</u>. Ed. First Last Name. City: Publisher, year. Pages of the story.

2. Main Character(s)

Describe each main character, and explain why you think each is a main character.

3. Supporting Characters

Describe each supporting character, and explain why you think each is a supporting character.

4. Setting

Describe the setting. Decide if this story can be changed and, if so, to where and when.

5. Sequence

Relate the events of the story in order.

6. Plot

Tell the story in no more than three sentences.

7. Conflicts

Identify and explain the conflicts involved here.

8. Significant Quotations

Explain the importance of each of these quotations. Record the page numbers in the parentheses.

a. "Only a man of Colonel Sartoris' generation and thought could have invented it, and only a woman could have believed it" (   ).

b. "The tax notice was also enclosed, without comment" (   ).

c. " 'Dammit, sir,' Judge Stevens said, 'will you accuse a lady to her face of smelling bad?' " (   ).

d. " 'I want arsenic' " (   ).

e. "The man himself lay in the bed" (   ).

9. Symbolism

Identify and explain the symbols in the story.

Follow-up Questions

10 Short Questions

*Select the **best** answer for each.*

1. Miss Emily is
    a. very friendly.
    b. very lively.
    c. very reserved.

2. Miss Emily is
    a. a modern woman.
    b. a young woman.
    c. of a past generation.

3. Miss Emily thinks
    a. that she is poor.
    b. that she is rich.
    c. that she is in between.

4. Miss Emily thinks she is
    a. beneath the towns-people.
    b. better than the towns-people.
    c. the same as the towns-people.

5. The servant is
    a. dishonest.
    b. disloyal.
    c. loyal.

6. The servant is
    a. silent.
    b. noisy.
    c. nosy.

7. After her father dies, Miss Emily
    a. easily accepts her father's death.
    b. denies his death.
    c. does not know where her father is.

8. Miss Emily's family
    a. has a history of insanity.
    b. is sane and solid.
    c. is very normal.

9. Miss Emily probably
    a. married Homer.
    b. scared Homer away.
    c. poisoned Homer.

10. Miss Emily's actions seem
    a. normal.
    b. grotesque.
    c. humorous.

5 Significant Quotations

Explain the importance of each of these quotations.

1. "But garages and cotton gins had encroached and obliterated even the august names of that neighborhood; only Miss Emily's house was left [. . .] —an eyesore among eyesores."

2. "On the first of the year they mailed her a tax notice. February came, and there was no reply."

3. "[. . .] so they were not surprised when the smell developed."

4. " 'Arsenic,' Miss Emily said. 'Is that a good one?' "

5. "Then we noticed that in the second pillow was the indentation of a head."

2 COMPREHENSION ESSAY QUESTIONS

Use specific details and information from the story to answer these as completely as possible.

1. Describe Miss Emily's relationships with the men in her life. Use specific details and information from the story to support your descriptions.

2. Explain the townspeople's perceptions of Miss Emily. Use specific details and information from the story to support your explanation.

WRITING

Use each of these ideas for writing an essay.

1. Miss Emily's neighbors keep a close watch on Miss Emily. All of us have had interesting neighbors—noisy, nosy, lively, strange, and so forth. Describe an interesting incident that you or someone you know has had with a neighbor.

2. Miss Emily does not handle death well. Think of a loss—the loss of a home when moving, the loss of a favorite thing, the loss of a pet or a loved one—that you or someone you know has experienced. Tell the story of this loss and of how you or someone you know handled the loss.

Further Writing

1. Although Faulkner said he did not use symbols in "A Rose for Emily," many would disagree. Read analyses of this story (which can be found in a library), and relate what you find about symbolism in this story.

2. Read a biography of Lizzie Borden (which can be found in a library), and consider aristocratic assumptions made by the aristocracy in her case. Compare the defense in the Borden trial with the protection Miss Emily enjoys.

3. Compare and contrast Miss Emily with the narrator in Edgar Allan Poe's "The Tell-Tale Heart" (page 77).

The Masque of the Red Death

 EDGAR ALLAN POE

PRE-READING VOCABULARY
CONTEXT

Use context clues to define these words before reading. Use a dictionary as needed.

1. The flu with aches and fever and dizziness can be a terrible *pestilence*.
   Pestilence means _____.

2. When the man rubbed against poison ivy, he got a *hideous* rash of
   white and red sores over his arms. *Hideous* means _____.

3. When the dam broke, the released water was so *profuse* that it flooded
   the valley below. *Profuse* means _____.

4. When the child dropped the candy in a glass of water, it turned into a
   dissolution of water and sugar. *Dissolution* means _____.

5. The store manager put a *ban* on large shopping bags when he thought
   shoppers were hiding stolen goods. *Ban* means _____.

6. When the moth flew into the spider's web, it reached its *termination*.
   Termination means _____.

7. The king ruled over all his lands and *dominions* with kindness and
   patience. *Dominion* means _____.

8. If you take your vitamins and eat healthy foods, you will probably be
   quite *hale* and have few illnesses. *Hale* means _____.

9. The king gave the brave *knight* a large piece of land because he had
   protected the people in the village. *Knight* means _____.

10. Restaurants usually have an *ingress* door to go into the kitchen and an *egress* door to get out of the kitchen. *Ingress* means _____ and *egress* means _____.

11. The fans were in a *frenzy* when their favorite group sang their favorite song. *Frenzy* means _____.

12. Flora thought it was sheer *folly* to try to get money from the selfish landlord. *Folly* means _____.

13. Children dress up in different costumes to *masquerade* for Halloween. *Masquerade* means _____.

14. Isabel is usually calm and logical, but when she had a fever with the flu, she talked and acted in a *bizarre* way. *Bizarre* means

_____.

15. The presidential *chambers* are the rooms where the President and his family live in the White House. *Chamber* means _____.

16. *Ebony* is a fine black wood that grows in Africa. *Ebony* means

_____.

17. The slow drip of the leaking faucet went on and on and on and became *monotonous*. *Monotonous* means _____.

18. The teacher expected the students to use their ears and to *hearken* to her directions. *Hearken* means _____.

19. Dressed in beautiful gowns and formal evening suits, the *waltzers* glided with the music around the ballroom floor. *Waltzer* means

_____.

20. Not knowing the day or where he was, Jan felt very confused and *disconcerted* with his surroundings. *Disconcerted* means

_____.

21. Since all the little girls were giggling and having so much fun at the birthday party, it was hard to tell who was *giddiest. Giddiest* means

_____.

22. When the team made the winning touchdown, the crowd went wild, and the noise was *tumultuous. Tumultuous* means _____.

23. When Gabriella does her yoga exercises, she concentrates deeply in quiet *meditation. Meditation* means _____.

24. All the guests had a wonderful time joining in the party's *revelry. Revelry* means _____.

25. Acting like a savage beast is considered *barbaric* behavior. *Barbaric* means _____.

26. The murderer ranted and raved, and his craziness made him seem quite *mad. Mad* means _____.

27. For her parents' fiftieth anniversary, Robin ordered a caterer, invited many guests, and planned a grand *fête. Fête* means _____.

28. The gigantic spider costume with its hairy arms and horrible jaws was *grotesque. Grotesque* means _____.

29. When Lusumba could not sleep, he tossed and turned and *writhed* in sleeplessness. *Writhe* means _____.

30. The teacher ordered a *cessation* of all talking, and the room became silent. *Cessation* means _____.

31. Matt dressed as a terrible devil for Halloween, and his *phantasm* scared everyone at the party. *Phantasm* means _____.

32. When Delia went on a diet, she became too thin, and her *gaunt* face looked like a skeleton. *Gaunt* means _____.

33. Dodee went to her closet and carefully chose her *habiliments* for her job interview. *Habiliment* means _____.

34. After their grandfather died, the grandchildren visited his *grave* and planted flowers by the headstone. *Grave* means _____.

35. You could tell by Sarah's happy *visage* that she was delighted to win the award. *Visage* means _____.

36. After his heart stopped beating, his *corpse* was sent to the funeral home. *Corpse* means _____.

37. During a seizure, one may *convulse* with uncontrolled actions. *Convulse* means _____.

38. The dog went crazy when the *intruder* tried to break into our house. *Intruder* means _____.

39. The fans stood in *awe* of the rock star who was standing in their presence. *Awe* means _____.

40. The man, intending to stab someone, drew a small *dagger* out of his pocket and was arrested. *Dagger* means _____.

PRE-READING VOCABULARY
WORD ATTACK

Define these words by solving the parts. Use a dictionary as needed.

1. depopulated
2. castellated
3. precaution
4. irregularly
5. disregarded
6. *decora*
7. feverishly
8. whirlingly
9. stiffened
10. thoughtful
11. whisperingly
12. besprinkled
13. reddened
14. nameless
15. maddening
16. hurriedly
17. uninterruptedly
18. unutterable
19. untenanted
20. bedewed
21. illimitable

PRE-READING QUESTIONS

Try answering these questions as you read.

What is happening in the story?

Who is Prince Prospero?

What does Prince Prospero try to do?

Who is the figure?

The Masque of the Red Death

EDGAR ALLAN POE

Edgar Allan Poe was born in 1809 and orphaned at a young age. He was adopted by John Allan, a rather militaristic businessman from Richmond, Virginia. Adoption by a person of means was not uncommon and would have been fortunate for the young Poe, except that his free spirit and his father's precision clashed. John Allan provided Poe with study at the University of Virginia—but Poe withdrew, due to drinking problems—and then at West Point—but Poe was dismissed, due to a disciplinary problem. Poe later married his very young cousin, Virginia Clemm, but the probable nonconsummation of this marriage and the early death of young Virginia contributed to Poe's idealization of both real and imagined women. His life, in fact, was one of continual disappointments. After Virginia's death, Poe sank into intermittent depressions, suffered bouts of insanity, and experienced hallucinations. Writing for many others, he wanted to publish his own magazine, but this dissolved in financial failure. He eventually died in Baltimore in 1849.

However, it is from these very problems that Poe's genius soars. He envelops the reader with his perceived worlds of the sane and insane, the rational and macabre, with equal ease. Credited with developing the modern mystery form, Poe's every word and every action draw the reader in, mixing reality with irreality, sane with insane. His other works include "The Pit and the Pendulum" and "The Fall of the House of Usher."

The "Red Death" had long devastated the country. No pestilence had ever been so fatal, or so hideous. Blood was its Avatar and its seal—the redness and the horror of blood. There were sharp pains, and sudden dizziness, and then profuse bleeding at the pores, with dissolution. The scarlet stains upon the body and especially upon the face of the victim, were the pest ban which shut him out from the aid and from the sympathy of his fellow-men. And the whole seizure, progress, and termination of the disease, were the incidents of half an hour.

2   But the Prince Prospero was happy and dauntless and sagacious. When his dominions were half depopulated, he summoned to his presence a thousand hale and light-hearted friends from among the knights and dames of his court, and with these retired to the deep seclusion of one of his castellated abbeys. This was an extensive and magnificent structure, the creation of the prince's own eccentric yet august taste. A strong and lofty wall girdled it in. This wall had gates of iron. The courtiers, having entered, brought furnaces and massy hammers and welded the bolts. They resolved to leave means neither of ingress nor egress to the sudden impulses of despair or of frenzy from within. The abbey was amply provisioned. With such precautions the courtiers might bid defiance to contagion. The external world could take care of itself. In the meantime it was folly to grieve, or to think. The prince had provided all the appliances of pleasure. There were buffoons, there were improvisatori, there were ballet-dancers, there were musicians, there was Beauty, there was wine. All these and security were within. Without was the "Red Death."

3   It was toward the close of the fifth or sixth month of his seclusion, and while the pestilence raged most furiously abroad, that the Prince Prospero entertained his thousand friends at a masked ball of the most unusual magnificence.

4   It was a voluptuous scene, that masquerade. But first let me tell of the rooms in which it was held. There were seven—an imperial suite. In many palaces, however, such suites form a long and straight vista, while the folding doors slide back nearly to the walls on either hand, so that the view of the whole extent is scarcely impeded. Here the case was very different; as might have been expected from the duke's love of the *bizarre.* The apartments were so irregularly disposed that the vision embraced but little more than one at a time. There was a sharp turn at every twenty or thirty yards, and at each turn a novel effect. To the right and left, in the middle of each wall, a tall and narrow Gothic window looked out upon a closed corridor which pursued the windings of the suite. These windows were of stained glass whose color varied in accordance with the prevailing hue of the decorations of the chamber

into which it opened. That at the eastern extremity was hung, for example, in blue—and vividly blue were its windows. The second chamber was purple in its ornaments and tapestries, and here the panes were purple. The third was green throughout, and so were the casements. The fourth was furnished and lighted with orange—the fifth with white—the sixth with violet. The seventh apartment was closely shrouded in black velvet tapestries that hung all over the ceiling and down the walls, falling in heavy folds upon a carpet of the same material and hue. But in this chamber only, the color of the windows failed to correspond with the decorations. The panes here were scarlet—a deep blood color. Now in no one of the seven apartments was there any lamp or candelabrum, amid the profusion of golden ornaments that lay scattered to and fro or depended from the roof. There was no light of any kind emanating from lamp or candle within the suite of chambers. But in the corridors that followed the suite, there stood, opposite to each window, a heavy tripod, bearing a brazier of fire, that projected its rays through the tinted glass and so glaringly illumined the room. And thus were produced a multitude of gaudy and fantastic appearances. But in the western or black chamber the effect of the fire-light that streamed upon the dark hangings through the blood-tinted panes was ghastly in the extreme, and produced so wild a look upon the countenances of those who entered, that there were few of the company bold enough to set foot within its precincts at all.

5 It was in this apartment, also, that there stood against the western wall, a gigantic clock of ebony. Its pendulum swung to and fro with a dull, heavy, monotonous clang; and when the minute-hand made the circuit of the face, and the hour was to be stricken, there came from the brazen lungs of the clock a sound which was clear and loud and deep and exceedingly musical, but of so peculiar a note and emphasis that, at each lapse of an hour, the musicians of the orchestra were constrained to pause, momentarily, in their performance, to hearken to the sound; and thus the waltzers perforce ceased their evolutions; and there was a brief disconcert of the whole gay company; and, while the chimes of the clock yet rang, it was observed that the giddiest grew pale, and the more aged and sedate passed their hands over their brows as if in confused revery or meditation. But when the echoes had fully ceased, a light laughter at once pervaded the assembly; the musicians looked at each other and smiled as if at their own nervousness and folly, and made whispering vows, each to the other, that the next chiming of the clock should produce in them no similar emotion; and then, after the lapse of sixty minutes (which embrace three thousand and six hundred seconds of the Time that flies), there came yet another

chiming of the clock, and then were the same disconcert and tremulousness and meditation as before.

6   But, in spite of these things, it was a gay and magnificent revel. The tastes of the duke were peculiar. He had a fine eye for colors and effects. He disregarded the *decora* of mere fashion. His plans were bold and fiery, and his conceptions glowed with barbaric lustre. There are some who would have thought him mad. His followers felt that he was not. It was necessary to hear and see and touch him to be *sure* that he was not.

7   He had directed, in great part, the movable embellishments of the seven chambers, upon occasion of this great *fête;* and it was his own guiding taste which had given character to the masqueraders. Be sure they were grotesque. There were much glare and glitter and piquancy and phantasm—much of what has been since seen in "Hernani." There were arabesque figures with unsuited limbs and appointments. There were delirious fancies such as the madman fashions. There were much of the beautiful, much of the wanton, much of the *bizarre,* something of the terrible, and not a little of that which might have excited disgust. To and fro in the seven chambers there stalked, in fact, a multitude of dreams. And these—the dreams—writhed in and about, taking hue from the rooms, and causing the wild music of the orchestra to seem as the echo of their steps. And, anon, there strikes the ebony clock which stands in the hall of the velvet. And then, for a moment, all is still, and all is silent save the voice of the clock. The dreams are stiff-frozen as they stand. But the echoes of the chime die away—they have endured but an instant—and a light, half-subdued laughter floats after them as they depart. And now again the music swells, and the dreams live, and writhe to and fro more merrily than ever, taking hue from the many-tinted windows through which stream the rays from the tripods. But to the chamber which lies most westwardly of the seven there are now none of the maskers who venture; for the night is waning away; and there flows a ruddier light through the blood-colored panes; and the blackness of the sable drapery appals; and to him whose foot falls upon the sable carpet, there comes from the near clock of ebony a muffled peal more solemnly emphatic than any which reaches *their* ears who indulge in the more remote gaieties of the other apartments.

8   But these other apartments were densely crowded, and in them beat feverishly the heart of life. And the revel went whirlingly on, until at length there commenced the sounding of midnight upon the clock. And then the music ceased, as I have told; and the evolutions of the waltzers were quieted, and there was an uneasy cessation of all things as before. But now there were twelve strokes to be sounded by the bell

of the clock; and thus it happened, perhaps, that more of thought crept, with more of time, into the meditations of the thoughtful among those who revelled. And thus too, it happened, perhaps, that before the last echoes of the last chime had utterly sunk into silence, there were many individuals in the crowd who had found leisure to become aware of the presence of a masked figure which had arrested the attention of no single individual before. And the rumor of this new presence having spread itself whisperingly around, there arose at length from the whole company a buzz, or murmur, expressive of disapprobation and surprise—then, finally, of terror, of horror, and of disgust.

9   In an assembly of phantasms such as I have painted, it may well be supposed that no ordinary appearance could have excited such sensation. In truth the masquerade license of the night was nearly unlimited; but the figure in question had out-Heroded Herod, and gone beyond the bounds of even the prince's indefinite decorum. There are chords in the hearts of the most reckless which cannot be touched without emotion. Even with the utterly lost, to whom life and death are equally jests, there are matters of which no jest can be made. The whole company, indeed, seemed now deeply to feel that in the costume and bearing of the stranger neither wit nor propriety existed. The figure was tall and gaunt, and shrouded from head to foot in the habiliments of the grave. The mask which concealed the visage was made so nearly to resemble the countenance of a stiffened corpse that the closest scrutiny must have had difficulty in detecting the cheat. And yet all this might have been endured, if not approved, by the mad revellers around. But the mummer had gone so far as to assume the type of the Red Death. His vesture was dabbled in *blood*—and his broad brow, with all the features of the face, was besprinkled with the scarlet horror.

10   When the eyes of Prince Prospero fell upon this spectral image (which, with a slow and solemn movement, as if more fully to sustain its *rôle*, stalked to and fro among the waltzers) he was seen to be convulsed, in the first moment with a strong shudder either of terror or distaste; but, in the next, his brow reddened with rage.

11   "Who dares"—he demanded hoarsely of the courtiers who stood near him—"who dares insult us with this blasphemous mockery? Seize him and unmask him—that we may know whom we have to hang, at sunrise, from the battlements!"

12   It was in the eastern or blue chamber in which stood the Prince Prospero as he uttered these words. They rang throughout the seven rooms loudly and clearly, for the prince was a bold and robust man, and the music had become hushed at the waving of his hand.

13   It was in the blue room where stood the prince, with a group of pale courtiers by his side. At first, as he spoke, there was a slight rushing movement of this group in the direction of the intruder, who, at the moment was also near at hand, and now, with deliberate and stately step, made closer approach to the speaker. But from a certain nameless awe with which the mad assumptions of the mummer had inspired the whole party, there were found none who put forth hand to seize him; so that, unimpeded, he passed within a yard of the prince's person; and, while the vast assembly, as if with one impulse, shrank from the centres of the rooms to the walls, he made his way uninterruptedly, but with the same solemn and measured step which had distinguished him from the first, through the blue chamber to the purple—through the purple to the green—through the green to the orange—through this again to the white—and even thence to the violet, ere a decided movement had been made to arrest him. It was then, however, that the Prince Prospero, maddening with rage and the shame of his own momentary cowardice, rushed hurriedly through the six chambers, while none followed him on account of a deadly terror that had seized upon all. He bore aloft a drawn dagger, and had approached, in rapid impetuosity, to within three or four feet of the retreating figure, when the latter, having attained the extremity of the velvet apartment, turned suddenly and confronted his pursuer. There was a sharp cry— and the dagger dropped gleaming upon the sable carpet, upon which, instantly afterward, fell prostrate in death the Prince Prospero. Then, summoning the wild courage of despair, a throng of the revellers at once threw themselves into the black apartment, and, seizing the mummer, whose tall figure stood erect and motionless within the shadow of the ebony clock, gasped in unutterable horror at finding the grave cerements and corpse-like mask, which they handled with so violent a rudeness, untenanted by any tangible form.

14   And now was acknowledged the presence of the Red Death. He had come like a thief in the night. And one by one dropped the revellers in the blood-bedewed halls of their revel, and died each in the despairing posture of his fall. And the life of the ebony clock went out with that of the last of the gay. And the flames of the tripods expired. And Darkness and Decay and the Red Death held illimitable dominion over all.

The Masque
of the Red Death

JOURNAL

1. MLA Works Cited

Using this model, record this reading here.

*Author's Last Name, First Name. "Title of the Story." <u>Title of the Book</u>. Ed.
First Name Last Name. City: Publisher, year. Pages of the story.*

2. Main Character(s)

*Describe each main character, and explain why you think each is a main
character.*

3. Supporting Characters

*Describe each supporting character, and explain why you think each is a
supporting character.*

4. Setting

*Describe the setting. Decide if this setting can be changed and, if so, to where
and when.*

5. Sequence

Relate the events of the story in order.

6. Plot

Tell the story in no more than three sentences.

7. Conflicts

Identify and explain the conflicts involved here.

8. Significant Quotations

Explain the importance of each of these quotations. Record the page number in the parentheses.

a. "The 'Red Death' had long devastated the country" (   ).

b. "The prince had provided all the appliances of pleasure" (   ).

c. "It was a voluptuous scene, that masquerade" (   ).

d. "And, anon, there strikes the ebony clock which stands in the hall of the velvet" (   ).

e. "And now was acknowledged the presence of the Red Death" (   ).

9. Symbolism

Identify and explain the symbols used in the story.

Follow-up Questions

10 Short Questions

Select the best answer for each.

____ 1. As a victim of the Red Death bleeds, one
   a. has the help and support of friends.
   b. does not have the help and support of friends.
   c. gets better rapidly.

____ 2. Prince Prospero
   a. cares about the general population.
   b. is kind to the general population.
   c. shows little concern for the general population.

____ 3. Prince Prospero
   a. thinks he can escape the Red Death.
   b. thinks he cannot escape the Red Death.
   c. does not know about the Red Death.

____ 4. He and his court
   a. think they will be infected with the disease.
   b. think they will not be infected with the disease.
   c. do not know about the disease.

____ 5. The castle rooms are
   a. all the same.
   b. one big room.
   c. separated and different.

____ 6. The black room's only other color is
   a. white.
   b. blue.
   c. blood red.

____ 7. The clock has
   a. an unsettling chime.
   b. a pleasant chime.
   c. a sweet, musical chime.

____ 8. The mummer enters
   a. an afternoon party.
   b. a formal ball.
   c. a masked ball.

____ 9. The mummer
   a. is wearing a mask.
   b. is not wearing a mask.
   c. is wearing heavy makeup.

____ 10. The prince and his guests
   a. escape the Red Death.
   b. never see the Red Death.
   c. die from the Red Death.

5 Significant Quotations

Explain the importance of each of these quotations.

1. "No pestilence had ever been so fatal, or so hideous."

2. "When his dominions were half depopulated, he summoned to his presence a thousand hale and light-hearted friends [. . .] and with these retired to the deep seclusion of one of his castellated abbeys."

3. "It was toward the close of [. . .] his seclusion, and while the pestilence raged most furiously abroad, that the Prince Prospero entertained his thousand friends at a masked ball of the most unusual magnificence."

4. "It was in this apartment, also, that there stood against the western wall, a gigantic clock of ebony."

5. "Then, summoning the wild courage of despair, a throng of revellers at once threw themselves into the black apartment, and, seizing the mummer [. . .] gasped in unutterable horror at finding the grave cerements and corpse-like mask [. . .] untenanted by any tangible form."

2 COMPREHENSION ESSAY QUESTIONS

Use specific details and information from the story to answer these as completely as possible.

1. Explain how the black chamber prepares you for the figure's appearance. Use specific details and information from the story to support your explanation.

2. Explain what happens to Prince Prospero. Use specific details and information from the story to support your explanation.

WRITING

Use each of these ideas for writing an essay.

1. We have all been to strange places. Describe a place you have been to that seemed to reek of disease or evil.

2. We have all met scary or gloomy people. Describe your encounter with a scary person and how you handled the situation.

Further Writing

1. Read literary analyses of "The Masque of the Red Death" (which can be found in a library). Then discuss whom or what beyond biological disease the figure of Red Death might represent in this story.

2. Research the AIDS/HIV virus, and use this story in your introduction to your research.

The Bell-Tower

HERMAN MELVILLE

PRE-READING VOCABULARY
CONTEXT

Use context clues to define these words before reading. Use a dictionary as needed.

1. When Raoul was in ancient Greece, he visited the leftover *ruins* of many ancient buildings. *Ruin* means _____.

2. When Lauren took the clapper out of the bell, the bell would no longer *chime*. *Chime* means _____.

3. Ironically, a *foundling* is a child without parents, and a *foundry* is a place where metals are produced. *Foundling* means _____, and *foundry* means _____.

4. In ancient times, the people of *Babel* tried to build a tower to reach heaven; but the tower was struck down, and the people then talked nonsense. *Babel* means _____.

5. Many campuses have a *bell-tower*, a tall building with a clock that rings out each hour. *Bell-tower* means _____.

6. The *architect* studied art, geology, and physics so that she could design large buildings. *Architect* means _____.

7. When Jorge wanted to build a brick wall, he called the *masons* to build it. *Mason* means _____.

8. The mountain climbers intended to reach the top and refused to stop until they reached the *summit*. *Summit* means _____.

9. The wrestler *smote* the other wrestler with a folding chair; then he turned to *smite* another one. *Smote* and *smite* mean

   _____ .

10. When Mom saw the ripped paper all over the floor, she knew the puppy was the guilty *culprit*. *Culprit* means _____ .

11. The metalworker formed a vase in a mold so that he could pour metal in the mold and *cast* many vases. *Cast* means _____ .

12. The cake that came out of the oven was perfect, except for a bubble *blemish* on the top. *Blemish* means _____ .

13. *Homo*– means "man" and –*cide* mans "to kill." *Homicide* means

    _____ .

14. Arson, armed robbery, and murder are all considered to be *felonies*. *Felony* means _____ .

15. Josette kept her valuable jewelry in *seclusion* in a safe hidden inside of a closet so that no one could find her jewelry. *Seclusion* means

    _____ .

16. The opening at the top of a steeple or tower where a bell hangs so that it can ring and be heard is called a *belfry*. *Belfry* means

    _____ .

17. The new gloves Amy bought were so soft and *pliant* that they felt like a second skin on her hands. *Pliant* means _____ .

18. The mayor and the town council members are usually considered to be the *magistrates* of the town. *Magistrate* means _____ .

19. Fatima decided to masquerade as a *domino,* wearing a mask and a long cloak; she scared one person after another in a *domino* effect. *Domino* means _____ .

20. Danielle was *apprehensive* about taking another algebra test because she had failed her first two tests. *Apprehensive* means _____.

21. The lords and ladies, who were born very rich and who live in large mansions, invited other *nobles* to their parties. *Noble* means

    _____.

22. *Vulcan*, the ugly Roman god of fire and metalworking, was married to the beautiful Venus. *Vulcan* means _____.

23. In the Bible, *Deborah* is able to see into the future and advises Barak to destroy the evil Sisera. *Deborah* means _____.

24. The man was buried in the churchyard after the *fatal* plane crash. *Fatal* means _____.

25. Although Sophia had been asleep, she awakened when her dog walked around upstairs, and she heard his every *footfall*. *Footfall* means

    _____.

26. Christians believe that after someone dies, his or her *soul* rises to heaven. *Soul* means _____.

27. In the biblical story of Deborah, *Jael* comes to the rescue and kills the evil Sisera. *Jael* means _____.

28. The criminals were *manacled* by tying their hands behind their backs when they were arrested. *Manacled* means _____.

29. Edmund kept the fifteenth-century *arquebuss* in his collection of rare guns. *Arquebuss* means _____.

30. The witnesses were sworn in to *aver* the facts of what they had seen. *Aver* means _____.

31. The drummers who play with the Beach Boys often create a very colorful *percussion* beat. *Percussion* means _____.

32. When Francis had a paper to write, he read several books and then took take time to *opine* in a list what he wanted to use. *Opine* means

_____.

33. The *agent* represented several other people and did their paperwork for them. *Agent* means _____.

34. The car without wheels stood still and had no *locomotion* until Dimitri added the wheels and moved it. *Locomotion* means

_____.

35. The giants among the ancient gods were called Titans, and their size was called *titanic. Titanic* means _____.

36. *Helots* and *serfs* served as slaves for wealthy nobles. *Helot* and *serf* mean _____.

37. The parents looked on their newborn baby as a gift from God and a *divine creation. Divine creation* means _____.

38. Henry Ford's *original* design, the Model A, was the first car built on an assembly line. *Original* means _____.

39. Although they felt they could not wait for the concert to begin, the fans *bided* their time by playing cards. *Bide* means _____.

40. While her roommates waited to shower for work, Sue was *oblivious* to their needs and spent an hour in the shower. *Oblivious* means

_____.

PRE-READING VOCABULARY
WORD ATTACK

Define these words by solving the parts. Use a dictionary as needed.

1. immeasurable
2. lengthening
3. lessening
4. falsity
5. metallic
6. mechanician
7. snail-like
8. overtopped
9. self-esteem
10. climax-stone
11. unrailed
12. prosperously
13. bell-tower
14. clock-tower
15. state-bell
16. undeterred
17. mythological
18. sickly
19. assistance
20. withdrew
21. spring-like
22. unease
23. earthen
24. artistic
25. unemployed
26. restlessness
27. milder
28. innumerable
29. footfall
30. fore-looking
31. unusual
32. encamp
33. blindwork
34. suspiciously
35. feverish
36. foretell
37. hair's breadth
38. scarcely
39. blankly
40. unforeseen
41. unbeknown
42. becloaked
43. uplifted
44. uncertainty
45. steely
46. sword-blade
47. upward
48. rehooded
49. unavoidably
50. unscientific
51. indirectly
52. comparatively
53. elephantine
54. erroneous
55. craziest
56. irrationality
57. vice-bench
58. railway
59. clangorous
60. superstructure

Try defining this word by using Melville's words around it.

"*Talus*, iron slave to Bannadonna, and through him, to man."

Talus means _____.

Read Chapters 4 and 5 of Judges in the Bible (which can be found in Appendix A, page 445) to help solve the biblical references in "The Bell-Tower."

Pre-reading Questions

Try answering these questions as you read.

Who is Bannadonna?

What does Bannadonna propose to do?

Who is Haman?

What happens to Bannadonna?

The Bell-Tower

HERMAN MELVILLE

Herman Melville was born in New York City in 1819 to a prosperous family with roots in the American Revolution and the Boston Tea Party. Melville enjoyed his early schooling. However, failing family finances, the family's move to Albany, and his father's mental instability and early death left Melville in personal and career confusion. After working briefly as an accountant and then as a teacher, Melville took to the sea, sailing around the Pacific from 1841 to 1846. During this period, he gained his richest material. In 1847 he married Elizabeth Knopp Shaw, the daughter of a close family friend, and left the sea for a more sedate life that enabled him to write. Between 1846 and 1851 he produced his major novels, including *Moby Dick*. From 1850 to 1851 he lived close to and visited with Nathaniel Hawthorne, whom he highly respected; in fact, he dedicated *Moby Dick* to Hawthorne. He returned to New York City, living out his life as a customs inspector. Preceded by two of his sons, Melville died in 1891.

His complex works can be read as narratives and as allegories , or symbolic tales, that concern good and evil and often center on relationships with God and the devil. "The Bell-Tower" takes on the very taboo of creation and is filled with rich biblical references (see Judges 4 and 5 in Appendix A, page 445) and references to the Renaissance and to ancient Greece.

In the south of Europe, nigh a once frescoed capital, now with dank mould cankering its bloom, central in a plain, stands what, at distance, seems the black mossed stump of some immeasurable pine, fallen, in forgotten days, with Anak and the Titan.

2   As all along where the pine tree falls, its dissolution leaves a mossy mound—last-flung shadow of the perished trunk; never lengthening, never lessening; unsubject to the fleet falsities of the sun; shade immutable, and true gauge which cometh by prostration—so westward from what seems the stump, one steadfast spear of lichened ruin veins the plain.

3   From that tree-top, what birded chimes of silver throats had rung. A stone pine; a metallic aviary in its crown: the Bell-Tower, built by the great mechanician, the unblest foundling, Bannadonna.

4   Like Babel's, its base was laid in a high hour of renovated earth, following the second deluge, when the waters of the Dark Ages had dried up, and once more the green appeared. No wonder that, after so long and deep submersion, the jubilant expectation of the race should, as with Noah's sons, soar into Shinar aspiration.

5   In firm resolve, no man in Europe at that period went beyond Bannadonna. Enriched through commerce with the Levant, the state in which he lived voted to have the noblest Bell-Tower in Italy. His repute assigned him to be architect.

6   Stone by stone, month by month, the tower rose. Higher, higher; snail-like in pace, but torch or rocket in its pride.

7   After the masons would depart, the builder, standing alone upon its ever-ascending summit, at close of every day, saw that he over-topped still higher walls and trees. He would tarry till a late hour there, wrapped in schemes of other and still loftier piles. Those who of saints' days thronged the spot—hanging to the rude poles of scaffolding, like sailors on yards, or bees on boughs, unmindful of lime and dust, and falling chips of stone—their homage not the less inspirited him to self-esteem.

8   At length the holiday of the Tower came. To the sound of viols, the climax-stone slowly rose in air, and, amid the firing of ordnance, was laid by Bannadonna's hands upon the final course. Then mounting it, he stood erect, alone, with folded arms, gazing upon the white summits of blue inland Alps, and whiter crests of bluer Alps off-shore—sights invisible from the plain. Invisible, too, from thence was that eye he turned below, when, like the cannon booms, came up to him the people's combustions of applause.

9   That which stirred them so was, seeing with what serenity the builder stood three hundred feet in air, upon an unrailed perch. This none but he durst do. But his periodic standing upon the pile, in each stage of its growth—such discipline had its last result.

10   Little remained now but the bells. These, in all respects, must correspond with their receptacle.

11   The minor ones were prosperously cast. A highly enriched one followed, of a singular make, intended for suspension in a manner before unknown. The purpose of this bell, its rotary motion, and connection with the clock-work, also executed at the time, will, in the sequel, receive mention.

12   In the one erection, bell-tower and clock-tower were united, though, before that period, such structures had commonly been built distinct; as the Campanile and Torre del 'Orologio of St. Mark to this day attest.

13   But it was upon the great state-bell that the founder lavished his more daring skill. In vain did some of the less elated magistrates here caution him; saying that though truly the tower was Titanic, yet limit should be set to the dependent weight of its swaying masses. But undeterred, he prepared his mammoth mould, dented with mythological

devices; kindled his fires of balsamic firs; melted his tin and copper, and, throwing in much plate, contributed by the public spirit of the nobles, let loose the tide.

14 The unleashed metals bayed like hounds. The workmen shrunk. Through their fright, fatal harm to the bell was dreaded. Fearless as Shadrach, Bannadonna, rushing through the glow, smote the chief culprit with his ponderous ladle. From the smitten part, a splinter was dashed into the seething mass, and at once was melted in.

15 Next day a portion of the work was heedfully uncovered. All seemed right. Upon the third morning, with equal satisfaction, it was bared still lower. At length, like some old Theban king, the whole cooled casting was disinterred. All was fair except in one strange spot. But as he suffered no one to attend him in these inspections, he concealed the blemish by some preparation which none knew better to devise.

16 The casting of such a mass was deemed no small triumph for the caster; one, too, in which the state might not scorn to share. The homicide was overlooked. By the charitable that deed was but imputed to sudden transports of esthetic passion, not to any flagitious quality. A kick from an Arabian charger; not sign of vice, but blood.

17 His felony remitted by the judge, absolution given him by the priest, what more could even a sickly conscience have desired.

18 Honoring the tower and its builder with another holiday, the republic witnessed the hoisting of the bells and clock-work amid shows and pomps superior to the former.

19 Some months of more than usual solitude on Bannadonna's part ensued. It was not unknown that he was engaged upon something for the belfry, intended to complete it, and surpass all that had gone before. Most people imagined that the design would involve a casting like the bells. But those who thought they had some further insight, would shake their heads, with hints, that not for nothing did the mechanician keep so secret. Meantime, his seclusion failed not to invest his work with more or less of that sort of mystery pertaining to the forbidden.

20 Ere long he had a heavy object hoisted to the belfry, wrapped in a dark sack or cloak—a procedure sometimes had in the case of an elaborate piece of sculpture, or statue, which, being intended to grace the front of a new edifice, the architect does not desire exposed to critical eyes, till set up, finished, in its appointed place. Such was the impression now. But, as the object rose, a statuary present observed, or thought he did, that it was not entirely rigid, but was, in a manner, pliant. At last, when the hidden thing had attained its final height, and,

obscurely seen from below, seemed almost of itself to step into the bel-fry, as if with little assistance from the crane, a shrewd old blacksmith present ventured the suspicion that it was but a living man. This sur-mise was thought a foolish one, while the general interest failed not to augment.

21   Not without demur from Bannadonna, the chief-magistrate of the town, with an associate—both elderly men—followed what seemed the image up the tower. But, arrived at the belfry, they had little rec-ompense. Plausibly entrenching himself behind the conceded myster-ies of his art, the mechanician withheld present explanation. The mag-istrates glanced toward the cloaked object, which, to their surprise, seemed now to have changed its attitude, or else had before been more perplexingly concealed by the violent muffling action of the wind without. It seemed now seated upon some sort of frame, or chair, con-tained within the domino. They observed that nigh the top, in a sort of square, the web of the cloth, either from accident or design, had its warp partly withdrawn, and the cross threads plucked out here and there, so as to form a sort of woven grating. Whether it were the low wind or no, stealing through the stone lattice-work, or only their own perturbed imaginations, is uncertain, but they thought they discerned a slight sort of fitful, spring-like motion, in the domino. Nothing, how-ever incidental or insignificant, escaped their uneasy eyes. Among other things, they pried out, in a corner, an earthen cup, partly cor-roded and partly encrusted, and one whispered to the other, that this cup was just such a one as might, in mockery, be offered to the lips of some brazen statute, or, perhaps, still worse.

22   But, being questioned, the mechanician said, that the cup was sim-ply used in his founder's business, and described the purpose; in short, a cup to test the condition of metals in fusion. He added, that it had got into the belfry by the merest chance.

23   Again, and again, they gazed at the domino, as at some suspicious incognito at a Venetian mask. All sorts of vague apprehensions stirred them. They even dreaded lest, when they should descend, the mechanician, though without a flesh and blood companion, for all that, would not be left alone.

24   Affecting some merriment at their disquietude, he begged to relieve them, by extending a coarse sheet of workman's canvas between them and the object.

25   Meantime he sought to interest them in his other work; nor, now that the domino was out of sight, did they long remain insensible to the artistic wonders lying round them; wonders hitherto beheld but in their unfinished state; because, since hoisting the bells, none but the

caster had entered within the belfry. It was one trait of his, that, even in details, he would not let another do what he could, without too great loss of time, accomplish for himself. So, for several preceding weeks, whatever hours were unemployed in his secret design, had been devoted to elaborating the figures on the bells.

26   The clock-bell, in particular, now drew attention. Under a patient chisel, the latent beauty of its enrichments, before obscured by the cloudings incident to casting, that beauty in its shyest grace, was now revealed. Round and round the bell, twelve figures of gay girls, garlanded, hand-in-hand, danced in a choral ring—the embodied hours.

27   "Bannadonna," said the chief, "this bell excels all else. No added touch could here improve. Hark!" hearing a sound, "was that the wind?"

28   "The wind, Excellenza," was the light response. "But the figures, they are not yet without their faults. They need some touches yet. When those are given, and the —— block yonder," pointing towards the canvas screen, "when Haman there, as I merrily call him,—him? it, I mean —— when Haman is fixed on this, his lofty tree, then, gentlemen, will I be most happy to receive you here again."

29   The equivocal reference to the object caused some return of restlessness. However, on their part, the visitors forbore further allusion to it, unwilling, perhaps, to let the foundling see how easily it lay within his plebeian art to stir the placid dignity of nobles.

30   "Well, Bannadonna," said the chief, "how long ere you are ready to set the clock going, so that the hour shall be sounded? Our interest in you, not less than in the work itself, makes us anxious to be assured of your success. The people, too,—why, they are shouting now. Say the exact hour when you will be ready."

31   "To-morrow, Excellenza, if you listen for it,—or should you not, all the same—strange music will be heard. The stroke of one shall be the first from yonder bell," pointing to the bell adorned with girls and garlands, "that stroke shall fall there, where the hand of Una clasps Dua's. The stroke of one shall sever that loved clasp. To-morrow, then, at one o'clock, as struck here, precisely here," advancing and placing his finger upon the clasp, "the poor mechanic will be most happy once more to give you liege audience, in this his littered shop. Farewell till then, illustrious magnificoes, and hark ye for your vassal's stroke."

32   His still, Vulcanic face hiding its burning brightness like a forge, he moved with ostentatious deference towards the scuttle, as if so far to escort their exit. But the junior magistrate, a kind-hearted man, troubled at what seemed to him a certain sardonical disdain, lurking beneath the foundling's humble mien, and in Christian sympathy

more distressed at it on his account than on his own, dimly surmising what might be the final fate of such a cynic solitaire, not perhaps uninfluenced by the general strangeness of surrounding things, this good magistrate had glanced sadly, sideways from the speaker, and thereupon his foreboding eye had started at the expression of the unchanging face of the Hour Una.

33   "How is this, Bannadonna?" he lowly asked, "Una looks unlike her sisters."

34   "In Christ's name, Bannadonna," impulsively broke in the chief, his attention, for the first attracted to the figure, by his associate's remark, "Una's face looks just like that of Deborah, the prophetess, as painted by the Florentine, Del Fonca."

35   "Surely, Bannadonna," lowly resumed the milder magistrate, "you meant the twelve should wear the same jocundly abandoned air. But see, the smile of Una seems but a fatal one. 'Tis different."

36   While his mild associate was speaking, the chief glanced, inquiringly, from him to the caster, as if anxious to mark how the discrepancy would be accounted for. As the chief stood, his advanced foot was on the scuttle's curb.

37   Bannadonna spoke:

38   "Excellenza, now that, following your keener eye, I glance upon the face of Una, I do, indeed perceive some little variance. But look all round the bell, and you will find no two faces entirely correspond. Because there is a law in art— but the cold wind is rising more; these lattices are but a poor defense. Suffer me, magnificoes, to conduct you, at least, partly on your way. Those in whose well-being there is a public stake, should be heedfully attended."

39   "Touching the look of Una, you were saying, Bannadonna, that there was a certain law in art," observed the chief, as the three now descended the stone shaft, "pray, tell me then—."

40   "Pardon; another time, Excellenza;—the tower is damp."

41   "Nay, I must rest, and hear it now. Here,—here is a wide landing, and through this leeward slit, no wind, but ample light. Tell us of your law; and at large."

42   "Since, Excellenza, you insist, know that there is a law in art, which bars the possibility of duplicates. Some years ago, you may remember, I graved a small seal for your republic, bearing, for its chief device, the head of your own ancestor, its illustrious founder. It becoming necessary, for the customs' use, to have innumerable impressions for bales and boxes, I graved an entire plate, containing one hundred of the seals. Now, though, indeed, my object was to have those hundred heads identical, and though, I dare say, people think them so, yet, upon

closely scanning an uncut impression from the plate, no two of those five-score faces, side by side, will be found alike. Gravity is the air of all; but, diversified in all. In some, benevolent; in some, ambiguous; in two or three, to a close scrutiny, all but incipiently malign, the variation of less than a hair's breadth in the linear shadings round the mouth sufficing to all this. Now, Excellenza, transmute that general gravity into joyousness, and subject it to twelve of those variations I have described, and tell me, will you not have my hours here, and Una one of them? But I like—."

43   "Hark! is that —— a footfall above?"

44   "Mortar, Excellenza; sometimes it drops to the belfry-floor from the arch where the stone-work was left undressed. I must have it seen to. As I was about to say: for one, I like this law forbidding duplicates. It evokes fine personalities. Yes, Excellenza, that strange, and—to you—uncertain smile, and those fore-looking eyes of Una, suit Bannadonna. very well."

45   "Hark!—sure we left no soul above?"

46   "No soul, Excellenza; rest assured, no *soul.*—Again the mortar."

47   "It fell not while we were there."

48   "Ah, in your presence, it better knew its place, Excellenza," blandly bowed Bannadonna.

49   "But, Una," said the milder magistrate, "she seemed intently gazing on you; one would have almost sworn that she picked you out from among us three."

50   "If she did, possibly, it might have been her finer apprehension, Excellenza."

51   "How, Bannadonna? I do not understand you."

52   "No consequence, no consequence, Excellenza—but the shifted wind is blowing through the slit. Suffer me to escort you on; and then, pardon, but the toiler must to his tools."

53   "It may be foolish, Signor," said the milder magistrate, as, from the third landing, the two now went down unescorted, "but, somehow, our great mechanician moves me strangely. Why, just now, when he so superciliously replied, his walk seemed Sisera's, God's vain foe, in Del Fonca's painting. And that young, sculptured Deborah, too. Ay, and that—."

54   "Tush, tush, Signor!" returned the chief. "A passing whim. Deborah?—Where's Jael, pray?"

55   "Ah," said the other, as they now stepped upon the sod, "Ah, Signor, I see you leave your fears behind you with the chill and gloom; but mine, even in this sunny air, remain. Hark!"

56   It was a sound from just within the tower door, whence they had emerged. Turning, they saw it closed.

57   "He has slipped down and barred us out," smiled the chief; "but it is his custom."

58   Proclamation was now made, that the next day, at one hour after meridian, the clock would strike, and—thanks to the mechanician's powerful art—with unusual accompaniments. But what those should be, none as yet could say. The announcement was received with cheers.

59   By the looser sort, who encamped about the tower all night, lights were seen gleaming through the topmost blind-work, only disappearing with the morning sun. Strange sounds, too, were heard, or were thought to be, by those whom anxious watching might not have left mentally undisturbed—sounds, not only of some ringing implement, but also—so they said—half-suppressed screams and plainings, such as might have issued from some ghostly engine, overplied.

60   Slowly the day drew on; part of the concourse chasing the weary time with songs and games, till, at last, the great blurred sun rolled, like a football, against the plain.

61   At noon, the nobility and principal citizens came from the town in cavalcade, a guard of soldiers, also, with music, the more to honor the occasion.

62   Only one hour more. Impatience grew. Watches were held in hands of feverish men, who stood, now scrutinizing their small dial-plates, and then, with neck thrown back, gazing toward the belfry, as if the eye might foretell that which could only be made sensible to the ear; for, as yet, there was no dial to the tower-clock.

63   The hour hands of a thousand watches now verged within a hair's breadth of the figure 1. A silence, as of the expectation of some Shiloh, pervaded the swarming plain. Suddenly a dull, mangled sound—naught ringing in it; scarcely audible, indeed, to the outer circles of the people—that dull sound dropped heavily from the belfry. At the same moment, each man stared at his neighbor blankly. All watches were upheld. All hour-hands were at—had passed—the figure 1. No bell-stroke from the tower. The multitude became tumultuous.

64   Waiting a few moments, the chief magistrate, commanding silence, hailed the belfry, to know what thing unforeseen had happened there.

65   No response.

66   He hailed again and yet again.

67   All continued hushed.

68   By his order, the soldiers burst in the tower-door; when, stationing guards to defend it from the now surging mob, the chief, accompanied by his former associate, climbed the winding stairs. Half-way up, they stopped to listen. No sound. Mounting faster, they reached the belfry; but, at the threshold, started at the spectacle disclosed. A spaniel, which, unbeknown to them, had followed them thus far, stood shivering as before some unknown monster in a brake: or, rather, as if it snuffed footsteps leading to some other world. Bannadonna lay, prostrate and bleeding, at the base of the bell which was adorned with girls and garlands. He lay at the feet of the hour Una; his head coinciding, in a vertical line, with her left hand, clasped by the hour Dua. With downcast face impending over him, like Jael over nailed Sisera in the tent, was the domino; now no more becloaked.

69   It had limbs, and seemed clad in a scaly mail, lustrous as a dragon-beetle's. It was manacled, and its clubbed arms were uplifted, as if, with its manacles, once more to smite its already smitten victim. One advanced foot of it was inserted beneath the dead body, as if in the act of spurning it.

70   Uncertainty falls on what now followed.

71   It were but natural to suppose that the magistrates would, at first, shrink from immediate personal contact with what they saw. At the least, for a time, they would stand in involuntary doubt; it may be, in more or less of horrified alarm. Certain it is, that an arquebuss was called for from below. And some add, that its report, followed by a fierce whiz, as of the sudden snapping of a main-spring, with a steely din, as if a stack of sword-blades should be dashed upon a pavement, these blended sounds came ringing to the plain, attracting every eye far upward to the belfry, whence, through the lattice-work, thin wreaths of smoke were curling.

24   Some averred that it was the spaniel, gone mad by fear, which was shot. This, others denied. True it was, the spaniel never more was seen; and, probably, for some unknown reason, it shared the burial now to be related of the domino. For, whatever the preceding circumstances may have been, the first instinctive panic over, or else all ground of reasonable fear removed, the two magistrates, by themselves, quickly rehooded the figure in the dropped cloak wherein it had been hoisted. The same night, it was secretly lowered to the ground, smuggled to the beach, pulled far out to sea, and sunk. Nor to any after urgency, even in free convivial hours, would the twain ever disclose the full secrets of the belfry.

73   From the mystery unavoidably investing it, the popular solution of the foundling's fate involved more or less of supernatural agency. But

some few less unscientific minds pretended to find little difficulty in otherwise accounting for it. In the chain of circumstantial inferences drawn, there may, or may not, have been some absent or defective links. But, as the explanation in question is the only one which tradition has explicitly preserved, in dearth of better, it will here be given. But, in the first place, it is requisite to present the supposition entertained as to the entire motive and mode, with their origin, of the secret design of Bannadonna; the minds above-mentioned assuming to penetrate as well into his soul as into the event. The disclosure will indirectly involve reference to peculiar matters, none of the clearest, beyond the immediate subject.

74   At that period, no large bell was made to sound otherwise than as at present, by agitation of a tongue within, by means of ropes, or percussion from without, either from cumbrous machinery, or stalwart watchmen, armed with heavy hammers, stationed in the belfry, or in sentry-boxes on the open roof, according as the bell was sheltered or exposed.

75   It was from observing these exposed bells, with their watchmen, that the foundling, as was opined, derived the first suggestion of his scheme. Perched on a great mast or spire, the human figure, viewed from below, undergoes such a reduction in its apparent size, as to obliterate its intelligent features. It evinces no personality. Instead of bespeaking volition, its gestures rather resemble the automatic ones of the arms of a telegraph.

76   Musing, therefore, upon the purely Punchinello aspect of the human figure thus beheld, it had indirectly occurred to Bannadonna to devise some metallic agent, which should strike the hour with its mechanic hand, with even greater precision than the vital one. And, moreover, as the vital watchman on the roof, sallying from his retreat at the given periods, walked to the bell with uplifted mace, to smite it, Bannadonna had resolved that his invention should likewise possess the power of locomotion, and, along with that, the appearance, at least, of intelligence and will.

77   If the conjectures of those who claimed acquaintance with the intent of Bannadonna be thus far correct, no unenterprising spirit could have been his. But they stopped not here; intimating that though, indeed, his design had, in the first place, been prompted by the sight of the watchman, and confined to the devising of a subtle substitute for him: yet, as is not seldom the case with projectors, by insensible gradations, proceeding from comparatively pigmy aims to Titanic ones, the original scheme had, in its anticipated eventualities, at last, attained to an unheard of degree of daring. He still bent his efforts upon the

locomotive figure for the belfry, but only as a partial type of an ulterior creature, a sort of elephantine Helot, adapted to further, in a degree scarcely to be imagined, the universal conveniences and glories of humanity; supplying nothing less than a supplement to the Six Days' Work; stocking the earth with a new serf, more useful than the ox, swifter than the dolphin, stronger than the lion, more cunning than the ape, for industry an ant, more fiery than serpents, and yet, in patience, another ass. All excellences of all God-made creatures, which served man, were here to receive advancement, and then to be combined in one. Talus was to have been the all-accomplished Helot's name. Talus, iron slave to Bannadonna, and, through him, to man.

78   Here, it might well be thought that, were these last conjectures as to the foundling's secrets not erroneous, then must he have been hopelessly infected with the craziest chimeras of his age; far outgoing Albert Magus and Cornelius Agrippa. But the contrary was averred. However marvelous his design, however apparently transcending not alone the bounds of human invention, but those of divine creation, yet the proposed means to be employed were alleged to have been confined within the sober forms of sober reason. It was affirmed that, to a degree of more than skeptic scorn, Bannadonna had been without sympathy for any of the vain-glorious irrationalities of his time. For example, he had not concluded, with the visionaries among the metaphysicians, that between the finer mechanic forces and the ruder animal vitality some germ of correspondence might prove discoverable. As little did his scheme partake of the enthusiasm of some natural philosophers, who hoped, by physiological and chemical inductions, to arrive at a knowledge of the source of life, and so qualify themselves to manufacture and improve upon it. Much less had he aught in common with the tribe of alchemists, who sought, by a species of incantations, to evoke some surprising vitality from the laboratory. Neither had he imagined, with certain sanguine theosophists, that, by faithful adoration of the Highest, unheard-of powers would be vouchsafed to man. A practical materialist, what Bannadonna had aimed at was to have been reached, not by logic, not by crucible, not by conjuration, not by altars; but by plain vice-bench and hammer. In short, to solve nature, to steal into her, to intrigue beyond her, to procure some one else to bind her to his hand;—these, one and all, had not been his objects; but, asking no favors from any element or any being, of himself, to rival her, outstrip her, and rule her. He stooped to conquer. With him, common sense was theurgy; machinery, miracle; Prometheus, the heroic name for machinist; man, the true God.

79   Nevertheless, in his initial step, so far as the experimental automaton for the belfry was concerned, he allowed fancy some little play; or, perhaps, what seemed his fancifulness was but his utilitarian ambition collaterally extended. In figure, the creature for the belfry should not be likened after the human pattern, nor any animal one, nor after the ideals, however wild, of ancient fable, but equally in aspect as in organism be an original production; the more terrible to behold, the better.

80   Such, then, were the suppositions as to the present scheme, and the reserved intent. How, at the very threshold, so unlooked for a catastrophe overturned all, or rather, what was the conjecture here, is now to be set forth.

81   It was thought that on the day preceding the fatality, his visitors having left him, Bannadonna had unpacked the belfry image, adjusted it, and placed it in the retreat provided—a sort of sentry-box in one corner of the belfry; in short, throughout the night, and for some part of the ensuing morning, he had been engaged in arranging everything connected with the domino; the issuing from the sentry-box each sixty minutes; sliding along a grooved way, like a railway; advancing to the clock-bell, with uplifted manacles; striking it at one of the twelve junctions of the four-and-twenty hands; then wheeling, circling the bell, and retiring to its post, there to bide for another sixty minutes, when the same process was to be repeated; the bell, by a cunning mechanism, meantime turning on its vertical axis, so as to present, to the descending mace, the clasped hands of the next two figures, when it would strike two, three, and so on, to the end. The musical metal in this time-bell being so managed in the fusion, by some art, perishing with its originator, that each of the clasps of the four-and-twenty hands should give forth its own peculiar resonance when parted.

82   But on the magic metal, the magic and metallic stranger never struck but that one stroke, drove but that one nail, severed but that one clasp, by which Bannadonna clung to his ambitious life. For, after winding up the creature in the sentry-box, so that, for the present, skipping the intervening hours, it should not emerge till the hour of one, but should then infallibly emerge, and, after deftly oiling the grooves whereon it was to slide, it was surmised that the mechanician must then have hurried to the bell, to give his final touches to its sculpture. True artist, he here became absorbed; and absorption still further intensified, it may be, by his striving to abate that strange look of Una; which, though, before others, he had treated with such unconcern, might not, in secret, have been without its thorn.

83   And so, for the interval, he was oblivious of his creature; which, not oblivious of him, and true to its creation, and true to its heedful winding up, left its post precisely at the given moment; along its well-oiled route, slid noiselessly towards its mark; and, aiming at the hand of Una, to ring one clangorous note, dully smote the intervening brain of Bannadonna, turned backwards to it; the manacled arms then instantly up-springing to their hovering poise. The falling body clogged the thing's return; so there it stood, still impending over Bannadonna, as if whispering some post-mortem terror. The chisel lay dropped from the hand, but beside the hand; the oil-flask spilled across the iron track.

84   In his unhappy end, not unmindful of the rare genius of the mechanician, the republic decreed him a stately funeral. It was resolved that the great bell—the one whose casting had been jeopardized through the timidity of the ill-starred workman—should be rung upon the entrance of the bier into the cathedral. The most robust man of the country round was assigned the office of bell-ringer.

85   But as the pall-bearers entered the cathedral porch, naught but a broken and disastrous sound, like that of some lone Alpine land-slide, fell from the tower upon their ears. And then, all was hushed.

86   Glancing backwards, they saw the groined belfry crashed sideways in. It afterwards appeared that the powerful peasant, who had the bell-rope in charge, wishing to test at once the full glory of the bell, had swayed down upon the rope with one concentrate jerk. The mass of quaking metal, too ponderous for its frame, and strangely feeble somewhere at its top, loosed from its fastening, tore sideways down, and tumbling in one sheer fall, three hundred feet to the soft sward below, buried itself inverted and half out of sight.

87   Upon its disinterment, the main fracture was found to have started from a small spot in the ear; which, being scraped, revealed a defect, deceptively minute, in the casting; which defect must subsequently have been pasted over with some unknown compound.

88   The remolten metal soon reassumed its place in the tower's repaired superstructure. For one year the metallic choir of birds sang musically in its belfry-bough-work of sculptured blinds and traceries. But on the first anniversary of the tower's completion—at early dawn, before the concourse had surrounded it—an earthquake came; one loud crash was heard. The stone-pine, with all its bower of songsters, lay overthrown upon the plain.

89   So the blind slave obeyed its blinder lord; but, in obedience, slew him. So the creator was killed by the creature. So the bell was too heavy for the tower. So the bell's main weakness was where man's blood had flawed it. And so pride went before the fall.

The Bell-Tower

Journal

1. MLA Works Cited

Using this model, record this reading here.

Author's Last Name, First Name. "Title of the Story." <u>Title of the Book</u>. Ed. First Last Name. City: Publisher, year. Pages of the story.

2. Main Character(s)

Describe each main character, and explain why you think each is a main character.

3. Supporting Characters

Describe each supporting character, and explain why you think each is a supporting character.

4. Setting

Describe the setting. Decide if this setting can be changed and, if so, to where and when.

5. Sequence

Relate the events of the story in order.

6. Plot

Tell the story in no more than three sentences.

7. Conflicts

Identify and explain the conflicts involved here.

8. Significant Quotations

Explain the importance of each of these quotations. Record the page number in the parentheses.

a. "In firm resolve, no man in Europe at that period went beyond Bannadonna" (   ).

b. "In the one erection, bell-tower and clock-tower were united, though, before that period, such structures had commonly been built distinct [. . .]" (   ).

c. "Fearless at Shadrach, Bannadonna, rushing through the glow, smote the chief culprit with his ponderous ladle" ( ).

d. "At last, when the hidden thing had attained its final height, and, obscurely seen from below, seemed almost of itself to step into the belfry, as if with little assistance from the crane, a shrewd old blacksmith present ventured the suspicion that it was but a living man" ( ).

e. "He lay at the feet of the hour Una; his head coinciding, in a vertical line, with her left hand, clasped by the hour Dua. With downcast face impending over him, like Jael over nailed Sisera in the tent, was the domino [. . .]" ( ). [*Note:* You will find that reading Judges 4 and 5 (Appendix A, page 445) may help you explain the importance of this quotation.]

9. Symbolism

Identify and explain the symbols used in the story.

Follow-up Questions

10 Short Questions

*Select the **best** answer for each.*

_____ 1. Bannadonna is
    a. just starting his career.
    b. a recognized artisan.
    c. not a recognized artisan.

_____ 2. Bannadonna
    a. is comfortable in his tower.
    b. is not comfortable in his tower.
    c. does not go up in his tower.

_____ 3. The bell has a flaw because
    a. it is too large.
    b. it has different figures.
    c. a man has been killed and melted in the process.

_____ 4. The figures are designed to unclasp hands so that
    a. each may stand alone.
    b. the bell will sound differently at each hour.
    c. they may move more easily.

_____ 5. Haman seems
    a. to move alone.
    b. not to move alone.
    c. never to move at all.

_____ 6. Una's face seems to
    a. look happy.
    b. look like her sisters.
    c. predict a fatal future.

_____ 7. The younger magistrate
    a. has suspicions about what Bannadonna is doing.
    b. does not have suspicions about what Bannadonna is doing.
    c. gets killed.

_____ 8. Haman relates to
    a. Jael.
    b. Bannadonna.
    c. Sisera.

_____ 9. In mechanical terms, Bannadonna
    a. should have oiled Haman's path more.
    b. does not oil Haman's path enough.
    c. oils Haman's path too well.

_____ 10. In mystical terms, the creation
    a. is ruled by the creator.
    b. slays the creator.
    c. is good to the people.

5 Significant Quotations

Explain the importance of each of these quotations.

1. "But it was upon the great state-bell that the founder lavished his more daring skill."

2. "All was fair except in one strange spot. [. . .]
    "[. . .] The homicide was overlooked."

3. " 'When those are given, and the—block yonder,' pointing towards the canvas screen, 'when Haman there, as I merrily call him,—-him? *it*, I mean—when Haman is fixed on this, his lofty tree, then, gentlemen, will I be most happy to receive you here again.' "

4. "He lay at the feet of the hour Una; his head coinciding, in a vertical line, with her left hand, clasped by the hour Dua. With downcast face impending over him, like Jael over nailed Sisera in the tent, was the domino; now no more becloaked."

5. "In short, to solve nature, to steal from her, to intrigue beyond her, to procure some one else to bind her to his hand;—these, one and all, had not been his objects; but, asking no favors from any element or any being, of himself, to rival her, outstrip her, and rule her."

2 COMPREHENSION ESSAY QUESTIONS

Use specific details and information from the story to answer these as completely as possible.

1. How does the title relate to the story? Explain the significance of the title using specific details and information from the story.

2. Hubris means self-pride wherein a person arrogantly thinks he or she is better than God. Explain how hubris relates to this story using specific details and information from the story.

WRITING

Use each of these ideas for writing an essay.

1. Think of one machine you depend on, and write an essay explaining both the good side and the bad side of your dependence.

2. Think of a machine that you wish you had or perhaps one you might invent. Describe the machine, and explain specifically how this machine would help you.

Further Writing

1. Research current genetic studies, and explain how new research relates to Bannadonna.

2. Read Judges 4 and 5 from the Bible (Appendix A, page 445), and relate these chapters to Bannadonna.

3. Read Sophocles's *Oedipus Rex* (which can be found in a library), and compare the consequences of the *hubris* of Oedipus and that of Bannadonna.

Appendix A

Judges

CHAPTER 4

¹Deborah and Barak deliver them from Jabin and Sisera. ¹⁸Jael killeth Sisera.

♦♦¹And the children of Israel again did evil in the sight of the LORD when Ehud was dead. ²And the LORD sold them into the hand of Jabin king of Canaan, who reigned in Hazor, the captain of whose host was Sisera, who dwelt in Harosheth of the Gentiles. ³And the children of Israel cried unto the LORD; for he had nine hundred chariots of iron, and twenty years he mightily oppressed the children of Israel.

⁴And Deborah, a prophetess, the wife of Lapidoth, judged Israel at that time. ⁵And she dwelt under the palm tree of Deborah between Ramah and Bethel in Mount Ephraim, and the children of Israel came up to her for judgment. ⁶And she sent and called Barak the son of Abinoam out of Kedesh-naphtali, and said unto him, "Hath not the LORD God of Israel commanded, saying, 'Go and draw near Mount Tabor, and take with thee ten thousand men of the children of Naphtali and of the children of Zebulun; ⁷and I will draw unto thee Sisera, the captain of Jabin's army, with his chariots and his multitude to the River Kishon;* and I will deliver him into thine hand'?" ♦ ⁸And, Barak said unto her, "If thou wilt go with me, then I will go; but if thou wilt riot go with me, then I will not go." ⁹And she said, "I will surely go with thee. Notwithstanding, the journey that thou takest shall not be for thine honor, for the LORD shall sell Sisera into the hand of a woman." And Deborah arose, and went with Barak to Kedesh. ¹⁰And Barak called Zebulun and Naphtali to Kedesh, and he went up with, ten thousand men at his heels; and Deborah went up with him. ¹¹(Now Heber the Kenite, who was of the children of Hobab the father-in-law of Moses,* had severed himself from the Kenites and pitched his tent unto the plain of Zaanaim, which is by Kedesh.)

¹²And they showed Sisera that Barak the son of Abinoam had gone up to Mount Tabor. ¹³And Sisera gathered together all his chariots, even nine hundred chariots of iron, and all the people who were with him, from Harosheth of the Gentiles unto the river of Kishon. ¹⁴And Deborah said unto Barak, "Up! For this is the day, in which the LORD hath delivered Sisera into thine hand. Has not the LORD gone out before thee?" So Barak went down from Mount Tabor, and ten thousand men after him. ¹⁵And the LORD discomfited Sisera and all his chariots and all his host with the edge of the sword before Barak, so that Sisera alighted down off his chariot and fled away on his feet.* ¹⁶But Barak pursued after the chariots and after the host unto Harosheth of the Gentiles; and all the host of Sisera fell upon the edge of the sword, and there was not a man left.

*7 Ps 83:9–10.   *11 Num 10:29.   *15 Ps 83:10.

¹⁷However Sisera fled away on his feet to the tent of Jael the wife of Heber the Kenite, for there was peace between Jabin the king of Hazor and the house of Heber the Kenite. ¹⁸And Jael went out to meet Sisera, and said unto him, "Turn in, my lord, turn in to me. Fear not." And when he had turned in unto her into the tent, she covered him with a mantle. ¹⁹And he said unto her, "Give me, I pray thee, a little water to drink; for I am thirsty." And she opened a bottle of milk, and gave him drink, and covered him.* ²⁰Again he said unto her, "Stand in the door of the tent, and it shall be, when any man doth come and inquire of thee and say, 'Is there any man here?' that tho, shalt say, 'No.'" ²¹Then Jael, Heber's wife, took a nail of the tent and took a hammer in her hand, and went softly unto him and smote the nail into his temples, and fastened it into the ground; for he was fast asleep and weary. So he died. ²²And behold, as Barak pursued Sisera, Jael came out to meet him and said unto him, "Come, and I will show thee the man whom thou seekest." And when he came into her tent, behold, Sisera lay dead, and the nail was in his temples.

²³So God subdued on that day Jabin the king of Canaan before the children of Israel. ²⁴And the hand of the children of Israel prospered, and prevailed against Jabin the king of Canaan, until they had destroyed Jabin king of Canaan.

CHAPTER 5

¹The song of Deborah and Barak.

¹Then sang Deborah and Barak, the son of Abinoam, on that day, saying:
²"Praise ye the LORD for the avenging of Israel,
    when the people willingly offered themselves.

³Hear, O ye kings;
    give ear, O ye princes.
I, even I, will sing unto the LORD;
    I will sing praise to the LORD God of Israel.

⁴"LORD, when Thou wentest out of Seir,*
    when Thou marched out of the field of Edom,
the earth trembled and the heavens dropped,
    the clouds also dropped water.
⁵The mountains melted from before the LORD,*
    even that Sinai, from before the LORD God of Israel.*

⁶"In the days of Shamgar the son of Anath,*
in the days of Jael,*
    the highways were unoccupied,
    and the travelers walked through byways.
⁷The inhabitants of the villages ceased,
    they ceased in Israel,
        until I, Deborah, arose,
        I arose a mother in Israel.
⁸They chose new gods;
    then was war in the gates.

---

*19 Jdg 5:25.   *4 Dt4:11.   *5a Ps 97:5.   *5b Ex 19:18.   *6a Jdg 3:31.   *6b Jdg 4:18.

Was there a shield or spear seen
among forty thousand in Israel?
⁹ My heart is toward the governors of Israel
that offered themselves willingly among the people.
Bless ye the LORD.

¹⁰ "Speak, ye that ride on white asses,
ye that sit in judgment and walk by the way.
¹¹ They that are delivered from the noise of archers
in the places of drawing water,
there shall they rehearse the righteous acts of the LORD,
even the righteous acts toward the inhabitants
of His villages in Israel.
Then shall the people of the LORD go down to the gates.

¹² "Awake, awake, Deborah!
Awake, awake, utter a song!
Arise, Barak, and lead thy captivity captive,
thou son of Abinoam.

¹³ "Then He made him that remaineth have dominion
over the nobles among the people;
the LORD made me have dominion over the mighty.
¹⁴ Out of Ephraim was there a root of them against Amalek;
after thee, Benjamin, among thy people;
out of Machir came down governors,
and out of Zebulun they that handle the pen
of the writer.
¹⁵ And the princes of Issachar were with Deborah,
even Issachar, and also Barak;
he was sent on foot into the valley.
In the divisions of Reuben there were great thoughts of
heart.
¹⁶ Why abodest thou among the sheepfolds,
to hear the bleatings of the flocks?
In the divisions of Reuben there were great
searchings of heart.
¹⁷ Gilead abode beyond the Jordan;
and why did Dan remain in ships?
Asher continued on the seashore
and abode in his sheltered coves.
¹⁸ Zebulun and Naphtali were a people
that jeopardized their lives unto the death
in the high places of the field.

¹⁹ "The kings came and fought;
then fought the kings of Canaan
in Taanach by the waters of Megiddo;
they took no gain of money.
²⁰ They fought from heaven;
the stars in their courses fought against Sisera.

²¹ The river of Kishon swept them away,
    that ancient river, the river Kishon.
        O my soul, thou hast trodden down strength!
²² Then were the horsehoofs broken
    by the means of the prancings,
        the prancings of their mighty ones.
²³ " 'Curse ye Meroz,' said the angel of the L ORD;
        'curse ye bitterly the inhabitants thereof,
    because they came not to the help of the L ORD,
        to the help of the L ORD against the mighty.'

²⁴ "Blessed above women
    shall Jael the wife of Heber the Kenite be;
        blessed shall she be above women in the tent.
²⁵ He asked water, and she gave him milk;
        she brought forth butter in a lordly dish.
²⁶ She put her hand to the nail,
        and her right hand to the workmen's hammer.
    And with the hammer she smote Sisera;
        she smote off his head, when she had pierced and
        stricken through his temples.
²⁷ At her feet he bowed, he fell, he lay down;
    at her feet he bowed, he fell;
        where he bowed, there he fell down dead.

²⁸ "The mother of Sisera looked out at a window,
    and cried through the lattice:
        'Why is his chariot so long in coming?
        Why tarry the wheels of his chariots?'
²⁹ Her wise ladies answered her,
        yea, she returned answer to herself:
³⁰ 'Have they not sped?
        Have they not divided the prey:
    to every man a damsel or two,
        to Sisera a prey of divers colors,
        a prey of divers colors of needlework,
    of divers colors of needlework on both sides,
        meet for the necks of them that take the spoil?'

³¹ "So let all Thine enemies perish, O L ORD!
        But let them that love Him be as the sun
        when he goeth forth in his might."

And the land had rest forty years.

Glossary of Prefixes and Suffixes

Some words in the Pre-Reading Vocabulary—Word Attack are simple words that have been combined or have extra syllables, which make these words look strange or difficult. When you take these words apart, they are usually quite simple to define.

When two or more words are combined to form a new word, the new word is called a **compound word.** By combining the meaning of each of the words, you can define the new word. Look at the word *everyday.* Here, two simple words—*every* and *day*—combine to mean "all the time." Look at the word *worn-whiskered.* *Worn* means "tired" or "old," and *whiskered* implies "old man" or "mature man." Thus, *worn-whiskered* is a word used to describe an old man.

Another way to build a new word is to add a prefix or suffix to a **root** word, or a core word. A **prefix** is a syllable added to front of the root word that often changes the meaning of the word. A **suffix** is a syllable added to the end of the root word that may alter the use or the meaning of the word. Prefixes and suffixes are called **affixes.** As you define the words in the Pre-reading Vocabulary—Word Attack exercises, look for and define the root word, and then define the affixes added on to the root word.

For instance, look at the word *provider. Provide* is the root word and is a verb that means "to supply." The suffix *–er* at the end means "one who." Thus, the verb *provide* becomes a person, and the noun *provider* means "a person who supplies something." Now, look at the word *nonprovider.* The prefix *non–* at the beginning means "not" and greatly changes the meaning of the word. *Nonprovider* means "a person who does *not* supply something."

To define the words in Pre-Reading Vocabulary—Word Attack, you need to know the prefixes and suffixes that are listed in Tables G-1 and G-2. Prefixes are defined and are listed in alphabetical order. Suffixes are arranged alphabetically in definition groups. Use the lists to help you in defining these words.

Prefixes

A prefix is added to the beginning of a root word. A prefix usually changes the meaning of the root word. *Be especially aware of prefixes because they can greatly change the meaning of a word.* Note that some prefixes have more than one meaning and these meanings may be different.

TABLE G-1
Prefixes

Prefix	Meaning	Application
a–	full of	*Acrawl* means "creeping or spreading everywhere." The town was *acrawl* with gossip when people learned the mayor was arrested.
a–	total absence	*Amoral* means "totally unable to tell right from wrong." When a shark kills, it is *amoral* because a shark does not know right from wrong.
be–	full of	*Beloved* means "very much loved." The soldier dearly missed his *beloved* wife.
counter–	against	*Counterplot* means "a plan to work against another plan." The police developed a *counterplot* to ruin the criminals' robbery plan.
de–	against, wrong	*Deform* means "badly or wrongly formed." The fire *deformed* the house and left it twisted and falling down.
de–	out of	*Deplane* means "to get off the airplane." The team claimed their luggage after they *deplaned*.
dis–	not, against	*Distrust* means "not to trust." Fatima felt *distrust* toward the salesman who lied to her.
en–	within, into	*Encircle* means "to place in the middle" or "to surround." The floodwaters *encircled* the house.
il–	not	*Illegal* means "not legal." Many laws state that stealing is *illegal* and will place you in jail.
il–	more so	*Illuminate* means "to light up brightly." The fireworks *illuminated* the night sky so brightly that it looked like daylight.
im–	not	*Immeasurable* means "not able to be measured." The joy Horace felt when he won the championship was *immeasurable*.
im–	more so	*Impoverished* means "very poor." The *impoverished* family did not even have enough money for food.
in–	not	*Incurable* means "not able to be healed." Doug caught an *incurable* disease, which he will have for the rest of his life.
in–	in, into	*Inside* means "to go in the side" or "to enter through the side." Jumana walked through the door to get *inside* the room.
inter–	between, among	*Intercollegiate* means "between two or more colleges." Michigan defeated Alabama in *intercollegiate* football.

TABLE G-1 (Cont'd)

Prefix	Meaning	Application
kin–	relative	*Kinfolk* means "the people you are related to or your family." All my *kinfolk* will gather together at Thanksgiving for a family reunion.
non–	not	*Nonaccompanied* means "no company or alone." Will preferred to attend the party alone, *nonaccompanied* by others.
pre–	before	*Predictable* means "able to tell beforehand." José's speeding ticket was *predictable* because he always drives too fast.
re–	again	*Refamiliarize* means "become familiar with again." To pass the test, Sue will *refamiliarize* herself with her notes.
self–	alone, one's own	*Self-satisfied* means "satisfied with oneself." After passing the test, Charlie felt good about himself and was quite *self-satisfied*.
semi–	half	*Semiconscious* means "only half or partly aware." With all the noise at the concert, Rich was only *semiconscious* of the sirens outside.
sub–	under	*Subway* means "a road that goes underground." When there is too much traffic on the city roads, it is easier to take the *subway*.
super–	larger, above	*Superman* means "a man larger or better than other men." Bravely running in a burning building to help others is the act of a *superman*.
un–	not	*Unperceived* means "not noticed." Joan usually notices everything, but this time the dirty room went *unperceived*.
under–	below	*Underbrush* means "low plants that grow under the bushes." Carl decided to weed out the *underbrush* that was growing under his garden plants.
trans–	across	*Transoceanic* means "across the ocean." Steve will catch a *transoceanic* flight from New York to Paris.

Suffixes

A suffix is added to the end of a root word. A suffix may have very little effect on the meaning of a word, but a suffix will often change the part of speech of a root word.

What is the part of speech of a word? The part of speech of a word is, very simply, the function or use of the word. For instance, look at the word *ski*. In the sentence "Sue's *ski* was damaged," *ski* is a noun—the thing Sue had that was damaged. In "Sue and Bill *ski* downhill," *ski* is a verb—the action Sue and Bill do. In "Sue took *ski* lessons," *ski* is an adjective that describes the kind of lessons that Sue took. The word *ski* remains the same three letters, but the function it serves and the information it communicates change slightly depending on the part of speech it demonstrates. Note that although the use changes—from thing to action to description—the basic idea of a downhill sport remains the same.

In the same way, a suffix may often change the part of speech of a root word while leaving the root word's basic meaning largely unchanged. For instance, if we add *-ed* to the noun and say, "Sue *skied* down the hill," the noun becomes a verb, and the action is in the past. Thus, Sue is still involved with skiing, but now she has done it in the past.

In Table G-2, suffixes you will need to know are listed alphabetically within definition groups and with the relevant parts of speech noted. You will see several words from Pre-Reading Vocabulary—Word Attack.

TABLE G-2
Suffixes

Suffix   Application

The following suffixes mean "one who" or "that which." Each turns a root word into a noun because the root word becomes the person or the thing that does something.

–ant   A *servant* is "one who serves." The *servants* cleaned the mansion before the guests arrived.

–ary   A *visionary* is "one who sees clearly or into the future." Einstein was a *visionary* of nuclear energy to come.

–ee   A *payee* is "one to whom things are paid." When Sara owed her brother money, she wrote a check to him and made him the *payee.*

–ent   A *student* is "one who studies." College *students* are usually serious about their studies and work for good grades.

–er   A *fancier* is "one who fancies or likes something." Jen is a proven cat *fancier* and currently has four cats that she loves living in her home.

–ess   A *princess* is "a female who acts like a prince." The *princess* sat on the throne next to her husband, the prince.

–folk   *Townsfolk* are "people of the town." The *townsfolk* held a general meeting so that they could all meet the new mayor.

–ian   A *musician* is "one who plays music." Jessica hired several *musicians* so that people would be able to dance at her party.

–ist   A *futurist* is "one who looks into the future." *Futurists* advise those in the government in Washington about issues on which they may need to enact laws in the future.

–man   A *horseman* is "a male who rides horses." Dave is a fine *horseman* who often rides his horse around the park.

–or   A *survivor* is "one who survives or lasts." Rich lasted the longest on the deserted island and was named the *survivor.*

The following suffixes make a root word an adjective, and each changes the meaning of the root word.

–able   *Distinguishable* means "able to tell apart or distinguish." The dirty spots made the dirty clothes *distinguishable* from the clean clothes.

–er   *Lovelier* means, by comparison, "more lovely than another." Carmen's garden, filled with blooms, is *lovelier* than Cheryl's weed patch.

–est   *Kindliest* means, by comparison, "the most kind of all." The mother's gentle pat was the *kindliest* touch of all.

–ful   *Frightful* means "full of fright or awful." With all its costumes and noisy bell ringing, Halloween is a *frightful* night.

–less   *Hapless* means "without happiness or luck" or "unfortunate." The *hapless* student had two flat tires and got a headache on his way to school.

–most   *Uppermost* means "most high" or "important." With a record of no accidents for two years, safety is the company's *uppermost* concern.

–ous   *Nervous* means "full of nerves" or "tense." Kirk was so *nervous* before his test that his hands were shaking.

TABLE G-2 (Cont'd)

The following suffixes mean "related to," "like," or "having the quality of" and generally change the meaning of a root word very little. Mostly, they change the parts of speech of the root word.

–al	The noun *cone* means "circular point" and becomes the adjective *conical*. The tip of the space shuttle is rounded and *conical*.
–ance	The verb *repent* means "to feel sorry about" and becomes the noun *repentance*. After he broke his Mom's favorite vase, Jim felt awful and was filled with *repentance*.
–ant	The verb *observe* means "to see" and becomes the adjective *observant*. Lydia watches everything closely and is very *observant*.
–ed	The noun *candy* means "something sweet" and becomes the adjective *candied*. Mom used lots of sugar to sweetly coat the *candied* apples.
–ed	The noun *ink* means "writing fluid" and becomes the past-tense verb *inked*. Jefferson took pen and *inked* his signature on the Declaration he wrote.
–en	The verb *chose* means "selected" and becomes the adjective *chosen*. He had joined the Marines and became one of the *chosen* few.
–ence	The verb *depend* means "to rely" and becomes the noun *dependence*. When Jill paid her own bills, she knew her *dependence* on her parents would end.
–ic	The noun *metal* means "shiny, element" and becomes the adjective *metallic*. Laura's silvery dress had a *metallic* shine.
–ing	The verb *terrify* means "to scare" and becomes the adjective *terrifying*. The *terrifying* thunder scared all of us as it seemed to shake the whole house.
–ish	The noun *fever* means "internal heat" and becomes the adjective *feverish*. Joel felt *feverish* from the heat of his sunburn.
–ism	The adjective *ideal* means "perfect" and becomes the noun *idealism*, which means "belief in perfection." George's *idealism* often leaves him disappointed because things are not always perfect.
–ity	The adjective *stupid* means "unthinking" and becomes the noun *stupidity*. Alice could not believe her *stupidity* when she locked her keys in the car.
–ive	The noun *feast* means "cheerful meal" and becomes the adjective *festive*. The wedding, with all its foods and colorful flowers, was a most *festive* affair.
–ly, –li	The adjective *stealthy* means "moving quietly" and becomes the adverb *stealthily*. Ken crept so *stealthily* in the back door that no one knew he had entered the house.
–ment	The verb *confine* means "to restrain" and becomes the noun *confinement*. When the children misbehaved, Dad sent them to their rooms for silent *confinement*.

-ness The adjective *nervous* means "tense" and becomes the noun *nervousness*. It was very hard for the groom to overcome his *nervousness* on his wedding day.

-tation The adjective *ornamental* means "decorated" and becomes the noun *ornamentation*. Her diamond rings and pearl necklaces created *ornamentation* fit for a queen.

-ty The adjective *frail* means "delicate" and becomes the noun *frailty*. At Aunt Alice's ninetieth birthday, we were all concerned about her *frailty*.

-y The noun *stone* means "hard item" and becomes the adjective *stony*. The policeman had a *stony* look when the boy who was driving did not have a license.

Credits

Chapter 1: *Page 26:* "A Worn Path" from A CURTAIN OF GREEN AND OTHER STORIES. Copyright 1941 and renewed 1969 by Eudora Welty. Reprinted by permission of Harcourt, Inc. *Page 42:* "Zulema" from INTAGLIO: A NOVEL IN SIX STORIES by Roberta Fernandez. Reprinted with permission from the publisher Arte Publico Press, Houston, TX, 1990. *Page 64:* "The Secret Life of Walter Mitty" from the book, MY WORLD AND WELCOME TO IT © 1942 by James Thurber. Copyright © renewed by Helen Thurber and Rosemary A. Thurber. Reprinted by arrangement with Rosemary A. Thurber and The Barbara Hogenson Agency. *Page 90:* "There Will Come Soft Rains" by Ray Bradbury is reprinted by permission of Don Congdon Associates, Inc. Copyright © 1950 by Crowell-Collier Publishing, renewed 1977 by Ray Bradbury.

Chapter 2: *Page 175:* "Everyday Use" from IN LOVE AND TROUBLE: STORIES OF BLACK WOMEN. Copyright © 1973 by Alice Walker. Reprinted by permission of Harcourt, Inc.

Chapter 3: *Page 207:* One Friday Morning" from SHORT STORIES by Langston Hughes. Copyright © 1996 by Ramona Bass and Arnold Rampersad. Reprinted by permission of Hill and Wang, a division of Farrar, Straus & Giroux, LLC. *Page 224:* "No Name Woman" from THE WOMAN WARRIOR by Maxine Hong Kingston. Copyright © 1975, 1976 by Maxine Hong Kingston. Reprinted by permission of Alfred A. Kopf, a division of Random House, Inc. *Page 243:* "The Lottery" from THE LOTTERY AND OTHER STORIES by Shirley Jackson. Copyright © 1948, 1949 by Shirley Jackson. Copyright renewed 1976, 1977 by Laurence Hyman, Barry Hyman, Mrs. Sarah Webster, and Mrs. Joanne Schnurer. Reprinted by permission of Farrar, Straus and Giroux, LLC. *Page 259:* "Good Country People" from A GOOD MAN IS HARD TO FIND AND OTHER STORIES. Copyright © 1955 by Flannery O'Connor and renewed 1983 by Reginia O'Connor. Reprinted by permission of Harcourt, Inc.

Chapter 4: *Page 329:* "The Wonderful Old Gentleman," copyright 1926, renewed © 1954 by Dorothy Parker, from THE PORTABLE DOROTHY PARKER by Dorothy Parker. Used by permission of Viking Penguin, a division of Penguin Putnam, Inc. *Page 348:* "Sweat" as taken from THE COMPLETE STORIES by ZORA NEALE THURSTON. Introduction copyright © 1995 by Henry Louis Gates, Jr., and Sieglinde Lemke. Compilation copyright © 1995 by Vivian Bowden, Lois J. Hurston Gaston, Clifford Hurston, Lucy Ann Hurston, Winifred Hurston Clark, Zora Mack Goins, Edgar Hurston, Sr., and Barbara Hurston Lewis. Afterward and bibliography copyright © 1995 by Henry Louis Gates. Reprinted by permission of HarperCollins Publishers, Inc.

Chapter 5: *Page 390:* "A Rose for Emily" from COLLECTED STORIES OF WILLIAM FAULKNER by William Faulkner. Copyright © 1930 & renewed 1958 by William Faulkner. Reprinted by permission of Random House, Inc.

Index of
Authors, Titles, and Terms